CHARLTON STANDAR[D]

ROYAL DOULTON JUGS

SIXTH EDITION

By
Jean Dale

Introduction By
Louise Irvine

W.K. Cross
Publisher

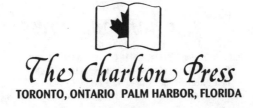

The Charlton Press

TORONTO, ONTARIO PALM HARBOR, FLORIDA

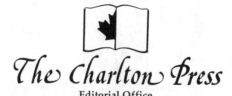

The Charlton Press

Editorial Office
P. O. BOX 94, THORNHILL, ONTARIO L3T 3N1
Telephone: (416) 488-1418 Fax: (416) 488-4656
Telephone: (800) 442-6042 Fax: (800) 442-1542
www.charltonpress.com   e-mail: chpress@charltonpress.com

EDITORIAL

Editor	Jean Dale
Graphic technician	Davina Rowan

ACKNOWLEDGEMENTS

The Charlton Press wishes to thank those who have helped with the sixth edition of *The Charlton Standard Catalogue of Royal Doulton Jugs*.

Special Thanks

The publishers would like to thank Louise Irvine for writing the introduction to the *The Charlton Standard Catalogue of Royal Doulton Jugs*. Louise Irvine is an independent writer and lecturer on Royal Doulton's history and products and is not connected with the pricing of this catalogue.

Our thanks also go to the staff of Royal Doulton, who have helped with additional technical information, especially Valerie Baynton, Ian Howe and Kevin Moyer.

Contributors To The Sixth Edition

The publisher would also like to thank the following individuals and companies who graciously supplied photographs or information or allowed us acess to their collection for photographic purposes: **Mrs. H. W. Babchyck**, Dedham, Massachusetts; **George Bagnall**, Precious Memories, Charlottetown, P.E.I.; **David Bearman**, Ohio; **Peter Bellis**, St. Helens, England; **Anthony Cross**, Anthony Cross and The Englishman, Blackburn, England; **William T. Cross**, William Cross Antiques and Collectibles, Burnaby, B.C.; **Tom Duenes**, Portland, Oregon; **Michael Lynch**; **Reg. G. Morris**, Chesterfield, Ohio; **Mark Oliver**, Phillips, London, England; **Sam Ginsburg**, Bronx, New York; **David Readdy**, Vero Beach, Florida; **Ronald Thompson**, West Midlands, England; **Betty Wheeler,** Pittsburgh, Pennsylvania; **Derek Woolf**, Solihull, England; **Roger Wilkinson**, England

A SPECIAL NOTE TO COLLECTORS

We welcome and appreciate any comments or suggestions in regard to *The Charlton Standard Catalogue of Royal Doulton Jugs*. If any errors or omissions come to your attention, please write to us, or if you would like to participate in pricing or supply previously unavailable data or information, please contact Jean Dale at (416) 488-1418, or e-mail us at chpress@charltonpress.com.

DISCLAIMER

Canadian Cataloguing In Publication Data

The National Library of Canada has catalogued this publication as follows:

The Charlton standard catalogue of Royal Doulton jugs

Biennial

1st ed. ([1991]) –

3rd to 5th editions have title: The Charlton standard catalogue of Royal Doulton Beswick jugs; editions beginning with the 6th have title: Charlton standard catalogue Royal Doulton jugs.

ISSN 1183-711X
ISBN 0-88968-256-9 (6th ed.)

      1. Charlton Press II. Title: Royal Doulton jugs III. Title: The Charlton standard catalogue of Royal Doulton Beswick jugs.

NK4695.C518C442   738.8'0294   C92-030326-9 rev

**Printed in Manitoba
in the Province of Winnipeg**

HOW TO USE THIS CATALOGUE

THE PURPOSE

As with the other catalogues in Charlton's Royal Doulton reference and pricing library, this publication has been designed to serve two specific purposes. First, to furnish the Royal Doulton enthusiast with accurate listings containing vital information and photographs to aid in the building of a rewarding collection. Secondly, this publication provides Royal Doulton collectors and dealers with current market prices for Royal Doulton jugs. Human subjects are covered in *The Charlton Standard Catalogue of Royal Doulton Figurines*, and animals are cover in *The Charlton Standard Catalogue of Royal Doulton Animals*.

STYLES AND VARIATIONS

On the pages that follow, Royal Doulton jugs are listed, illustrated and described in alphabetical order within their categories.

STYLES: When two or more jugs have the same name but different physical modelling characteristics, they are listed as **Style One**, **Style Two**, and so on. Such jugs will also have different D numbers.

VARIATIONS: A change in colour is a variation.

When known, the jug's modeller or **Designer** is listed next. What follows is a statistics table which gives the **D number** assigned to the jug, the size and height, as well as the date (or dates) when the jug was **Issued.** A description of the jug's **Handle** is next, followed by the actual **Colour** (or colours) of the jug.

The pricing table gives the **Price** (the current market value) of the jug described. The price appears in U.S. dollars, Canadian dollars and pounds sterling.

Although the publisher has made every attempt to obtain and photograph all jugs and their varieties, several pieces, naturally, have not come into the publisher's possession.

A WORD ON PRICING

In addition to providing accurate information, this catalogue gives the readers the most up-to-date retail prices for Royal Doulton jugs in American, Canadian and British currencies.

To accomplish this, The Charlton Press continues to access an international pricing panel of experts who submit prices based on both dealer and collector retail-price activity, as well as current auction results in the U.S.A., Canada and the U.K. These market prices are carefully averaged to reflect accurate valuations for jugs in each of these markets. All discontinued jugs are priced in this manner.

Please be aware that all prices given in a particular currency are for jugs within that particular country. The prices published herein have not been calculated using exchange rates exclusively. They have been determined solely by supply and demand within the country in question.

A necessary word of caution: no pricing catalogue can be, or should be, a fixed price list. This catalogue, therefore, should be considered as a pricing guide only — showing the most current retail prices based on market demand within a particular region for the various models.

Current models, however, are priced according to the manufacturer's suggested retail price. Please be aware that price or promotional sales discounting is always possible and can result in lower prices than those listed.

The prices listed herein are for jugs in mint condition. Collectors are cautioned that a repaired or restored piece may be worth as little as 25 per cent of the value of the same model in mint condition.

One exception, however, occurs in the case of current jugs or recent limited editions issued in only one of the three markets. Since such items were priced by Doulton only in the country in which they were to be sold, prices for the other markets are not shown.

ROYAL DOULTON YEAR CYPHERS

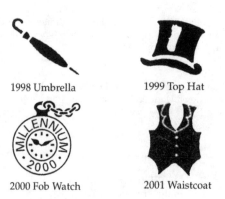

1998 Umbrella   1999 Top Hat

2000 Fob Watch   2001 Waistcoat

CONTENTS

THE INTERNET AND PRICING

Over three years ago we wrote a column for the introduction of our guides dealing with the Internet and the impact it would have on the collecting industry. In this column we gave the reasons why the Internet would affect collectables and their selling price, and also how it would impact and change the way collectors acquire items for their collections.

All this is certainly happening. The industry is now in the sea of change. On the World Wide Web it makes no difference what you collect - coins, stamps, ceramics, art pottery, glass, books - all and sundry are impacted. Naturally, the Van Gogh's are not, but leaving out the high priced items or the exotics, all collectables are and will be affected.

The Web has lowered the transaction cost between the buyer and the seller to a point where land-based sellers (dealers, auction houses) cannot compete under the old rules.

Collectables and collections used to flow through the old supply chain: estate or non-collector/picker/ dealer/collector/land auction/dealer/collector. Naturally, the chain could be interrupted or jumped when convenient.

The new chain which moves items at a much faster rate, and at a much lower cost, maybe outlined as follows: estate, non-collector, picker, collector, dealer/on-line auction/dealer/collector.

Retail stores and malls have closed. Collectable/ Antique Fairs and Shows are losing dealers simply because collectors are changing their buying habits. Collectable Shows are too long and too drawn out. High-end Antique/Decorator Shows can still support long openings, for besides being fairs, they are a form of entertainment.

The following is a chart of the number of items, by type, that appear on a major on-line auction site:

Category	Items Daily	Items Projected To Yearly Basis
Coins	6,000	2,190,000
Disney	37,500	13,687,500
Harry Potter	2,300	839,500
Lalique	650	237,250
Moorcroft	250	91,250
Royal Doulton	3,500	1,277,500
Royal Worcester	600	219,000
Stamps	12,750	4,654,000
Star Wars	19,000	6,935,000

As you can see, the numbers are staggering. This major site advertises "over 5 million items for sale." That is over 1.8 billion items yearly.

Of course, these are not all collectables but one can become easily dismayed by such numbers. Turning to a positive point of view, it also signifies tremendous interest and awareness in things collectable. This major on-line auction has sites in Australia, Austria, Canada, France, Germany, Italy, Japan, the United Kingdon and the United States. Three years ago it was only the United States. What happens now, will the rest of the world (China, India) join in? When they do, the interest and awareness will only continue to build.

Certainly, collecting is a function of disposable income, but that is also improving worldwide. What is happening to prices? We, Charlton, come from a numismatic background, based in the 1960s, 70s and 80s. Our experience derives from a market that has seen wild gyrations in the supply and demand for over a forty-year period. Equating the numismatic market to the collectable market, what appears to be happening in the collectable field is exactly what occurred in the great coin melts of the late sixties to early eighties. The flood gates opened - attics, basements, garages, storage rooms, grandma's and grandpa's houses all disgorged their (coins) goodies. Today's collectables are being rushed to an on-line auction site (the melting pot), where they may be disposed of regardless of price.

How long will this go on? In the coin market, the melts lasted (as long as the precious metal prices rose) nearly 20 years. The rise in the intrinsic value of coins drew all and sundry out onto the market, identical to what is now happening to the on-line auctions and all collectables.

Everyone is rushing, looking for the next item to list on the on-line auction. When some item makes a tremendous splash (at a very high price), the hunt is on to find another like it.

With supply rising, prices will fall. Competition in the early stages will not be demand driven, but supply driven. With more competition, prices will fall. So what's the forecast?

Now, remember, this is over a long time period. Prices will move down from highs of the late-nineties, into lows for the mid-2000, and then rise again in mid-2010. The time frame mentioned may be over-estimated for we do deal with an infinite supply and the rate at which items change hands is certainly rapid.

Our guide prices will, over time, have the look of a large saucer-shaped curve for prices will rise.

Now this will not apply across the board, for what is now scarce will probably remain scarce. However, some will turn from scarce to plentiful as the flood changes the supply. The reverse will also be true, some things that are thought to be plentiful will be found to be scarce. There is one certainty: it will be an interesting time.

THE ORIGINS OF THE TOBY JUG
Louise Irvine

Pottery jugs in the image of human beings have been made since the dawn of civilisation, and some impressive examples have survived from Greek and Roman times, as well as from the ancient cultures of South America. In Medieval England, potters poked fun at their contemporaries by creating figurative jugs, and these primitive vessels also provide interesting precedents for the toby jug, which first appeared in the Staffordshire Potteries in the late 18th century.

The toby jug traditionally represents a seated drinking character with a pot of foaming ale balanced on his knee. He is dressed in typical costume of the period, with a long coat and knee breeches, and his large tricorn hat forms the spout of the jug. There are several theories as to the origin of his name. Some suggest a connection with Shakespeare's convivial character Sir Toby Belch, others believe the notorious Yorkshire toper Henry Elwes was the model. He died in 1761 having consumed some 2,000 gallons of Stingo, a particularly strong ale, and was known as "Toby Fillpot." Potters might also have been inspired by an old English drinking song, *The Brown Jug*, written by the Reverend Francis Fawkes, which paid tribute to Toby Fillpot, "a thirsty old soul" who excelled in boozing. The popular verses were first published in 1761 and were soon distributed in print form, accompanied by a caricature of an enthusiastic drinker with a ruddy complexion and a huge beer belly.

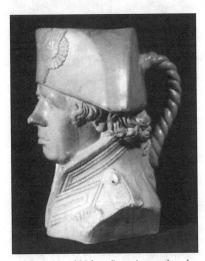

Admiral Lord Nelson figure jug produced
at the Doulton and Watts factory

By the early years of the 19th century, the Staffordshire potters were producing many variations on the original toby type, including standing figures flourishing pipes, sporting squires, jolly sailors and even female characters. Toby jugs were also made in other parts of England, notably London, where the Lambeth potteries used their favoured brown salt-glaze stoneware material to produce genial tobies astride barrels.

DOULTON LAMBETH JUGS

Brown stoneware tobies were amongst the earliest products of the Doulton and Watts factory, which was established on the banks of the river Thames in London in 1815. As well as complete figure jugs, the company also produced face jugs of famous personalities. The most impressive and best known is their portrait of the great naval hero Lord Nelson. Two different models are marked with the company's early trademark, Doulton and Watts. The complete bust stands 11¾" tall and the smaller head and shoulder design was made in three different sizes, the largest 7½" tall. Replicas of both these models, clearly marked as such, were later made to celebrate the centenary of the Battle of Trafalgar in 1905, but even these are difficult to find today.

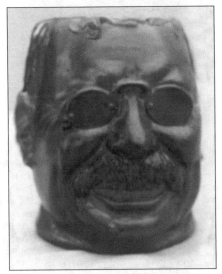

Stoneware portrait jug of Theodore Roosevelt
modelled by Leslie Harradine

Nelson's great antagonist Napoleon has also been portrayed as a stoneware jug, and there are similar tributes to Wellington, the Iron Duke, but these are unmarked and could have been made by any of the London potters, as they frequently copied each other's ideas. The Doulton pottery went on to honour many other military heroes, politicians and statesmen on flasks, jugs and vases, but the idea of the face jug was not revived until the early 1900s, when the celebrated modeller Leslie Harradine produced a stoneware portrait jug of Theodore Roosevelt, the 26th President of the United States. This was followed by a curious pair of Veteran Motorist jugs, an ugly Highwayman, a beaming Old King Cole and a humorous caricature of Mr. Pecksniff, from Dickens's *Martin Chuzzlewit*. The pattern books also refer to a Wee Mac jug in 1908, but to date this has not materialised and there may well be others still to come to light. Harradine left the Lambeth studio in 1912, but his colleague Mark

Marshall occasionally dabbled in the toby tradition, producing a Soldier toby jug and a face jug, which bears a strong resemblance to John Barleycorn, the first character jug made at Royal Doulton's other factory in Burslem, Stoke-on-Trent.

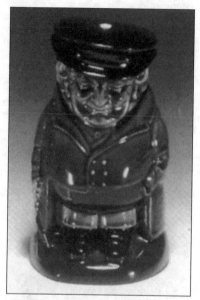

Old King Cole modelled by Leslie Harradine

Charles Noke, the Burslem art director, was a regular visitor to Lambeth and was undoubtedly influenced by the achievements of the stoneware modellers. He was particularly impressed with the work of Harry Simeon, who contorted Toby Fillpot into a variety of useful shapes, including three styles of toby jugs, tobacco jars, ashpots, inkwells, candlesticks, decanters and even a teapot. A publicity leaflet of the mid 1920s indicates that the Simeon toby jugs were available in several sizes with modelling variations and alternative colourways. In addition the waistcoat could be coloured in a bright red enamel for a surcharge of 25 percent on the list price.

Simeon's toby wares all feature the full seated figure, with the exception of one model that depicts a happy smiling face on the marriage day, but when it is turned upside down, scowling features reveal what happens after marriage. The Marriage mug was made in three sizes and was included in the publicity leaflet for the rest of the stoneware toby collection. Although most of the Lambeth tobies were made of slip cast stoneware and produced in small editions, they are very hard to find today and count amongst the rarest of the Royal Doulton jugs.

BURSLEM CHARACTER AND TOBY JUGS

The Doulton family extended their business to Burslem, Stoke-on-Trent, in 1877, but initially they concentrated on the production of tablewares and other useful wares for the Victorian home. Gradually an art studio was developed, and in 1889 Charles Noke, who had trained at the Worcester

factory, was appointed as a modeller of ornamental vases, mainly for exhibition purposes. Before long Noke was also producing figure models and had embarked on a mission to revive the Staffordshire figurative tradition. In 1913, following the launch of his famous HN collection of figures, he was promoted to art director, and he soon turned his attention to the revival of the toby jug.

His first models were quite different in style from the traditional smoking topers with brimful tankards of ale. In 1918, he introduced a portrait of the great silent movie star Charlie Chaplin in the form of a large toby jug, and this was followed a few years later by a similar portrait of George Robey, the popular music-hall comedian. In both models the characters' bowler hats come off to reveal the jugs underneath. George Robey, the "Prime Minister of Mirth," visited the Burslem factory in 1925, and the toby jug was probably made at that time.

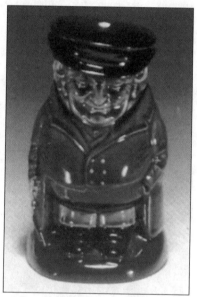

The Kingsware Huntsman modelled by
Charles Noke, 1919

Another early toby jug depicts a huntsman in scarlet, D4090, and this 1919 model was re-launched in more subdued colours as part of an extensive collection of tobies in 1950. The Huntsman was also issued in Kingsware, a distinctive treacle-brown ware which was developed by Noke in the early 1900s and used primarily for whisky flasks. A Kingsware Squire toby jug was also produced and a face jug of a Highlander was made around 1930 for D & J McCallum distillers in Edinburgh. It may have been this commission which gave Noke the idea for a collection of face jugs, for by 1933 he had modelled two designs, John Barleycorn, the personification of barley, and Old Charley, a typical night watchman, and they were launched the following year.

With the help of his chief modeller, Harry Fenton, Noke quickly introduced more personalities from literature, legend, folk-lore and song, and by 1935 the first models were also available in a small size (around 4") as an alternative to the original large size (around 6½"). A miniature size (around 2½") was added to the range by 1939, and the following year the first tinies (1¼") were launched. These became the four standard sizes for the character jug range, although the dimensions have altered over the years, with some large-size jugs now measuring over 7½". There have also been occasional medium- or intermediate-size jugs (around 4½"), as with the Dickens, Wild West and Beatles collections and an extra-large Tony Weller character jug, but these are exceptions to the usual sizes.

Although Charles Noke was in his mid seventies when he introduced character jugs, his fertile imagination was still working overtime, and by 1939 he had adapted the most popular personalities from the range to create a collection of useful gift items now known as the derivatives; for example, musical jugs, wall vases, tobacco jars, ashtrays, sugar bowls and teapots. He also developed a new range of toby jugs, several of which were closely based on early models by Harry Simeon at Doulton's Lambeth factory, in particular Double XX, Honest Measure and The Squire.

The bombing of the Burslem studio during the Second World War briefly interrupted Noke's creative output, but the conflict gave him an opportunity to pay tribute to the great war leader Winston Churchill, the first contemporary personality to be portrayed as a character and toby jug. Unfortunately Noke's character jug portrait, an unusual two-handled model in white, was not considered a good likeness and was quickly withdrawn from the range. It was the first character jug to be discontinued, and because of its brief production period, it is now very sought after. Early in 1941 Noke made a couple of attempts to remodel and colour the portrait, but only prototypes of these experiments are known to exist. Harry Fenton had considerably more success with his toby jug portrait of Churchill, which was launched in 1940 and remained in production for 50 years.

Charles Noke died in 1941, at the age of 83, and for several years Harry Fenton was the sole modeller. He continued to create excellent likenesses of contemporary characters, such as Monty and Smuts, but he was equally at home with historical or fictional characters, for example the Samuel Johnson and Robin Hood jugs which impart a vivid sense of reality. In 1949 Max Henk, who had been appointed as a tableware modeller, became interested in character jugs and his Uncle Tom Cobbleigh was introduced in 1952. When Fenton died in 1953, Henk was able to step into the breach and he soon set a new style for character jugs, which is most obvious in his approach to their handles. He fully exploited the handle's potential for elaborating on the story of the character portrayed; thus Scaramouche has his guitar and the handle of The Ugly Duchess is a flamingo, which she used as a croquet mallet in the story of Alice in Wonderland. Henk obviously loved delving into literature and legend for symbolic allusions such as these, and they add a new dimension to character jugs for the curious collector.

Apart from his own work, Henk had responsibility for training the next generation of artists. Geoff Blower was generally regarded as Henk's protégé and even before he had completed his five-year apprenticeship, he was contributing to the character jug range. His first jug in 1952 was Lord Nelson, and he followed this with several other popular models, such as Rip Van Winkle, which was in production for 40 years. Blower left the Burslem studio in 1956 to take up a career in teaching, but on his retirement he began modelling character jugs again and worked on the Collecting World series. His former colleague Garry Sharpe also started his career at Doulton but moved overseas in 1960, by which time he had modelled some of the best-selling character jugs in the range, including Old Salt and Merlin (style one). Perhaps his success had something to do with Fenton's modelling tools, which Henk gave him in 1953 with the challenging remark, "If there is any of Harry's magic left in these modelling tools, you certainly need it!"

Henk's third apprentice was David Biggs, who joined the team in 1958 after an art school training. Working on his first jug, the Town Crier, he soon found out how difficult it is to create one face which typifies a profession or a hobby, but he then went on to specialise in this field, modelling the Golfer, the Yachtsman, the Punch and Judy Man and many other representative characters. When stuck for a particular expression, he would often reach for a mirror and manoeuvre his own face to achieve the desired effect.

To make way for all the exciting jugs from this new generation of modellers, around 30 early models were withdrawn from production in 1960. A few years later, Royal Doulton decided to discontinue the traditional earthenware body and make all the jugs in the newly developed English Translucent China. David Biggs was given the task of making all the new, more detailed models of existing jugs, which were required for the new process, and several more jugs were withdrawn at this stage to avoid all the costly remodelling. The changeover took place between 1968 and 1970, but the fine china jugs were only made for a few years before earthenware production was resumed in 1973 at the newly acquired John Beswick factory. The fine china jugs are therefore highly valued by collectors and can be recognised most easily by the slight difference in size. Biggs continued to model new character jugs until the early 1970s, and for the next 20 years he concentrated on tableware modelling, occasionally reviving his character jug design skills, notably for W.C. Fields and Louis Armstrong in the Celebrity series. In recent years some of his models for the character jug range include H. G. Wells, Quasimodo, and the Character Jug of the Year for 1998, Lewis Carroll.

In 1972 a special studio was established for the development of figures and character jugs, and Eric Griffiths was appointed the new head of sculpture, ultimately becoming art director. Griffiths was a portrait painter by training and he particularly enjoyed modelling famous people for the jug range, notably Henry VIII, Mark Twain and Ronald Reagan. He also portrayed John Doulton, the founder of the company, as the first character jug especially for members of the Royal Doulton International Collectors Club, which was founded in 1980. There have been many more exclusive commissions for members in the intervening years, including a revival of the tiny size for the Beefeater and Old King Cole jugs.

The 1980s was an exciting time for character jug fans. The club provided a lot of useful information on the subject, stimulating many new collections, and the first major reference book by Desmond Eyles had just been published in 1979. Another informative book was produced by Jocelyn

Lukins to celebrate the 50th anniversary of character jugs in 1984, and there were a number of price guides reflecting the buoyant market. New record prices were continuously being set in the sale rooms and amongst the most exceptional was the Toby Gillette jug, which was modelled by Eric Griffiths in a limited edition of three for a popular British TV show, "Jim'll Fix It." The jug sold for over £15,000 at Christie's auction rooms in 1984 to raise money for charity.

Several limited edition collections of character jugs were launched during the 1980s, beginning with the novel two-faced portraits for the Antagonists series by Michael Abberley, a young Royal Doulton figure painter who taught himself to model jugs in his spare time. The Antagonists were extremely popular, and the edition of 9,500 was soon over-subscribed. Abberley followed his first success with another two-faced collection, the Star-Crossed Lovers, and he also worked on some unlimited series, including the Wives of Henry VIII and characters from Shakespeare.

Such was the popularity of character jugs by the mid 1980s that many independent companies requested special designs for advertising purposes. This was not a new idea, as famous firms such as Charringtons had commissioned specially branded tobies in the 1930s and in 1956 the American industrialist Cliff Cornell even had a toby jug made in his own image to impress his customers. Thirty years later another American firm, Quaker Oats, ordered a character jug of Mr. Quaker and Pick Kwik Wines and Spirits of Derby purchased a large range of character jug containers for their liquor during the 1980s. Mail order companies, fair organisers and leading retailers all wanted exclusive jugs for promotional events and colourways of existing jugs were sold in special editions. At first the very small editions were snapped up , as with the colourway of the Mad Hatter made to commemorate the opening of the Royal Doulton Shop at Higbees of Cleveland in 1985, but collectors eventually became jaded with the number of colourways, and the company concentrated resources on new subjects instead.

Since the 1980s most new character jug subjects have been conceived as part of sets, thus creating interesting themes for collectors. In response to the demand for American subjects, Royal Doulton introduced the Wild West and the Celebrity series. The 50th anniversary of the Second World War led to several commemorative series, the Heroic Leaders, the Armed Forces and Heroes of the Blitz, and other important historical events have inspired individual jugs, notably Columbus, which was produced to mark the 500th anniversary of his famous voyage to the New World. Established themes have also been developed to create new series; for example, the Beefeater was joined by lots of other London characters, and Henk's early characters from *Alice's Adventures in Wonderland* were joined by The Red Queen and The March Hare. To date this is the only animal character in the range, but the designer Bill Harper has also considered a grinning Cheshire Cat and White Rabbit, so it will be interesting to see if any others appear in the future. Harper is perhaps best known as a figure modeller, but he has

produced a number of character jugs, as well as the amusing Doultonville collection of 25 small-size tobies, which were produced between 1983 and 1991.

Since 1992 there have also been limited-edition toby jugs of traditional characters, such as the Jester and the Clown. These were designed by Stan Taylor, a retired art teacher from Bristol, and he has been responsible for the majority of character jugs introduced since 1982. His subjects are extremely diverse, ranging from portraits of circus performers to typical characters encountered on a journey through Britain, such as a postman and a policeman. He also allowed his imagination to run riot for his Witch and Genie jugs. These are now in demand, having only been in production for six months because of the extensive withdrawal of character jugs at the end of 1991. The range was reduced from 157 models to 59 — all the early toby jugs were withdrawn and the miniature-size jug was discontinued altogether.

The rationalisation of the character jug range coincided with the appointment of a new art director, Amanda Hughes-Lubeck, who is in charge of all the Royal Doulton design studios. She continues to commission character jugs from Stan Taylor and Bill Harper but other younger modellers from the John Beswick studio, notably Martyn Alcock and Warren Platt, have also been encouraged to try their hands at modelling jugs. They work under the guidance of studio manager Graham Tongue, who has several advertising jugs to his credit, including the superb portrait of William Grant.

As well as all this new talent, recent marketing initiatives have also been well received by collectors. The Character Jug of the Year concept has proved very successful, with huge sales for Winston Churchill, the 1992 exclusive. The prestige limited-edition jugs with two or more handles have also been popular, notably the Henry VIII and William Shakespeare designs. After a brief period of concern about wide-ranging withdrawals and colourways, the future now looks very bright for character jug collectors.

BUILDING A COLLECTION

Collections start in many different ways. Often a surprise gift will be responsible for starting a life-long enthusiasm or it could be a legacy that starts an instant collection. Perhaps a chance discovery in an antique market might also spark off a new collector's curiosity and hunting for more will become an absorbing hobby. One thing is certain, the first acquisition is rarely alone for long.

A few dedicated collectors have acquired all the Royal Doulton character and toby jugs in the standard range and then gone on to add rare prototypes, colourways, modelling variations and unusual backstamps. However, this goal requires considerable time and energy as well as substantial financial resources. Most collectors are content to concentrate on specific themes, sizes or types of jugs and can build some fascinating collections in this way.

Collecting By Type

Lambeth Stoneware Jugs

The scarcity of the early jugs from the Lambeth factory has meant that they are not as widely publicised as the Burslem models. However, there is a committed group of collectors who specialise in English stonewares and seek out the Doulton tobies and face jugs along with other brown salt-glaze stoneware products, such as reform flasks, hunting jugs, bottles, mugs and jars. Competition is stiff, therefore, to include representative examples in Doulton jug collections. A little more accessible are the Lambeth toby wares, modelled by Harry Simeon, which were made in small editions during the 1920s. A number of collectors have specialised in this field, delighting in all the ingenious uses devised for Toby Fillpots, be it a candlestick, tobacco jar, ink pot or traditional jug. One of the largest collections, built up over ten years, included more than 75 examples in various sizes and colour schemes. Collectors' discoveries have added greatly to the archive information over the years, but it is still impossible to produce a definitive list, which is part of the fun of collecting these Simeon tobies.

Toby Jugs

The term "toby" is frequently used to describe all Royal Doulton jugs, but strictly speaking it should only be applied to jugs in the form of a full seated or standing figure. Although Royal Doulton began by producing toby jugs at their Burslem factory, they are better known for their character jugs, which feature only the head and shoulders. Nevertheless, there is a lot of scope for collectors in the toby jug range alone.

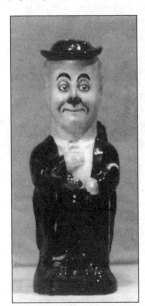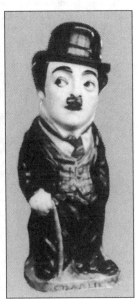

George Robey (c.1925) and Charlie Chaplin (1918)
designed by Charles Noke, Art Director

Two of the earliest Burslem tobies are also the rarest, the large portraits of Charlie Chaplin and George Robey, which stand around 11" tall. Most of the traditional tobies, with their tankards of foaming ale, were introduced in 1939, and the majority remained in production for over 50 years, so they are relatively easy to find. The best-selling toby portrait of Winston Churchill is also readily available in three different sizes and should not be confused, as has often happened, with the rare Churchill character jug. Also confusing is the similarity between the Winston Churchill toby and the toby of Cliff Cornell. This American industrialist was a great admirer of Churchill, and in 1956 he commissioned a portrait toby of himself in the image of the great statesman — even smoking a cigar. Three different colourways were produced in two sizes, with Cornell wearing either a brown, blue or tan suit and various matching ties. The base was suitably inscribed to promote his Cleveland Flux company, and he sent them to his friends and associates as Thanksgiving gifts. Today they are becoming hard to find, particularly the tan suit variation, which was made in smaller quantities than the others. Advertising toby jugs were also commissioned by Charrington's to promote their Toby Ale, and three versions with different inscriptions have been recorded from the 1930s.

Completely different in style from the rest of the range are the little Dickens tobies (4½" high), which verge on caricature. There are six characters to find in this desirable collection, which was produced between 1948 and 1960, and there is a lot of competition from Dickens fans. This whimsical style of toby jug was revived by Bill Harper for his Doultonville collection in 1983. He created 25 larger-than-life characters from the imaginary town of Doultonville for this appealing set and all have appropriate comical names. One of the rarest is Albert Sagger, the Potter, which was only made for a six-month period especially for Collectors Club members.

In 1992 Royal Doulton launched their first limited-edition toby jugs in a new style and size (5½"). The collection has grown rapidly and their instant popularity has inspired a revival of interest in Royal Doulton tobies. The subjects have varied from traditional characters, like the Jester and the Clown, to unusual double-sided designs like The Judge and Thief.

In 1994, Royal Doulton launched a new tiny size for their toby jugs, reinterpreting some of the first toby designs, such as Old Charley and Happy John, in this miniature scale. The set of six tiny tobies has been well received and it will be interesting to see if more follow.

Character Jugs

The standard character jug range has included around 300 different subjects, not to mention all the different sizes which have been available, so there is a lot of scope for collectors. It is the ambition of many keen collectors to find all of them, but as the range expands, so the task becomes more daunting and choices have to be made.

The most accessible jugs are the ones in current production, which can be purchased in local china shops or by mail order through specialist dealers. The Doulton catalogues currently list around 40 different subjects, some of which are available in large size, some in small size and some in both. There are also limited editions, subject to availability, and a few special commissions from Lawleys By Post and other companies. This number changes every year as new designs are added and models are withdrawn from production.

Once a piece has been discontinued in the Doulton catalogues, it is only available on the secondary market. Prices will depend on the demand for the retired model, which is often influenced by how long it was in production. Obviously there will be lots of Bacchus jugs around, as it was made for over 30 years before being discontinued in 1991, whereas the Genie and the Witch jugs were in production for less than a year before being caught up in the sweeping withdrawals of 1991.

There are different styles of discontinued character jugs, and it may be that a specific era or the work of a particular artist appeals. Harry Fenton, who was active in the 1930s and 40s, modelled rugged, wrinkly faces (with warts and all!), whereas in the 1950s and 60s his successor, Max Henk, favoured smoother complexions with exaggerated features. It was Henk and his assistants who saw the potential of the character jug's handle which had been mostly plain and functional in the early years, and many collectors delight in the creativity and ingenuity of the designs, which have included animals, birds, boats, various weapons, sporting equipment, musical instruments and even parts of buildings. Miniature faces or figures have often been incorporated in the handle and the latest representation of Henry VIII features all six of his wives on two handles — seven portraits in one jug! There has even been a prestigious three-handled jug recently, King Charles I. Occasionally new handles have been modelled for promotional purposes or just to ring the changes, and in the case of the Santa Claus and Father Christmas jugs, several different handles have been issued over the years.

Themes and Series

Part of the fun of collecting character jugs is researching the symbolism of the handles and finding out more about the characters behind the jugs. For bookworms there have been lots of characters from literature, beginning with the novels of Charles Dickens, a particular favourite of the art director, Charles Noke. Just looking for all the different Dickens character jugs, tobies, derivatives and limited-edition jugs could keep a collector very busy for several years. Those interested in England's past will find an abundance of kings and queens, colourful London characters and military heroes to create a historical pageant of jugs. As an island nation, the sea has been particularly important in British history, and not surprisingly there are many seafaring characters which could form part of a nautical collection. Patriotic Americans can look out for all the presidents, Civil War generals, Williamsburg pioneers, Hollywood film stars and Wild West cowboys represented in the collection. In many cases these have been presented in themed sub-collections, some in limited editions, and issued on an annual basis by Royal Doulton. A list of all the different self-contained series is listed on pages 655 to 658 for easy reference.

Collecting by Size

Potential display space is one of the factors to consider when embarking on a collection of character jugs as many subjects have been available in four different sizes — large, small, miniature and tiny. Some keen collectors purchase their favourite jugs in all the sizes along with the toby version and the various derivatives, and in the case of Sairey Gamp, that makes 12 different portraits of her to collect!

The majority of collectors look out for one specific size of character jug and the large has tended to be the most popular. In the past Royal Doulton always launched the large size first and, if it was well received, smaller versions would follow within a few years. Sometimes the subject never appeared in the small or miniature sizes, much to the chagrin of those who were collecting these. In recent years, the Royal Doulton International Collectors Club has commissioned a number of small-size jugs exclusively for their members, and Lawleys By Post, the mail-order division of the company, also prefers the small size for their special series, and these are not produced in any other size.

The smaller the jug, the less detail it is possible to achieve, and the costs do not decrease in proportion to the scale, which has tended to make the miniature-size character jug the least popular choice. In 1992 Royal Doulton discontinued this size jug altogether, so there are now set limits to a miniature character jug collection. However, some models will be hard to find, notably Trapper and Lumberjack, which were not officially launched, yet some examples have appeared on the market. On several occasions miniature prototypes were developed many years before they were put into production, as with The Golfer, where the miniature followed 15 years after the large size, or Old Salt, where there was an interval of 23 years.

To date Royal Doulton have only produced 40 tiny-size character jugs, making this a diminutive collection in more ways than one. Their obvious appeal is reflected in the high prices commanded by the original set of 12, which are out of all proportion to their Lilliputian scale. The tinies require expert decorating skills, and the artists have to balance the minute jugs on the end of their little fingers, which is very time consuming and consequently expensive. Such tiny jugs are also difficult to display in china shops, which has meant that models have tended to be special commissions; for example, a set of Kings and Queens of the Realm characters for Lawleys By Post customers and the tiny Beefeater and Old King Cole jugs for members of the RDICC.

LIMITED AND SPECIAL-EDITION CHARACTER AND TOBY JUGS

Limited-edition jugs are comparatively recent developments, as the first character jug was not commissioned until 1978 and the first toby in 1992. It was Michael Doulton's first American tour that inspired the reproduction of the company's very first jug, John Barleycorn, and it was issued in a limited edition of 7,500, appropriately numbered and marked on the base. A few years later, in 1983, the first limited-edition collection was launched with Grant and Lee as the initial pair of Antagonists. The novel two-faced design proved to be very popular, and the edition of 9,500 was quickly sold out. The other three jugs in the series were also very successful, and so they were quickly followed in 1985 by the Star-Crossed Lovers, another two-faced collection.

In 1984 Royal Doulton had the honour of designing a character jug portrait of President Ronald Reagan as a fund-raiser for the Republican National Committee, and number one of the edition of 2,000 was presented to the President at the White House. This prestigious commission was followed by many other requests for special character jugs to promote various companies, products and events. A character jug of Mr. Quaker was produced in a limited edition of 3,500 to mark the 85th year of Quaker Oats Limited in 1985, and the restricted distribution amongst this company's customers and employees has made this a very desirable jug today. Pick-Kwik Wines and Spirits of Derby commissioned a range of small-size character jugs, some adapted as liquor containers, to promote their various whiskies. As well as the traditional pre-announced limited editions, they also issued collectors editions and special editions — new terms coined to describe commissions by independent companies that are not individually numbered limited editions in the strictest sense. Special editions have included colourways (discussed in the section on colour variations) and entirely new jugs, such as the Collecting World Series for Kevin Francis and the Great Generals series for UK International Ceramics.

There have also been occasional special commissions, which are limited by time and distribution rather than by numbers. For example, in 1984 only members of the Royal Doulton International Collectors Club could purchase a small- size Henry Doulton character jug, and in 1986 the offer was a small Doultonville toby of Albert Sagger, the Potter. Similarly, only customers attending Michael Doulton's special appearances in 1988 and 1989 could buy the character jug portrait of him. In 1991 Royal Doulton launched their new Character Jug of the Year concept, which limits the model to one year's production, and this has proved very popular.

In the last few years there has been a new approach to limited character jugs with the launch of several exceptionally complex and detailed models in low editions at premium prices. Some of these prestige jugs had two handles, or even three, and gold or silver embellishments. The first of this type was Henry VIII, issued in 1991 in a limited edition of 1,991 to mark the 500th anniversary of his birth. The edition was quickly oversubscribed, endorsing collectors' very positive reactions to these ambitious designs. Another recent development which has generated a lot of interest is the collection of limited-edition toby jugs, which began in 1992 with the Jester.

PROTOTYPES AND VARIATIONS

Once all the standard range jugs have been acquired, the ultimate challenge for many serious collectors is to find as many prototypes and variations as possible. This usually requires a very healthy bank balance, as huge sums of money can change hands for these rare pieces.

Prototypes

Prototype jugs are the samples taken from the master mould, and they are often described as pilots or trials. Usually two or three jugs are cast at this early stage, any more would wear down the detail in the master mould, and they are given different decorative treatments. If one of the prototypes is approved, then lots of production moulds will be made, but if it is rejected, the model will only exist in prototype form. There have been lots of character jugs and at least a few toby jugs that did not get past the prototype stage for various reasons.

In the 1920s Charles Noke modelled a toby jug of John Wesley, the founder of Methodism, but when the prototypes came from the kiln, he had misgivings about the propriety of portraying a strict abstainer as a toby. He therefore abandoned the project, giving one of the prototype jugs to the decorator Ted Eley, another was later presented to the Museum of the Wesley Church in Tasmania.

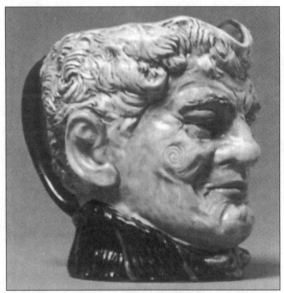

Prototype of The Maori modelled by Harry Fenton in 1939

During the 1930s most of the jugs that were modelled seem to have gone into production, but the war interrupted several plans. In the Royal Doulton archives there are references to an Old Scrooge jug and one called Red Wing, but no illustrations have survived. Harry Fenton modelled two portraits of a New Zealand Maori, one of which was approved in July 1939, but it did not subsequently go into the general range. A few examples survive in private collections around the world, and the last one to come on the market in 1998 sold for £21,000. No records survive for the Buffalo Bill jug, which presumably also dates from the war years and was modelled by Fenton.

The 1950s seem to have passed with only two casualties. The Scarlet Pimpernell, which was submitted by Geoff Blower, surfaced in 1987 and changed hands for over £15,000. Blower's colleague Garry Sharpe remembered his portrait of Alice in Wonderland being turned down in 1959 because of copyright restrictions, but no examples have come to light, so perhaps it did not get beyond the clay stage.

During the 1960s a rejected Village Blacksmith was rescued from a Doulton rubbish skip by a factory labourer, and his family sold it, in 1993, at Phillips Auction rooms in London for over £7,000. It is probably the work of design manager Max Henk, and it was given a pattern number D6549 in 1961, so it is strange that it was never launched.

David Biggs was responsible for many of the successful character jugs produced during the 1960s, but several of his prototypes were rejected at the end of the decade, possibly because of the re-appraisal of the collection and the change-over to bone china production, which took place at that time. He remembers submitting a Racing Driver, but this has not come to light. However, his models of of a Fisherman (1968), John Gilpin (1968) and two colourways of The Baseball Player (1971) are in private collections, and his ambitious Pilgrim Father was discovered at Royal Doulton in 1988.

Several new modellers joined the design department in the 1970s, and inevitably some of their early work was not accepted for production. Robert Tabbenor's character jug of Uncle Tom Cobbleigh was rejected in 1975 and Peter Gee's Jester toby in 1977. Although both artists later produced popular jugs, they made figure modelling their speciality. Michael Abberley's Cabinet Maker of Williamsburg, which he modelled in 1979, caused a lot of confusion, as it was publicised in the 1981 catalogue but was not launched then, as it was decided to discontinue the Williamsburg range. In August 1995 it finally joined the collection at the RDICC convention in Williamsburg to mark the 15th anniversary of the club. Bill Harper's first character jug of a pirate was rejected in 1976, but he has gone on to contribute a wide range of subjects to the range. Unfortunately his admirable portrait of Pierre Trudeau (1986) missed the boat as the Canadian Prime Minister had left office before the jug was ready to be launched. In 1987 Bill was keen to produce a Canterbury Tales series of jugs but it was felt that the Miller and The Wife of Bath were not sufficiently well-known internationally, and so they remain in prototype form in Royal Doulton's own collection. Bill also submitted a portrait of Elvis Presley for the Celebrity collection, but it was not approved by the singer's estate. Several stars in this hapless series did not get beyond the prototype stage, but they have found their way on to the market. In 1992 one of the Marilyn Monroe prototypes was auctioned in Canada for $17,500 and a Humphrey Bogart prototype has also changed hands for a significant sum. A portrait of Clark Gable had got beyond the prototype stage and several hundred had been made in 1984 before it was recalled for copyright reasons, so although not unique, it is still a rare model.

A few more jugs "got away" in the late 1980s, including a portrayal of Robin Hood by Eric Griffiths, Uncle Sam by Harry Sales and a Prison Warder by Stan Taylor, and no doubt there will be more in the future, although the art director's ideal is not to reach the expensive prototype stage until all the production problems have been ironed out. For this reason original clay models are smashed or left to dry out and crumble to dust if they do not come up to scratch.

Often the design of the character jug is basically acceptable, but there are reservations about the handle. Usually this is resolved at the clay stage, as with the Collectors Club jug of Henry Doulton, which originally incorporated a drainpipe in the handle to symbolise the firm's original achievements. It was felt that this was too mundane a reminder and the vase motif was emphasised instead. Occasionally alternative handles have been moulded, and for the Catharine of Aragon character jug two different designs featuring a cornet and a scroll were considered before the version with the tower was agreed upon.

It is not only aesthetic considerations which lead to modifications, cost is also an important factor and handles occasionally need to be simplified. For example, the prototype of Groucho Marx included the other Marx brothers peeping out from behind his cigar, and they were subsequently removed for the production model. Eagle-eyed collectors have often noticed other minor modifications. The original version of the Fireman character jug, which was used for publicity purposes, featured the badge of the London Fire Brigade, but this was changed when permission to use it was not granted. Discrepancies such as these have always had a particular fascination for jug collectors, and premium prices are paid when original-version prototypes come up for sale.

Modelling Variations

If a character jug is altered once it has gone into production, it can no longer be described as a prototype, but there is still a lot of interest in such modelling variations, and there are more of them around for collectors to find. The Anne of Cleves character jug is a celebrated example. When it was launched in 1980, the ears on the horse handle were erect, but as these were easily chipped they were soon remodelled to lie flat. A premium is now paid for the first "ears up" version. Similarly with the original handle of the Macbeth jug, the large protruding noses on the witches were prone to damage and consequently the heads were turned inwards. It would appear that only a few of the original jugs had been made before modification, so the "noses out" version is extremely rare.

Some of the early character jugs have also been modified, although the reasons for the changes are not so apparent. Harry Fenton's Granny, which was introduced in 1935, was revamped within a few years. The proportions of her face were altered and a white frill was added to the front of her bonnet, but the most significant addition was a prominent front tooth. This resulted in the original version being dubbed the "Toothless Granny," and she commands considerably more in the marketplace than the second version, which continued in production until 1983. Fenton's Cavalier also exists in two versions; the original from 1940 features a goatee beard, which is missing from the later version, but it now makes a big difference in price if he is bearded.

The war years seem to have been a period of change and reappraisal generally. Apart from the modifications already mentioned, Drake acquired a plumed hat, making the original, hatless version something of a rarity, and Pearly

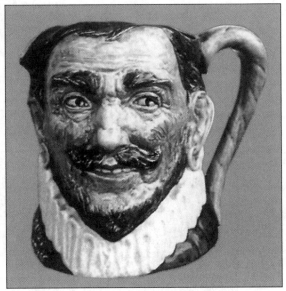

Style One: Hatless Drake

more special colourway editions followed this early success, but their appeal gradually diminished until ultimately the practice ceased at the end of the decade.

During long production runs, colours have frequently been altered for technical reasons, and the results of the new recipes are often noticed by serious collectors. The most obvious in recent years was the Beefeater, who received an on-glaze red jacket in 1987 instead of the early underglaze maroon shade. There have also been other modifications to this long-lived jug. In the first year or so of production, the Royal Cypher GR was picked out in gold, and this is now very rare. When Queen Elizabeth was crowned in 1953, the handle was altered again to feature her cypher ER.

Character and toby jugs are all painted individually by different artists, and so inevitably there will be slight variations in colour between one and another, even though everybody is following the same standard. Occasionally mistakes are made, colours might be reversed or omitted, and they can cause a lot of interest amongst collectors when they slip through the system. An interesting error was spotted in 1984, when the first Custer and Sitting Bull character jugs left the factory. The Indian chief was depicted with grey eyes and, when it was pointed out that this was genetically unlikely, the eyes were altered to brown. There are no prizes for guessing which variation is the most sought after! Around the same time a small quantity of Henry V jugs left the factory without the on-glaze red and gold decoration, and initially they caused some excitement in the marketplace before it was realised they were seconds. Colour variations do not always command premium prices, but it is still fun looking out for them.

Boy lost his relief-modelled buttons to become plain 'Arry. His companion, Pearly Girl, was not remodelled, but was decorated differently to become 'Arriet. The original Pearly Boy and Girl character jugs are now amongst the rarest production models to find.

Colour Variations

Changes of colour can make a significant difference to the desirability of jugs, as has been seen with the Pearly Girl. The presence of a lime green and pink hat, as opposed to the drab green worn by 'Arriet, will attract a substantial premium. Pearly Boy has also worn different coloured outfits, and the blue version is considered to be much rarer than the brown. Another expensive variation is Fenton's Old King Cole. The original, which dates from 1939, has a yellow crown, and the second common version an orange one. There are also slight modelling variations in the ruff, but the colour differences are the most pronounced.

The Clown character jug features the most radical of the early colour changes. In the first version, introduced in 1937, he has a white painted face with bright red hair, whilst the post-war version has natural flesh tones with white hair. There is also a brown-hair variation, which is contemporary with the red-haired model. All the clowns are desirable additions to a collection, but the red and brown-haired versions are priced higher.

In the early years alternative colour schemes for character jugs were unusual, but from the mid 1980s it became standard practice to offer the most popular models in different outfits. A few of these went into the general range, but most were special commissions in limited editions. The first, in 1985, was a colourway of the large-size Mad Hatter, which was produced in an edition of 250 to celebrate the opening of the Royal Doulton room at Higbees department store in the US, and it sold out on the day of issue. Many

DERIVATIVES

Novelty coupled with practicality became Charles Noke's maxim during the 1930s, as his fertile imagination contorted many of his favourite character jug personalities into all sorts of useful items, including teapots, tobacco jars, ashtrays and wall vases. Collecting these derivatives, as they are known, can add another dimension to Doulton displays. It is possible to find Old Charley in 15 different guises, including character jugs, tobies and derivatives, and Sairey Gamp comes a close second in the variety of her appearances, so putting together displays of these characters alone could be fun.

It may be that Noke was given the idea for the derivatives from the novel toby wares made by Harry Simeon at the Lambeth studio, and it is probably not a coincidence that the Burslem factory was also commissioned to model character decanters for Aspreys and Co. The resulting Scotsman and Irishman whisky containers were issued in 1934 and can be considered forerunners of the derivatives. Bookends, busts and napkin rings of Dickens personalities followed, and although they have more in common with Noke's figures from the HN series, they are still sought after by jug enthusiasts.

The first true character jug derivatives were the ashtrays of 1936, which are essentially miniature-size jugs with trays added. These must have been successful, for larger ashbowls and tobacco jars were soon added to the range. Generally only minor modifications were required to suit the character

xvi

LIST OF DERIVATIVES AVAILABLE

Ash Bowls

Auld Mac	109
Farmer John	182
John Barleycorn (style two)	232
Old Charley	293
Paddy	299
Parson Brown	300
Sairey Gamp	337

Ash Trays

Dick Turpin	165
John Barleycorn (style two)	232
Old Charley	293
Parson Brown	300

Bookends

Mr. Micawber (style one)	280
Mr. Pickwick (style one)	282
Sairey Gamp	337
Tony Weller	378

Busts

Buzfuz	128
Mr. Micawber (style one)	280
Mr. Pickwick (style one)	282
Sairey Gamp	337
Sam Weller	339
Tony Weller	378

Musical Jugs

Auld Mac	109
Granny	210
Old Charley	293
Old King Cole	294
Paddy	299
Tony Weller	378

Napkin Rings

Fat Boy	183
Mr. Micawber (style one)	280
Mr. Pickwick (style one)	282
Sairey Gamp	337
Sam Weller	339
Tony Weller	378

Sugar Bowls

Old Charley	293
Sairey Gamp	337
Tony Weller	378

Table Lighters

Bacchus	111
Beefeater	119
Buzfuz	128
Capt. Ahab	130
Cap'n Cuttle	133
Falstaff	181
Granny	210
The Lawyer	249
Long John Silver	256
Mr. Micawber (style one)	280
Mr. Pickwick (style one)	282
Old Charley	293
The Poacher	311
Porthos	313
Rip Van Winkle	326

Teapots

Falstaff	181
Long John Silver	256
Old Charley	293
Old Salt	296
Sairey Gamp	337
Tony Weller	378

Toothpick Holders

Fat Boy	183
Old Charley	293
Paddy	299
Sairey Gamp	337

Tobacco Jars

Old Charley	293
Paddy	299
Sairey Gamp	337

Wall Pockets

Jester	227
Old Charley	293

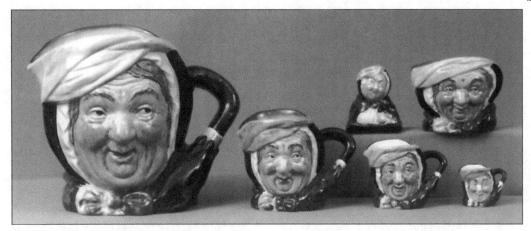

Complete set of Sairey Gamp character jugs together with a sugar bowl and bust

jugs for their new purposes. The musical jugs, for instance, had an extended hollow base to accommodate the Thorens Swiss movement which played the appropriate tune. In contrast, Harry Fenton's creative powers were fully stretched to incorporate Sairey Gamp, Tony Weller and Old Charley into teapots! Although it is highly unlikely that these figurative teapots were used, they soon had matching sugar bowls. Perhaps milk jugs would have followed if it had not been for the outbreak of war, which abruptly curtailed production of all these whimsical gift items. Consequently all the early derivatives are considered rare.

It was not until the late 1950s that designers were once again able to turn their attention to the novelty gift market. A range of table lighters in the form of jug personalities was launched in 1958, and some of these now prove elusive. As well as the 14 lighters recorded in the catalogues, a prototype Granny lighter has also made an appearance in the market. Most of the post-war derivatives have been liquor containers made to order for various distillers and bottlers, including W. Walklate, Pick-Kwik and William Grant, and perhaps there will be more in the future. The Royal Doulton International Collectors Club has also played its part in keeping the derivatives in focus by reviving the potty teapot tradition. In 1988 they commissioned the Old Salt Teapot especially for members, and this led to the introduction of several new character teapots of The Old Balloon Seller, Long John Silver and Falstaff. As they were only in the range for a brief period, they will eventually become as hard to find as some of the early derivatives.

LIMITED-EDITION LOVING CUPS AND JUGS

A few years before the successful launch of character jugs, Charles Noke and Harry Fenton had already collaborated on a spectacular range of limited-edition loving cups and jugs. These large, colourful pieces are vigorously modelled in low relief, and they feature many of the characters who were later portrayed as jugs. Thus in terms of subject and style, they are closely related to character and toby jugs, and consequently many keen collectors seek them out as display

centrepieces. Unfortunately they are not easy to find, as most were only made for a short period during the 1930s, and they were produced in very small editions of 300 to 1,000, some of which were never completed. Also it is inevitable that some have been broken in the intervening years, so not surprisingly, they are expensive when they do appear on the market.

These loving cups and jugs were Royal Doulton's very first limited-edition pieces and, as such, represent the zenith of Noke's achievements as art director. The accompanying certificates of authenticity are almost as splendid as the items they describe, with elaborate illustrations, ribboned seals and Noke's signature written in ink. Understandably many collectors have these documents framed as works of art in their own right. Further authentification and the unique number of the loving cup or jug appears on the base, which is usually equally decorative, with appropriate motifs or symbols. Perhaps the most novel is the treasure chart on the base of The Treasure Island jug.

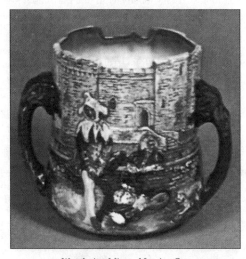

Wandering Minstrel Loving Cup

The majority of the loving cups and jugs stand around 10 inches high, and the scene unfolds in relief, painted in glowing underglaze colours. The handles are often ingeniously linked to the subject; for instance, the John Peel loving cup has a riding crop and fox head, whilst the Guy Fawkes jug has a flaming torch. It is interesting that symbolic handles such as these later became a major feature of the character jug range.

Many of the subjects reflect Noke's literary interests, which he regularly explored in the series ware, figures and character jug collections, in particular the writings of Dickens and Shakespeare and popular adventure stories such as The Three Musketeers and Treasure Island. The exploits of real-life seafaring heroes, such as Drake, Nelson and Cook, were also celebrated in the range.

Noke realised at an early stage that these prestige pieces were ideal for commemorating important historical and royal events, and so the bicentenary of the birth of George Washington in 1932 was marked with a patriotic American jug, bedecked in stars and stripes, whilst the anniversary of the founding of New South Wales was recalled by the launch of the Captain Phillip jug. There was no shortage of royal events to celebrate during the 1930s, and loving cups with portraits of the monarchs, emblazoned with flags and regalia, were issued for the Silver Jubilee of George V and the coronation of George VI. There are even three different coronation loving cups for Edward VIII, who, of course, was never crowned, but some of the editions had been sold before his abdication. Years later these ceremonial loving cups were revived for the Coronation and Silver Jubilee of Queen Elizabeth II in 1953 and 1977 respectively, and perhaps they will be used again for important royal occasions in the future.

In 1982 the Royal Doulton International Collectors Club commissioned a loving cup in traditional style depicting Pottery in the Past, and as it was only made in small numbers for members, it is becoming increasingly difficult to find.

Collecting all the limited-edition loving cups and jugs will prove to be something of a challenge, and as with all Royal Doulton wares, there are also some tantalising prototypes and variations. To date nobody has found the trials of Roger Solemel, Cobbler and I.T. Wigg, Broom-man, but one lucky collector has a prototype George Washington presentation jug with a different stars and stripes handle. This variation was not recorded in the Royal Doulton archives, and there may well be others to be found, so happy hunting.

MAKING CHARACTER AND TOBY JUGS

Each Royal Doulton character and toby jug goes through the hands of many skilled and experienced individuals. From ÿthe designer to the painter to the kiln manager, each person is responsible for ensuring the quality of the finished article.

Today the diverse ideas for new jugs usually originate in the company's marketing department, and following discussions with the design managers, the modeller is briefed about the required subject. A great deal of research goes into the initial concept. If a historical personality is to be depicted, contemporary paintings, photographs and other records are studied to ensure accuracy in features and costume. For a fictional character, the designer needs to read the relevant book and consider any illustrations before embarking on sketches. Some Royal Doulton artists submit drawings of their proposed subject, others prefer to work directly with the modelling clay to visualise their ideas.

A careful balance must be achieved between portraiture and caricature, good humour and dignity, to create a jug suitable for the Royal Doulton range. The symbolism of the handle, which is now such an important element of the design, also requires a lot of thought and ingenuity. When the modeller is completely satisfied with his work, it goes for approval to the art and marketing directors, who occasionally suggest modifications to improve the design or avert potting problems. It is vital that everybody is happy with the jug at this stage, because the lines and details of this master model will determine the exact appearance of the finished piece.

The mould-maker then takes over and carefully disects the original to create plaster of Paris moulds of each part. Usually a four-part mould is required, for the head and the handle are moulded separately. A few sample jugs, known as prototypes, will be cast from the master mould for further discussion and colour trials. Ideally only two or three prototypes are produced, as with each casting the intricate detail of the mould is gradually worn away. If the prototype is approved at one of the design conferences, a rubber working "case" is made from the master mould, and it is from this case that all the subsequent plaster of Paris production moulds are made.

In the casting department a liquid clay mixture known as slip is poured into the production moulds through a hole in the top. The porous plaster absorbs the water in the slip and a layer of solid clay is formed in the interior of the mould. When this has reached the required thickness, the excess slip is drained away and the mould is taken apart for the various cast sections to be extracted. The separate parts of the jug are assembled using slip as an adhesive and the rough edges and seams smoothed away in a process known as fettling.

After drying at a controlled temperature, the jugs are ready to receive their first firing in the electric tunnel kiln. This is known as the "biscuit" firing because of the texture of the jug when it emerges from the kiln. On completion the fragile clay body has shrunk by about an eighth of its original size, becoming hard and durable.

The white biscuit jug is then taken to the decorating studio, where special pigments suitable for underglaze painting are used. Painting directly onto the porous biscuit body gives the rugged character lines and wrinkles required in many jug subjects. Considerable care and expertise is required at this stage, as some colours can change during the fixing process in the hardening — on kiln.

After this second, low-temperature firing, the jug is ready to be glazed, and this is done by either spraying it with a liquid glass mixture or dipping it into a vat of the same mixture. The glossy, protective finish is achieved by firing the jug again, this time in a glost kiln. In many cases, this completes the process, but some brightly coloured jugs have a further coat of paint applied on top of the glaze, and they need to be fired a fourth time to seal the colours permanently. Before leaving the factory, the finished jugs are inspected by the quality control staff to ensure there are no flaws, and they are then packed for despatch all over the world.

BODIES AND GLAZES

Stoneware

The first Doulton jugs were produced at the Lambeth factory in London, and these were made of salt-glaze stoneware, a high-fired ceramic body which is literally glazed with salt thrown into the kiln at peak temperatures. Bodies range from a plain buff to a rich brown, which is sometimes dipped in a darker coloured slip to create a two-tone effect. Muted colours can be achieved in this high-temperature process, but only the Simeon toby wares were additionally coloured with a bright red on-glaze enamel colour.

Earthenware, Kingsware and China

The first character and toby jugs produced at Royal Doulton's factory in Nile Street, Burslem, were mostly made of white earthenware, although the treacle-coloured Kingsware body was used for some early commissions. For a brief period, between 1968 and 1973, character jugs were made in English Translucent China, a porcelain body pioneered by Doulton chemists in 1959. All the jugs had to be remodelled for this process, and so collectors will notice differences in detail between earthenware and ETC jugs. However, the most obvious variation is the size, as the china body fires about a half- inch smaller than the earthenware.

Following Royal Doulton's acquisition of the John Beswick factory, it was decided to concentrate the production of jugs at this location in Longton, and the earthenware body was revived. Consequently, since 1973 new models have been produced in earthenware and painted under the glaze, although some recent designs also have on-glaze decoration, particularly to achieve bright reds, blues or metallic effects.

In the early 1980s there was some research at the Nile Street factory to revive the china body for character jugs, in order to cope with the demand for the Antagonists and Beatles collections, and although the experiment was short-lived, occasional china examples come on to the market.

White Jugs

From time to time, white-glazed versions of standard character jugs appear on the market, and these are highly valued by collectors. Most were made from the late 1930s to the early 1950s when wartime restrictions prohibited the production of decorated china for the UK market. It is believed that white biscuit jugs with slight flaws, which could not be decorated for the export market, were glazed for sale to company employees.

These white substandard jugs should not be confused with the white character jug portrait of Winston Churchill, which was originally conceived undecorated, no doubt because of the UK embargo. Examples are rare because it did not remain in production for long.

During the 1930s D&J McCallum, the whisky distillers, commissioned a white version of their Highlander jug, as well as the better-known Kingsware variety. Numbers were limited to around 1,000 and they are hard to find today. Fifty years later Pick-Kwik Wines and Spirits of Derby commissioned two undecorated variations in their extensive range of promotional jugs. Only 100 of each were made of the Micawber character jug and spirit container for internal promotional use.

Occasionally modern white character jugs have turned up at local auctions and markets, but it would appear that these have "escaped" from the factory in an undecorated state and been glazed to cater for the strong market demand for white jugs.

CARE AND REPAIR

Character and toby jugs are relatively robust and easy to look after. The glaze seals and protects the colours permanently, and occasional dusting will maintain the shiny finish. If the jugs are displayed on open shelves, it is a good idea to fill the interior with crumpled tissue paper, as this catches the dust and can be replaced easily at cleaning times. When necessary, jugs can be washed in luke-warm water using a mild detergent, then rinsed thoroughly and dried naturally or buffed with a soft cloth. Care should be taken not to knock jugs against the tap or each other – the rims and handles are the most vulnerable parts. If an accident does happen, there are professional restorers who can make "invisible" repairs to chips and cracks, even hairlines.

Obviously when buying on the secondary market, it is advisable to check very carefully for restorations such as these, as they are not immediately obvious to the naked eye. Expert dealers have many different ways of spotting repairs. Rarely do they carry an ultraviolet lamp that will highlight problem areas, instead they become sensitive to the different vibrations given by the softer restored areas when tapped with a metallic object or even bitten with the teeth! Reputable dealers will stand by any guarantees they give regarding restorations. Prices should reflect the level of damage sustained and the quality of the ÿrestoration.

Occasionally old jugs have been used as containers, and these can appear at flea markets quite dirty and stained. If washing fails, petroleum jelly will usually remove stubborn rust marks. It is worth persevering — apparently the rare, coloured Churchill character jug, which made over £16,000 at auction in 1989, had originally been used as a storage jar under the kitchen sink.

A GUIDE TO BACKSTAMPS AND DATING

The marks on the base of a character jug can be a useful guide for dating the piece, particularly if it has been in production for a while. However, it is impossible to be precise, as stocks of old-style backstamps continued to be used up after changes had been implemented. Nevertheless, jugs can usually be placed in a specific time period and, very occasionally, if there is a date code, an exact year of manufacture can be determined.

The Royal Doulton Trademark

Most prominent on the base is the Royal Doulton factory mark, which has featured a lion standing on a crown ever since the company was awarded the Royal Warrant in 1901. It is unusual for a jug not to have a Royal Doulton trademark, but occasionally prototypes have been found with a blank base, and these have been authenticated by the company in Stoke-on-Trent.

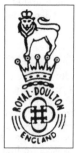 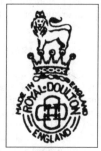

| Lion and Crown Backstamp 1901 to 1930s | Made in England was added in the 1930s |

The early Royal Doulton trademark is found on some of the first Burslem toby jugs, such as Charlie Chaplin, and on the McCallum character jugs. By the early 1930s, the words "Made in England" had been incorporated in the lion and crown trademark, and this style of backstamp has been recorded, with no other information, on some of the first character jugs. Most of the toby jugs issued between 1939 and 1950 are marked with this backstamp and the title of the character portrayed. Copyright information was either nonexistent or kept to a minimum, unlike the character jugs.

The 1930s

In order to protect their designs from being copied, Royal Doulton registered them at the UK patent office, and the resulting registration number (e.g. RdNo782778 for John Barleycorn) is often printed underneath the backstamp. The year the jug was registered can be worked out from the table of numbers published by the patent office. Usually registration was a year before the jug went into production, but on occasion the number was not issued in time and the words "Reg. applied for" were added to the backstamp (this has also been found misspelt "Registeration"). It should be noted that the registration number does not give the date of manufacture for a specific piece, only when the design was first protected.

Around 1938 Royal Doulton also began to register their designs in Australia, and the information "Regd in Australia" was added to the backstamp.

By the late 1930s, the name of the jug in inverted commas was usually included above the registration number (e.g. "The Cavalier"). Jugs produced during the 1930s might also have a hand-painted D pattern number, which was added by the decorator when the jug was completed. This practice continued until the Second World War.

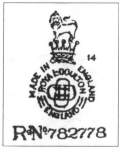 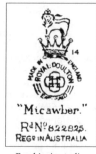

| Registered trademak below backstamp. Printed numeral '14' stands for 1941 | Regd in Australia. Name in inverted commas |

All the above details will help date a piece to the 1930s, but the only way to determine the exact year of manufacture is with the date code, if it has one. This numbering system began in 1928 with the number one. The date-code number is immediately to the right of the lion and crown symbol, and the year of manufacture can be calculated by adding it to 1927. Thus the code number 11 will give a date of 1938, and 15 indicates 1942. This code system can be found on character jugs from the 1930s and 40s.

The 1940s and 1950s

A capital A on the left of the lion and crown symbol is known as the A mark and it is a kiln control mark denoting a specific type of earthenware body known as Georgian. Sometimes an A mark appears on a character jug without any other information. It was used on a variety of Royal Doulton products between 1939 and 1955, so its presence on character jugs will date the piece to within that time period.

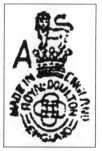 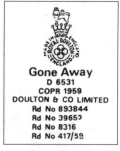

| 'A' to the left of the Lion and Crown | Copyright mark |

After the war Royal Doulton found it necessary to register their designs in more of their main export markets, and a new style backstamp was devised in 1947. This gives a copyright date for Doulton and Co Limited and four different registration numbers for the UK, Australia, South Africa and New Zealand. A few jugs introduced in 1950 only have three registration numbers.

From circa 1952 a printed D pattern number appears above the copyright date, and a few years later the inverted commas around the character's name were dropped. Several different typefaces appear to have been used.

The 1960s and 1970s

New UK copyright laws in 1966 gave protection in each country without separate design registrations. Protection was extended to articles previously registered, and as the period of registration ran out, the relevant numbers were withdrawn from the backstamp. By circa 1973 the lists had disappeared altogether and a new copyright symbol was adopted, "C" in place of "Copr." From 1975 the company's new name, Royal Doulton Tableware Ltd, began to appear in the copyright notice, and many collectors were puzzled by this reference to tableware on gift items.

The 1980s and 1990s

A large elegant script was adopted for the character names in the early 1980s, and by 1983 the first reference to hand made and hand decorated had been included underneath. The new Doultonville tobies also adopted this improved style. An entirely new design of backstamp was introduced in 1984, featuring the new styling for the company name, Royal Doulton, the subject of the jug in bold capitals, the modeller's facsimile signature and the words "Hand made and hand decorated" forming an arch around the lion and crown. These changes were implemented in order to acknowledge the talents of individual artists and to seek public recognition of the specialist production skills involved. Initials or dots and dashes on the base are decorator's marks, but no records exist to identify these.

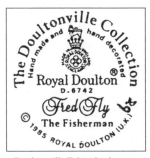
Doultonville Tobies backstamp

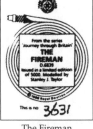
The Fireman backstamp

In the last ten years backstamps have become increasingly interesting and attractive, as evocative images and typefaces are chosen to capture the spirit of the subject matter; for example, the Journey through Britain series has lots of novel backstamp motifs, including a hose for the Fireman jug and postage stamp for the Postman. The Celebrity collection has a Hollywood-billboard typeface and relevant quotes from the characters portrayed. This is not a completely new idea, as one of the earliest jugs, Mephistopheles, was inscribed with a quotation about the devil by Rabelais. Not all the jugs carry this inscription, however, and keen collectors are prepared to pay a slight premium for this feature.

Promotional and Commemorative Backstamps

There are many other interesting backstamp variations which ardent collectors will seek out. During the 1930s several independent companies commissioned standard character jugs with their name printed on the base for promotional purposes, and this can now add to the value of the jug. Amongst the names to look for are Coleman's, Bentall's, Darley and Sons and the Salt River Cement Works. In 1967, to celebrate the Canadian Centenary, the North American Indian and Trapper jugs were launched with a special backstamp in North America only, and this was deleted for worldwide sales the following year. The presence of this commemorative backstamp will double the price of these jugs.

This practice of pre-releasing has continued in recent years for Royal Doulton's important customers. For example, the first two jugs in the Celebrity series, W.C. Fields and Mae West, were produced in a premier edition for American Express, and a small premium is payable for this backstamp.

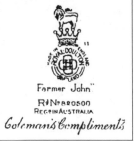
"Coleman's Compliments" backstamp

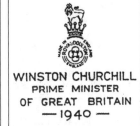
"Winston Churchill Prime Minister of Great Britain 1940"

Generally speaking the backstamps on toby jugs do not excite collectors, the exception being the portrait of Winston Churchill, which originally had a backstamp commemorating "Winston Churchill Prime Minister of Great Britain 1940." This was deleted after 1940, and so jugs with this mark are very rare and consequently expensive.

Other Guides to Dating

Much can obviously be gleaned from the backstamp as to the age of a character jug, but occasionally there are some other clues. It used to be the practice with large-size jugs to continue painting inside the rim, and this is referred to by collectors as bleeding. As this method was discontinued by 1973, it is possible to date jugs with this trait before then. Having checked the rim, look into the character's eyes! It is not as strange as it sounds, for early-style modelling was to indent the iris, and this continued until the early 1960s. For a few years between 1968 and 1973, character jugs were produced in a type of porcelain known as ETC, so pieces in this body must have been made during this short period.

Other clues are specific to certain models; for example, early versions of Auld Mac have "Owd Mac" on the backstamp and also impressed in the tammy. Toby Philpots was spelt with a double t until circa 1952, so those spelt Toby Philpotts date from the 1930s or 40s. The Beefeater has a couple of unique clues. Until circa 1953 it was called "Beefeaters" on the backstamp, and following the coronation of Queen Elizabeth in 1953, the handle was remodelled with a new Royal cypher (see Modelling Variations).

ROYAL DOULTON COLLECTORS CLUB AND GUILD

Royal Doulton International Collectors Club

Founded in 1980, the Royal Doulton International Collectors Club provides an information service on all aspects of the company's products, past and present. A club magazine, *Gallery*, is published four times a year with information on new products and current events that will keep the collector up-to-date on the happenings in the world of Royal Doulton. Upon joining the club, each new member will receive a free gift and invitations to special events and exclusive offers.

To join the Royal Doulton Collectors Club, please contact your local stockist, or contact the club directly at the address or telephone numbers below:

Minton House
London Road, Stoke-on-Trent
Staffordshire ST4 7QD, England

Telephone:
  U.K.: (01782) 292127
  U.S.A. and Canada: 1-800-747-3045 (toll free)
  Australia: 011-800-142624 (toll free)
Fax: U.K.: (01782) 292099
Attn.: Jill Daniels

Royal Crown Derby Collectors Guild

The Royal Crown Derby Collectors Guild was established in 1994 to establish contact with Royal Crown Derby Collectors. Membership entitles the collector to a yearly subscription to the quarterly Royal Crown Derby magazine, membership gift and free admission for the member to the Royal Crown Derby Visitor Centre.

To join the Royal Crown Derby Collectors Guild, please contact the guild at the address or telephone number below:

Royal Cown Derby
194 Ormaston Road, Derby DE23 8JZ
Tel.: (44) 1332 712846 Fax: (44) 1332 712899
Attn.: Jackie Banks

Caithness Glass Paperweight Collectors Society
Caithness Glass International
Paperweight Collectors Society

Formed in 1997, by Colin Terris, the society is the clearing house for all information on Caithness Glass Paperweights. Membership of the society entitles the collector to receive *Reflections*, the society's twice yearly magazine, plus three newsletters and a personal tour of the paperweight studios in Perth, Scotland, if you are ever in the area. An annual International Convention is held in Scotland in October.

To join the Caithness Glass Paperweight Collectors Society, please contact the society at one of the addresses or telephone numbers below:

In the U.K. and International
Caithness Glass Paperweight Collectors Scoiety
Caithness Glass Inc.
Inveralmond, Perth PH1 3TZ, Scotland
Tel.: (44) (0) 1738 637373
Fax: (44) (0) 1738 622494

In the U.S.A.
Caithness Glass Paperweight Collectors Society
Caithness Glass Inc.
141 Lanza Avenue, Building No. 12
Garfield, N.J. 07026, U.S.A.
Tel.: (973) 340-3330
Fax: (973) 340-9415

COLLECTOR CLUB CHAPTERS

Chapters of the RDICC have formed across North America and are worthy of consideration in those areas.

Detroit Chapter
Frank Americk, President
1771 Brody, Allen Park, MI 48101

Edmonton Chapter
Mildred's Collectibles
6813 104 Street, Edmonton, AB

New England Chapter
Robert Hicks, President; Lee Piper, Vice-President
Michael Lynch, Secretary; Scott Reichenberg, Treas.
E-mail: doingantiq@aol.com

Northern California Chapter
Edward L. Khachadourian, President
P.O. Box 214, Moraga, CA 94556-0214
Tel.: (925) 376-2221 Fax: (925) 376-3581
E-mail: khack@pacbell.net

Northwest, Bob Haynes, Chapter
Alan Matthew, President
15202 93rd Place N.E., Bothell, WA 98011
Tel.: (425) 488-9604

Ohio Chapter
Reg Morris, President; Dick Maschmeier, Treasurer
5556 White Haven Ave., North Olmstead, OH 44070
Tel.: (216) 779 5554

Rochester Chapter
Judith L. Trost President
103 Garfield Street, Rochester, N.Y. 14611
Tel.: (716) 436-3321

Western Pennsylvania Chapter
John Re, President
9589 Parkedge Drive, Allison Park, PA 15101
Tel.: (412) 366-0201 Fax: (412) 366-2558

VISITOR CENTRES

Royal Doulton Visitor Centre

Opened in the summer of 1996, the Royal Doulton Visitor Centre houses the largest collection of Royal Doulton figurines in the world. Demonstration areas offer the collector a first hand insight on how figurines are assembled and decorated. Also at the Visitor Centre is a cinema showing a 20 minute video on the history of Royal Doulton, plus a restaurant, and a retail shop offering both best quality ware and slight seconds.

Factory tours may be booked, Monday to Friday, at the Visitor Centre.

Nile Street, Burslem
Stoke-on-Trent, ST6 2AJ, England
Tel.: (01782) 292434
Fax: (01782) 292424
Attn.: Yvonne Wood

Royal Doulton John Beswick Studios

Tours of the John Beswick Factory and Museum are available Monday to Thursday by appointment only. Please book in advance.

Gold Street, Longton
Stoke-on-Trent, ST3 2JP, England
Tel.: (01782) 291213
Fax: (01782) 291279
Attn.: Margaret Burton

Royal Crown Derby Visitor Centre

Opened in the spring of 1998, the Visitor Centre was created to provide an insight into the tradition, history and skills that go into making Royal Crown Derby collectables. The centre houses the largest collection of Royal Crown Derby seen anywhere in the world, a demonstration area for skilled Royal Crown Derby artists and crafts people, restaurants, and shops.

Factory tours may be booked Monday to Friday at the centre, with advance bookings suggested.

194 Osmaston Road
Derby, DE23 8JZ, England
Tel.: (01332) 712841
Fax: (01332) 712899
Attn.: Stella Birks

Caithness Glass Visitor Centre

The Visitor Centre is home to the largest public display of Caithness Glass paperweights. Over 1200 designs are on display. A special viewing gallery enables visitors to watch the complete paperweight making process.

Inveralmond
Perth, PH1 3TZ, Scotland
Tel.: (44) (0)1738 637373
Fax: (44) (0)1738 622494

Factory Shops

Royal Doulton Visitor Centre
Nile Street, Burslem
Stoke-on-Trent, England
Tel.: (01782) 292451

Royal Doulton Group Factory Shop
Lawley Street, Longton
Stoke-on-Trent, ST3 2PH, England
Tel.: (01782) 291172

Royal Doulton Factory Shop
Minton House, London Road
Stoke-on-Trent, ST4 7QD, England
Tel.: (01782) 292121

Royal Doulton Factory Shop
Leek New Road, Baddeley Green,
Stoke-on-Trent ST2 7HS, England
Tel.: (01782) 291700

Royal Doulton Factory Shop
Victoria Road, Fenton,
Stoke-on-Trent ST4 2PJ, England
Tel.: (01782) 291869

Beswick Factory Shop
Barford Street, Longton,
Stoke-on-Trent. ST3 2JP, England
Tel.: (01782) 291237

Web Site and E-mail Addresses

Sites: www.royal-doulton.com
www.doulton-direct.com
www.caithnessglass.co.uk
E-mail:
Clubs: icc@royal-doulton.com
Visitor Centre: Visitor@royal-doulton.com
Consumer Enquiries: enquiries@royal-doulton.com
Museum Curator: heritage@royal-doulton.com
Doulton-Direct: direct@doulton-direct.com

WHERE TO BUY

Discontinued Doulton collectables can be found in antique shops, markets, auctions, shows and fairs. specialist dealers in Royal Doulton collectables attend many of the events listed below.

For Auction happenings it is necessary to subscribe to Auction Houses that hold 20th Century or Doulton Auctions.

UNITED KINGDOM
Auction Houses

BBR Auctions
Elsecar Heritage Centre
Nr. Barnsley,
South Yorkshire, S74 8HJ, England
Tel.: (01226) 745156
Fax: (01226) 351561
Attn: Alan Blakeman

Bonhams
65-69 Lots Road, Chelsea,
London, SW10 0RN, England
Tel.: (0208) 393-3900
Fax: (0208) 393-3906
www.bonhams.com
Attn: Neil Grenyer

Christie's South Kensington
85 Old Brompton Road
London, SW7 3LD, England
Tel.: (0207) 581 7611
Fax: (0207) 321-3321
www.christies.com
Attn: Michael Jeffrey

Potteries Specialist Auctions
271 Waterloo Road
Stoke-on-Trent
Staffordshire, ST6 3HR, England
Tel.: (01782) 286622
Fax: (01782) 213777
Attn: Stella ???

Louis Taylor
Britannia House
10 Town Road, Hanley,
Stoke-on-Trent, ST1 2QG
England
Tel.: (01782) 21411
Fax: (01782) 287874
Attn: Clive Hillier

Phillips
101 New Bond Street
London, W1Y 0AS, England
Tel.: (0207) 629-6602
Fax: (0207) 629-8876
www.phillips-auctions.com
Attn: Mark Oliver

Sotheby's
34-35 New Bond Street
London, W1A 2AA, England
Tel.: (0207) 293-5000
Fax: (0207) 293-5989
www.sothebys.com
Attn: Christina Donaldson

Sotheby's Sussex
Summers Place
Billingshurst, Sussex, RH14 9AF
England
Tel.: (01403) 833500
Fax: (01403) 833699

Thomson Roddick & Laurie
60 Whitesands
Dumfries, DG1 2RS
Scotland
Tel.: (01387) 255366
Fax: (01387) 266236
Attn: Sybelle Medcalf

Peter Wilson Auctioneers
Victoria Gallery, Market Street
Nantwich, Cheshire, CW5 5DG
England
Tel.: (01270) 623878
Fax: (01270) 610508
Attn: Stella Ashbrook or
      Robert Stone

Antique Fairs

Doulton and Beswick Collectors Fair
National Motorcycle Museum, Meriden, Birmingham,
Usually March and August
For information on times and dates:
Doulton and Beswick Dealers Association
(0208) 303 3316

Doulton and Beswick Collectors Fair
Dorking. Usually in October.
For information on times and location:
UK Fairs Ltd. 10 Wilford Bridge Spur,
Melton,Woodbridge, Suffolk, IP12 1 RJ
Tel.: (01394) 386663

20th Century Fairs
266 Glossop Road, Sheffield S10 2HS, England
Usually the last week in May or the first week in June.
For information on times and dates:
Tel.: (0114) 275-0333
Fax: (0114) 275-4443

International Antique & Collectors Fair
Newark, Nottinghamshire
Usually six fairs annually.
For information on times and dates:
International Antique & Collectors Fair Ltd.
P.O. Box 100, Newark, Nottinghamshire, NG2 1DJ
Tel.: (01636) 702326

West London Wade Beswick & Doulton Fair
Brunel University, Kingston Lane,
Uxbridge, Middlesex
For information on times and dates:
B & D Fairs, P.O. Box 273, Uxbridge,
Middlesex, UB9 4LP
Tel.: (01895) 834694 or 834357

Yesterdays Doulton Fair
Usually November.
For information on times and location:
Doulton and Beswick Dealers Association
Tel.: (0181) 303-3316

London Markets

Alfie's Antique Market
13-25 Church Street, London
Tuesday - Saturday

Camden Passage Market
Upper Street, London N1
Wednesday and Saturday

New Caledonia Market
Bermondsey Square, London
Friday morning

Portobello Road Market
Portobello Road, London
Saturday

UNITED STATES
Auction Houses

Christie's East
219 East 67th Street
New York, NY 10021
Tel.: (212) 606-0400
www.christies.com
Attn: Timothy Luke

Sotheby's Arcade Auctions
1334 York Avenue
New York, NY 10021
Tel.: (212) 606-7000
www.sothebys.com
Attn: Andrew Cheney

Collectable Shows

Atlantique City
New Atlantic City Convention Centre
Atlantic City, NJ
For information on times and dates:
Krause Publications
700 East State Street, Iola, WI 54990-0001
Tel.: (877) 746-9757   Fax: (715) 445-4389
E-mail: iceshow@krause.com
www.collectibleshow.com

Florida Doulton Convention & Sale
Sheraton Inn
1825 Griffin Road
Dania, Florida
Usually mid-January
For information on times and dates:
Pascoe and Company, 932 Ponce De Leon Blvd.
Coral Gables, Florida 33134. (305) 445-3229

O'Hare National Antiques Show & Sale
Rosemont Convention Centre,
Chicago, IL.
For information on times and dates:
Krause Publications
700 East State Street, Iola, WI 54990-0001
Tel.: (877) 746-9757   Fax: (715) 445-4389
E-mail: iceshow@krause.com
www.collectibleshow.com

Royal Doulton Convention & Sale
John S. Knight Convention Centre
77 E. Mill Street, Akron, Ohio 44308
Usually August.
For information on times and dates:
Colonial House Productions
182 Front Street, Berea, Ohio 44017
(800) 344-9299

CANADA

Auction Houses

Maynards
415 West 2nd Avenue, Vancouver, BC V5Y 1E3
Tel.: (604) 876-1311

Ritchie's
288 King Street East, Toronto, Ontario. M5A 1K4
Tel.: (416) 364-1864   Fax: (416) 364-0704
Attn: Caroline Kaiser

Waddington's
111 Bathurst Street, Toronto, Ontario M5V 2R1
Tel.: (416) 504-9100   Fax: (416) 504-0033
E-mail: info@waddingtonsauctions.com
www.waddingtonsauctions.com

Collectable Shows

Canadian Art & Collectibles Show & Sale
Kitchener Memorial Auditorium, Kitchener, Ontario.
Usually early May.
For information on times and location:

FURTHER READING

Animals, Figures and Character Jugs

Royal Doulton Figures by Desmond Eyles, Louise Irvine and Valerie Baynton
The Charlton Standard Catalogue of Beswick Animals by Diane & John Callow and Marilyn & Peter Sweet
The Charlton Standard Catalogue of Royal Doulton Animals by Jean Dale
The Charlton Standard Catalogue of Royal Doulton Beswick Figurines by Jean Dale
Collecting Character and Toby Jugs by Jocelyn Lukins
Collecting Doulton Animals by Jocelyn Lukins
Doulton Flambé Animals by Jocelyn Lukins
The Character Jug Collectors Handbook by Kevin Pearson
The Doulton Figure Collectors Handbook by Kevin Pearson

Storybook Figurines

The Charlton Standard Catalogue of Bunnykins by Jean Dale and Louise Irvine
The Charlton Standard Catalogue of Royal Doulton Beswick Storybook Figurines by Jean Dale
Cartoon Classics and other Character Figures by Louise Irvine
Royal Doulton Bunnykins Figures by Louise Irvine
Bunnykins Collectors Book by Louise Irvine
Beatrix Potter Figures and Giftware edited by Louise Irvine
The Beswick Price Guide by Harvey May

General

The Charlton Standard Catalogue of Beswick Pottery by Diane and John Callow
Discovering Royal Doulton by Michael Doulton
The Doulton Story by Paul Atterbury and Louise Irvine
Royal Doulton Series Ware by Louise Irvine (Vols. 1-5)
Limited Edition Loving Cups by Louise Irvine and Richard Dennis
Doulton for the Collector by Jocelyn Lukins
Doulton Kingsware Flasks by Jocelyn Lukins
Doulton Burslem Advertising Wares by Jocelyn Lukins
Doulton Lambeth Advertising Ware, by Jocelyn Lukins
The Doulton Lambeth Wares by Desmond Eyles
The Doulton Burslem Wares by Desmond Eyles
Hannah Barlow by Peter Rose
George Tinworth by Peter Rose
Sir Henry Doulton Biography by Edmund Gosse
Phillips Collectors Guide by Catherine Braithwaite
Royal Doulton by Jennifer Queree
John Beswick: A World of Imagination. Catalogue reprint (1950-1996)
Royal Doulton by Julie McKeown

Magazines and Newsletters

Rabbitting On (Bunnykins Newsletter) Contact Leah Selig: 2 Harper Street, Merrylands 2160
New South Wales, Australia. Tel./Fax 61 2 9637 2410 (International), 02 637 2410 (Australia)
Collect It! Contact subscription department at: P.O. Box 3658, Bracknell, Berkshire RG12 7XZ
Telephone: (1344) 868280 or e-mail: collectit@dialpipex.com
Collecting Doulton Magazine, P.O. Box 310, Richmond, Surrey TW9 1FS, England
Doulton News, published by Thorndon Antiques & Fine China Ltd., edited by David Harcourt
P.O. Box 12-076 (109 Molesworth Street), Wellington, New Zealand
Beswick Quarterly (Beswick Newsletter) Contact Laura J. Rock-Smith: 10 Holmes Ct., Sayville,
N.Y. 11782-2408, U.S.A. Tel./Fax 516-589-9027

DOULTON
LAMBETH
JUGS

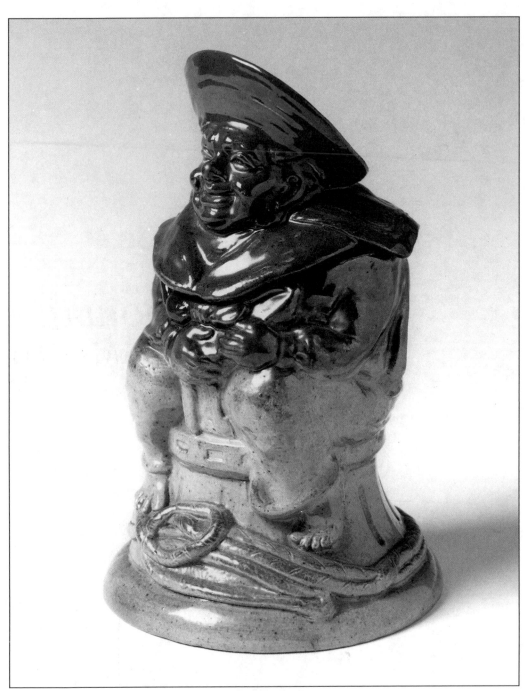

Sailor Tobacco Jar

John Broad
(1879-1919)

Triple Toby

TRIPLE TOBY

Designer:	Attributed to John Broad
Height:	9 ½", 24.0 cm
Issued:	c.1888
Handle:	Plain
Colourway:	1. Light brown overall glaze; no dark brown overglaze
	2. Light brown overall, upper section with dark brown overglaze
Backstamp:	Doulton Lambeth

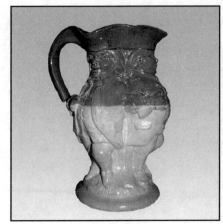

Triple Toby

Doulton Number	Current Market Value		
	U.K. £	U.S. $	Can. $
168903	Extremely rare		

Note: Variation No. 1 sold Phillips, New Bond Street, London, England, May 2000, £1,050.00.

LESLIE HARRADINE
(1902-1912)

Highwayman
Mr. Pecksniff
Old King Cole
The Standing Man
Theodore Roosevelt
Veteran Motorist

HIGHWAYMAN

This design by Leslie Harradine could very well be interpreted as the forerunner of the Doulton line of character jugs.

Designer: Leslie Harradine
Height: Unknown
Issued: c.1912-Unknown
Handle: Strands of hair
Colourway: Saltglaze
Backstamp: Doulton Lambeth

Model Number	Current Market Value		
	U.K. £	U.S. $	Can. $
Unknown		Extremely rare	

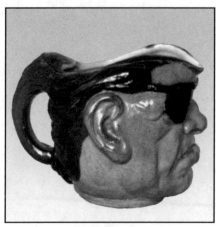

Highwayman

MR PECKSNIFF

Designer: Leslie Harradine
Height: 7 ½", 19.1 cm
Issued: c.1912-Unknown
Handle: Plain
Colourway: Variation No. 1   Ivory
　　　　　　Variation No. 2   Treacle glaze
Backstamp: Doulton Lambeth

Model Number	Variation	Colourway	Current Market Value		
			U.K. £	U.S. $	Can. $
5354	Var. 1	Ivory	1,750.00	3,000.00	3,750.00
5354	Var. 2	Treacle	1,750.00	2,750.00	3,500.00

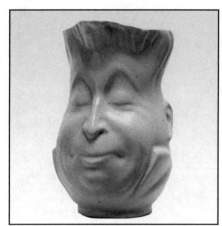

Mr Pecksniff

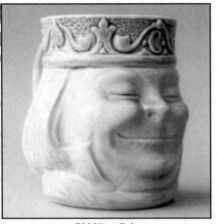

Old King Cole

OLD KING COLE

Designer:	Leslie Harradine
Height:	Unknown
Size:	Large
Issued:	c.1910-Unknown
Handle:	Plain
Colourway:	Saltglaze stoneware
Backstamp:	Doulton Lambeth

Model Number	Current Market Value		
	U.K. £	**U.S. $**	**Can. $**
—	Extremely rare		

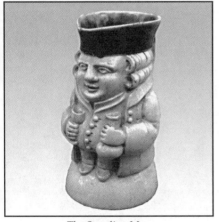

The Standing Man

THE STANDING MAN

This toby jug may well be the forerunner of the toby jugs later introduced by Harry Simeon, see X8573, page 26.

Designer:	Leslie Harradine
Height:	8 ½", 21.6 cm
Issued:	c.1912
Handle:	Plain
Colourway:	1. Buff Saltglaze stoneware
	2. Green and beige glaze, brown stoneware finish
Backstamp:	Doulton Lambeth

Model Number	Current Market Value		
	U.K. £	**U.S. $**	**Can. $**
H57	1,000.00	1,750.00	2,500.00

THEODORE ROOSEVELT

Designer:	Leslie Harradine
Height:	Unknown
Size:	4 ½"
Issued:	c.1910-Unknown
Handle:	Plain
Colourway:	Brown Saltglaze stoneware
Backstamp:	Doulton Lambeth

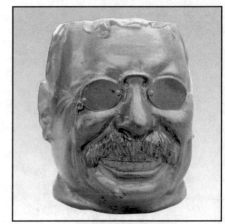

Model Number	Current Market Value		
	U.K. £	U.S. $	Can. $
—	Extremely rare		

Theodore Roosevelt

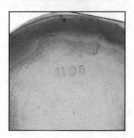

VETERAN MOTORISTS

STYLE ONE: GOGGLES OVER EYES

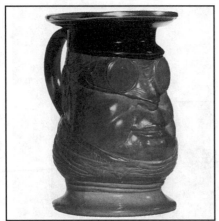

Designer: Leslie Harradine
Height: Unknown
Size: Large
Issued: c.1905-Unknown
Handle: Plain
Colourway: Saltglaze stoneware
Backstamp: Doulton Lambeth

Model Number	Style	Current Market Value U.K. £	U.S. $	Can. $
—	Style One	Extremely rare		

Veteran Motorist, Style One

STYLE TWO: GOGGLES AROUND CAP

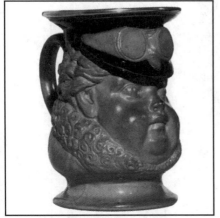

Designer: Leslie Harradine
Height: Unknown
Size: Large
Issued: c.1905-Unknown
Handle: Plain
Colourway: Saltglaze stoneware
Backstamp: Doulton Lambeth

Model Number	Style	Current Market Value U.K. £	U.S. $	Can. $
—	Style Two	Extremely rare		

Note: Both Style One and Style Two have sterling silver hallmarked rims dated 1906.

Veteran Motorist, Style Two

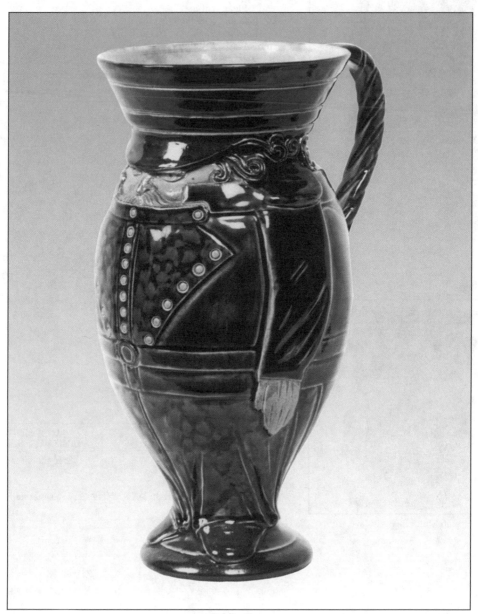

Soldier Boy

MARK MARSHALL
(1880-1912)

Soldier Boy

SOLDIER BOY

STYLE ONE: WITH THREE LINES OF
BUTTONS ON JACKET

Designer: Mark Marshall
Height: Unknown
Size: Large
Issued: c.1910-Unknown
Handle: Plain
Colourway: Saltglaze stoneware
Backstamp: Doulton Lambeth

Model Number	Size	Current Market Value		
		U.K. £	U.S. $	Can. $
—	Large	Extremely rare		

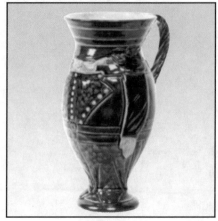

Soldier Boy, Style One

STYLE TWO: WITH ONE LINE OF
BUTTONS ON JACKET

Designer: Mark Marshall
Height: Unknown
Size: Large
Issued: c.1910-Unknown
Handle: Plain
Colourway: Blue, green and browns
Backstamp: Doulton Lambeth

Model Number	Size	Current Market Value		
		U.K. £	U.S. $	Can. $
—	Large	Extremely rare		

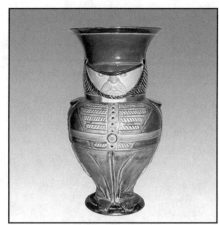

Soldier Boy, Style Two

HARRY SIMEON
(1894-1936)

Armchair Toby
The Best Is Not Too Good
Drummer
Gnome Smoking
Honest Measure
Marriage Day
Seated Toby
The Standing Man
Toby XX

LISTING OF HARRY SIMEON TOBIES
BY MODEL NUMBER

The pattern or model numbers do not run with any degree of accuracy. Different models are found with the same number, adding to the confusion of the series. Hopefully, over the next two or three editions we will get the listings right.

X7889	Miniature toper jug, as X8572, 2 ¾", high slip cast
X7890	Before and After Marriage, plain white, miniature slip cast mug
X8572	X8572, slip cast coloured, miniature, ½ pint, 1 pint, 1 ½ pint, 2 pint, 1925
X8573	As X8572, but plain
X8583	Toby inkstand and cover, 2 ¾"
X8584	Toby covered pot, as X8611 (lower part)
X8585	Candlestick, 3 ½"
X8586	Ashtray (chair) S/S, 4"
X8587	Ashtray (chair) L/S, 5 ½"
X8588	Toby jug, handled, 1/2 pint, 3 5/8"
X8589	Toby XX, S/S. 7"
X8590	Toby XX, L/S, 8 ¼"
X8591	Toby XX beaker
X8593	Tobacco jar and lid
X8594	Combined toby matchstand and ashtray
X8595	Miniature Marriage Mug, S/S, M/S - ¼ pint, L/S ½ pint
X8599	Miniature toby jug 3 ½"
X8607	Squat Toby with printed motto base
X8611	Seated Toby, as X8584 but with cocked hat fixed
X8612	Armchair Toby, as X8586 but cocked hat
X8613	Armchair Toby, as X8587 but cocked hat and cork hole for 13oz flagon
X8654	Toby teapot
X8655	Gnome Smoking, ashtray
X8762	Drummer, ashtray

ARMCHAIR TOBY
Plain Hat

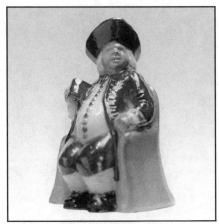

Seated Toby, Variation No. 1

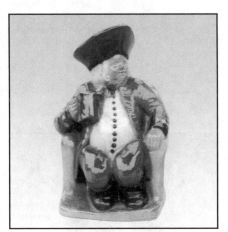

Seated Toby Derivative, Ash

STYLE ONE: PLAIN HAT, FEET ON FLOOR

Designer: Harry Simeon
Height: 4", 10.1 cm
Issued: c.1925-Unknown
Colour: 1. Blue jacket; cream waistcoat; dark brown breeches
2. Brown jacket; orange waistcoat; dark brown breeches
3. Royal blue jacket; burgundy waistcoat; green breeches
Backstamp: Doulton Lambeth

Model Number	Current Market Value		
	U.K. £	U.S. $	Can. $
X8586 (543)	475.00	900.00	1,200.00

Derivatives of Style One

Item: ASHPOT
Height: 4 ¼", 10.8 cm
Issued: c.1925-Unknown
Colourway: Green jacket; orange waistcoat; brown breeches
Backstamp: Doulton Lambeth

Model Number	Item	Current Market Value		
		U.K. £	U.S. $	Can. $
X8587 (543)	Ashpot	750.00	1,400.00	1,750.0

STYLE TWO: PLAIN HAT, FEET ON PLINTH

Designer: Harry Simeon
Height: 6", 15.0 cm
Issued: c.1925-Unknown
Colour: 1. Slate blue jacket; orange waistcoat; brown breeches
2. Blue jacket; white waistcoat; brown breeches
3. Green jacket; rust waistcoat; black breeches; Advertisement for "Ye Olde Cock Tavern 22 Fleet Street Founded 1549"
Backstamp: Doulton Lambeth

Model Number	Current Market Value		
	U.K. £	U.S. $	Can. $
X8587 (551)	600.00	1,100.00	1,400.00

Derivatives of Archair Toby, Plain Hat

Item: ASHPOT
Height: 6", 15.0 cm
Issued: c.1925-Unknown
Colourway: Green jacket; orange waistcoat; brown breeches
Backstamp: Doulton Lambeth

Model Number	Item	Current Market Value		
		U.K. £	U.S. $	Can. $
X8586 (543)	Ashpot	750.00	1,400.00	1,750.00

ARMCHAIR TOBY
Cocked Hat

STYLE ONE: COCKED HAT, FEET ON FLOOR

Designer: Harry Simeon
Height: 4", 10.1 cm
Issued: c.1925-Unknown
Colour: Unknown
Backstamp: Doulton Lambeth

Model Number	Current Market Value		
	U.K. £	U.S. $	Can. $
X8612	475.00	900.00	1,200.00

STYLE TWO: COCKED HAT, FEET ON PLINTH

Designer: Harry Simeon
Height: 6", 15.0 cm
Issued: c.1925-Unknown
Colour: Slate blue jacket; orange waistcoat; brown breeches
Backstamp: Doulton Lambeth

Model Number	Current Market Value		
	U.K. £	U.S. $	Can. $
X8612 (551)	600.00	1,100.00	1,400.00

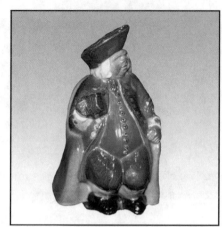

Armchair Toby, Cocked Hat, Style One

Derivatves of Armchair Toby, Cocked Hat

Item: BOOKEND
Height: 8", 20.3 cm
Issued: c.1925-Unknown
Colourway: Unknown
Backstamp: Doulton Lambeth

Item: LIQUOR FLASK
Height: 6", 15.0 cm
Issued: c.1925-Unknown
Colourway: Green jacket; orange waistcoat; brown breeches
Backstamp: Doulton Lambeth

Model Number	Item	Current Market Value		
		U.K. £	U.S. $	Can. $
X8613	Bookend	750.00	1,400.00	1,750.00
X8613	Liquor Flask	750.00	1,400.00	1,750.00

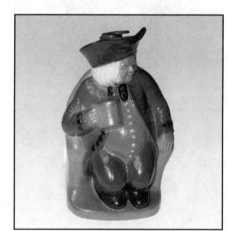

Armchair Toby, Style Two, Derivative,
Liquor Flask

THE BEST IS NOT TOO GOOD

STYLE ONE: SMILING FACE; EYES OPEN; LEFT HAND
HOLDING A PIPE; 15 BUTTONS

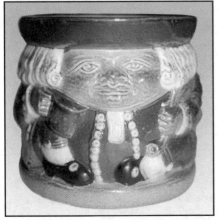

The Best is Not Too Good, Style One

Issued circa 1925, this jug by Harry Simeon was the forerunner of
The Best is not too Good by Harry Fenton. It is wider and darker than the
later version. The character has white hair, a closed mouth, a dark
waistcoat with 15 light-coloured buttons, a smooth face and his whole
hand encloses the pipe. The Harry Fenton jug is lighter, and the character
has dark hair, white teeth on a smiling face, no tie, a dark waistcoat with
11 buttons, his face is detailed and his index finger holds the pipe.

Designer:	Harry Simeon
Height:	4 ½", 11.9 cm
Size:	Small
Issued:	c.1925-Unknown
Handle:	Plain
Colourway:	Slate blue jacket, brown waistcoat and breeches
Backstamp:	Doulton Lambeth

Model Number	Size	Current Market Value U.K. £	U.S. $	Can. $
X8598	Small	500.00	1,000.00	1,250.00

Derivatives of Style One

Item:	LIDDED JAR
Height:	5", 12.7 cm
Issued:	c.1925-Unknown
Colourway:	Slate blue jacket, grey shirt, olive green breeches Inscription around base "Ye Olde Cock Tavern 22 Fleet St Founded 1549"

Item:	TOBACCO JAR
Height:	4 ½", 11.9 cm
Issued:	c.1925-Unknown
Colourway:	Slate blue jacket, grey shirt, olive green breeches
Backstamp:	Doulton Lambeth

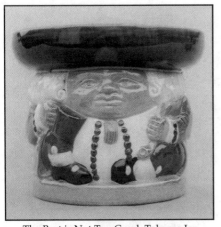

The Best is Not Too Good, Tobacco Jar

Model Number	Item	Current Market Value U.K. £	U.S. $	Can. $
X8598	Lidded Jar	1,000.00	2,000.00	2,500.00
X8598	Tobacco Jar	1,000.00	2,000.00	2,500.00

THE BEST IS NOT TOO GOOD

STYLE TWO: SMILING FACE; LEFT EYE WINKING;
LEFT HAND HOLDING A PIPE;
15 BUTTONS

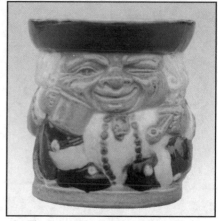

Designer:	Harry Simeon
Height:	3", 7.6 cm
Size:	Small
Handle:	Plain
Issued:	c.1925-Unknown
Colourway:	Slate blue jacket; white waistcoat; brown breeches
Backstamp:	Doulton Lambeth

Model Number	Current Market Value U.K. £	U.S. $	Can. $
X8588	400.00	800.00	900.00

The Best is Not Too Good, Style Two

Derivatives of Style Two

The neck of this flask is hallmarked sterling silver. The outer edge of the flask is blue.

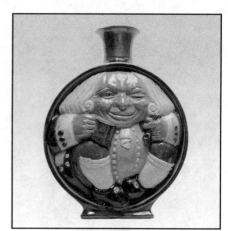

Item:	LIQUOR FLASK
Height:	8 ½", 21.6 cm
Issued:	c.1925-Unknown
Colourway:	Slate blue jacket; orange waistcoat; olive green breeches
Inscription:	No inscription around base
Backstamp:	Doulton Lambeth

Model Number	Item	Current Market Value U.K. £	U.S. $	Can. $
—	Liquor Flask	1,500.00	3,000.00	3,500.00

Note: See page 35 for the continuation of this jug in china.

The Best is Not Too Good, Liquor Flask

THE BEST IS NOT TOO GOOD

STYLE THREE: SOMBRE FACE; SQUINT EYES; LEFT HAND HOLDING LONG PIPE; 12 BUTTONS

Designer:	Harry Simeon
Height:	4 ½", 11.9 cm
Size:	Small
Issued:	c.1925-Unknown
Handle:	Plain
Colourway:	Slate blue jacket; red waistcoat; brown breeches
Backstamp:	Doulton Lambeth

Model		Current Market Value		
Number	Size	U.K. £	U.S. $	Can. $
X8588	Small	425.00	800.00	900.00

Photograph not available at press time

Derivatives of Style Three

Item:	LIDDED JAR
Height:	5", 12.7 cm
Issued:	c.1925-Unknown
Colourway:	Slate blue jacket; orange waistcoat; olive green breeches
Inscription:	No inscription around base
Backstamp:	Doulton Lambeth

Model		Current Market Value		
Number	Item	U.K. £	U.S. $	Can. $
X8593	Lidded Jar	1,000.00	2,000.00	2,500.00

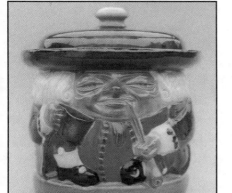

The Best is Not Too Good, Lidded Jar

STYLE FOUR: SMILING FACE; EYES OPEN; NO PIPE; LEFT HAND HOLDING LAPEL; 13 BUTTONS

Designer:	Harry Simeon
Height:	4", 10.1 cm
Size:	Small
Issued:	c.1925-Unknown
Handle:	Plain
Colourway:	1. Slate blue jacket; orange waistcoat; brown breeches
	2. Slate blue jacket; olive green waistcoat; brown breeches
Backstamp:	Doulton Lambeth

Model		Current Market Value		
Number	Variation	U.K. £	U.S. $	Can. $
X8588	Var. 1	500.00	1,000.00	1,200.00
X8588	Var. 2	500.00	1,000.00	1,200.00

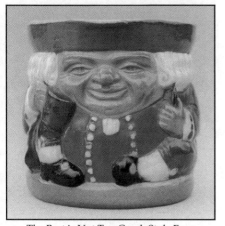

The Best is Not Too Good, Style Four

THE BEST IS NOT TOO GOOD

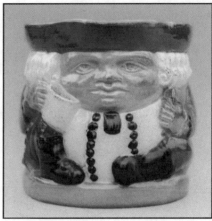

STYLE FIVE: SOMBRE FACE; EYES OPEN; NO PIPE;
LEFT HAND HOLDING LAPEL;
13 BUTTONS

Designer:	Harry Simeon
Height:	3 ¾", 9.5 cm
Issued:	c.1925-Unknown
Handle:	Plain
Colourway:	**Variation No. 1** Slate blue jacket; white waistcoat; olive-green breeches
	Variation No. 2 Olive green jacket; white waistcoat; blue breeches; black hat
Backstamp:	Doulton Lambeth

Model Number	Variation	Current Market Value U.K. £	U.S. $	Can. $
X8584	Var. 1	425.00	900.00	1,100.00
X8584	Var. 2	425.00	900.00	1,100.00

The Best is Not Too Good, Style Five

Derivative of Style Five

Item:	TOBACCO JAR
Height:	4 ½", 11.9 cm
Issued:	c.1925-Unknown
Colourway:	Slate blue jacket; white waistcoat; olive green breeches
Backstamp:	Doulton Lambeth

Model Number	Item	Current Market Value U.K. £	U.S. $	Can. $
X8593	Tobacco Jar	1,000.00	2,000.00	2,500.00

STYLE SIX: SMILING FACE; EYES OPEN; 16 BUTTONS

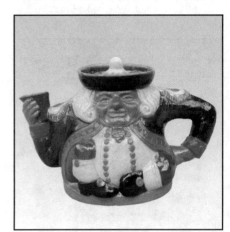

Item:	TEAPOT
Designer:	Harry Simeon
Height:	4 ¾", 12.1 cm
Issued:	c.1925-Unknown
Colourway:	Slate blue jacket with red edging and gold epaulettes; white waistcoat; olive green breeches; white stockings
Backstamp:	Doulton Lambeth

Model Number	Item	Current Market Value U.K. £	U.S. $	Can. $
X8654	Teapot	1,000.00	2,000.00	2,500.00

The Best is Not Too Good, Teapot

THE BEST IS NOT TOO GOOD

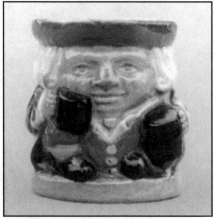

The Best Is Not Too Good, Style Seven,
Knees Apart

STYLE SEVEN: KNEES APART

Designer:	Harry Simeon
Height:	See below
Size:	Tiny
Issued:	c.1925-Unknown
Colourway:	Slate blue jacket; olive green waistcoat; brown breeches
Backstamp:	Doulton Lambeth

Model Number	Height	Current Market Value U.K. £	U.S. $	Can. $
X8594	2 ½", 6.4 cm	750.00	1,400.00	1,750.00
X8588	2", 5.0 cm	750.00	1,400.00	1,750.00

Photograph not
available
at press time

Derivatives of Style Seven

Item:	CANDLESTICK HOLDER
Height:	2" - 2 ¾", 5.0 - 7.0 cm
Issued:	c.1925-Unknown
Colourway:	1. Slate blue jacket; white waistcoat
	2. Cream jacket; tan waistcoat
	3. Slate blue jacket; brown waistcoat
	4. Slate blue jacket; olive green waistcoat; olive green breeches
Backstamp:	Doulton Lambeth

Model Number	Current Market Value U.K. £	U.S. $	Can. $
X8594	450.00	900.00	1,200.00

DRUMMER

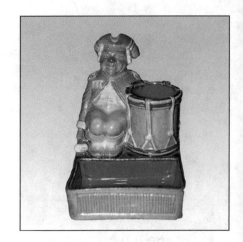

Item:	MATCH HOLDER
Designer:	Harry Simeon
Height:	5", 12.7 cm
Issued:	1891-1901
Colourway:	Browns, white and green
Backstamp:	Doulton Lambeth

Model Number	Current Market Value		
	U.K. £	U.S. $	Can. $
X8762	Extremely rare		

GNOME SMOKING

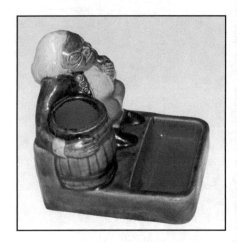

Item:	MATCH HOLDER
Designer:	Harry Simeon
Height:	3 ½", 8.9 cm
Issued:	c.1925-Unknown
Colourway:	Blue-green jacket; white waistcoat, cuffs, stockings and hair; green breeches; brown barrel and base; blue wells
Backstamp:	Doulton Lambeth

Model Number	Current Market Value		
	U.K. £	U.S. $	Can. $
X8655	400.00	900.00	1,100.00

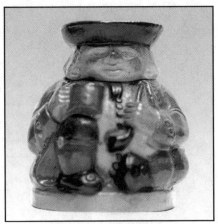

Honest Measure, Ink Pot

HONEST MEASURE
(Removable Head)

Item:	INK STAND AND COVER
Designer:	Harry Simeon
Height:	2 ¾", 7.0 cm
Issued:	c.1925-Unknown
Colourway:	1. Olive green jacket; orange waistcoat; slate blue breeches
	2. Brown jacket; white waistcoat; black breeches
Backstamp:	Doulton Lambeth

Model	Current Market Value		
Number	U.K. £	U.S. $	Can. $
X8583	600.00	1,100.00	1,400.00

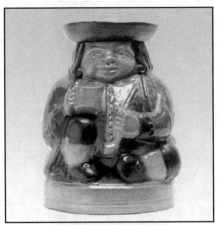

Honest Measure, Ash Pot

HONEST MEASURE
(Removable Hat)

Item:	COVERED POT
Designer:	Harry Simeon
Height:	1. 4", 10.1 cm
	2. 2 ¾", 7.0 cm
Issued:	c.1925-Unknown
Colourway:	1. Olive green jacket; dark green waistcoat; black breeches
	2. Olive green jacket; orange waistcoat; slate blue breeches
	3. Brown jacket; saltglazed waistcoat; blue breeches
	4. Cream jacket; blue waistcoat; brown breeches
Backstamp:	Doulton Lambeth

Model		Current Market Value		
Number	Height	U.K. £	U.S. $	Can. $
X8584	4", 10.1 cm	600.00	1,150.00	1,400.00
X8583	2 ¾", 7.0 cm	600.00	1,150.00	1,400.00

Note: Model X8611 exists which is similar in style to X8583/4, but without the removable hat or head. The hat is cocked and fixed. This model is 4 ¼" in height.

MARRIAGE DAY

This saltglaze jug was issued with the words "Marriage Day" and "After Marriage" inscribed atop either a smiling or frowning face resulting in two variations.

Designer:	Harry Simeon
Size:	½ Pint — 4 ¾", 12.1 cm
	¼ Pint — 3 ½", 8.9 cm
	Miniature — 2", 5.0 cm
Issued:	**1.** X7890 — c.1912
	2. X8595 — c.1925-Unknown
	3. X8596 — c.1925-Unknown
Handle:	Plain
Colourway:	**1.** White
	2. Blue, brown and white
Backstamp:	Doulton Lambeth

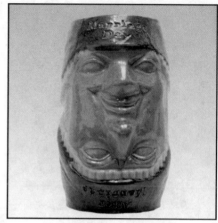

Marriage Day / Smile upright

Doulton Number	Size	Description	Current Market Value U.K. £	U.S. $	Can. $
X7890	Unknown	Unknown		Rare	
X8595	½ pint	Frown upright	500.00	1,100.00	1,400.00
X8595	½ pint	Smile upright	500.00	1,100.00	1,400.00
X8596	¼ pint	Frown upright	450.00	1,000.00	1,300.00
X8596	¼ pint	Smile upright	450.00	1,000.00	1,300.00
X8595	Miniature	Frown upright	950.00	1,400.00	1,750.00
X8595	Miniature	Smile upright	950.00	1,400.00	1,750.00

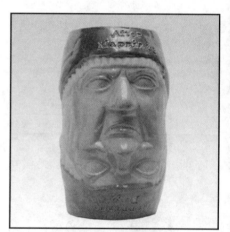

After Marriage/ Frown upright

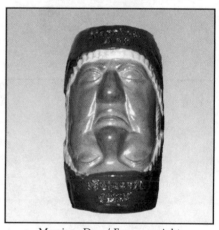

Marriage Day / Frown upright

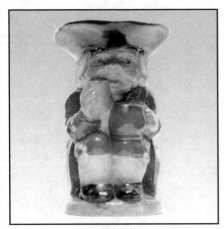

Seated Toby

SEATED TOBY

Designer:	Harry Simeon
Handle:	Plain
Height:	3 ¼", 8.3 cm
Issued:	c.1925-Unknown
Colourway:	1. Slate blue jacket; orange waistcoat; olive green breeches
	2. Slate blue jacket; olive green waistcoat; white breeches
Backstamp:	Doulton Lambeth

Model Number	Current Market Value U.K. £	U.S. $	Can. $
X8599	500.00	900.00	1,000.00

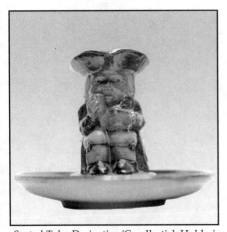

Seated Toby Derivative 'Candlestick Holder'

Derivatives of Seated Toby

Item:	CANDLESTICK HOLDER
Height:	3 ¾", 9.5 cm
Issued:	c.1925-Unknown
Colourway:	Slate blue jacket; orange breeches
Backstamp:	Doulton Lambeth

Model Number	Item	Current Market Value U.K. £	U.S. $	Can. $
X8585	Candlestick Holder	600.00	1,000.00	1,300.00

THE STANDING MAN

STYLE ONE: SMILING FACE

Designer: Harry Simeon
Issued: c.1925-Unknown
Handle: Plain
Backstamp: Doulton Lambeth

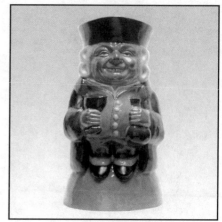

The Standing Man, Style One

VARIATION No. 1 **Colourway** — Slate blue jacket; orange waistcoat; brown breeches

Height:
1. Large — 8 ¾", 22.2 cm
2. Medium — 6"-7", 15.0-17.8 cm
3. Small — 4 ½", 11.9 cm

Colourway: Slate blue jacket; orange waistcoat; brown breeches; waistcoat buttons are either white or gold

Model Number	Size	Waistcoat Buttons	Current Market Value U.K. £	U.S. $	Can. $
1A. X8572	Large	White	500.00	950.00	1,150.00
1B. X8572	Large	White/silver rim	600.00	1,100.00	1,400.00
1C. X8572	Large	White	500.00	950.00	1,150.00
2A. X8572	Medium	Gold	475.00	900.00	1,100.00
2B. X8572	Medium	White/silver rim	600.00	1,100.00	1,400.00
2C. X8572	Medium	Gold/silver rim	600.00	1,100.00	1,400.00
2D. X8572	Medium	White	475.00	900.00	1,100.00
2E. X8572	Medium	White/silver rim	600.00	1,100.00	1,400.00
2F. X8572	Medium	White	475.00	900.00	1,100.00
3. X8572	Small	White	450.00	850.00	1,000.00

VARIATION No. 2 **Colourway** — Slate blue jacket; olive green waistcoat; olive green breeches

Height: 6", 15.0 cm
Size: Medium
Colourway: Slate blue jacket; olive green waistcoat and breeches

Model Number	Size	Colourways	Current Market Value U.K. £	U.S. $	Can. $
X8572	Medium	Slate blue	475.00	900.00	1,100.00

Note:
1. For the Leslie Harradine model of the Standing Man toper jug see page 7.
2. Large and medium size jugs are found with sterling silver rims hallmarked Birmingham, 1928 or 1929.
3. Five sizes of this jug exist, 2 pint (extra large), 1 ½ pint (large), 1 pint (medium), and miniature. We have not listed all five sizes of the 'Smiling Face' version due to sighting irrgularities.
4. Model number X8573 is known plain.

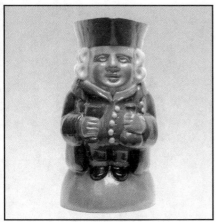

The Standing Man, Style Two

THE STANDING MAN

STYLE TWO: SOMBRE FACE

The sombre-face, standing-man variety has two buttons on the left lapel of his jacket.

Designer: Harry Simeon
Height: 1. Large — 8 ¾", 22.2 cm
2. Medium — 6 ¼", 15.9 cm
3. Small — 4 ½", 11.9 cm
4. Miniature — 2 ¾", 7.0 cm
Issued: c.1925-Unknown
Handle: Plain
Colourway: Slate blue jacket; brown waistcoat; brown breeches; white or gold waistcoat buttons
Backstamp: Doulton Lambeth

Model Number	Size	Waistcoat Buttons	Current Market Value		
			U.K. £	U.S. $	Can. $
X8572	Large	White	550.00	1,000.00	1,300.00
X8572	Large	Gold	600.00	1,100.00	1,400.00
X8572	Medium	White	500.00	900.00	1,200.00
X8572	Small	White	400.00	700.00	1,000.00
X8572	Tiny	White	750.00	1,400.00	1,950.00

Note: Five sizes of this jug exist, 2 pint (extra large), 1 ½ pint (large), 1 pint (medium), and miniature. We have not listed all five sizes of the 'Sombre Face' version due to sighting irrgularities

TOBY XX

HAND HOLDS JUG OF ALE, WITH HANDLE

STYLE TWO: SALTGLAZE COLOURED STONEWARE

Designer: Harry Simeon
Height: 1. X8590 — 8", 20.3 cm
    2. X8592 — 8", 20.3 cm
    3. X8589 — 6 ¾", 17.2 cm
Issued: c.1925-Unknown
Handle: Strands of hair
Colourway: 1. Slate blue jacket; brown waistcoat; green breeches
    2. Slate blue jacket; orange waistcoat; green breeches
    3. Slate blue jacket; brown waistcoat; brown breeches
    4. Slate blue jacket; orange waistcoat; olive green breeches
    5. Slate blue jacket; green waistcoat; olive green breeches
    6. Black jacket; olive green waistcoat; slate blue breeches
    7. Slate blue jacket; white waistcoat; brown breeches
Backstamp: Doulton Lambeth

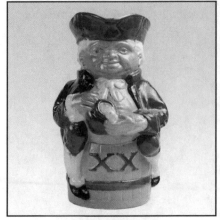

Toby XX, Style Two

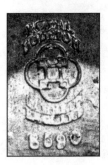

Model Number	Height	Current Market Value U.K. £	U.S. $	Can. $
X8590	8", 20.3 cm	500.00	1,000.00	1,300.00
X8592	8", 20.3 cm	500.00	1,000.00	1,300.00
X8589	6 ½", 16.5 cm	450.00	900.00	1,200.00

Derivative of Toby XX Style Two

This liquor container is supported by a silver-plated stand, produced by Finnigans Limited, Manchester.

Item: LIQUOR CONTAINER
Height: 10 ¼", 26.0 cm
Issued: c.1925-Unknown
Handle: None
Colourway: Slate blue jacket; orange waistcoat; brown breeches
Backstamp: Doulton Lambeth

Model Number	Item	Current Market Value U.K. £	U.S. $	Can. $
X8589	Liquor Container	1,100.00	2,000.00	2,500.00

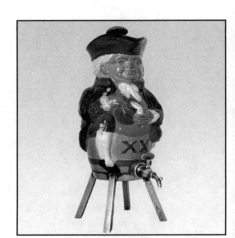

Toby XX Derivative, Liquor container

TOBY XX

BEAKER, HANDS REST ON KNEES

VARIATION No. 1: SALTGLAZE STONEWARE

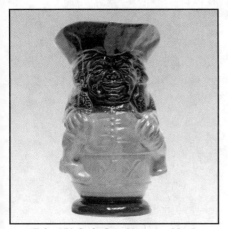

Toby XX, Style One, Variation No. 1

Designer: (Harry Simeon)
Height: 5 ¾", 14.6 cm
Issued: Unknown
Handle: None
Colourway: 1. Light brown overall glaze; no dark brown overglaze
2. Light brown overall; different sections with dark brown overglaze
Backstamp: A. Doulton Lambeth
B. Doulton Lambeth, Phillips Oxford St. London

Model Number	Colourway	Backstamp	Current Market Value		
			U.K. £	U.S. $	Can. $
8547	1	A	500.00	900.00	1,200.00
8547	2	B	500.00	900.00	1,200.00

Note: The style of glazing dates Variation No. 1 much earlier than c.1925.

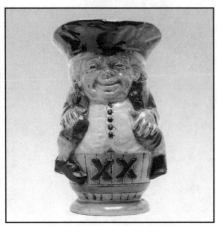

Toby XX, Style One, Variation No. 2

VARIATION No. 2: SALTGLAZE COLOURED STONEWARE

Designer: Harry Simeon
Height: 5 ½" - 5 ¾", 14.0 - 14.6 cm
Issued: c.1925-Unknown
Handle: None
Colourway: 1. Olive green jacket; white waistcoat; olive green breeches
2. Slate blue jacket; orange waistcoat; brown breeches
3. Slate blue jacket; green waistcoat; green breeches
Backstamp: Doulton Lambeth

Model Number	Variation	Height	Current Market Value		
			U.K. £	U.S. $	Can. $
X8591	Var. 1	5 ¾", 14.6 cm	450.00	800.00	1,000.00
X8591	Var. 2	5 ½", 14.0 cm	450.00	800.00	1,000.00
(8)547	Var. 3	5 ½", 14.0 cm	450.00	800.00	1,000.00

Toby XX, Style Two, Saltglaze Coloured Stoneware

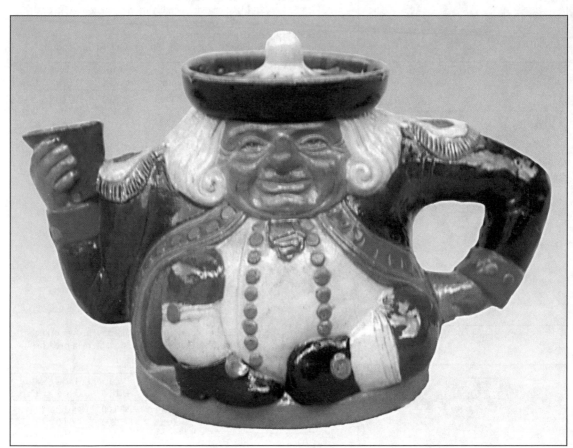

The Best Is Not Too Good, Teapot

UNKNOWN DESIGNERS

Admiral Lord Nelson
Sailor
Saved
Toby XX
Wee Mac

ADMIRAL LORD NELSON

STYLE ONE: NELSON MODELLED TO THE CHEST

The Admiral Lord Nelson jug was produced in the 1820s by Doulton and Watts in Lambeth. Although originally called a figure mug, this jug must be considered one of the first character jugs. This jug was reissued in 1905 to commemorate the 100th anniversary of the Battle of Trafalgar in which Nelson defeated the French fleet.

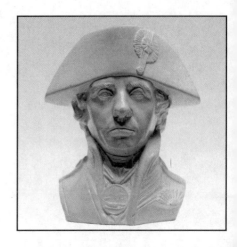

Designer:	Unknown
Height:	1. Large — 7 ¾", 19.7 cm
	Large, replica — 8", 20.3 cm
	2. Small — 6 ½", 16.5 cm
	3. Miniature — 5", 12.7 cm
Issued:	See below
Handle:	Rope
Colourway:	Saltglaze; light tan
Backstamp:	**A.** Doulton & Watts
	B. Doulton & Watts, Lambeth Pottery London
	C. Doulton & Watts Replica

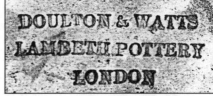

Backstamp B - Doulton & Watts

Jug No.	Model No.	Size	Issued	Current Market Value U.K. £	U.S. $	Can. $
1A.	—	Large	1821-1830	700.00	1,100.00	1,350.00
1B.	—	Large	1821-1830	700.00	1,100.00	1,350.00
1C.	—	Large	1905	475.00	675.00	800.00
2A.	—	Small	1821-1830	600.00	900.00	1,100.00
2B.	—	Small	1821-1830	600.00	900.00	1,100.00
3A.	—	Miniature	1821-1830	425.00	700.00	800.00
3B.	—	Miniature	1821-1830	425.00	700.00	800.00

Note: The above sizes and dates are only approximate, there are differences.

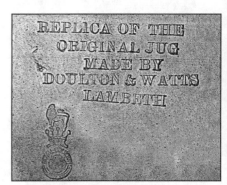

Backstamp C - Doulton & Watts Replica

ADMIRAL LORD NELSON

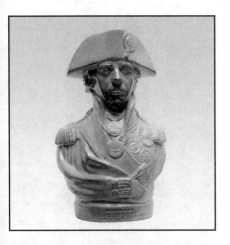

STYLE TWO: NELSON MODELLED TO THE WAIST

The inscription around the base of this jug is Nelson's famous words spoken before the Battle of Trafalgar, "England Expects Every Man to do his Duty." As in Style One, this jug was reproduced in 1905 to commemorate the 100th anniversary of the Battle of Trafalgar.

Designer:	Unknown
Height:	11 ¾", 29.8 cm
Size:	Large
Issued:	See below
Handle:	Hair tied with a bow
Colourway:	Saltglaze; light brown
Backstamp:	**A.** Doulton & Watts, Lambeth Pottery, London
	B. Doulton Burslem

Model Number	Backstamp	Issued	U.K. £	U.S. $	Can. $
—	A	1845-Unknown	1,500.00	2,750.00	3,000.00
—	B	1905-1905	1,250.00	2,250.00	2,500.00

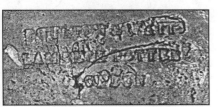

Backstamp B - Doulton & Watts

SAILOR

Item:	TOBACCO JAR
Designer:	Unknown
Height:	7 ¾", 19.7 cm
Issued:	1894
Handle:	Rope design
Colourway:	Saltglaze stoneware
Backstamp:	Doulton Lambeth

Model Number	Current Market Value		
	U.K. £	U.S. $	Can. $
3581	Extremely rare		

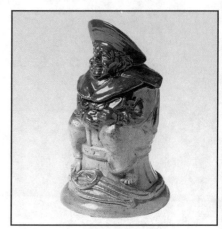

Sailor Tobacco Jar

SAVED

Item:	MATCH HOLDER
Designer:	Unknown
Height:	3 ¼", 8.3 cm
Issued:	1890
Colourway:	Saltglaze stoneware
Backstamp:	Doulton Lambeth

Model Number	Current Market Value		
	U.K. £	U.S. $	Can. $
162582	Extremely rare		

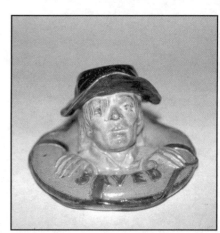

'Saved' Match Holder

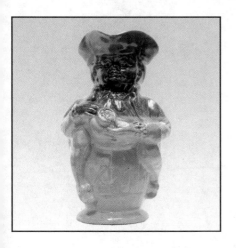

TOBY XX

HAND HOLDS JUG OF ALE, WITH HANDLE

STYLE ONE: SALTGLAZE STONEWARE

Designer: Unknown
Height: See below
Issued: See below
Handle: Hair tied with a bow
Colourway: See below
Backstamp: Doulton Lambeth

VARIATION No. 1: Light brown overall glaze; no dark brown overglaze

Model Number	Height	Issued	Current Market Value U.K. £	U.S. $	Can. $
6365	14 ½", 36.8 cm	1863-Unk.	1,000.00	1,800.00	2,200.00
6365	8 ½", 21.6 cm	1863-Unk.	500.00	1,000.00	1,300.00

VARIATION No. 2: Light brown overall glaze, different sections with dark brown overglaze

Model Number	Height	Issued	Current Market Value U.K. £	U.S. $	Can. $
6365	12 ½", 31.7 cm	1863-Unk.	800.00	1,500.00	1,900.00
6365	10 ½", 26.7 cm	1863-Unk.	650.00	1,200.00	1,500.00
6365	8 ½", 21.6 cm	1863-Unk.	500.00	1,000.00	1,300.00

VARIATION No. 3: Light brown overall glaze; "XX" is replaced with "W. Dow & Co. India Pale Ale" on barrel

Model Number	Height	Issued	Current Market Value U.K. £	U.S. $	Can. $
6365	14 ½", 36.8 cm	1891-Unk.	Rare		

Note: 1. Some examples carry a registration number 169753, which is a design registration by Doulton, circa 1891.
2. Some of the above jugs are found with sterling silver rims, usually hallmarked Birmingham, 1928 or 1929.
   These jugs will command a premium of 10% to 20% over the catalogue price.

WEE MAC

Designer:	Unknown
Height:	Unknown
Issued:	c.1908-Unknown
Handle:	Unknown
Colourway:	Saltglaze stoneware
Backstamp:	Doulton Lambeth

Model Number	Current Market Value		
	U.K. £	U.S. $	Can. $
X7247	Extremely rare		

TOBY JUGS

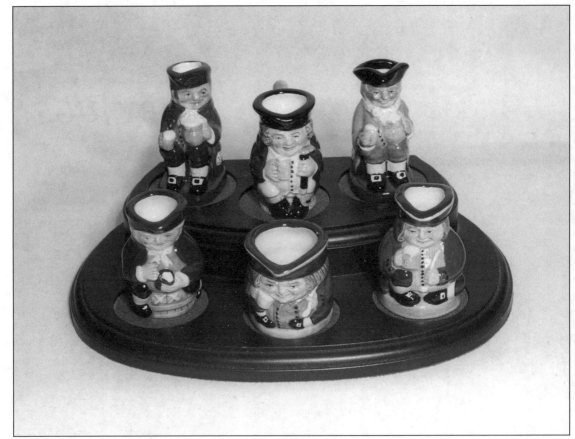

Tiny Tobies Set

ALBERT SAGGER THE POTTER

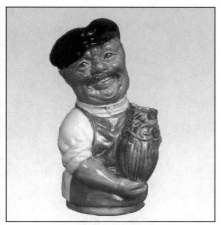

Albert Sagger The Potter

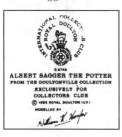

This jug was issued for the Royal Doulton International Collectors Club in 1986.

Designer: William K. Harper

Statistics:	Doulton Number	Size	Height	Issued
	D6745	Small	4", 10.1 cm	1986-1986

Handle: Plain

Colourway: Brown apron; white shirt; dark green cap; light green vase

Backstamp: Doulton/RDICC

Series: 1. The Doultonville Collection
2. RDICC

	Current Market Value		
Size	U.K. £	U.S. $	Can. $
Small	85.00	150.00	225.00

ALDERMAN MACE THE MAYOR

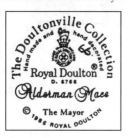

Alderman Mace The Mayor

Designer: William K. Harper

Statistics:	Doulton Number	Size	Height	Issued
	D6766	Small	4", 10.1 cm	1987-1991

Handle: Plain

Colourway: Red coat trimmed with gold; white collar and scarf; black hat trimmed with gold and white feathers

Backstamp: Doulton

Series: The Doultonville Collection

	Current Market Value		
Size	U.K. £	U.S. $	Can. $
Small	55.00	90.00	135.00

THE BEST IS NOT TOO GOOD

STYLE TWO: BURSLEM, 11 BUTTONS

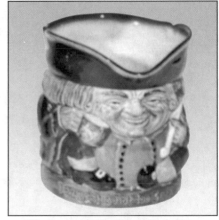

This jug was modelled on an earlier Harry Simeon Lambeth design of about 1920. There are, however, several obvious differences on this later piece. See page 17 for an outline of these differences.

Designer: Harry Fenton

	Doulton			
Statistics:	**Number**	**Size**	**Height**	**Issued**
	See below	Small	4 ½", 11.9 cm	1939-1960

Handle: Plain
Colourway: Green jacket; burgundy breeches; mustard waistcoat with double row of black buttons; brown hat with gold trim
Inscription: "The Best is not too Good"
Backstamp: Doulton

The Best is Not Too Good, Style Two

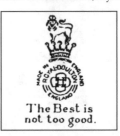

The Best is not too good.

Size	Model Number	Doulton Number	Current Market Value		
			U.K. £	**U.S. $**	**Can. $**
Small	8338	D6107	300.00	525.00	725.00

Note: For the tiny version of this jug see Tiny Tobies set page 83.

BETTY BITTERS THE BARMAID

Designer: William K. Harper

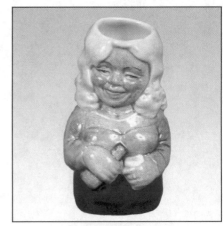

	Doulton			
Statistics:	**Number**	**Size**	**Height**	**Issued**
	D6716	Small	4", 10.1 cm	1984-1990

Handle: Plain
Colourway: Green blouse; burgundy skirt; yellow hair
Backstamp: Doulton
Series: The Doultonville Collection

Size	Current Market Value		
	U.K. £	**U.S. $**	**Can. $**
Small	45.00	85.00	125.00

Betty Bitters The Barmaid

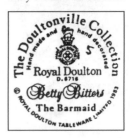

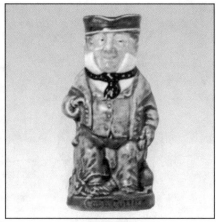

Cap'n Cuttle

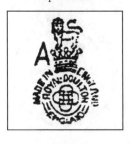

CAP'N CUTTLE

Designer: Harry Fenton

Statistics:

	Doulton Number	Size	Height	Issued
	D6266	Small	4 ½", 11.9 cm	1948-1960

Handle: Plain
Colourway: Light brown suit; blue highlights on jacket lapels and waistcoat
Backstamp: Doulton
Series: Dickens Tobies

	Current Market Value		
Size	U.K. £	U.S. $	Can. $
Small	150.00	225.00	325.00

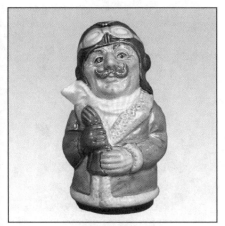

Captain Prop The Pilot

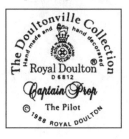

CAPTAIN PROP THE PILOT

Designer: William K. Harper

Statistics:

	Doulton Number	Size	Height	Issued
	D6812	Small	4", 10.1 cm	1989-1991

Handle: Plain
Colourway: Brown coat and gloves; grey cap; cream scarf
Backstamp: Doulton
Series: The Doultonville Collection

	Current Market Value		
Size	U.K. £	U.S. $	Can. $
Small	75.00	110.00	160.00

CAPT. SALT THE SEA CAPTAIN

Designer: William K. Harper

Statistics:	Doulton Number	Size	Height	Issued
	D6721	Small	4", 10.1 cm	1985-1991

Handle: Plain
Colourway: Blue-black coat; blue-black cap trimmed with yellow
Backstamp: Doulton
Series: The Doultonville Collection

	Current Market Value		
Size	U.K. £	U.S. $	Can. $
Small	55.00	90.00	135.00

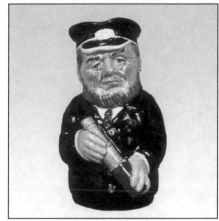

Capt. Salt The Sea Captain

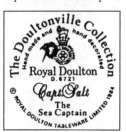

CELSIUS AND FAHRENHEIT

Ander Celsius, a Swede, created his temperature scale in 1742. Gabriel Fahrenheit invented his scale in 1717. This double toby, available through Lawleys By Post in a limited edition of 2,500, includes a working thermometer.

Designer: William K. Harper

Statistics:	Doulton Number	Size	Height	Issued
	D7143	Small	4", 10.1 cm	See below

Issued: 1999 in a limited edition of 2,500
Handle: Plain
Colourway: Celsius — Black hat with grey trim; blue jacket; green waistcoat and pantaloons; white stockings; black shoes with silver buckles
Fahrenheit — Burgundy hat with yellow trim; red jacket; tan pantaloons; white stockings; brown shoes
Backstamp: Doulton
Series: Double Toby Jugs

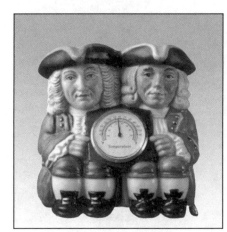

Celsius and Fahrenheit

	Current Market Value		
Size	U.K. £	U.S. $	Can. $
Small	170.00	280.00	—

CHARLES DICKENS

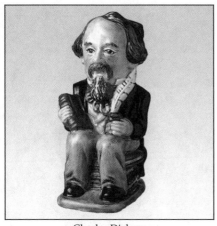

Charles Dickens

The 125th anniversary of the death of Charles Dickens was commemorated in 1995 with this toby jug of Dickens. The jug, issued in a limited edition of 2,500, was available through Lawleys By Post.

Designer: Stanley J. Taylor

Statistics:	Doulton Number	Size	Height	Issued
	D6997	Small	5", 12.7 cm	See below

Issued: 1995 in a limited edition of 2,500
Handle: Plain
Colourway: Black and grey
Backstamp: Doulton

	Current Market Value		
Size	**U.K. £**	**U.S. $**	**Can. $**
Small	125.00	175.00	250.00

Note: For the character jug Charles Dickens see page 144, and for the Charles Dickens Commemorative Set see page 143.

CHARLIE

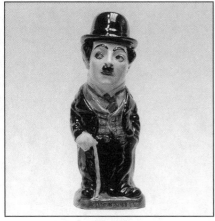

Charlie

This figure of Charlie Chaplin has a removable bowler hat. He stands on a green base and the name "Charlie" is incised around the base.

Designer: Unknown

Statistics:	Doulton Number	Size	Height	Issued
	D —	Large	11 ¼", 28.5 cm	1918-Unk.

Handle: Plain
Colourway: Black suit and bowler hat; green and red plaid waistcoat; red-brown tie; green base
Backstamp: Doulton

	Current Market Value		
Size	**U.K. £**	**U.S. $**	**Can. $**
Large	2,250.00	4,000.00	6,000.00

Note: For the character jug Charlie Chaplin see page 145.

CHARLIE CHEER THE CLOWN

Designer: William K. Harper

Statistics:

Doulton Number	Size	Height	Issued
D6768	Small	4", 10.1 cm	1987-1991

Handle: Plain
Colourway: Orange jacket; blue tie; green cap; yellow hair; pink sausages
Backstamp: Doulton
Series: The Doultonville Collection

	Current Market Value		
Size	**U.K. £**	**U.S. $**	**Can. $**
Small	75.00	110.00	150.00

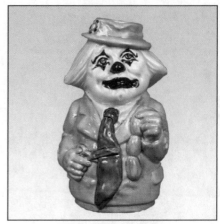

Charlie Cheer the Clown

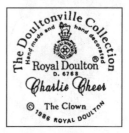

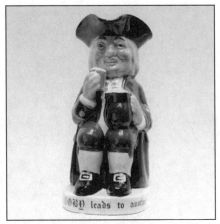

Variation No. 2 "One Toby Leads to Another"

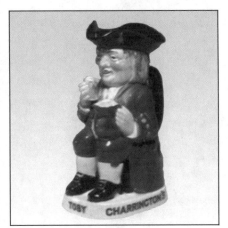

Variation No. 3 "Charrington's Toby"

CHARRINGTON & CO. LTD.

According to the Bass Museum, Burton-on-Trent, Staffordshire, these jugs originated from Hoare & Co., a London brewery which had been purchased by Charrington, another London brewery. The original Charrington toby jugs were made by Doulton, but there are no records of the numbers manufactured. The three variations below were made as promotional pieces for Charrington & Co., Mile End, London. They differ only in the wording on their bases and were in production during the 1930s. Charrington closed Hoare & Co. in 1933.

Designer:	Unknown			
	Doulton			
Statistics:	**Number**	**Size**	**Height**	**Issued**
	D8074	Large	See below	See below
Handle:	Plain			
Colourway:	Black hat; green coat; maroon trousers			
Inscription:	See below			
Backstamp:	Doulton			

VARIATION No. 1: Inscription around base — "Toby Ale"

			Current Market Value		
Variation	Height	Issued	U.K. £	U.S. $	Can. $
Var. 1	9", 22.9 cm	1934-1938	375.00	575.00	775.00

VARIATION No. 2: Inscription around base — "One Toby Leads to Another"

			Current Market Value		
Variation	Height	Issued	U.K. £	U.S. $	Can. $
Var. 2	9", 22.9 cm	1937-1938	450.00	725.00	1,000.00

VARIATION No. 3: Inscription around base — "Charrington's Toby"

			Current Market Value		
Variation	Height	Issued	U.K. £	U.S. $	Can. $
Var. 3	9 ¼", 23.5 cm	1938-1939	450.00	725.00	1,000.00

CLIFF CORNELL

In 1956 an American industrialist commissioned these toby jugs as gifts to friends and associates. The inscription on the base reads, "Greetings Cliff Cornell 'Famous Cornell Fluxes' Cleveland Flux Company." Approximately 500 pieces were issued for the large size blue and dark brown jugs, and 375 pieces for the small sizes. The number of light brown jugs produced is unknown.

Designer: Unknown

Statistics:	Doulton Number	Size	Height	Issued
1.	D —	Large	9", 22.9 cm	1956-1956
2.	D —	Small	5 ½", 14.0 cm	1956-1956

Handle: Plain
Colourway: See below
Backstamp: Doulton

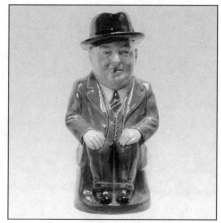

Variation No. 1

VARIATION No. 1: Colourway — Light brown suit; brown and cream striped tie

Jug No.	Size	Variation	Current Market Value U.K. £	U.S. $	Can. $
1.	Large	Var. 1	300.00	525.00	700.00
2.	Small		1,200.00	1,750.00	2,250.00

VARIATION No. 2: Colourway — Dark blue suit; red tie with cream polka dots

Jug No.	Size	Variation	Current Market Value U.K. £	U.S. $	Can. $
1.	Large	Var. 2	200.00	300.00	450.00
2.	Small		200.00	300.00	450.00

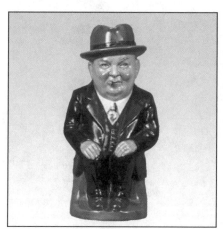

Variation No. 2

VARIATION No. 3: Colourway — Dark brown suit; green, black and blue design on tie

Jug No.	Size	Variation	Current Market Value U.K. £	U.S. $	Can. $
1.	Large	Var. 3	200.00	300.00	450.00
2.	Small		200.00	325.00	475.00

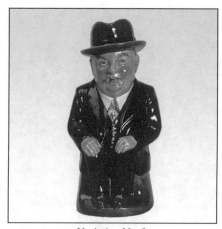

Variation No. 3

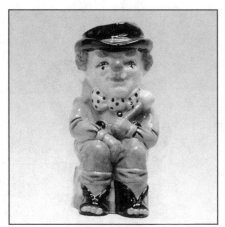

The Clown

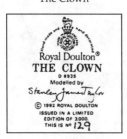

THE CLOWN

Designer:	Stanley J. Taylor

	Doulton			
Statistics:	**Number**	**Size**	**Height**	**Issued**
	D6935	Small	5 ½", 14.0 cm	See below

Issued:	1993 in a limited edition of 3,000
Handle:	Plain, black
Colourway:	Green shirt; blue trousers; yellow bow tie with blue polka dots; yellow and red drum
Backstamp:	Doulton

	Current Market Value		
Size	**U.K. £**	**U.S. $**	**Can. $**
Small	70.00	150.00	200.00

DR JEKYLL AND MR HYDE

Designer: Stanley J. Taylor

Statistics:	**Doulton Number**	**Size**	**Height**	**Issued**
	D7024	Small	5", 12.7 cm	1996-1998

Handle: Plain
Colourway: Black, white and brown
Backstamp: Doulton
Series: Two-sided Tobies

	Current Market Value		
Size	**U.K. £**	**U.S.$**	**Can.$**
Small	75.00	135.00	200.00

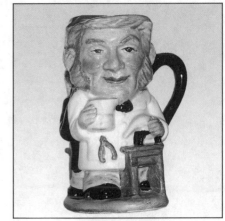

Dr. Jekyll

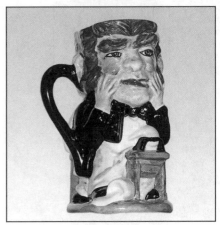

Mr. Hyde

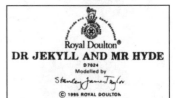

DR. PULSE THE PHYSICIAN

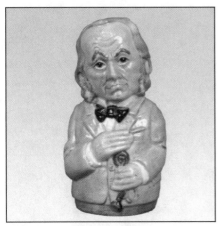

Dr. Pulse The Physician

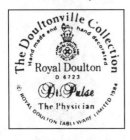

Designer: William K. Harper

	Doulton			
Statistics:	**Number**	**Size**	**Height**	**Issued**
	D6723	Small	4", 10.1 cm	1985-1991

Handle: Plain
Colourway: Light brown jacket; grey hair
Backstamp: Doulton
Series: The Doultonville Collection

	Current Market Value		
Size	**U.K. £**	**U.S. $**	**Can. $**
Small	50.00	80.00	100.00

FALSTAFF

Sir John Falstaff is a fat, good-humoured braggart who figures in Shakespeare's *Henry IV* and *The Merry Wives of Windsor*.

Designer: Charles Noke

	Doulton			
Statistics:	**Number**	**Size**	**Height**	**Issued**
1.	D6062	Large	8 ½", 21.6 cm	1939-1991
2.	D6063	Small	5 ¼", 13.3 cm	1939-1991

Handle: Plain
Colourway: Burgundy clothes; black hat with burgundy feathers
Backstamps: A. Sir John Falstaff
B. Falstaff

Jug		**Current Market Value**		
No.	**Size**	**U.K. £**	**U.S. $**	**Can. $**
1.	Large	80.00	135.00	200.00
2.	Small	55.00	90.00	125.00

Note: For the character jug Falstaff see page 181.

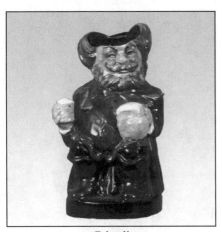

Falstaff

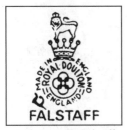

Backstamp B - Falstaff

FAT BOY

Designer: Harry Fenton

	Doulton			
Statistics:	**Number**	**Size**	**Height**	**Issued**
	D6264	Small	4 ½", 11.9 cm	1948-1960

Handle: Plain
Colourway: Brown
Backstamp: Doulton
Series: Dickens Tobies

	Current Market Value		
Size	**U.K. £**	**U.S. $**	**Can. $**
Small	150.00	250.00	350.00

Note: For the character jug Fat Boy see page 183.

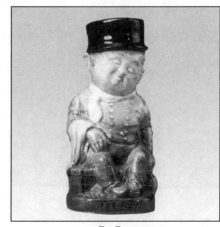

Fat Boy

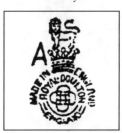

FATHER CHRISTMAS

A holly wreath is incorporated into the backstamp of the Father Christmas toby jug. Produced in a limited edition of 3,500, each jug is issued with a certificate of authenticity.

Designer: William K. Harper

	Doulton			
Statistics:	**Number**	**Size**	**Height**	**Issued**
	D6940	Small	5 ½", 14.0 cm	See below

Issued: 1993 in a limited edition of 3,500
Handle: Plain
Colourway: Red and white
Backstamp: Doulton

	Current Market Value		
Size	**U.K. £**	**U.S. $**	**Can. $**
Small	85.00	150.00	200.00

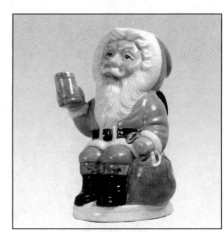

Father Christmas

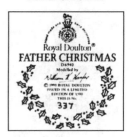

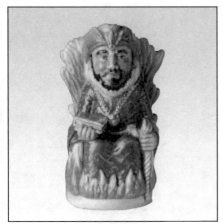

The Fire King

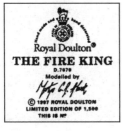

THE FIRE KING and THE ICE QUEEN

This is the first-ever matched pair of toby jugs. Both characters hail from the realm of the mystica, the imaginative. He holds his book of ancient rites for passing judgments; she can rely on her flask of 'snow gems' to deal with wrongdoers by turning them into frozen statues of ice. Embellished with 22 carat gold and platinum, these jugs were issued by Lawleys By Post, numbered and sold as a pair, in a limited edition of 1,500.

Designer: Martyn C. R. Alcock

	Doulton			
Statistics:	**Number**	**Size**	**Height**	**Issued**
1.	D7070	Medium	5", 12.7 cm	See below
2.	D7071	Medium	5", 12.7 cm	See below

Issued: 1998 in a limited edition of 1,500 each
Handle: Plain
Colourway: 1. Fire King — Red, yellow, orange and gold
               2. Ice Queen — Blue, pink, white and gold
Backstamp: Doulton

Jug No.	Doulton Number	Name	Current Market Value U.K. £	U.S. $	Can. $
1.	D7070	Fire King	175.00	250.00	350.00
2.	D7071	Ice Queen		Price for pair	

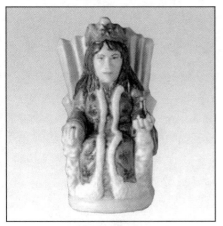

The Ice Queen

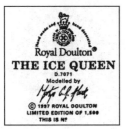

FLORA FUCHSIA THE FLORIST

Designer: William K. Harper

	Doulton			
Statistics:	**Number**	**Size**	**Height**	**Issued**
	D6767	Small	4", 10.1 cm	1987-1990

Handle: Plain
Colourway: Light blue uniform; brown hair; red, yellow and white flowers
Backstamp: Doulton
Series: The Doultonville Collection

	Current Market Value		
Size	**U.K. £**	**U.S. $**	**Can. $**
Small	80.00	125.00	175.00

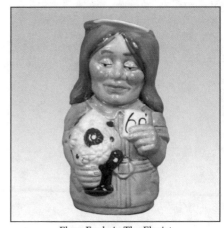

Flora Fuchsia The Florist

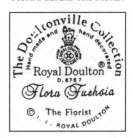

FRED FEARLESS THE FIREMAN

Designer: William K. Harper

	Doulton			
Statistics:	**Number**	**Size**	**Height**	**Issued**
	D6809	Small	4", 10.1 cm	1989-1991

Handle: Plain
Colourway: Dark blue uniform with green buttons; yellow helmet
Backstamp: Doulton
Series: The Doultonville Collection

	Current Market Value		
Size	**U.K. £**	**U.S. $**	**Can. $**
Small	70.00	110.00	150.00

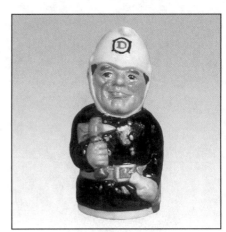

Fred Fearless The Fireman

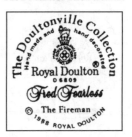

FRED FLY THE FISHERMAN

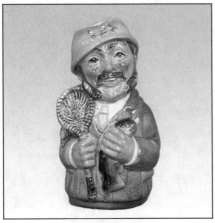

Fred Fly The Fisherman

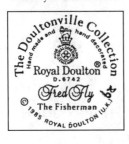

Designer: William K. Harper

Statistics:	**Doulton Number**	**Size**	**Height**	**Issued**
	D6742	Small	4", 10.1 cm	1986-1991

Handle: Plain
Colourway: Light brown coat; tan hat; grey fish and net
Backstamp: Doulton
Series: The Doultonville Collection

	Current Market Value		
Size	**U.K. £**	**U.S. $**	**Can. $**
Small	60.00	90.00	125.00

GEORGE ROBEY

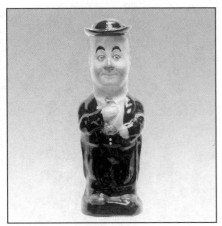

George Robey

George Robey, a star of the British Music Hall, entertained thousands during his long career. The hat on this jug is detachable, and his name is incised on the base.

Designer: Charles Noke

Statistics:	**Doulton Number**	**Size**	**Height**	**Issued**
	D —	Large	9 ¾", 24.7 cm	c.1925-Unk.

Handle: Plain
Colourway: Black suit and hat; grey shirt; green base
Backstamp: Doulton

	Current Market Value		
Size	**U.K. £**	**U.S. $**	**Can. $**
Large	2,250.00	4,500.00	6,000.00

HAPPY JOHN

Designer: Harry Fenton

Statistics:

	Doulton Number	Size	Height	Issued
1.	D6031	Large	8 ½", 21.6 cm	1939-1991
2.	D6070	Small	5 ¼", 13.3 cm	1939-1991

Handle: Plain
Colourway: Black hat; light green coat; yellow scarf with blue polka dots; orange breeches
Backstamp: Doulton

Jug No.	Size	Current Market Value U.K. £	U.S. $	Can. $
1.	Large	85.00	125.00	175.00
2.	Small	60.00	90.00	125.00

Note: For the tiny version of Happy John, see Tiny Tobies, page 83.

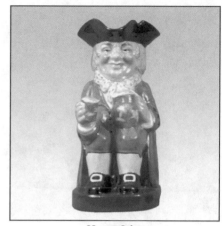

Happy John

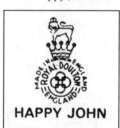

HONEST MEASURE

Designer: Harry Fenton

Statistics:

Doulton Number	Size	Height	Issued
D6108	Small	4 ¼", 10.8 cm	1939-1991

Handle: Plain
Colourway: Green coat; orange waistcoat with black buttons; burgundy breeches; brown hat with gold trim
Inscription: "Honest Measure: Drink at Leisure"
Backstamp: Doulton

Size	Current Market Value U.K. £	U.S. $	Can. $
Small	75.00	110.00	150.00

Note: For the tiny version of Honest Measure, see Tiny Tobies, page 83.

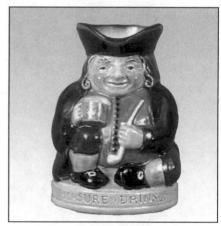

Honest Measure

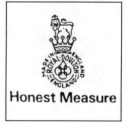

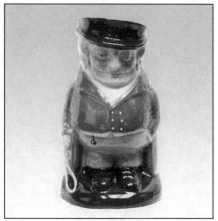

Variation No. 1

THE HUNTSMAN

Designer: Charles Noke
Handle: Plain

VARIATION No. 1: Doulton Burslem
            Colourway — Bright orange coat

Statistics:	**Doulton** **Model No**	**Size**	**Height**	**Issued**
	4090	Large	8", 20.3 cm	c.1919-Unk.

Colourway: Bright orange coat; yellow waistcoat;
              silver rim around top of hat
Backstamp: Doulton Burslem

		Current Market Value		
Size	**Variation**	**U.K. £**	**U.S. $**	**Can. $**
Large	Var. 1		Extremely rare	

VARIATION No. 2: Doulton Burslem
            Colourway — Red coat

This variation may be found with or without the sterling silver rim around the hat. The variety recorded has a silver rim.

Statistics:	**Doulton** **Model No**	**Size**	**Height**	**Issued**
	4090	Large	7 ¾", 19.7 cm	c.1919-1930

Colourway: Red coat with yellow buttons; yellow waistcoat;
              white shirt
Backstamp: Doulton Burslem

		Current Market Value		
Size	**Variation**	**U.K. £**	**U.S. $**	**Can. $**
Large	Var. 2		Extremely rare	

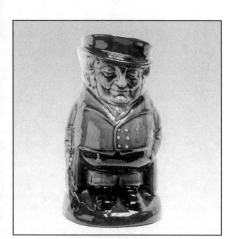

Variation No. 2

VARIATION No. 3: Kingsware
            Colourway — Browns

Statistics:	**Doulton** **Model No**	**Size**	**Height**	**Issued**
	—	Large	7 ¼", 18.4 cm	1910-c.1927

Colourway: Browns
Backstamp: Doulton

		Current Market Value		
Size	**Variation**	**U.K. £**	**U.S. $**	**Can. $**
Large	Var. 3	750.00	1,200.00	1,500.00

Variation No. 3

THE HUNTSMAN (cont.)

VARIATION No. 4:   Doulton
                            Colourway — Black hat; maroon coat

This is the Harry Fenton adaptation of Noke's original design.

Designer: Harry Fenton

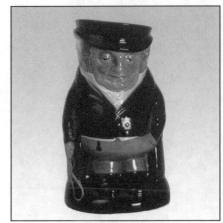

Variation No. 4

Statistics:	Doulton Number	Size	Height	Issued
	D6320	Large	7", 17.8 cm	1950-1991

Colourway: Black hat; maroon coat; white shirt;
                  gold waistcoat; grey trousers
Backstamp: Doulton

Size	Variation	Current Market Value		
		U.K. £	U.S. $	Can. $
Large	Var. 4	85.00	125.00	175.00

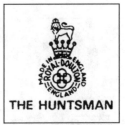

THE HUNTSMAN

Variation No. 4

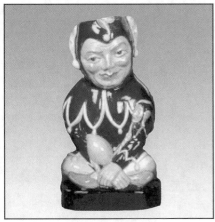

The Jester, Prototype

THE JESTER

PROTOTYPE

Designer: Peter A. Gee

	Doulton			
Statistics:	**Number**	**Size**	**Height**	**Issued**
	See below	Large	9", 22.9 cm	See below

Modelled: 1977
Issued: Not put into production
Handle: Plain
Colourway: Green and maroon costume with yellow trim; grey tights and balloon; black base
Backstamp: Doulton

	Model	**Doulton**	**Current Market Value**		
Size	**Number**	**Number**	**U.K. £**	**U.S. $**	**Can. $**
Large	2595	D6662	Extremely rare Sold November 21, 1999 Phillips, New Bond Street London, England, £6,000.00		

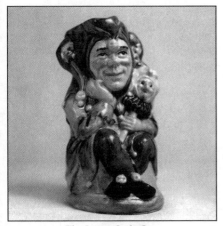

The Jester, Style One

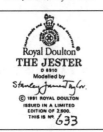

REGULAR ISSUE

STYLE ONE: JESTER HOLDING PUNCH

Designer: Stanley J. Taylor

	Doulton			
Statistics:	**Number**	**Size**	**Height**	**Issued**
	D6910	Small	5", 12.7 cm	See below

Issued: 1992 in a limited edition of 2,500
Handle: Plain, black
Colourway: Mauve and brown costume with yellow bobbles
Backstamp: Doulton

	Current Market Value		
Size	**U.K. £**	**U.S. $**	**Can. $**
Small	125.00	200.00	275.00

THE JESTER and THE LADY JESTER

STYLE TWO: JESTER HOLDING BALLOON

These jugs, in a green and pink colourway which resembles the Parian ware Jester figure (HN 3922), was issued, numbered and sold as a pair in a limited edition of 1,500 by Lawleys By Post.

Designer: David B. Biggs

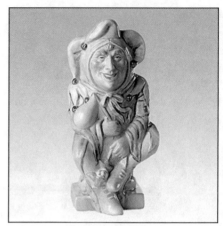

The Jester, Style Two

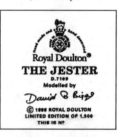

Statistics:	Doulton Number	Size	Height	Issued
1.	D7109	Medium	5", 12.7 cm	See below
2.	D7110	Medium	5", 12.7 cm	See below

Issued: 1998 in a limited edition 1,500
Handle: Plain
Colourway: Pale green and pink, gold bobbles
Backstamp: Doulton

Jug No.	Doulton Number	Name	Current Market Value U.K. £	U.S. $	Can. $
1.	D7109	Jester	175.00	250.00	325.00
2.	D7110	Lady Jester		Price for pair	

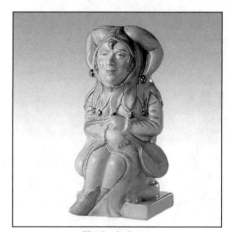

The Lady Jester

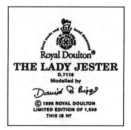

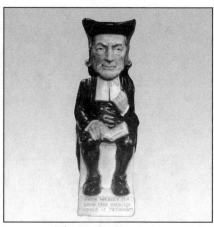

John Wesley, Prototype

JOHN WESLEY

PROTOTYPE

Designer: Charles Noke

	Doulton			
Statistics:	**Number**	**Size**	**Height**	**Issued**
	—	Large	Unknown	c.1925-Unk.

Handle: Plain
Colourway: Black
Backstamp: Doulton

	Current Market Value		
Size	**U.K. £**	**U.S. $**	**Can. $**
Large		Only two known	

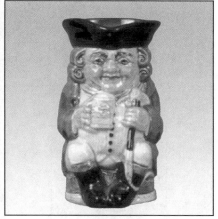

Jolly Toby

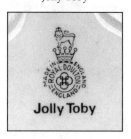

Jolly Toby

JOLLY TOBY

Designer: Harry Fenton

	Doulton			
Statistics:	**Number**	**Size**	**Height**	**Issued**
	D6109	6", 15.0 cm	6", 15.0 cm	See below

Height: 6", 15.0 cm
Issued: 1. 1939-1991
      2. Unknown
Handle: Riding crop
Colourway: 1. Black hat; burgundy coat; yellow vest;
        white breeches
      2. Black hat; burgundy coat; yellow vest;
        blue breeches
Backstamp: Doulton

Jug			**Current Market Value**		
No.	**Size**	**Colourway**	**U.K. £**	**U.S. $**	**Can. $**
1.	Medium	White breeches	75.00	125.00	175.00
2.		Blue breeches	300.00	450.00	650.00

Note: For the tiny version of Jolly Toby, see Tiny Tobies, page 83.

THE JUDGE AND THIEF

This is a double-sided toby jug with the caricatures of a stern judge and a smirking thief.

Designer: Stanley J. Taylor

	Doulton			
Statistics:	**Number**	**Size**	**Height**	**Issued**
	D6988	Small	5 ¼", 13.3 cm	1995-1998

Handle: Plain
Colourways: Red, white, black and brown
Backstamp: Doulton
Series: Two-sided Tobies

	Current Market Value		
Size	**U.K. £**	**U.S. $**	**Can. $**
Small	75.00	150.00	225.00

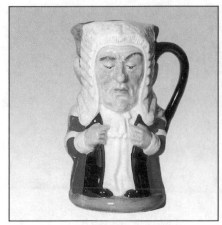

The Judge

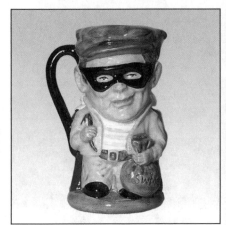

The Thief

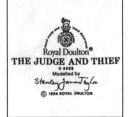

KING AND QUEEN OF CLUBS

This is the second jug issued in this series. It was produced in 1995 in a limited edition of 2,500.

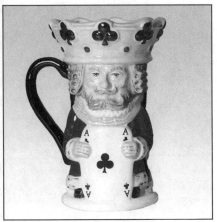

King of Clubs

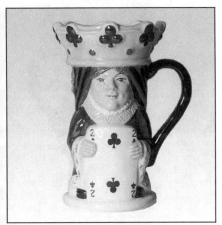

Queen of Clubs

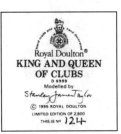

Designer: Stanley J. Taylor

	Doulton			
Statistics:	**Number**	**Size**	**Height**	**Issued**
	D6999	Small	5", 12.7 cm	See below

Issued: 1995 in a limited edition of 2,500
Handle: Plain
Colourway: King in red; Queen in blue; both wear yellow crowns
Backstamp: Doulton
Series: 1. Suites From Playing Cards
2. Two-sided Tobies

	Current Market Value		
Size	**U.K. £**	**U.S. $**	**Can. $**
Small	90.00	150.00	225.00

KING AND QUEEN OF DIAMONDS

This is one of a series of four tobies illustrating the four suites of playing cards. This is the first double-sided toby jug in this series, and it was issued in a limited edition of 2,500.

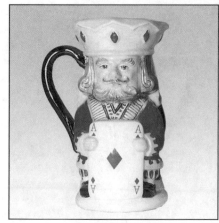

King of Diamonds

Designer: Stanley J. Taylor

Statistics:	**Doulton Number**	**Size**	**Height**	**Issued**
	D6969	Small	5", 12.7 cm	See below

Issued: 1994 in a limited edition of 2,500
Handle: Plain
Colourway: King in red; Queen in blue; both wear yellow crowns
Backstamp: Doulton
Series: 1. Suites From Playing Cards
2. Two-sided Tobies

	Current Market Value		
Size	**U.K. £**	**U.S. $**	**Can. $**
Small	90.00	150.00	225.00

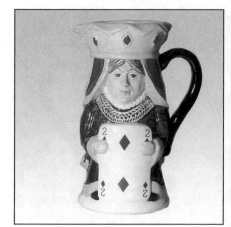

Queen of Diamonds

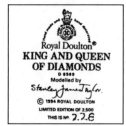

KING AND QUEEN OF HEARTS

This is the third jug in this series. It was issued in 1996 in a limited edtion of 2,500.

Designer: Stanley J. Taylor

	Doulton			
Statistics:	**Number**	**Size**	**Height**	**Issued**
	D7037	Small	5", 12.7 cm	See below

Issued: 1996 in a limited edition of 2,500
Handle: Plain
Colourway: King in red, Queen in blue; both wear yellow crowns
Backstamp: Doulton
Series: 1. Suites From Playing Cards
2. Two-sided Tobies

	Current Market Value		
Size	**U.K. £**	**U.S. $**	**Can. $**
Small	90.00	150.00	225.00

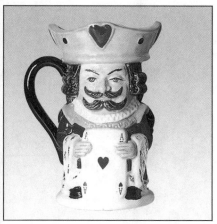

King of Hearts

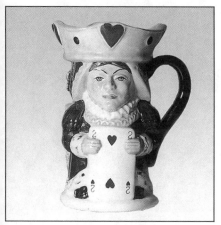

Queen of Hearts

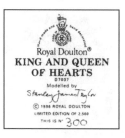

KING AND QUEEN OF SPADES

This is the fourth and last jug in this series. It was issued in 1997 in a limited edtion of 2,500.

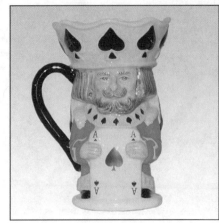

King of Spades

Designer: Stanley J. Taylor

Statistics:	**Doulton** **Number**	**Size**	**Height**	**Issued**
	D7087	Small	5", 12.7 cm	See below

Issued: 1997 in a limited edition of 2,500
Handle: Plain
Colourway: King in red, Queen in blue; both wear yellow crowns
Backstamp: Doulton
Series: 1. Suites From Playing Cards
2. Two-sided Tobies

	Current Market Value		
Size	**U.K. £**	**U.S. $**	**Can. $**
Small	90.00	150.00	225.00

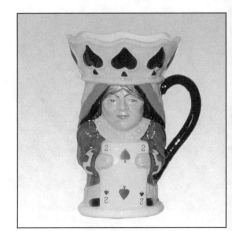

Queen of Spades

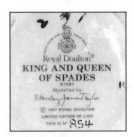

KING HENRY VIII

Commissioned by Lawleys By Post in a limited edition of 2,500, this piece was issued singly or with the six wives on a presentation stand.

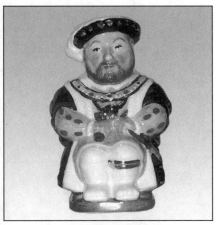

King Henry VIII

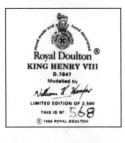

Designer: William K. Harper

	Doulton			
Statistics:	**Number**	**Size**	**Height**	**Issued**
	D7047	Small	3 ½", 8.9 cm	See below

Issued: 1996 in a limited edition of 2,500
Handle: Plain
Colourway: Black, white, yellow and gold
Backstamp: Doulton

	Current Market Value		
Size	**U.K. £**	**U.S. $**	**Can. $**
Small	75.00	150.00	200.00

Note: Character jugs: For Henry VIII (Style One) see page 222, for Henry VIII (Style Two) see Kings and Queens of the Realm, page 247. For King Henry VIII see page 246. For the Six Wives of Henry VIII series, see page 364.

LEN LIFEBELT THE LIFEBOATMAN

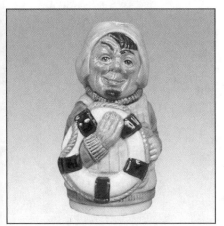

Len Lifebelt The Lifeboatman

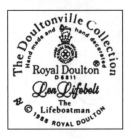

Designer: William K. Harper

	Doulton			
Statistics:	**Number**	**Size**	**Height**	**Issued**
	D6811	Small	4", 10.1 cm	1989-1991

Handle: Plain
Colourway: Yellow life jacket and sou'wester; blue sweater; white life preserver
Backstamp: Doulton
Series: The Doultonville Collection

	Current Market Value		
Size	**U.K. £**	**U.S. $**	**Can. $**
Small	60.00	90.00	135.00

LEPRECHAUN

This jug was issued in a worldwide limited edition of 2,500. It was sold out in 1994.

Designer: Stanley J. Taylor

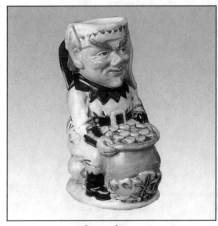

Statistics:	**Doulton Number**	**Size**	**Height**	**Issued**
	D6948	Small	5", 12.7 cm	See below

Issued: 1994 in a limited edition of 2,500
Handle: Plain
Colourways: Light and dark green and brown
Backstamp: Doulton

	Current Market Value		
Size	**U.K. £**	**U.S. $**	**Can. $**
Small	85.00	125.00	175.00

Leprechaun

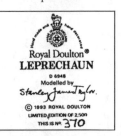

LEWIS CARROLL

The centenary of the death of Lewis Carroll, author of *Alice in Wonderland,* was commemorated by the issue of this toby jug. The jug was commissioned by Lawleys By Post in a limited edition of 1,500.

Designer: David B. Biggs

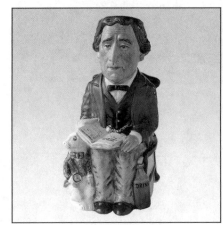

Statistics:	**Doulton Number**	**Size**	**Height**	**Issued**
	D7078	Medium	6 ½", 16.5 cm	See below

Issued: 1997 in a limited edition of 1,500
Handle: Plain
Colourway: Red, black, white and grey
Backstamp: Doulton

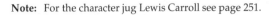

	Current Market Value		
Size	**U.K. £**	**U.S. $**	**Can. $**
Medium	90.00	150.00	225.00

Lewis Carroll

Note: For the character jug Lewis Carroll see page 251.

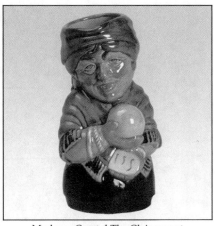

Madame Crystal The Clairvoyant

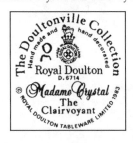

MADAME CRYSTAL THE CLAIRVOYANT

Designer: William K. Harper

Statistics:

	Doulton Number	Size	Height	Issued
	D6714	Small	4", 10.1 cm	1984-1989

Handle: Plain
Colourway: Green headscarf; burgundy skirt; mauve shawl with blue fringe
Backstamp: Doulton
Series: The Doultonville Collection

	Current Market Value		
Size	U.K. £	U.S. $	Can. $
Small	60.00	90.00	125.00

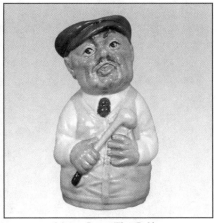

Major Green The Golfer

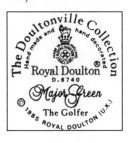

MAJOR GREEN THE GOLFER

Designer: William K. Harper

Statistics:

	Doulton Number	Size	Height	Issued
	D6740	Small	4", 10.1 cm	1986-1991

Handle: Plain
Colourway: Light brown waistcoat; yellow shirt; green cap
Backstamp: Doulton
Series: The Doultonville Collection

	Current Market Value		
Size	U.K. £	U.S. $	Can. $
Small	75.00	110.00	175.00

MANSION HOUSE DWARF
FATHER

The companion to Mansion House Dwarf Son, this model was available through Lawleys By Post in 1999 in a limited edition of 1,500. The quote on the dwarf's hat reads "Royal Doulton Visit Their New Showroom".

Modeller: William K. Harper

Statistics:	Doulton Number	Size	Height	Issued
	D7134	Small	4 ¾", 12.1 cm	See below

Issued: 1999 in a limited edition of 1,500
Handle: Plain
Colourway: Black hat with white band; purple jacket with gold buttons; green pantaloons; white stockings; black shoes with purple bows
Backstamp: Doulton

	Current Market Value		
Size	U.K. £	U.S. $	Can. $
Small	100.00	150.00	225.00

Photograph not available at press time

MANSION HOUSE DWARF
SON

The inspiration for this jug was derived from London's Mansion House Dwarves in Tudor times who seemed to fulfil the function of walking billboards by displaying advertising on their large hats for upcoming events. The quote on the dwarf's hat reads "Royal Doulton Potteries / There can be no better gift - call in today!". The jug was issued by Lawleys By Post in a limited edition of 1,500, along with a signed limited edition print of William K. Harper's working sketches.

Modeller: William K. Harper

Statistics:	Doulton Number	Size	Height	Issued
	D7135	Small	4 ¾", 12.1 cm	See below

Issued: 1998 in a limited edition of 1,500
Handle: Plain
Colourway: Black hat with pink feathers; blue and white vest with gold buttons; pink sleeves and pantaloons; white stockings; black shoes with blue bows
Backstamp: Doulton

	Current Market Value		
Size	U.K. £	U.S. $	Can. $
Small	100.00	150.00	225.00

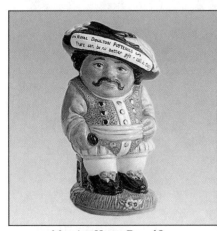

Mansion House Dwarf Son

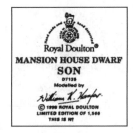

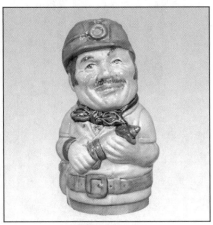

Mike Mineral The Miner

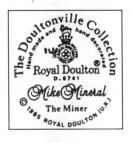

MIKE MINERAL THE MINER

Designer: William K. Harper

Statistics:	**Doulton Number**	**Size**	**Height**	**Issued**
	D6741	Small	4", 10.1 cm	1986-1989

Handle: Plain
Colourway: Light green shirt; grey helmet; blue scarf; light brown belt
Backstamp: Doulton
Series: The Doultonville Collection

	Current Market Value		
Size	U.K. £	U.S. $	Can. $
Small	100.00	150.00	200.00

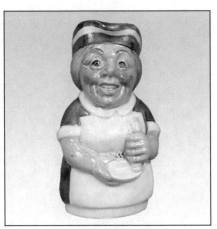

Miss Nostrum The Nurse

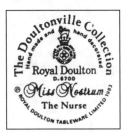

MISS NOSTRUM THE NURSE

Designer: William K. Harper

Statistics:	**Doulton Number**	**Size**	**Height**	**Issued**
	D6700	Small	4", 10.1 cm	1983-1991

Handle: Plain
Colourway: Blue uniform; white apron; blue and white cap
Backstamp: Doulton
Series: The Doultonville Collection

	Current Market Value		
Size	U.K. £	U.S. $	Can. $
Small	55.00	75.00	110.00

MISS STUDIOUS THE SCHOOLMISTRESS

Designer: William K. Harper

Statistics:	**Doulton Number**	**Size**	**Height**	**Issued**
	D6722	Small	4", 10.1 cm	1985-1989

Handle: Plain
Colourway: Yellow blouse; green waistcoat; dark burgundy skirt
Backstamp: Doulton
Series: The Doultonville Collection

	Current Market Value		
Size	**U.K. £**	**U.S. $**	**Can. $**
Small	70.00	110.00	150.00

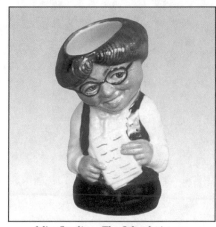

Miss Studious The Schoolmistress

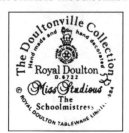

MONSIEUR CHASSEUR THE CHEF

Designer: William K. Harper

Statistics:	**Doulton Number**	**Size**	**Height**	**Issued**
	D6769	Small	4", 10.1 cm	1987-1991

Handle: Plain
Colourway: White chef 's coat and hat; blue scarf
Backstamp: Doulton
Series: The Doultonville Collection

	Current Market Value		
Size	**U.K. £**	**U.S. $**	**Can. $**
Small	70.00	110.00	150.00

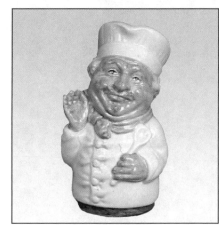

Monsieur Chasseur The Chef

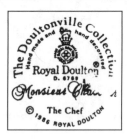

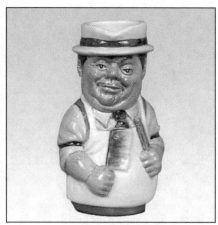

Mr. Brisket The Butcher

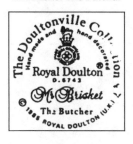

MR. BRISKET THE BUTCHER

Designer: William K. Harper

Statistics:	Doulton Number	Size	Height	Issued
	D6743	Small	4", 10.1 cm	1986-1991

Handle: Plain
Colourway: Pale blue shirt; white apron; yellow hat with brown band
Backstamp: Doulton
Series: The Doultonville Collection

Size	Current Market Value		
	U.K.£	U.S. $	Can. $
Small	60.00	90.00	125.00

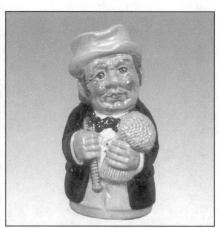

Mr. Furrow The Farmer

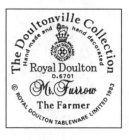

MR. FURROW THE FARMER

Designer: William K. Harper

Statistics:	Doulton Number	Size	Height	Issued
	D6701	Small	4", 10.1 cm	1983-1989

Handle: Plain
Colourway: Dark brown coat; cream trousers; light brown hat
Backstamp: Doulton
Series: The Doultonville Collection

Size	Current Market Value		
	U.K. £	U.S. $	Can. $
Small	55.00	85.00	125.00

MR. LITIGATE THE LAWYER

Designer:	William K. Harper			

	Doulton			
Statistics:	**Number**	**Size**	**Height**	**Issued**
	D6699	Small	4", 10.1 cm	1983-1991

Handle:	Plain
Colourway:	Black robes; yellow waistcoat; grey wig and trousers
Backstamp:	Doulton
Series:	The Doultonville Collection

	Current Market Value		
Size	**U.K. £**	**U.S. $**	**Can. $**
Small	60.00	90.00	125.00

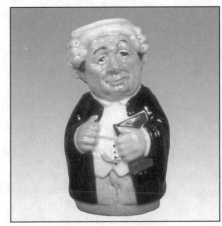

Mr. Litigate The Lawyer

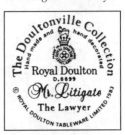

MR. MICAWBER

Designer:	Harry Fenton			

	Doulton			
Statistics:	**Number**	**Size**	**Height**	**Issued**
	D6262	Small	4 ½", 11.9 cm	1948-1960

Handle:	Plain
Colourway:	Browns
Backstamp:	Doulton
Series:	Dickens Tobies

	Current Market Value		
Size	**U.K. £**	**U.S. $**	**Can. $**
Small	150.00	225.00	300.00

Note: For the character jug Mr. Micawber see page 280.

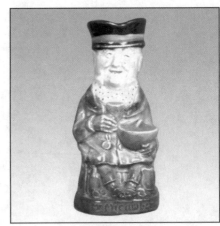

Mr. Micawber

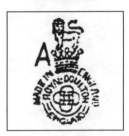

MR. PICKWICK

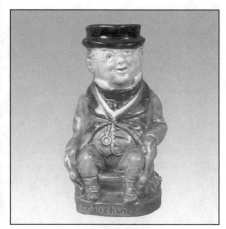

Mr. Pickwick

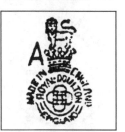

| | Designer: | Harry Fenton | | | |

		Doulton			
Statistics:	**Number**	**Size**	**Height**	**Issued**
	D6261	Small	4 ½", 11.9 cm	1948-1960

Handle:	Plain
Colourway:	Browns
Backstamp:	Doulton
Series:	Dickens Tobies

	Current Market Value		
Size	**U.K. £**	**U.S. $**	**Can. $**
Small	150.00	225.00	300.00

Note: For the character jug Mr. Pickwick see page 282.

MR. TONSIL THE TOWN CRIER

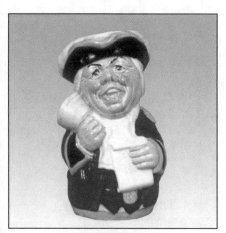

Mr. Tonsil The Town Crier

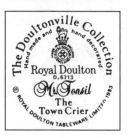

| | Designer: | William K. Harper | | | |

		Doulton			
Statistics:	**Number**	**Size**	**Height**	**Issued**
	D6713	Small	4", 10.1 cm	1984-1991

Handle:	Plain
Colourway:	Burgundy coat trimmed with gold; brown hat trimmed with gold; white scarf
Backstamp:	Doulton
Series:	The Doultonville Collection

	Current Market Value		
Size	**U.K.£**	**U.S. $**	**Can. $**
Small	55.00	90.00	125.00

MRS. LOAN THE LIBRARIAN

Designer: William K. Harper

Statistics:

	Doulton			
	Number	**Size**	**Height**	**Issued**
	D6715	Small	4", 10.1 cm	1984-1989

Handle: Plain
Colourway: Dark green blouse trimmed with white;
light green skirt; yellow book
Backstamp: Doulton
Series: The Doultonville Collection

	Current Market Value		
Size	U.K. £	U.S. $	Can. $
Small	55.00	90.00	125.00

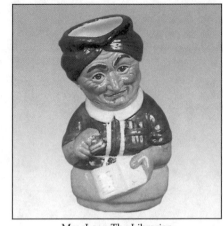

Mrs. Loan The Librarian

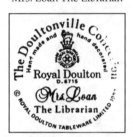

OLD CHARLIE

Designer: Harry Fenton

Statistics:

	Doulton			
	Number	**Size**	**Height**	**Issued**
1.	D6030	Large	8 ½", 21.6 cm	1939-1960
2.	D6069	Small	5", 12.7 cm	1939-1960

Handle: Plain
Colourway: Brown hat; green coat; burgundy trousers
Backstamp: Doulton

Jug		Current Market Value		
No.	Size	U.K. £	U.S. $	Can. $
1.	Large	250.00	400.00	550.00
2.	Small	175.00	300.00	450.00

Note: For the tiny version of Old Charlie see the Tiny Tobies Series
page 83.

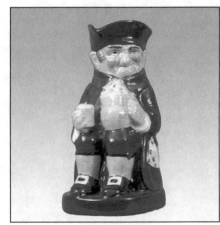

Old Charlie

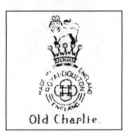

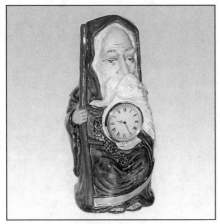

Old Father Time

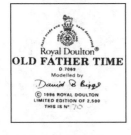

OLD FATHER TIME

For the first time Royal Doulton have incorporated a working clock into a toby jug. This jug was released by Lawleys By Post in a limited edition of 2,500.

Designer: David B. Biggs

	Doulton			
Statistics:	**Number**	**Size**	**Height**	**Issued**
	D7069	Medium	6 ½", 16.5 cm	See below

Issued: 1996 in a limited edition of 2,500
Handle: Hour glass and hat
Colourway: Dark blue, white and brown
Backstamp: Doulton

	Current Market Value		
Size	**U.K. £**	**U.S. $**	**Can. $**
Medium	90.00	150.00	225.00

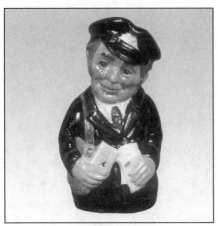

Pat Parcel The Postman

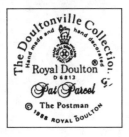

PAT PARCEL THE POSTMAN

Designer: William K. Harper

	Doulton			
Statistics:	**Number**	**Size**	**Height**	**Issued**
	D6813	Small	4", 10.1 cm	1989-1991

Handle: Plain
Colourway: Dark blue uniform trimmed with red; grey postbag
Backstamp: Doulton
Series: The Doultonville Collection

	Current Market Value		
Size	**U.K. £**	**U.S. $**	**Can. $**
Small	55.00	80.00	125.00

REV. CASSOCK THE CLERGYMAN

Designer: William K. Harper

Statistics:	**Doulton Number**	**Size**	**Height**	**Issued**
	D6702	Small	4", 10.1 cm	1983-1990

Handle: Plain
Colourway: Black coat; grey shirt; brown cap
Backstamp: Doulton
Series: The Doultonville Collection

Size	Current Market Value		
	U.K. £	**U.S. $**	**Can. $**
Small	50.00	85.00	110.00

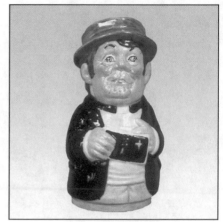

Rev. Cassock The Clergyman

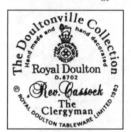

ROMANY MALE and FEMALE

Produced in a limited edition of 2,500, these jugs were issued as a pair with matching edition numbers from Lawleys by Post.

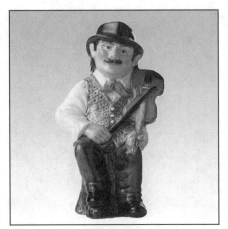

Romany Male

Designer: David B. Biggs

	Doulton			
Statistics:	**Number**	**Size**	**Height**	**Issued**
1.	D7139	Medium	6 ½", 16.5 cm	See below
2.	D7140	Medium	6 ½", 16.5 cm	See below

Issued: 1999 in a limited edition of 2,500
Handle: Plain
Colourway: 1. Male — Black hat; yellow shirt; green vest; red neckerchief; brown violin; dark green pants
2. Female — Yellow kerchief; cream sleeves; green bodice; red skirt with green trim
Backstamp: Doulton

Jug No.	Doulton Number	Name	Current Market Value U.K.£	U.S. $	Can. $
1.	D7139	Romany Male	199.50	—	—
2.	D7140	Romany Female		Price for pair	

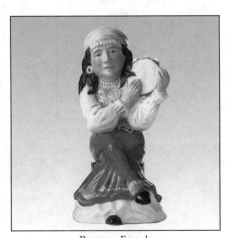

Romany Female

SAIREY GAMP

Designer: Harry Fenton

	Doulton			
Statistics:	**Number**	**Size**	**Height**	**Issued**
	D6263	Small	4 ½", 11.9 cm	1948-1960

Handle: Plain
Colourway: Browns
Backstamp: Doulton
Series: Dickens Tobies

	Current Market Value		
Size	**U.K.£**	**U.S. $**	**Can. $**
Small	150.00	225.00	300.00

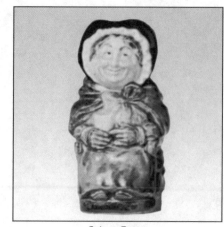

Sairey Gamp

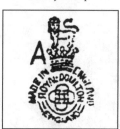

SAM WELLER

Designer: Harry Fenton

	Doulton			
Statistics:	**Number**	**Size**	**Height**	**Issued**
	D6265	Small	4 ½", 11.9 cm	1948-1960

Handle: Plain
Colourway: Browns
Backstamp: Doulton
Series: Dickens Tobies

	Current Market Value		
Size	**U.K.£**	**U.S. $**	**Can. $**
Small	150.00	225.00	300.00

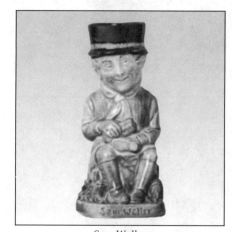

Sam Weller

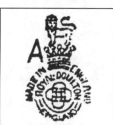

SGT. PEELER THE POLICEMAN

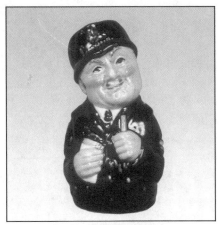

Sgt. Peeler The Policeman

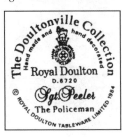

Designer: William K. Harper

Statistics:	Doulton Number	Size	Height	Issued
	D6720	Small	4", 10.1 cm	1985-1991

Handle: Plain
Colourway: Blue-black uniform
Backstamp: Doulton
Series: The Doultonville Collection

	Current Market Value		
Size	U.K.£	U.S. $	Can. $
Small	55.00	90.00	125.00

SHERLOCK HOLMES

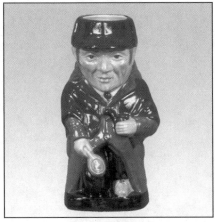

Sherlock Holmes

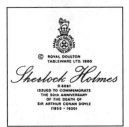

The inscription on the base of this jug reads "Issued to Commemorate the 50th Anniversary of the Death of Sir Arthur Conan Doyle (1859 - 1930)."

Designer: Robert Tabbenor

Statistics:	Doulton Number	Size	Height	Issued
	D6661	Large	9", 22.9 cm	1981-1991

Handle: Plain, black
Colourway: Green hat and cloak; green-brown coat
Backstamp: Doulton

	Current Market Value		
Size	U.K.£	U.S. $	Can. $
Large	85.00	150.00	200.00

Note: For the character jug Sherlock Holmes, see the "Sherlock Holmes Set" page 354. For the Sherlock Holmes and Dr Watson Bookends see page 406.

SIR FRANCIS DRAKE

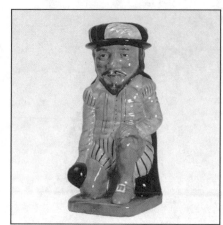

The inscription on the base of this jug reads "Issued to commemorate the 400th Anniversary of the circumnavigation of the world."

Designer: Michael Abberley

	Doulton			
Statistics:	**Number**	**Size**	**Height**	**Issued**
	D6660	Large	9", 22.9 cm	1981-1991

Handle: Plain
Colourway: Black hat with white feather; yellow with brown tunic; tan boots
Backstamp: Doulton

	Current Market Value		
Size	**U.K.£**	**U.S. $**	**Can. $**
Large	85.00	150.00	225.00

Sir Francis Drake

Note: For the character jug Drake, see page 169, and for the character jug Sir Francis Drake, see page 357.

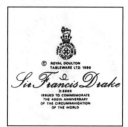

THE SPOOK and THE BEARED SPOOK

The Spook and Bearded Spook are based on the original figures designed by C. J. Noke. They were remodelled by Robert Tabbenor. This pair of jugs was issued, numbered and sold as a set in a limited edition of 1,500 by Lawleys By Post.

Designer: C. J. Noke
Modeller: Robert Tabbenor

Statistics:	Doulton Number	Size	Height	Issued
1.	D7132	Small	5 ¾", 14.6 cm	See below
2.	D7133	Small	5 ¼", 13.3 cm	See below

Issued: 1998 in a limited edition of 1,500
Handle: Plain
Colourway: Blue-grey robes; black caps; brown handles and bases
Backstamp: Doulton

Jug No.	Doulton Number	Name	Current Market Value U.K.£	U.S. $	Can. $
1.	D7132	Spook	125.00	200.00	300.00
2.	D7133	Bearded Spook		Price for pair	

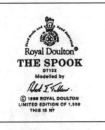

The Spook

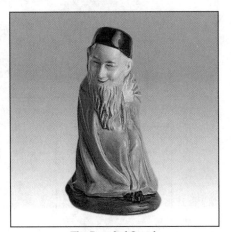

The Bearded Spook

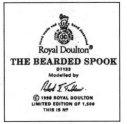

THE SQUIRE

Designer: Unknown

VARIATION No. 1: Kingsware
                            Colourway — Browns; sterling silver rim
                            around neck of jug

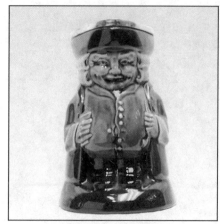

	Doulton			
Statistics:	**Number**	**Size**	**Height**	**Issued**
	D —	Medium	6", 15.0 cm	c.1910-Unk.

Handle: Plain
Backstamp: Doulton

Colourway: Browns; sterling silver rim around neck of jug

Size	Variation	Current Market Value		
		U.K.£	**U.S. $**	**Can. $**
Medium	Var. 1	750.00	1,200.00	1,600.00

Variation No. 1 - Kingsware

VARIATION No. 2: Earthenware
                            Colourway — Green coat; brown hat

Designer: Harry Fenton

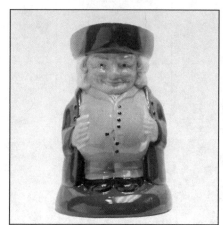

	Doulton			
Statistics:	**Number**	**Size**	**Height**	**Issued**
	D6319	Medium	6", 15.0 cm	1950-1969

Colourway: Brown hat; green coat; mustard waistcoat
                    with black buttons

Size	Variation	Current Market Value		
		U.K.£	**U.S. $**	**Can. $**
Medium	Var. 2	350.00	550.00	750.00

Variation No. 2 - Earthenware

Note: 1. We believe there is a possibility that an early Squire jug, issued circa 1910, exists in earthenware. If anyone has any information regarding this jug, please contact us.
       2. A Kingsware jug exists with a silver lid.

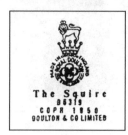

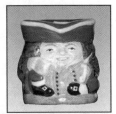

The Best Is Not Too
Good

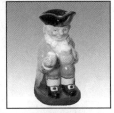

Happy John

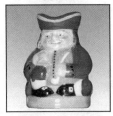

Honest Measure

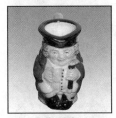

Jolly Toby

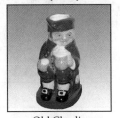

Old Charlie

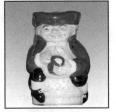

Toby XX

TINY TOBIES

The Harry Fenton designs of the 1930s were authentically reproduced by William K. Harper in a new tiny size for 1994. The limited edition of 2,500 was sold only as a set and was available with a presentation stand.

Designer: William K. Harper

Statistics:	Doulton Number	Size	Height	Issued
1.	D6974	Tiny	2", 6.4 cm	See below
2.	D6975	Tiny	2", 6.4 cm	
3.	D6976	Tiny	2", 6.4 cm	
4.	D6977	Tiny	1 ½", 3.8 cm	
5.	D6978	Tiny	2 ½", 6.4 cm	
6.	D6979	Tiny	2 ½", 6.4 cm	

Issued: 1994 in a limited edition of 2,500
Handle: Plain
Colourway: 1. **Honest Measure** — Green, yellow and brown
2. **Toby XX** — Burgundy, mustard, black and white
3. **Jolly Toby** — Burgundy, yellow and black
4. **Best Is Not Too Good (The)** — Green, mustard and brown
5. **Old Charlie** — Green, brown and mustard
6. **Happy John** — Light green, mustard and black
Backstamp: Doulton

Jug No.	Doulton Number	Name	Current Market Value U.K.£	U.S $	Can. $
1.	D6974	Honest Measure	50.00	85.00	125.00
2.	D6975	Toby XX	50.00	85.00	125.00
3.	D6976	Jolly Toby	50.00	85.00	125.00
4.	D6977	Best Is Not Too Good	50.00	85.00	125.00
5.	D6978	Old Charlie	50.00	85.00	125.00
6.	D6979	Happy John	50.00	85.00	125.00
		Complete set / presentation stand	300.00	500.00	750.00

TOBY XX

STYLE FOUR: BURSLEM, EARTHENWARE,
BURGUNDY COAT, WITH HANDLE

Style Four is a modification of the 1925 design by Harry Simeon.
Toby XX is also known as The Man on the Barrel and Double XX.

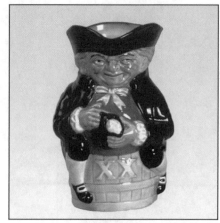

Toby XX

Designer: Harry Fenton

	Doulton			
Statistics:	**Number**	**Size**	**Height**	**Issued**
	See below	Medium	7", 17.8 cm	1939-1969

Handle: Strands of hair
Colourway: Burgundy coat; orange shirt; blue bow tie; black
trousers; dark brown hat; green-grey hair; cream barrel
Backstamp: Doulton

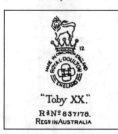

	Model	Doulton	Current Market Value		
Size	Number	Number	U.K.£	U.S. $	Can. $
Medium	8337	D6088	250.00	500.00	600.00

Note: See page 35 for the early stoneware Toby XX tobies. For the tiny
version of Toby XX, see the Tiny Tobies Series, page 83.

TOWN CRIER

Designer: Stanley J. Taylor

	Doulton			
Statistics:	**Number**	**Size**	**Height**	**Issued**
	D6920	Medium	5", 12.7 cm	See below

Issued: 1992 in a limited edition of 2,500
Handle: Plain, black
Colourway: Scarlet great coat trimmed with yellow; black
tricorn hat trimmed with yellow; white feather
Backstamp: Doulton

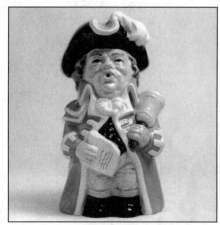

Town Crier

	Current Market Value		
Size	U.K.£	U.S. $	Can. $
Medium	125.00	200.00	250.00

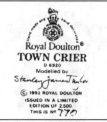

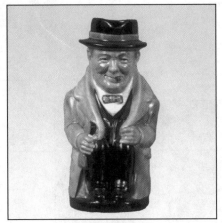

Winston Churchill

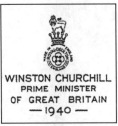

Backstamp A

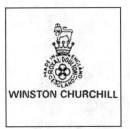

Backstamp B

WINSTON CHURCHILL

Designer: Harry Fenton

Statistics:	Doulton Number	Size	Height	Issued
1.	D6171	Large	9", 22.9 cm	See below
2.	D6172	Medium	5 ½", 14.0 cm	
3.	D6175	Small	4", 10.1 cm	

Issued: A. 1940-1940
B. 1941-1991
Handle: Plain
Colourway: Black hat; brown overcoat; black-green suit
Backstamps: A. "Winston Churchill Prime Minister of Great Britain 1940" Model No. 8360B
B. "Winston Churchill"

Jug No.	Size	Current Market Value		
		U.K.£	U.S. $	Can. $
1A.	Large	275.00	475.00	650.00
1B.	Large	80.00	125.00	150.00
2A.	Medium	225.00	400.00	575.00
2B.	Medium	60.00	90.00	100.00
3A.	Small	150.00	225.00	350.00
3B.	Small	55.00	80.00	90.00

Note: For the character jug Churchill, see page 151, for the character jug Sir Winston Churchill, see page 363 and for the character jug Winston Churchill, see page 397.

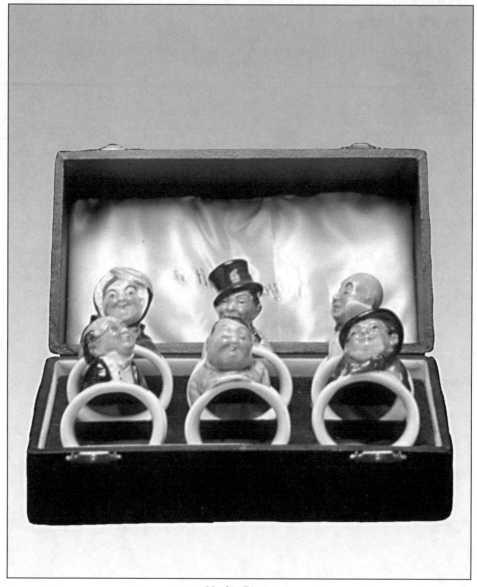

Napkin Rings
Sairey Gamp, Sam Weller, Mr. Micawber
Mr. Pickwick, Fat Boy, Tony Weller

ROYAL DOULTON CHARACTER JUGS

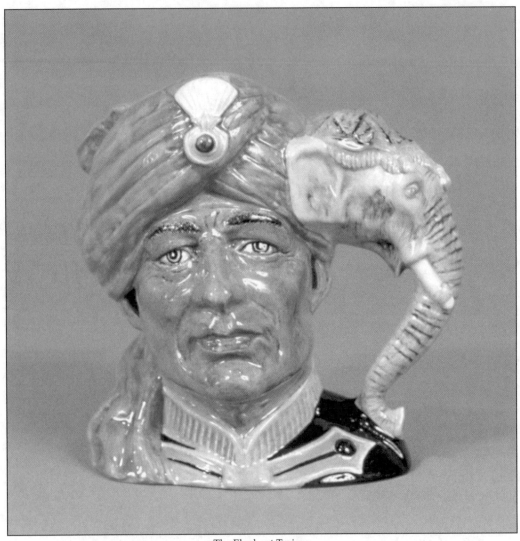

The Elephant Trainer

ABRAHAM LINCOLN

First in a series of Presidents of the United States of America, issued in a limited edition of 2,500. The American flag and Lincoln's famous speech that begins "Four score and seven years ago..." form the handle.

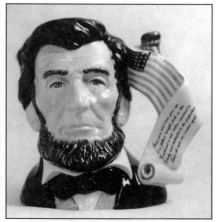

Abraham Lincoln

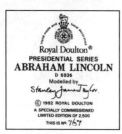

Designer: Stanley J. Taylor

Statistics:	Doulton Number	Size	Height	Issued
	D6936	Large	6 ¾", 17.2 cm	See below

Issued: 1992 in a limited edition of 2,500
Handle: U.S. flag and Gettysburg Address
Colourway: Black and white
Backstamp: Doulton
Series: Presidents of the United States

Size	Current Market Value		
	U.K. £	U.S. $	Can. $
Large	250.00	325.00	400.00

THE AIRMAN
(Royal Air Force)

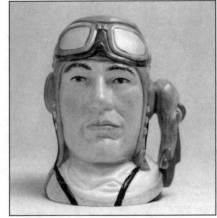

STYLE ONE: HANDLE — GERMAN PLANE

This series pays tribute to those servicemen of the Royal Air Force, the Royal Army and the Royal Navy who fought in World War II. An airman belongs to the Royal Air Force, as either a pilot or another member of the crew.

Designer: William K. Harper

VARIATION No. 1:   White scarf without cypher

	Doulton			
Statistics:	**Number**	**Size**	**Height**	**Issued**
	D6870	Small	4 ½", 11.9 cm	1991-1996

The Airman, Style One, Variation No. 1

Handle: German fighter plane shot down in flames
Colourway: Light brown cap; dark brown flight jacket with cream collar; white scarf
Backstamp: Doulton
Series: Armed Forces

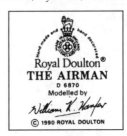

		Current Market Value		
Size	**Variation**	**U.K. £**	**U.S. $**	**Can. $**
Small	Var. 1	45.00	85.00	135.00

(Royal Canadian Air Force)

The Royal Canadian Air Force variation was commissioned by The British Toby of Ontario, Canada, in a limited edition of 250 pieces. It sold originally as part of a set of three at Can. $465.00.

VARIATION No. 2:   Red scarf with cypher "RCAF"

	Doulton			
Statistics:	**Number**	**Size**	**Height**	**Issued**
	D6903	Small	4 ½", 11.9 cm	See below

Issued: 1991 in a limited edition of 250
Handle: German fighter plane shot down in flames
Colourway: Dark brown cap; flight jacket with beige collar; red scarf with cypher
Backstamp: Doulton
Series: The Canadians

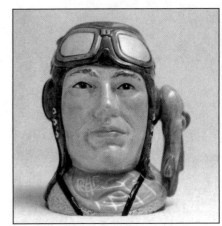

The Airman, Style One, Variation No. 2

		Current Market Value		
Size	**Variation**	**U.K. £**	**U.S. $**	**Can. $**
Small	Var. 2	175.00	300.00	350.00

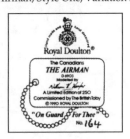

THE AIRMAN

Commissioned by Lawleys By Post, one could have a National Service Number incorporated within the accompanying certificate.

STYLE TWO: HANDLE — OXYGEN MASK

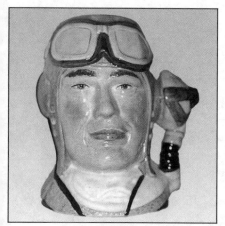

The Airman, Style Two

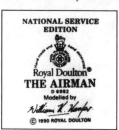

Designer: William K. Harper

	Doulton			
Statistics:	**Number**	**Size**	**Height**	**Issued**
	D6982	Small	4 ½", 11.9 cm	See below

Issued: 1994 in a special edition
Handle: An oxygen mask
Colourway: Cream, brown and grey
Backstamp: Doulton
Series: National Service Edition

	Current Market Value		
Size	**U.K. £**	**U.S. $**	**Can. $**
Small	85.00	165.00	225.00

ALADDIN'S GENIE

Issued in a limited edition of 1,500, this was the first jug to be decorated in flambé.

Designer: David B. Biggs

	Doulton			
Statistics:	**Number**	**Size**	**Height**	**Issued**
	D6971	Large	7 ½", 19.1 cm	See below

Issued: 1994 in a limited edition of 1,500
Handle: Lamp, ghost form and tassel
Colourway: Flambé
Backstamp: Doulton
Series: Flambé

	Current Market Value		
Size	U.K. £	U.S. $	Can. $
Large	300.00	600.00	700.00

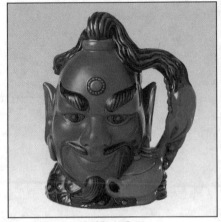

Aladdin's Genie

ALBERT EINSTEIN

Designer: Stanley J. Taylor

	Doulton			
Statistics:	**Number**	**Size**	**Height**	**Issued**
	D7023	Large	7", 17.8 cm	1995-1997

Handle: Molecule, theory of relativity, scroll $E=mc^2$
Colourway: White, blue and red
Backstamp: Doulton/Albert Einstein
Licensed by The Roger Richman
Agency, Inc. Beverley Hills. CA

	Current Market Value		
Size	U.K. £	U.S. $	Can. $
Large	115.00	200.00	225.00

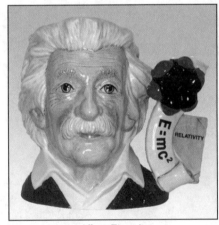

Albert Einstein

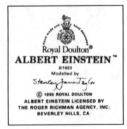

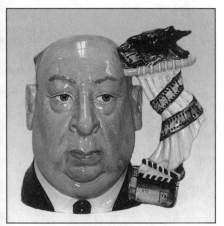

Alfred Hitchcock

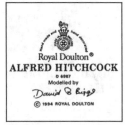

Backstamp A - Doulton

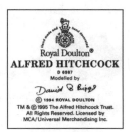

Backstamp B -
Doulton/MCA
Universal Copyright

ALFRED HITCHCOCK

This jug commemorates the achievements of Alfred Hitchcock (1899-1990) in producing superb movie thrillers. The handle features the shower curtain from *Psycho* and a bird from *The Birds*.

The original design of this jug had the shower curtain painted pink and the backstamp was the usual Royal Doulton design. This was later changed to a white shower curtain with blue shading and a backstamp that incorporated the MCA Universal Copyright.

Designer: David B. Biggs
Handle: Shower curtain, bird and film

Statistics:	**Doulton Number**	**Size**	**Height**	**Issued**
	D6987	Large	7 ½", 19.1 cm	1995

VARIATION No. 1: **Colourway** — White shower curtain with pink shading

Issued: 1995
Colourway: White shower curtain with pink shading
Backstamp: **A.** Doulton
B. Doulton/MCA Universal Copyright

Jug No.	Size	Current Market Value U.K. £	U.S. $	Can. $
A.	Large	1,250.00	1,750.00	2,250.00
B.	Large	1,250.00	1,850.00	2,250.00

VARIATION No. 2: **Colourway** — White shower curtain with blue shading

Issued: 1995-1995
Colourway: White shower curtain with blue shading
Backstamp: Doulton/MCA Universal Copyright

Jug No.	Size	Current Market Value U.K. £	U.S. $	Can. $
B.	Large	125.00	200.00	225.00

THE ANGEL

This jug was issued in the U.S.A. only, but made available to all members of the Royal Doulton International Collectors Club. This is the last jug in the Christmas Miniature Series of Santa, Mrs. Claus, The Elf, Snowman and Caroler.

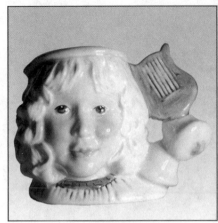

The Angel

Designer: Martyn C. R. Alcock

Statistics:

Doulton Number	Size	Height	Issued
D7051	Miniature	2 ¾", 7.0 cm	1996-1997

Handle: Harp and bells
Colourway: White, light brown and yellow
Backstamp: Doulton
Series: Christmas Miniatures

Size	Current Market Value		
	U.K. £	U.S. $	Can. $
Miniature	40.00	65.00	100.00

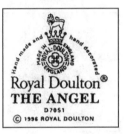

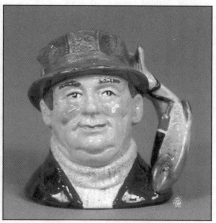

The Angler, Style One

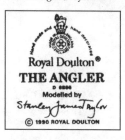

THE ANGLER

STYLE ONE: HANDLE — FISH AND LURE

Designer: Stanley J. Taylor

Statistics:	**Doulton Number**	**Size**	**Height**	**Issued**
	D6866	Small	4", 10.1 cm	1990-1995

Handle: A fish and lure
Colourway: Green jacket; brown hat; cream pullover
Backstamp: Doulton
Series: Characters From Life

	Current Market Value		
Size	**U.K. £**	**U.S. $**	**Can. $**
Small	45.00	85.00	110.00

STYLE TWO: HANDLE — FISHING NET AND REEL

Designer: David B. Biggs

Statistics:	**Doulton Number**	**Size**	**Height**	**Issued**
	D7065	Small	4 ¾", 12.1 cm	1997 to the present

Handle: Fishing net and reel
Colourway: Green jacket; yellow pullover; tan hat
Backstamp: Doulton

	Current Market Value		
Size	**U.K. £**	**U.S. $**	**Can. $**
Small	55.00	145.00	285.00

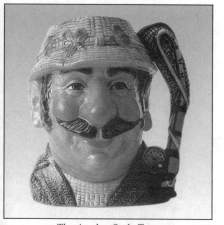

The Angler, Style Two

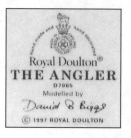

ANNE BOLEYN

Anne Boleyn (1502-1536) became the second wife of Henry VIII in a secret ceremony performed in January 1533. Their marriage was officially sanctioned in May by the Archbishop of Canterbury, Thomas Cranmer, and she was crowned Queen on June 1, 1533, in Westminster Hall. Unable to produce the son Henry VIII desired, Anne was imprisoned in the Tower of London on false grounds of adultery. She was beheaded with a sword on May 19, 1536, in a courtyard of the Tower of London (the modeller's use of an axe to form the handle was incorrect). Anne Boleyn was the mother of Queen Elizabeth I, born on September 7, 1533.

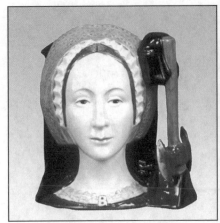

Anne Boleyn, Style One

STYLE ONE: HANDLE IN FORM OF AN AXE

Designer: Douglas V. Tootle

Statistics:	Doulton Number	Size	Height	Issued
1.	D6644	Large	7 ¼", 18.4 cm	1975-1990
2.	D6650	Small	3 ½", 8.9 cm	1980-1990
3.	D6651	Miniature	2 ½", 6.4 cm	1980-1990

Handle: An axe and chopping block
Colourway: Black and grey
Backstamp: Doulton
Series: Henry VIII and His Six Wives

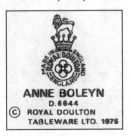

ANNE BOLEYN
D.6644
© ROYAL DOULTON
TABLEWARE LTD. 1975

Jug No.	Size	Current Market Value U.K. £	U.S. $	Can. $
1.	Large	100.00	150.00	175.00
2.	Small	65.00	95.00	125.00
3.	Miniature	65.00	85.00	100.00

Note: For Anne Boleyn, Style Two, see "The Six Wives of Henry VIII," page 364.

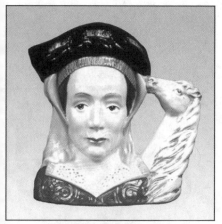

Anne of Cleves, Style One, Variation No. 2

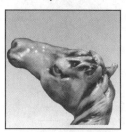

Variation No. 1, Horse's
ears pointing up

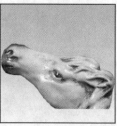

Variation No. 2, Horse's
ears flat against head

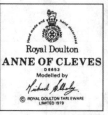

Backstamp D6653,
Large size jug

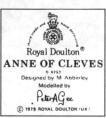

Backstamp D6753,
Small size jug

ANNE OF CLEVES

In a political arrangement by Thomas Cromwell, Anne of Cleves (1515-1557) was chosen to marry Henry VIII. Upon seeing his dull and unattractive betrothed, whom he later referred to as his "Flanders Mare," Henry attempted unsuccessfully to break the contract. Anne became his fourth wife on January 6, 1540, for only a brief time. Henry had the marriage annulled on July 8th of that year and gave Anne a pension for life.

STYLE ONE: HANDLE IN THE SHAPE OF A HORSE'S HEAD

VARIATION No. 1: **Handle** — Horse's ears pointing up

Designer: Michael Abberley

Statistics:	**Doulton** **Number**	**Size**	**Height**	**Issued**
	D6653	Large	7 ¼", 18.4 cm	1980-1981

Handle: Head of a horse; ears pointing up
Colourway: Black and red
Backstamp: Doulton
Series: Henry VIII and His Six Wives

			Current Market Value		
Size	**Variation**		**U.K. £**	**U.S. $**	**Can. $**
Large	Var. 1		185.00	275.00	325.00

VARIATION No. 2: **Handle** — Horse's ears flat against head. Because the upright ears tended to break off during packaging and shipping, the design was changed so the ears lay flat against the head.

Designer: Large size: Michael Abberley
Small and miniature size: Peter Gee

Statistics:	**Doulton** **Number**	**Size**	**Height**	**Issued**
1.	D6653	Large	7 ¼", 18.4 cm	1980-1990
2.	D6753	Small	4 ¼", 10.8 cm	1987-1990
3.	D6754	Miniature	2 ½", 6.4 cm	1987-1990

Handle: Head of a horse; ears flat
Colourway: Black and red
Backstamp: Doulton
Series: Henry VIII and His Six Wives

Jug			Current Market Value		
No.	Size	Variation	U.K. £	U.S. $	Can. $
1.	Large	Var. 2	100.00	150.00	200.00
2.	Small		100.00	150.00	150.00
3.	Miniature		100.00	150.00	150.00

Note: For Anne of Cleves, Style Two, see "The Six Wives of Henry VIII," page 364.

ANNIE OAKLEY

Phoebe Anne Moses (1860-1926) learned to shoot at the age of eight and helped support her family by killing game for a hotel in Cincinnati, Ohio. At 15, she defeated professional marksman Frank Butler in a shooting contest. She married him in 1876 and became a regular performer in shooting exhibitions, using the stage name Annie Oakley. She was a star of Buffalo Bill's Wild West Show from 1885 until 1901, when she was injured in a train accident and forced to retire. During World War I she trained American soldiers in marksmanship.

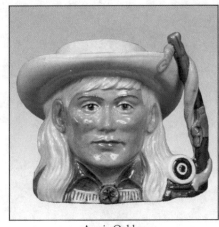

Annie Oakley

Designer: Stanley J. Taylor

Statistics:	Doulton Number	Size	Height	Issued
	D6732	Mid	5 ¼", 13.3 cm	1985-1989

Handle: Rifle and belt
Colourway: Yellow hair; cream hat; brown tunic
Backstamp: Doulton
Series: The Wild West Collection

Size	Current Market Value		
	U.K.£	U.S. $	Can. $
Mid	75.00	125.00	150.00

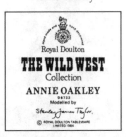

THE ANTIQUE DEALER

This jug was commissioned by Kevin Francis Ceramics Ltd. in 1988 in a special edition of 5,000 pieces. It is interesting to note that Kevin Francis jugs have the handle on the left side.

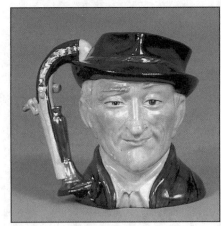

The Antique Dealer

Designer: Geoff Blower

Statistics:	Doulton Number	Size	Height	Issued
	D6807	Large	7 ¼", 18.4 cm	See below

Issued: 1988 in a special edition of 5,000
Handle: Flintlock handgun and candlestick
Colourway: Black hat; blue coat
Backstamp: Doulton/Kevin Frances Ceramics
Series: The Collecting World

Size	Current Market Value		
	U.K.£	U.S. $	Can. $
Large	100.00	200.00	225.00

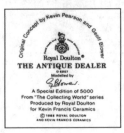

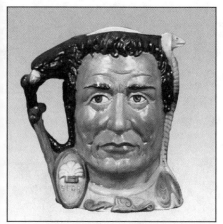

Antony, Prototype

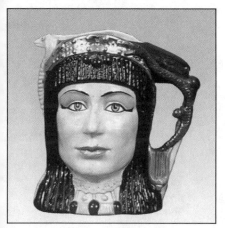

Cleopatra, Prototype

ANTONY AND CLEOPATRA

PROTOTYPE

A prototype of this character jug exists where Antony has a pudgy face, wide eyes and brown hair, and Cleopatra has lighter eye make-up, lighter beads around her neck and a dark red headdress. Only one is known to exist.

Designer: Michael Abberley

Statistics:	**Doulton Number**	**Size**	**Height**	**Issued**
	D6728	Large	7 ¼", 18.4 cm	See below

Modelled: 1984
Issued: Not put into production
Handle: Eagle's head, dagger and shield; asp and harp
Colourway: Black, grey, brown
Backstamp: Doulton

		Current Market Value		
Size	**Description**	**U.K. £**	**U.S. $**	**Can. $**
Large	Prototype		Unique	

ANTONY AND CLEOPATRA

REGULAR ISSUE

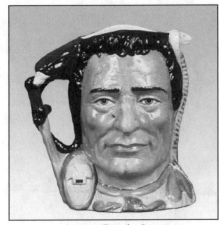

Antony, Regular Issue

Marcus Antonius (83-30 B.C.) was a skilled soldier and co-ruler of Rome with Caesar's nephew Octavian from 43 to 32 B.C.

Cleopatra (68-30 B.C.), well known for her charm and beauty, was Queen of Egypt and an ally and lover of Julius Caesar. In 41 B.C. Antony and Cleopatra met and fell in love, marrying in 37 B.C. Antony gave Cleopatra and their children a share of his Roman provinces in 34 B.C., a move which enraged Octavian, who waged war on the couple, pursuing them in their defeat to Alexandria.

Antony, hearing a false rumour of Cleopatra's death, stabbed himself in grief. He was carried to her and died in her arms. In turn, Cleopatra committed suicide by placing an asp on her chest, apparently from fear of Octavian.

The jugs were issued in 1985 in a limited edition of 9,500 pieces.

Designer: Michael Abberley

Statistics:

	Doulton Number	Size	Height	Issued
	D6728	Large	7 ¼", 18.4 cm	See below

Issued: 1985 in a limited edition of 9,500
Handle: Eagle's head, dagger and shield; asp and harp
Colourway: Black, grey, brown
Backstamp: Doulton
Series: The Star-Crossed Lovers Collection (Two-faced jug)

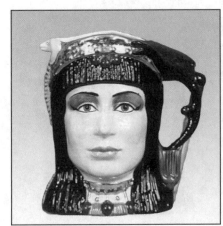

Cleopatra, Regular Issue

Size	Description	Current Market Value		
		U.K. £	U.S. $	Can. $
Large	Regular Issue	75.00	100.00	125.00

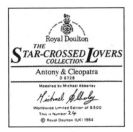

APOTHECARY

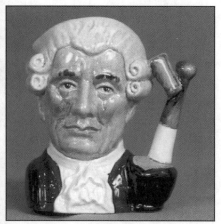

Apothecary

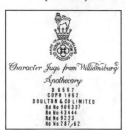

Along with the other characters in the Williamsburg Series, the apothecary was central to colonial life in 18th century America.

Designer: Max Henk

	Doulton			
Statistics:	**Number**	**Size**	**Height**	**Issued**
1.	D6567	Large	7", 17.8 cm	1963-1983
2.	D6574	Small	4", 10.1 cm	1963-1983
3.	D6581	Miniature	2 ½", 6.4 cm	1963-1983

Handle: Mortar and pestle
Colourway: Green coat with white cravat; white wig
Backstamp: Doulton
Series: Characters From Williamsburg

Jug				**Current Market Value**		
No.	Size	Comp.	Issued	U.K. £	U.S. $	Can. $
1.	Large	EW	1963-1983	100.00	150.00	175.00
		ETC	1968-1971	150.00	250.00	300.00
2.	Small	EW	1963-1983	60.00	85.00	125.00
		ETC	1968-1971	75.00	125.00	175.00
3.	Miniature	EW	1963-1983	60.00	85.00	110.00
		ETC	1968-1971	75.00	125.00	150.00

ARAMIS

One of the three musketeers, Aramis joined Athos, Porthos and D'Artagnan in a life of adventure in Alexandre Dumas's 19th century novel, following their code "All for one, and one for all."

The wording "One of the Three Musketeers" was included in the earlier backstamp to indicate that Aramis was one of the famous Musketeers.

Designer: Max Henk
Handle: Handle of a sword

VARIATION No. 1: Colourway — Black hat; white feather; brown tunic

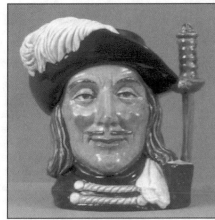

Aramis, Variation No. 1

Statistics:	**Doulton Number**	**Size**	**Height**	**Issued**
1.	D6441	Large	7 ¼", 18.4 cm	1956-1991
2.	D6454	Small	3 ½", 8.9 cm	1956-1991
3.	D6508	Miniature	2 ½", 6.4 cm	1960-1991

Colourway: Black hat; white feather; brown tunic
Backstamps: A. Doulton
B. Doulton/One of the "Three Musketeers"
Series: The Three Musketeers / Characters From Literature

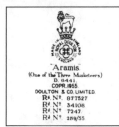

Backstamp B -
Doulton/"One of"

Jug No.	Size	Comp.	Issued	Current Market Value		
				U.K. £	**U.S. $**	**Can. $**
1.	Large	EW	1956-1991	65.00	90.00	110.00
		ETC	1968-1971	75.00	125.00	175.00
2.	Small	EW	1956-1991	55.00	75.00	100.00
		ETC	1968-1971	65.00	110.00	150.00
3.	Miniature	EW	1960-1991	45.00	65.00	90.00
		ETC	1968-1971	55.00	90.00	125.00

VARIATION No. 2: Colourway — Yellow hat; maroon tunic

This jug was commissioned by Peter Jones China Ltd., England, and issued in 1988 in a limited edition of 1,000.

Statistics:	**Doulton Number**	**Size**	**Height**	**Issued**
	D6829	Large	7 ¼", 18.4 cm	See below

Issued: 1988 in a limited edition of 1,000
Colourway: Yellow hat; maroon tunic
Backstamp: Doulton

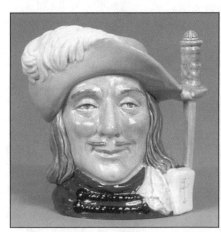

Aramis, Variation No. 2

Size	Variation	Current Market Value		
		U.K. £	**U.S. $**	**Can. $**
Large	Var. 2	125.00	200.00	225.00

Note: Price differentials between backstamps are no longer significant.

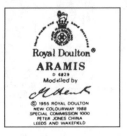

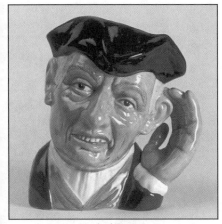

'Ard of 'Earing

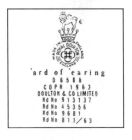

'ARD OF 'EARING

With hand held to cup his ear, this cockney gentleman is a comic representation of a deaf man. After being discontinued in 1967, this jug has increased in value and is difficult to find.

Designer: David B. Biggs

Statistics:	Doulton Number	Size	Height	Issued
1.	D6588	Large	7 ½", 19.1 cm	1964-1967
2.	D6591	Small	3 ½", 8.9 cm	1964-1967
3.	D6594	Miniature	2 ½", 6.4 cm	1964-1967

Handle: A hand held to the ear
Colourway: Dark purple tricorn; green, white and yellow clothing
Backstamp: Doulton

Jug No.	Size	Current Market Value U.K. £	U.S. $	Can. $
1.	Large	1,300.00	2,000.00	2,400.00
2.	Small	800.00	1,150.00	1,500.00
3.	Miniature	950.00	1,400.00	1,800.00

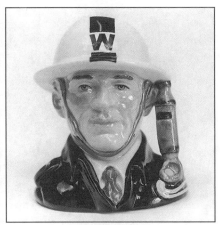

A.R.P. Warden

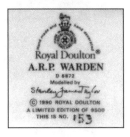

A.R.P. WARDEN

The A.R.P. (Air Raids Precautions) Wardens were charged with the responsibility of insuring that people were as secure as possible during an air raid. Armed only with his whistle, he would patrol the streets enforcing the "lights out please" signal and see that all citizens took cover as quickly as possible. The Heroes of the Blitz jugs were commissioned by Lawleys By Post in a limited edition of 9,500 sets.

Designer: Stanley J. Taylor

Statistics:	Doulton Number	Size	Height	Issued
	D6872	Small	4", 10.1 cm	See below

Issued: 1991 in a limited edition of 9,500
Handle: Grey whistle
Colourway: Dark blue jacket; white helmet with black stripe and the initial W (Warden)
Backstamp: Doulton
Series: Heroes of the Blitz

Size	Current Market Value U.K. £	U.S. $	Can. $
Small	115.00	190.00	275.00

'ARRIET

'Arriet is a coster or costermonger, a cockney woman who sold fruits and vegetables from a barrow in the streets of London. She is a variation of the Pearly Girl character jug (see page 304).

Designer: Harry Fenton

Statistics:	Doulton Number	Size	Height	Issued
1.	D6208	Large	6 ½", 16.5 cm	1947-1960
2.	D6236	Small	3 ¼", 8.3 cm	1947-1960
3.	D6250	Miniature	2 ¼", 5.7 cm	1947-1960
4.	D6256	Tiny	1 ¼", 3.1 cm	1947-1960

Handle: Hat feather
Colourway: Green hat; brown coat; yellow scarf
Backstamp: Doulton

Jug No.	Size	Current Market Value		
		U.K. £	U.S. $	Can. $
1.	Large	135.00	195.00	235.00
2.	Small	70.00	100.00	125.00
3.	Miniature	60.00	85.00	100.00
4.	Tiny	125.00	200.00	250.00

Note: For the Pearly Girl see page 304.

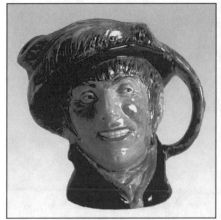

"Arriet

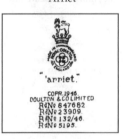

'ARRY

'Arriet's husband 'Arry is also a costermonger, plying his trade in London. He is a variation of the Pearly Boy (see page 302) character jug. The original design featured the word "Blimey" across the back, but it was never produced.

Designer: Harry Fenton

Statistics:	Doulton Number	Size	Height	Issued
1.	D6207	Large	6 ½", 16.5 cm	1947-1960
2.	D6235	Small	3 ½", 8.9 cm	1947-1960
3.	D6249	Miniature	2 ½", 6.4 cm	1947-1960
4.	D6255	Tiny	1 ½", 3.8 cm	1947-1960

Handle: Plain
Colourway: Brown hat and coat; red and yellow scarf
Backstamp: Doulton

Jug No.	Size	Current Market Value		
		U.K. £	U.S. $	Can. $
1.	Large	135.00	195.00	235.00
2.	Small	70.00	100.00	125.00
3.	Miniature	60.00	85.00	100.00
4.	Tiny	125.00	200.00	250.00

Note: For the Pearly Boy see page 302.

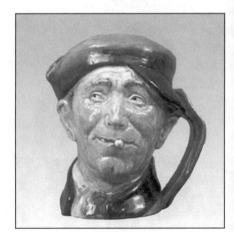

"Arry

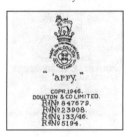

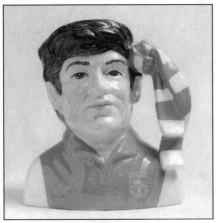

Arsenal (Football Club)

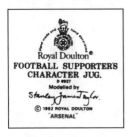

ARSENAL (FOOTBALL CLUB)

Designer: Stanley J. Taylor

Statistics:	**Doulton Number**	**Size**	**Height**	**Issued**
	D6927	Small	5", 12.7 cm	1992-1999

Handle: Team coloured scarf
Colourway: Red and white uniform
Backstamp: Doulton
Series: The Football Supporters

	Current Market Value		
Size	**U.K. £**	**U.S. $**	**Can. $**
Small	60.00	125.00	150.00

ARTFUL DODGER

For the character jug Artful Dodger, see the "Charles Dickens Commemorative Set" page 143.

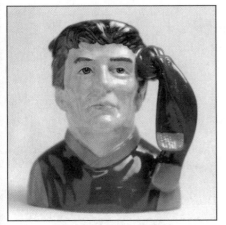

Aston Villa (Football Club)

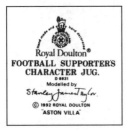

ASTON VILLA (FOOTBALL CLUB)

Designer: Stanley J. Taylor

Statistics:	**Doulton Number**	**Size**	**Height**	**Issued**
	D6931	Small	5", 12.7 cm	1992-1999

Handle: Team coloured scarf
Colourway: Maroon and blue uniform
Backstamp: Doulton
Series: The Football Supporters

	Current Market Value		
Size	**U.K. £**	**U.S. $**	**Can. $**
Small	60.00	125.00	150.00

ATHOS

Under the banner of "All for one and one for all," Athos was one of the original musketeers in the 19th-century novel by Alexandre Dumas. First issued as one of four in the Three Musketeers Series, Athos is now incorporated into the larger series, Characters from Literature.

Designer: Max Henk
Handle: Upper half of a sword

VARIATION No. 1: **Mould** — Feathers along rim of hat
Colourway — Black hat; white feather; green tunic with gold trim

	Doulton Number	Size	Height	Issued
Statistics:				
1.	D6439	Large	7 ¼", 18.4 cm	1956-1991
2.	D6452	Small	3 ¾", 9.5 cm	1956-1991
3.	D6509	Miniature	2 ½", 6.4 cm	1960-1991

Colourway: Black hat; white feather; green tunic with gold trim
Backstamps: A. Doulton
B. Doulton /One of the "Three Musketeers"
The wording "One of the Three Musketeers" was included in the early backstamp to indicate that Athos was one of the famous Musketeers.
Series: The Three Musketeers / Characters from Literature

Jug No.	Size	Comp.	Issued	Current Market Value		
				U.K. £	U.S. $	Can. $
1.	Large	EW	1956-1991	65.00	85.00	90.00
		ETC	1968-1971	75.00	100.00	125.00
2.	Small	EW	1956-1991	40.00	60.00	65.00
		ETC	1968-1971	50.00	75.00	100.00
3.	Miniature	EW	1960-1991	30.00	45.00	50.00
		ETC	1968-1971	40.00	60.00	65.00

Note: Price differentials between backstamps are no longer significant.

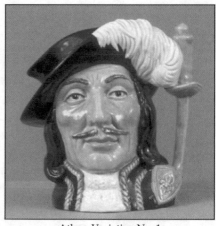

Athos, Variation No. 1

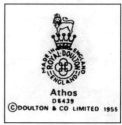

Backstamp A - Doulton

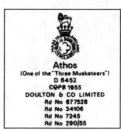

Backstamp B -
Doulton/"One of"

ATHOS (cont.)

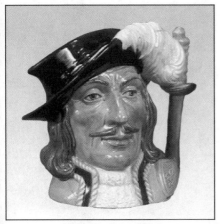

Athos, Variation No. 2

There were two different moulds used in the production of the Peter Jones Colourway, variation 2 and variation 3. A total of 1,000 jugs were issued, but how many of each variation were produced is unknown.

	Doulton			
Statistics:	Number	Size	Height	Issued
	D6827	Large	7 ¼", 18.4 cm	See below

Issued:	Variation No. 2 — 1988 in a limited edition of 1,000
	Variation No. 3 — 1988 (included in above)
Handle:	Upper half of a sword
Colourway:	Black hat; white feather; yellow tunic with blue trim
Backstamp:	Doulton/Peter Jones China Ltd.
	Commissioned by Peter Jones China Ltd.,
	England. Issued in 1988 in a limited
	edition of 1,000.

VARIATION No. 2: **Mould** — Feather along rim of hat

VARIATION No. 3: **Mould** — Feathers above rim of hat

		Current Market Value		
Size	Variation	U.K. £	U.S. $	Can. $
Large	Var. 2	125.00	200.00	225.00
Large	Var. 3	125.00	200.00	225.00

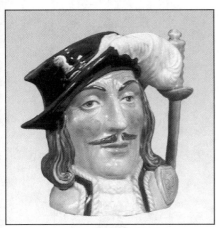

Athos, Variation No. 3

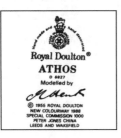

THE AUCTIONEER

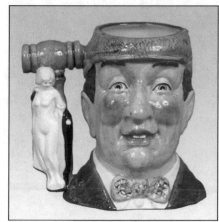

The Auctioneer

Commissioned by Kevin Francis Ceramics Ltd., The Auctioneer jug was issued in 1988 in a limited edition of 5,000. Characteristic of Kevin Francis, this is a left-handed jug.

Designer: Geoff Blower

Statistics:	Doulton Number	Size	Height	Issued
	D6838	Large	6 ¼", 15.9 cm	See below

Issued: 1988 in a special edition of 5,000
Handle: Auctioneer's gavel and The Bather (HN687)
Colourway: Green coat and bow tie; light brown cap
Backstamp: Doulton/Kevin Frances Ceramics
Series: The Collecting World

Size	Current Market Value		
	U.K. £	U.S. $	Can. $
Large	125.00	225.00	265.00

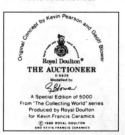

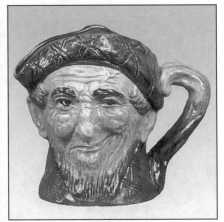

Auld Mac

AULD MAC

A song by Sir Harry Lauder, a 20th-century singer and comedian, called "Bang Went Saxpence," inspired this piece. In it a Scotsman named Mac found the prices too high in London because every time he made a move, "bang went saxpence," which is incised on the back of his tam, below "Auld Mac."

Designer:	Harry Fenton			

	Doulton			
Statistics:	**Number**	**Size**	**Height**	**Issued**
1.	D5823	Large	6 ¼", 15.9 cm	1937-1986
2.	D5824	Small	3 ¼", 8.3 cm	1937-1985
3.	D6253	Miniature	2 ¼", 5.7 cm	1946-1985
4.	D6257	Tiny	1 ¼", 3.1 cm	1946-1960

Handle: A brier
Colourway: Green tam; brown coat

Backstamp:
A. Doulton/"Owd Mac": "Owd Mac" was incised in the tam and printed in the backstamp, c.1937.
B. Doulton/Auld Mac: "Auld Mac" was incised in the tam in 1938, but "Owd Mac" continued in the backstamp until c.1940.
C. Doulton/Auld Mac: "Auld Mac" was incised in the tam and printed in the backstamp

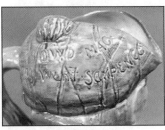

"OWD MAC"

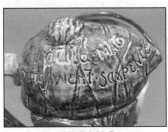

AULD MAC

Jug.				**Current Market Value**		
No.	**Size**	**Comp.**	**Issued**	**U.K. £**	**U.S. $**	**Can. $**
1A.	Large	EW	1937-c.1937	350.00	525.00	675.00
1B.		EW	1938-1940	150.00	325.00	450.00
1C.		EW	1940-1986	65.00	90.00	100.00
1C.		ETC	1968-1971	80.00	125.00	150.00
2A.	Small	EW	1937-1937	250.00	400.00	500.00
2B.		EW	1938-1940	100.00	150.00	175.00
2C.		EW	1940-1985	30.00	50.00	70.00
2C.		ETC	1968-1971	55.00	85.00	100.00
3.	Miniature	EW	1946-1985	30.00	50.00	70.00
3.		ETC	1968-1971	55.00	85.00	100.00
4.	Tiny	EW	1946-1960	100.00	175.00	225.00

Note: Jugs 1A and 2A are also found in white gloss.

Auld Mac Derivatives

Item:	MUSICAL JUG		**Item:**	ASH BOWL
Height:	6 ¼", 15.9 cm		**Height:**	3", 7.6 cm
Issued:	1938-c.1939		**Issued:**	1938-1960

Doulton		**Current Market Value**		
Number	**Item**	**U.K. £**	**U.S. $**	**Can. $**
D5889	Musical Jug	600.00	1,000.00	1,250.00
D6006	Ash Bowl	100.00	150.00	175.00

Note: The musical jug plays the tune "The Campbells are Coming."

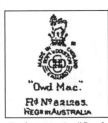

"Owd Mac".
Rd Nº 821285.
REGᵈ ᴵⁿ AUSTRALIA

Backstamp A - "Owd Mac"

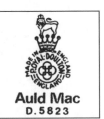

Auld Mac
D.5823

Backstamp B - "Auld Mac"

AUXILIARY FIREMAN

Large numbers of volunteer firemen were needed to assist the regular firemen during the World War II bombing of London and other cities of Great Britain. It was through the courage of the Auxiliary Fire Service (A.F.S.) that many of the fires of the air raids were held in check. The Heroes of the Blitz set of jugs was commissioned by Lawleys By Post in a limited edition of 9,500 sets.

Designer: Stanley J. Taylor

Statistics:

Doulton Number	Size	Height	Issued
D6887	Small	4", 10.1 cm	See below

Issued: 1991 in a limited edition of 9,500
Handle: Hose and nozzle
Colourway: Black jacket; grey helmet with white initials "A.F.S."
Backstamp: Doulton
Series: Heroes of the Blitz

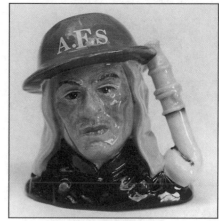

Auxiliary Fireman

Size	Current Market Value		
	U.K. £	U.S. $	Can. $
Small	100.00	175.00	250.00

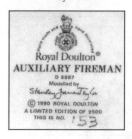

BACCHUS

In Greek and Roman mythology, Bacchus was the god of wine and nature, inspiring men and women to appreciate music and poetry. "Bacchanalia," the harvest celebrations to honour him, were reputed to be such orgies of excess that the Roman government had them banned.

Some of the earlier versions of the miniature jug had the leaves on the vine handle painted green. There is no current premium value for this variety.

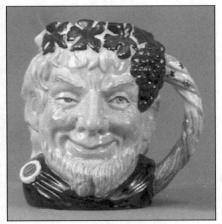

Bacchus

Designer: Max Henk

Statistics:	Doulton Number	Size	Height	Issued
1.	D6499	Large	7", 17.8 cm	1959-1991
2.	D6505	Small	4", 10.1 cm	1959-1991
3.	D6521	Miniature	2 ½", 6.4 cm	1960-1991

Handle: Grapevine
Colourway: Maroon robes; green leaves and purple grapes adorn the head
Backstamps: A. Doulton
B. Doulton/City of Stoke-on-Trent Jubilee Year 1959 - 1960 With the compliments of Lord Mayor and Lady Mayoress Alderman Harold Clowes, O.B.E., J.P. and Miss Christine Clowes

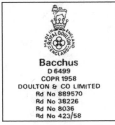

Bacchus
D 6499
COPR 1958
DOULTON & CO LIMITED
Rd No 889570
Rd No 38226
Rd No 8036
Rd No 423/58

Backstamp A - Doulton

CITY OF
STOKE-ON-TRENT
JUBILEE YEAR
1959-1960
WITH THE COMPLIMENTS OF
LOAD MAYOR AND LADY MAYORESS
ALDERMAN HAROLD CLOWES O.B.E. J.P.
AND
MISS CHRISTINE CLOWES

Backstamp B - City of Stoke-on-Trent

Jug No.	Size	Comp	Issued	Current Market Value U.K. £	U.S. $	Can. $
1A.	Large	EW	1959-1991	65.00	100.00	125.00
1A.		ETC	1968-1971	100.00	150.00	185.00
1B.		EW	1959-1960	4,500.00	7,500.00	9,000.00
2A.	Small	EW	1959-1991	40.00	55.00	65.00
2A		ETC	1968-1971	50.00	75.00	95.00
3A.	Miniature	EW	1960-1991	40.00	60.00	70.00
3A.		ETC	1968-1971	55.00	90.00	100.00

Bacchus Derivative

Item: TABLE LIGHTER
Height: 3 ½", 8.9 cm
Issued: 1964-1974

Doulton Number	Item	Current Market Value U.K. £	U.S. $	Can. $
D6505	Table Lighter	175.00	325.00	385.00

BAHAMAS POLICEMAN

This jug was commissioned by Island Galleria, Nassau, Bahamas, in a special edition of 1,000 jugs. The D number 6912 is also the numerical designation of The Snake Charmer.

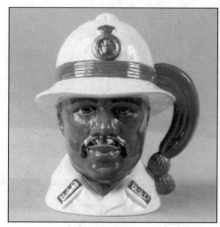

Bahamas Policeman

Designer: William K. Harper

Statistics:

Doulton Number	Size	Height	Issued
D6912	Large	7", 17.8 cm	See below

Issued: 1992 in a special edition of 1,000
Handle: Tassel
Colourway: White and red
Backstamp: Doulton/Island Galleria

Size	Current Market Value U.K. £	U.S. $	Can. $
Large	165.00	250.00	275.00

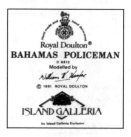

BASEBALL PLAYER

PROTOTYPE

Only two of these jugs are known to exist, and each is different. They are test pieces and were never put into production.

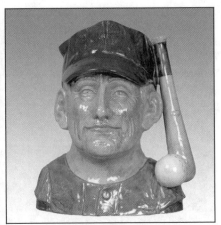

Baseball Player, Style One, Variation No. 1

Designer: David B. Biggs

Statistics:	Doulton Number	Size	Height	Issued
	D6624	Large	See below	See below

Modelled: 1970
Issued: Not put into production
Handle: Bat and ball
Colourway: See below
Backstamp: Doulton

VARIATION No. 1: Colourway — Blue-green jersey; red sleeves and cap

Height: 8 ¼", 21.0 cm

		Current Market Value		
Size	Variation	U.K. £	U.S. $	Can. $
Large	Var. 1			Extremely rare

Sold November 21, 1999
Phillips, New Bond Street
London, England, £16,000.00

VARIATION No. 2: Colourway — Striped blue and black jersey and cap

Height: 7", 17.8 cm

		Current Market Value		
Size	Variation	U.K. £	U.S. $	Can. $
Large	Var. 2			Extremely rare

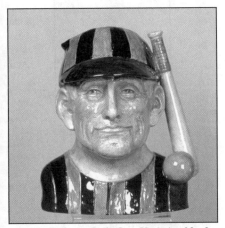

Baseball Player, Style One, Variation No. 2

Sold November 21, 1999
Phillips, New Bond Street
London, England, £10,000.00

THE BASEBALL PLAYER

REGULAR ISSUE

Designer: Stanley J. Taylor
Handle: Ball, bat and glove

Statistics:	Doulton Number	Size	Height	Issued
	D6878	Small	4 ¼", 10.8 cm	1991-1998

VARIATION No. 1: **General baseball player** — blue cap with lion and crown insignia

Issued: **A.** 1991-1998 For general issue, 1991.
B. 1991 in a special edition of 500
Colourway: Dark blue cap; white jersey with blue trim
Backstamps: **A.** Doulton
B. Doulton/Britannia Limited / Commissioned by Britannia Limited to celebrate the fifth anniversary of their Doulton Convention and Sale, January 1991. Issued in a special edition of 500 pieces.
Series: Characters From Life

Jug. No.	Size	Backstamp	Current Market Value		
			U.K. £	**U.S. $**	**Can. $**
1A.	Small	Doulton	50.00	100.00	135.00
1B.	Small	Doulton/Britannia	85.00	125.00	150.00

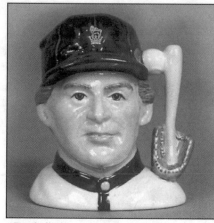

Baseball Player, Style Two, Variation No. 1

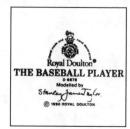

Backstamp A - Doulton

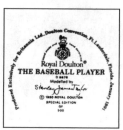

Backstamp B - Britannia Ltd.

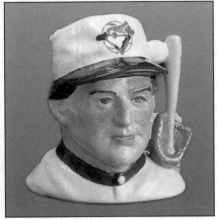

VARIATION No. 2: **Toronto Blue Jays** — blue cap with Toronto Blue Jays insignia

This character jug was issued to commemorate the Toronto Blue Jays, winner of the 1992 and 1993 World Series of baseball. It was produced in a limited edition of 2,500 worldwide.

	Doulton			
Statistics:	Number	Size	Height	Issued
	D6973	Small	4 ¼", 10.8 cm	See below

Issued: 1994 in a limited edition of 2,500
Colourway: Blue cap; white jersey with blue trim
Backstamp: Doulton/MLBPA/Blue Jays

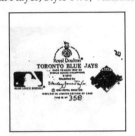

Baseball Player, Style Two, Variation No. 2

Size	Backstamp	Current Market Value		
		U.K. £	U.S. $	Can. $
Small	Doulton/MLBPA/BlueJays	75.00	125.00	175.00

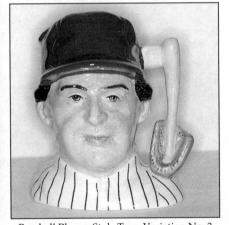

VARIATION No. 3: **Philadelphia** — red cap with Philadelphia Phillies insignia

Produced to celebrate the 125th anniversary of Strawbridge and Clothier in Philadelphia, this jug was available only through that retailer. It was issued in a limited edition of 2,500 pieces.

	Doulton			
Statistics:	Number	Size	Height	Issued
	D6957	Small	4 ¼", 10.8 cm	See below

Issued: 1993 in a limited edition of 2,500
Colourway: Red cap; white jersey with red stripes
Backstamp: Doulton "New Colourway 1993"

Size	Backstamp	Current Market Value		
		U.K. £	U.S. $	Can. $
Small	Doulton	100.00	150.00	225.00

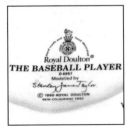

Baseball Player, Style Two, Variation No. 3

BEEFEATER (WITH KEYS)

PROTOTYPE

This jug was designed for a proposed commission by PWC Publishing. The head was from the standard Beefeater jug, originally modelled by Harry Fenton, and Harry Sales remodelled the keys from Simon the Cellarer to form the handle. Due to cost and quantity requirements, the project was not continued.

Variation 3 was not returned to Doulton and is now in a U.S. collection.

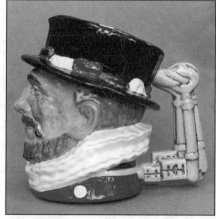

Beefeater (With Keys) side view

Designer: Head — Harry Fenton
Keys — Remodelled by Harry Sales

Statistics:	Doulton Number	Size	Height	Issued
	D —	Large	6 ½", 16.5 cm	See below

Modelled: 1984
Handle: See colourway variations above
Colourway: Scarlet tunic; white ruff; black hat
Backstamp: Doulton

VARIATION No. 1: **Colourway** — Grey keys; blue hat

VARIATION No. 2: **Colourway** — Yellow keys; blue hat; name highlighted in yellow

VARIATION No. 3: **Colourway** — Yellow keys; black hat with on-glaze red and blue band

Size	Variation	Current Market Value		
		U.K. £	U.S. $	Can. $
Large	Var. 1		Unique	
Large	Var. 2		Unique	
Large	Var. 3		Unique	

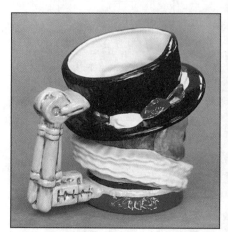

Beefeater (With Keys) back view

Note: Variation 3 sold November 21, 1999, at Phillips, New Bond Street, London, England, for £9,500.00.

BEEFEATER

REGULAR ISSUE

The Yeomen of the Guard and warders of the Tower of London are colloquially referred to as Beefeaters. The name "Beefeater" came from a visiting Grand Duke who was astonished by the large amounts of beef eaten by the Yeoman Guards. The monarch's cypher, GR, at the base of the handle is an abbreviation of George Rex, for King George VI. After his death in 1953, the cypher was changed to ER (Elizabeth Regina), for Queen Elizabeth II.

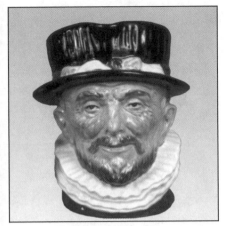

Beefeater, Regular Issue

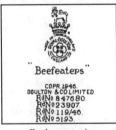

"Beefeaters"

COPR.1946.
DOULTON & CO LIMITED
RdNo 847680
RdNo23907.
RdNo 119/46.
RdNo 5193.

Backstamp A

Designer: Large, small and miniature — Harry Fenton
Tiny — Robert Tabbenor

Statistics:	Doulton Number	Size	Height	Issued
1.	D6206	Large	6 ½", 16.5 cm	See below
2.	D6233	Small	3 ¼", 8.3 cm	
3.	D6251	Miniature	2 ½", 6.4 cm	

Colourway: Black hat; white ruff; pink tunic
Backstamp: Doulton/"Beefeaters".
The pluralized name was used on all three sizes of jugs from 1947 through 1953

VARIATION No. 1: Colourway — Pink
Handle — Pink; "GR" cypher

Issued: 1947-1953
Handle: Pink with a "GR" cypher
Series: The London Collection

Jug No.	Size	Variation	Issued	Current Market Value		
				U.K. £	U.S. $	Can. $
1.	Large	Var. 1	1947-1953	80.00	175.00	225.00
2.	Small		1947-1953	55.00	100.00	125.00
3.	Miniature		1947-1953	55.00	100.00	125.00

VARIATION No. 2: Colourway — Pink with yellow highlights
Handle — Pink with yellow highlights; "GR" cypher

Issued: 1947-1947
Handle: Pink with yellow hightlights; "GR" cypher

Jug No.	Size	Variation	Issued	Current Market Value		
				U.K. £	U.S. $	Can. $
1.	Large	Var. 2	1947-1947	1,000.00	2,000.00	3,000.00
2.	Small		1947-1947	900.00	1,500.00	2,000.00
3.	Miniature		1947-1947		Rare	

Note: Large size "GR" jug is found in white gloss.

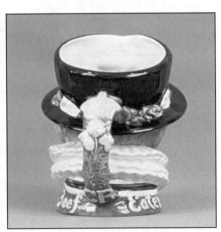

Var. 2 - Yellow highlights, "GR" cypher

REGULAR ISSUE (cont.)

VARIATION No. 3: **Colourway** — Pink
Handle — Pink; "ER" cypher

Statistics:	Doulton Number	Size	Height	Issued
1.	D6206	Large	6 ½", 16.5 cm	See below
2.	D6233	Small	3 ¼", 8.3 cm	
3.	D6251	Miniature	2 ½", 6.4 cm	

Issued: **A.** 1953-1953
B. 1953-1987
C. 1978-1978

Backstamps: **A.** Doulton/"Beefeaters"
The plural name was found only on early versions of the "ER" jugs.
B. Doulton/Beefeater
In late 1953 the backstamp was adjusted and the singular "Beefeater" name was incorporated.
C. Doulton/Beefeater
Fired in the last firing of a traditional Bottle Oven 1978 Longton Stoke-on-Trent, England

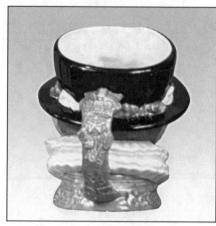

Var. 3 - Pink with an "ER" cypher

Jug No.	Size	Comp.	Issued	Current Market Value U.K. £	U.S. $	Can. $
1.	Large	EW	1953-1987	60.00	100.00	125.00
		ETC	1968-1971	150.00	225.00	250.00
1C.		EW	1978-1978		Rare	
2.	Small	EW	1953-1987	40.00	60.00	65.00
		ETC	1968-1971	60.00	85.00	95.00
3.	Miniature	EW	1953-1953	35.00	50.00	55.00
		ETC	1968-1971	50.00	75.00	85.00

Note: **1.** Some of the early George VI (GR cypher) jugs have yellow highlights on the handle. Jugs also exist with gilt highlights on the handle, however we do not have confirmation that the gilt was factory applied.
2. Price differentials in backstamps are no longer significant, except for the rare 1978 backstamp.

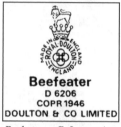

Beefeater
D 6206
COPR 1946
DOULTON & CO LIMITED

Backstamp B, Large size

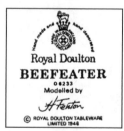

Royal Doulton
BEEFEATER
D 6233
Modelled by
H Fenton
© ROYAL DOULTON TABLEWARE LIMITED 1948

Backstamp B, Small size

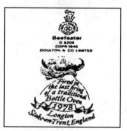

Backstamp C

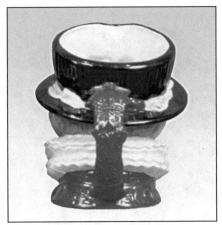

Var. 4, Scarlett with an "ER" cypher

REGULAR ISSUE *(cont.)*

VARIATION No. 4:   Colourway — Scarlet
Handle — Scarlett; "ER" cypher

Statistics:	Doulton Number	Size	Height	Issued
1.	D6206	Large	6 ½", 16.5 cm	1987-1996
2.	D6233	Small	3 ¼", 8.3 cm	1987-1996
3.	D6251	Miniature	2 ½", 6.4 cm	1987-1991
4.	D6806	Tiny	1 ½", 3.8 cm	1988-1988

Handle: Scarlet with an "ER" cypher
Colourway: Black hat; white ruff; scarlet tunic
Backstamps: **A.** Doulton/"Beefeater"
B. Doulton/Royal Doulton International Collectors Club
In 1988 Robert Tabbenor miniaturized Fenton's design of 1947 and created a tiny Beefeater, which was offered for sale to the members of the RDICC.

Jug No.	Size	Variation	Current Market Value U.K. £	U.S. $	Can. $
1A.	Large	Var. 4	50.00	85.00	100.00
2A.	Small		35.00	50.00	70.00
3A.	Miniature		35.00	50.00	70.00
4B.	Tiny		85.00	150.00	175.00

Beefeater Derivative

Item: TABLE LIGHTER
Height: 3 ½", 8.9 cm
Issued: 1958-1973

Doulton Number	Item	Current Market Value U.K. £	U.S. $	Can. $
D6233	Table Lighter	125.00	225.00	275.00

BEHTHOVEN

Designer:	Stanley J. Taylor			

	Doulton			
Statistics:	**Number**	**Size**	**Height**	**Issued**
	D7021	Large	7", 17.8 cm	1996-2001

Handle: Bar of music and quill
Colourways: Brown,white and maroon
Backstamp: Doulton
Series: Great Composers

	Current Market Value		
Size	**U.K. £**	**U.S. $**	**Can. $**
Large	100.00	225.00	300.00

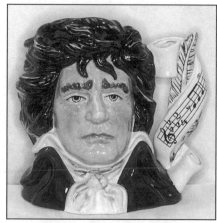

Beethoven

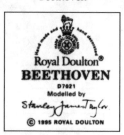

BENJAMIN FRANKLIN

An American publicist, scientist and statesman, Ben Franklin (1706-1790) was a signatory to the peace between Britain and the U.S.A. following the War of Independence. In 1748 he left his printing business to his foreman and devoted his life to science. His most famous discovery, that lightning is electricity, was accomplished with the simple objects of a knife and a key. It lead to the invention of the lightning rod, still used today to divert lightning harmlessly into the ground.

This jug was modelled for "The Queen's Table," Royal Doulton's exhibit at the United Kingdom Showcase at Walt Disney's Epcot Center in Orlando, Florida. It was sold exclusively to Epcot tourists visiting the exhibition during 1982, then released for general sale in 1983.

Designer:	Eric Griffiths			

	Doulton			
Statistics:	**Number**	**Size**	**Height**	**Issued**
	D6695	Small	4", 10.1 cm	1982-1989

Handle: A kite and key
Colourway: Black coat; white shirt; blue scarf
Backstamp: Doulton

	Current Market Value		
Size	**U.K. £**	**U.S. $**	**Can. $**
Small	75.00	125.00	150.00

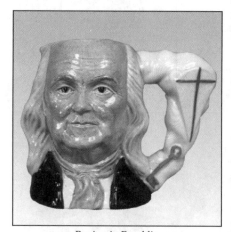

Benjamin Franklin

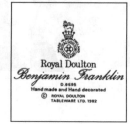

BETSY TROTWOOD

For the character jug Betsy Trotwood, see the "Charles Dickens Commemorative Set" page 143.

BILL SIKES

One of Dickens' most memorable characters is the infamous Bill Sikes, a character from *Oliver Twist*. This jug was commissioned by Lawleys By Post in a limited edition of 2,500.

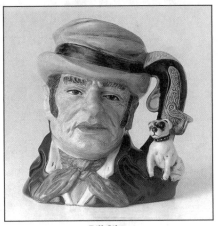

Bill Sikes

Designer: Stanley J. Taylor

Statistics:	Doulton Number	Size	Height	Issued
	D6981	Large	7", 17.8 cm	See below

Issued: 1994 in a limited edition of 2,500
Handle: Pistol and dog "Bull's-eye"
Colourway: Beige hat; green jacket; red scarf
Backstamp: Doulton

	Current Market Value		
Size	**U.K. £**	**U.S. $**	**Can. $**
Large	125.00	225.00	300.00

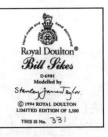

BILL SYKES

For the character jug Bill Sykes see the "Charles Dickens Commemorative Set" page 143.

BIRD WATCHER

PROTOTYPE

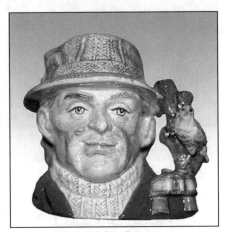

Bird Watcher, Prototype

Designer: Unknown
Height: Unknown
Size: Small
Issued: Not put into production
Handle: Brown and white bird, grey binoculars
Colourway: Light brown cap; green jacket; light green pullover
Backstamp: Doulton

Doulton Number	Current Market Value		
	U.K. £	**U.S. $**	**Can. $**
D6981	Extremely rare		

BLACKSMITH

PROTOTYPE

This large prototype of the Blacksmith jug has older features, a different hat and a different hair style. Only one copy is known to exist.

Designer: David B. Biggs

	Doulton			
Statistics:	**Number**	**Size**	**Height**	**Issued**
	—	Large	7 ¼", 18.4 cm	See below

Modelled: c.1963
Issued: Not put into production
Handle: Hammer, anvil and pliers
Colourway: Beige, white and black
Backstamp: Doulton

	Current Market Value		
Size	**U.K. £**	**U.S. $**	**Can. $**
Large		Unique	

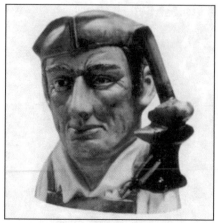

Blacksmith, Prototype

REGULAR ISSUE

Designer: David B. Biggs

	Doulton			
Statistics	**Number**	**Size**	**Height**	**Issued**
1.	D6571	Large	7 ¼", 18.4 cm	1963-1983
2.	D6578	Small	4", 10.1 cm	1963-1983
3.	D6585	Miniature	2 ½", 6.4 cm	1963-1983

Handle: Hammer, anvil and pliers
Colourway: Salmon hat; white shirt; light brown apron
Backstamp: Doulton
Series: Characters From Williamsburg

Jug				Current Market Value		
No.	Size	Comp.	Issued	U.K. £	U.S. $	Can. $
1A.	Large	EW	1963-1982	60.00	90.00	125.00
1B.		ETC	1968-1971	100.00	150.00	175.00
2A.	Small	EW	1963-1982	45.00	75.00	85.00
2B.		ETC	1968-1971	65.00	100.00	125.00
3A.	Miniature	EW	1963-1982	40.00	65.00	75.00
3B.		ETC	1968-1971	60.00	85.00	100.00

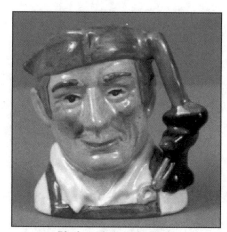

Blacksmith, Regular Issue

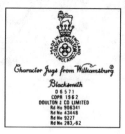

Character Jugs from Williamsburg
Blacksmith
D 6571
COPR 1962
DOULTON & CO LIMITED
Rd No 906341
Rd No 43468
Rd No 9227
Rd No 283/62

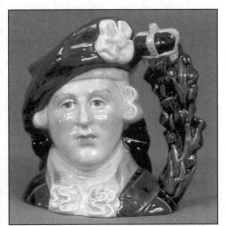

Bonnie Prince Charlie, Variation No. 1

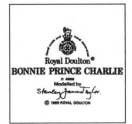

BONNIE PRINCE CHARLIE

James II's grandson, the "Young Pretender" (1720-1788), was born Charles Edward Stuart in Rome. He became the hopeful leader of the Jacobites, adherents to the Stuart line, and led them in an unsuccessful uprising in 1745. After being defeated at Culloden Moor in 1746, he escaped to France with the help of Flora McDonald. Charles roamed Europe, a drunkard, until settling in Rome where he passed the remainder of his life.

Designer: Stanley J. Taylor

Statistics:

	Doulton Number	Size	Height	Issued
	D6858	Large	6 ½", 16.5 cm	See below

Handle: Crown atop thistles
Colourway: See below
Backstamp: Doulton

VARIATION No. 1: Colourway — Blue plaid tam; red coat trimmed with yellow collar; white ruffles at the neck

Issued: 1990-1994
Backstamp: Doulton

Size	Variation	Current Market Value		
		U.K. £	U.S. $	Can. $
Large	Var. 1	125.00	200.00	250.00

VARIATION No. 2: Colourway — Mid-blue tam; green and blue coat trimmed with yellow collar

Issued: Not put into production
Backstamp: Doulton

Size	Variation	Current Market Value		
		U.K. £	U.S. $	Can. $
Large	Var. 2	Sold November 21, 1999 Phillips, New Bond Street London, England £1,500.00		

BOOTMAKER

PROTOTYPE

This large-size prototype of the Bootmaker jug has younger features and different hair, handle and hat designs. Only one copy is known to exist.

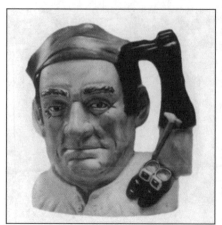

Designer: David B. Biggs

Statistics:	Doulton Number	Size	Height	Issued
Height:	D6572	Large	7 ½", 19.1 cm	See below

Modelled: c.1963
Issued: Not put into production
Handle: A boot and hammer, with a pair of shoes at the base
Colourway: Beige cap; white shirt; black shoes
Backstamp: Doulton

Bootmaker, Prototype

Size	Current Market Value U.K. £	U.S. $	Can. $
Large		Sold March 12, 1997 Sotheby's Arcade Auction New York, $1,955.00	

REGULAR ISSUE

Designer: David B. Biggs

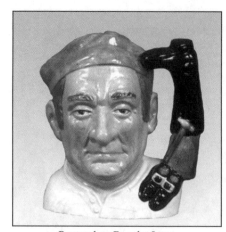

Statistics:	Doulton Number	Size	Height	Issued
1.	D6572	Large	7 ½", 19.1 cm	1963-1983
2.	D6579	Small	4", 10.1 cm	1963-1983
3.	D6586	Miniature	2 ½", 6.4 cm	1963-1983

Handle: A boot and hammer, with a pair of shoes at the base
Colourway: Salmon cap; white shirt
Backstamp: Doulton
Series: Characters From Williamsburg

Bootmaker, Regular Issue

Jug No.	Size	Comp.	Issued	Current Market Value U.K. £	U.S. $	Can. $
1A.	Large	EW	1963-1983	65.00	90.00	125.00
1B.		ETC	1968-1971	125.00	175.00	200.00
2A.	Small	EW	1963-1983	45.00	70.00	85.00
2B.		ETC	1968-1971	75.00	100.00	125.00
3A.	Miniature	EW	1963-1983	40.00	70.00	85.00
3B.		ETC	1968-1971	75.00	100.00	125.00

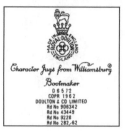

Character Jugs from Williamsburg
Bootmaker
D 6572
COPR 1962
DOULTON & CO LIMITED
Rd No 906342
Rd No 43449
Rd No 9228
Rd No 282/62

BOWLS PLAYER

Bowls is a British game played on a flat green (lawn) in lanes. Sir Francis Drake is reputed to have been playing bowls when the Spanish Armada was sighted in the English Channel.

Designer: Stanley J. Taylor

Statistics:	Doulton Number	Size	Height	Issued
	D6896	Small	4", 10.1 cm	1991-1995

Handle: Bowl, jack and measure
Colourway: White and yellow
Backstamp: Doulton
Series: Characters From Life

Size	Current Market Value		
	U.K. £	U.S. $	Can. $
Small	45.00	100.00	150.00

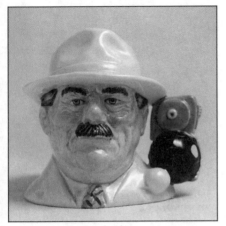

Bowls Player

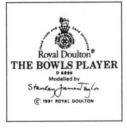

BUDDY HOLLY

A native of Lubbock, Texas, Buddy Holly left his mark on popular music, influencing later generations. He is best known for his song *Peggy Sue*. This jug was issued in a limited edition of 2,500 pieces.

Designer: David B. Biggs

Statistics:	Doulton Number	Size	Height	Issued
	D7100	Large	8", 20.3 cm	See below

Issued: 1998 in a limited edition of 2,500
Handle: A guitar, records, music sheet *Peggy Sue*
Colourway: Black and brown; resin glasses
Backstamp: Doulton/TM/© 1997 Maria Elena Holly By CMG Worldwide Indianapolis in USA

Size	Current Market Value		
	U.K. £	U.S. $	Can. $
Large	125.00	300.00	400.00

Note: Sold Phillips, New Bond Street, London, England, November 21st, 1999, (Jug No. 1 of 2,500) £550.00.

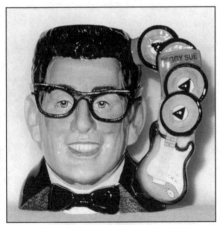

Buddy Holly

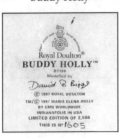

BUFFALO BILL

PROTOTYPE

This jug was piloted but never put into production, and only three jugs are known to exist. "W.F. Cody Buffalo Bill" is incised on the right shoulder in raised letters.

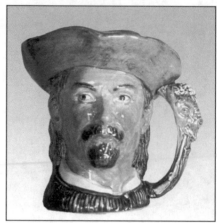

Buffalo Bill, Prototype

Designer: Unknown

Statistics:	Doulton Number	Size	Height	Issued
	D —	Large	7 ½", 19.1 cm	See below

Modelled: Unknown
Issued: Not put into production
Handle: A rifle and buffalo head
Colourway: Brown hat; grey moustache and goatee
Backstamp: Doulton

	Current Market Value		
Size	**U.K. £**	**U.S. $**	**Can. $**
Large	Extremely rare		

REGULAR ISSUE

William Frederick Cody (1846-1917) was a scout, plainsman, soldier in the Civil War, hotelier, rancher and showman. His expert marksmanship as a buffalo hunter earned him his nickname Buffalo Bill. In 1883, Cody and others formed "Buffalo Bill's Wild West Show," a theatrical shooting exhibition, which became very successful and travelled through the U.S. and Europe.

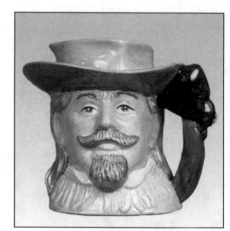

Buffalo Bill, Regular Issue

Designer: Robert Tabbenor

Statistics:	Doulton Number	Size	Height	Issued
	D6735	Mid	5 ½", 14.0 cm	1985-1989

Handle: Buffalo head and horn
Colourway: Light brown hat and buckskin jacket
Backstamp: Doulton
Series: The Wild West Collection

	Current Market Value		
Size	**U.K. £**	**U.S. $**	**Can. $**
Mid	55.00	85.00	110.00

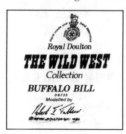

THE BUSKER

PROTOTYPE

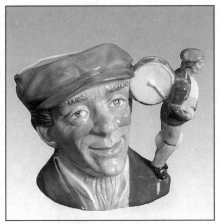

The Busker, Prototype

The prototype of The Busker jug had a one-man band for the handle; however, this was too complex for production and was replaced by a concertina.

Designer: Stanley J. Taylor

Statistics:	Model Number	Size	Height	Issued
	3025	Large	6 ½", 16.5 cm	See below

Modelled: 1986
Issued: Not put into production
Handle: One-man band
Colourway: Grey cap; green coat; white shirt; yellow scarf
Backstamp: Doulton

Size	Description	Current Market Value		
		U.K. £	U.S. $	Can. $
Large	Prototype		Unique	

REGULAR ISSUE

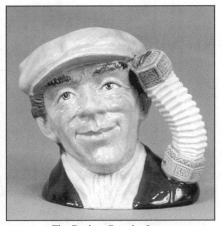

The Busker, Regular Issue

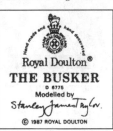

From its roots with the early wandering minstrels, entertaining in public places for money is still a way for artists to support themselves while gaining public exposure for their work.

Designer: Stanley J. Taylor

Statistics:	Doulton Number	Size	Height	Issued
	D6775	Large	6 ½", 16.5 cm	1988-1991

Handle: An open concertina
Colourway: Grey cap; green coat; yellow scarf
Backstamp: Doulton
Series: The London Collection

Size	Desription	Current Market Value		
		U.K. £	U.S. $	Can. $
Large	Regular Issue	100.00	175.00	200.00

BUZFUZ

This is an excellent example of the literary character designs of early character jugs. In Dickens' *Pickwick Papers*, Sergeant Buzfuz was the counsel of Mrs. Bardell in the breach of promise suit she brought against Mr. Pickwick.

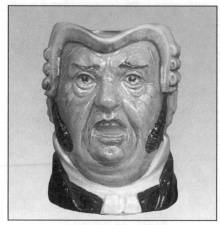

Buzfuz

Designer: Leslie Harradine
Harry Fenton

Statistics:	Doulton Number	Size	Height	Issued
	D5838	Mid	4 ¼", 10.8 cm	1938-1948
	D5838	Small	3 ¼", 8.3 cm	1948-1960

Handle: Plain
Colourway: White collar; brown waistcoat; dark green coat; black robe
Backstamp: Doulton

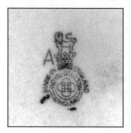

	Current Market Value		
Size	U.K. £	U.S. $	Can. $
Mid	125.00	225.00	275.00
Small	65.00	115.00	150.00

Buzfuz Derivatives

Item:	TABLE LIGHTER	**Item:**	BUST
Height:	3 ½", 8.9 cm	**Height:**	2 ½", 6.4 cm
Issued:	1958-1959	**Issued:**	1939-1960

Doulton		Current Market Value		
Number	Item	U.K. £	U.S. $	Can. $
D5838	Table Lighter	200.00	350.00	400.00
D6048	Bust	70.00	100.00	125.00

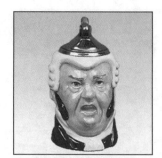

Buzfuz Table Lighter

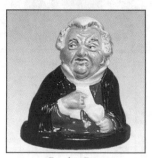

Buzfuz Bust

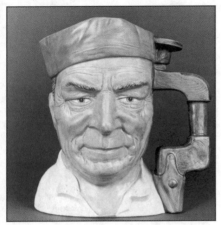

Cabinet Maker, Prototype

CABINET MAKER

In 1981 it was announced that a new jug in the Williamsburg series, the Cabinet Maker, would be produced. However, the series was cancelled in 1983, and the jug was not put into production at that time. In 1995 the decision was made to put the jug into production and to launch it at the 15th anniversary convention of the Royal Doulton International Collectors Club, held at Williamsburg. It was issued in a special edition of 1,500 pieces.

PROTOTYPE

Designer: Michael Abberley

Statistics:	Doulton Number	Size	Height	Issued
	D6659	Large	7 ½", 19.1 cm	See below

Modelled: 1979
Issued: Not put into production
Handle: Brace
Colourway: Red, white and brown
Backstamp: Doulton

Size	Description	Current Market Value		
		U.K. £	U.S. $	Can. $
Large	Prototype		Rare	

REGULAR ISSUE

Designer: Michael Abberley

Statistics:	Doulton Number	Size	Height	Issued
	D7010	Large	7 ½", 19.1 cm	See below

Issued: 1995 in a special edition of 1,500
Handle: Brace
Colourway: Red, white and brown
Backstamp: Doulton
Series: Characters From Williamsburg

Size	Description	Current Market Value		
		U.K. £	U.S. $	Can. $
Large	Regular issue	200.00	300.00	400.00

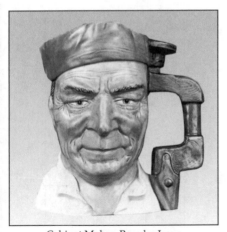

Cabinet Maker, Regular Issue

CAPT AHAB

Captain Ahab sailed the whaler, *Pequod*, in Herman Melville's great 19th-century American classic, *Moby Dick*. He lost a leg and then his life in pursuit of the great white whale, who triumphed in the chase and sunk his ship.

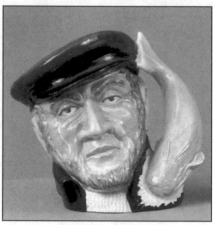

Capt Ahab

Designer: Garry Sharpe

Statistics:	Doulton Number	Size	Height	Issued
1.	D6500	Large	7", 17.8 cm	1959-1984
2.	D6506	Small	4", 10.1 cm	1959-1984
3.	D6522	Miniature	2 ½", 6.4 cm	1960-1984

Issued: See below
Handle: A grey whale
Colourway: Blue cap; black coat; white sweater
Backstamp: Doulton

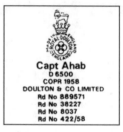

Capt Ahab
D 6500
COPR 1958
DOULTON & CO LIMITED
Rd No 889571
Rd No 38227
Rd No 8037
Rd No 422/58

Jug No.	Doulton No.	Comp.	Issued	Current Market Value U.K. £	U.S. $	Can. $
1.	Large	EW	1959-1984	85.00	125.00	150.00
		ETC	1968-1971	125.00	225.00	250.00
2.	Small	EW	1959-1984	55.00	85.00	110.00
		ETC	1968-1971	75.00	125.00	150.00
3.	Miniature	EW	1960-1984	45.00	75.00	100.00
		ETC	1968-1971	65.00	100.00	125.00

Capt Ahab Derivative

Item: TABLE LIGHTER
Height: 3 ½", 8.9 cm
Issued: 1964-1972

Doulton Number	Item	Current Market Value U.K. £	U.S. $	Can. $
D6506	Table Lighter	250.00	400.00	500.00

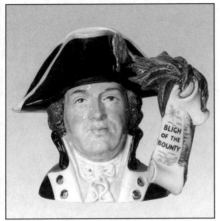

Captain Bligh, Style One

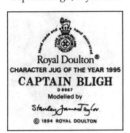

CAPTAIN BLIGH

This character jug of the year for 1995 commemorates Captain Bligh and the *Mutiny on the Bounty*. In 1789 the crew of the *Bounty*, under the leadership of Christian Fletcher, mutinied and set Bligh adrift in an open boat. He survived a 3,500-mile voyage before reaching land.

STYLE ONE: HANDLE ON RIGHT SIDE OF JUG

Designer: Stanley J. Taylor

Statistics:	Doulton Number	Size	Height	Issued
	D6967	Large	7", 17.8 cm	1995-1995

Handle: Navigation chart; palm tree and "Bligh of the Bounty"
Colourway: Black, cream, green, red and brown
Backstamp: Doulton/Character Jug of the Year, 1995
Series: Character Jug of the Year

	Current Market Value		
Size	U.K. £	U.S. $	Can. $
Large	150.00	225.00	350.00

CAPTAIN BLIGH AND FLETCHER CHRISTIAN

This pair of jugs was issued by Lawleys By Post, in a limited edition of 2,500.

STYLE TWO: CAPTAIN BLIGH — HANDLE ON LEFT SIDE OF JUG

Designer: Robert Tabbenor

Statistics:

	Doulton Number	Size	Height	Issued
1.	D7074	Small	4 ½", 11.9 cm	See below
2.	D7075	Small	4 ½", 11.9 cm	See below

Issued: 1997 in a limited edition of 2,500
Handle: 1. Captain Bligh — Palm tree and lifeboat
2. Fletcher Christian — Potted sapling
Colourway: 1. Captain Bligh — Black, white, yellow and brown
2. Fletcher Christian — Dark blue, white, grey and yellow
Backstamp: Doulton

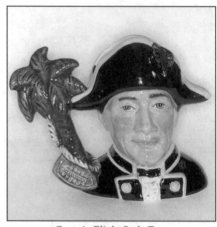

Captain Bligh, Style Two

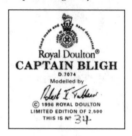

Jug No.	Doulton Number	Name	Current Market Value		
			U.K. £	U.S. $	Can. $
1.	D7074	Captain Bligh	100.00	250.00	300.00
2.	D7075	Fletcher Christian	Priced per pair		

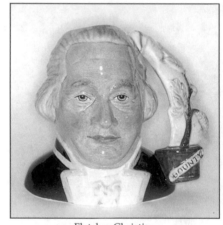

Fletcher Christian

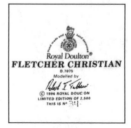

CAP'N CUTTLE

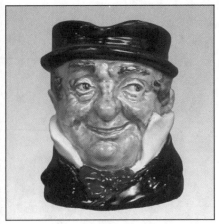

Cap'n Cuttle

The wonderful characters of Dickens' novels were the inspiration for many early jug designs. Captain Edward Cuttle was an eccentric English gentleman in *Dombey and Son* (1846), who is best known for saying, "When found, make a note of it."

Designer:	Leslie Harradine			
	Harry Fenton			

	Doulton			
Statistics:	**Number**	**Size**	**Height**	**Issued**
1.	D5842	Mid	4", 101. cm	1938-1948
2.	D5842	Small	3 ½", 8.9 cm	1948-1960

Handle: Plain
Colourway: Blue-black coat; grey-green hat; white collar; green bow tie
Backstamp: Doulton

Jug		**Current Market Value**		
No.	**Size**	**U.K. £**	**U.S. $**	**Can. $**
1.	Mid	125.00	200.00	225.00
2.	Small	65.00	100.00	125.00

Cap'n Cuttle Derivative

Item: TABLE LIGHTER
Height: 3 ½", 8.9 cm
Issued: 1958-1959

Doulton		**Current Market Value**		
Number	**Item**	**U.K. £**	**U.S. $**	**Can. $**
D5842	Table Lighter	225.00	375.00	425.00

CAPT HENRY MORGAN

A privateer and pirate leader in the West Indies, Morgan (1635-1688) also carried out commissions from the British authorities. His attack on Panama in 1671 violated a peace treaty between England and Spain. Sent to England to stand trial, he was instead knighted and became Lieutenant Governor of Jamaica, where he remained until his death.

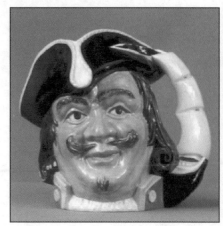

Capt Henry Morgan

Designer: Garry Sharpe
Handle: Sails of a ship

VARIATION No. 1: **Colourway:** Black tricorn trimmed with gold; blue collar trimmed with gold

	Doulton			
Statistics:	Number	Size	Height	Issued
1.	D6467	Large	6 ¾", 17.2 cm	1958-1982
2.	D6469	Small	3 ½", 8.9 cm	1958-1982
3.	D6510	Miniature	2 ½", 6.4 cm	1960-1982

Issued: See below
Colourway: Black tricorn; blue collar trimmed with gold
Backstamps: **A.** Doulton
B. Doulton/City of Stoke-on-Trent Jubilee Year 1959-1960/With the compliments of Lord Mayor and Lady Mayoress Alderman Harold Clowes, O.B.E., J.P., and Miss Christine Clowes

Jug				Current Market Value		
No.	Size	Comp.	Issued	U.K. £	U.S. $	Can. $
1A.	Large	EW	1958-1982	75.00	125.00	150.00
1A.		ETC	1968-1971	100.00	150.00	175.00
1B.		EW	1958-1959		Rare	
2A.	Small	EW	1958-1982	35.00	50.00	65.00
2A.		ETC	1968-1971	50.00	80.00	95.00
3A.	Miniature	EW	1960-1982	40.00	65.00	75.00
		ETC	1968-1971	50.00	80.00	95.00

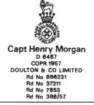

Backstamp A -

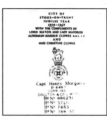

Backstamp B - City of Stoke-on-Trent

VARIATION No. 2: Black tricorn trimmed with red; black collar trimmed with red

Issued: Unknown
Colourway: Black tricorn trimmed with red; black collar trimmed with red
Backstamp: Doulton

	Current Market Value		
Size	U.K. £	U.S. $	Can. $
Large		Extremely rare	

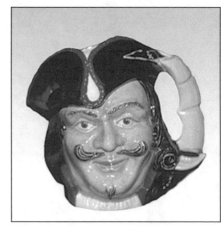

Capt Henry Morgan, Variation 2

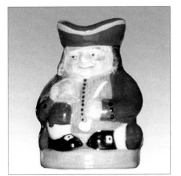

Honest Measure

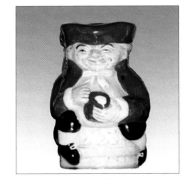

Toby XX

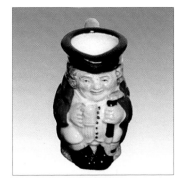

Jolly Toby

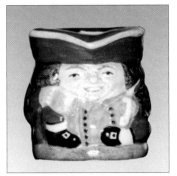

The Best is not Too Good

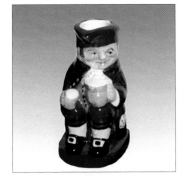

Old Charlie

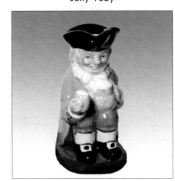

Happy John

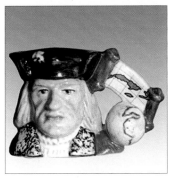

Columbus

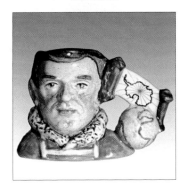

Scott

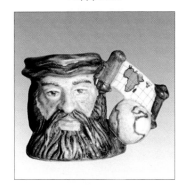

DaGama

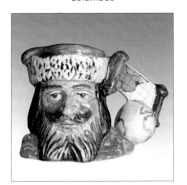

Marco Polo

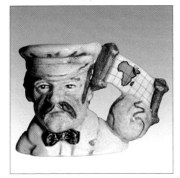

Dr. Livingstone

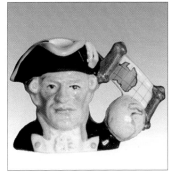

Cook

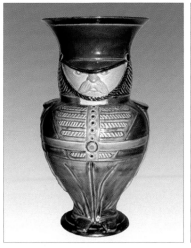

Soldier Boy (Style Two)

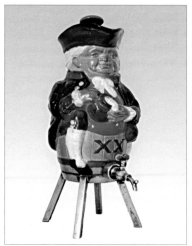

Toby XX Liquor Container

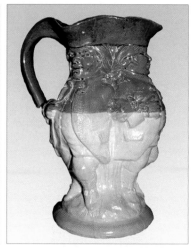

Triple Toby

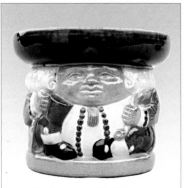

The Best is Not Too Good,
(Style One) Tobacco Jar

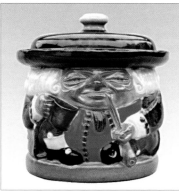

The Best is Not Too Good
(Style Three) Lidded Jar

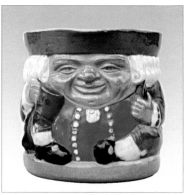

The Best is Not Too Good
(Style Four)

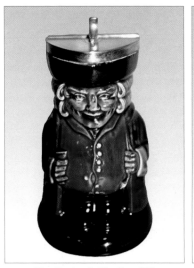

The Squire (with silver lid)

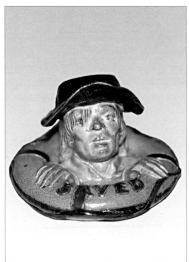

Saved Match Holder

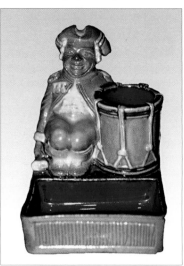

Drummer Match Holder

The Doultonville Collection

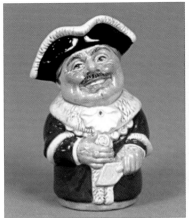

(D6766) Alderman Mace the Mayor

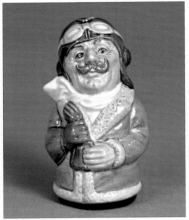

(D6812) Captain Prop the Pilot

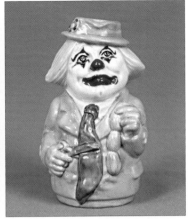

(D6768) Charlie Cheer the Clown

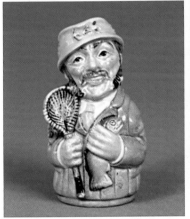

(D6742) Fred Fly the Fisherman

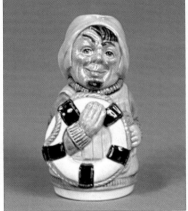

(D6811) Len Lifebelt the Lifeboatman

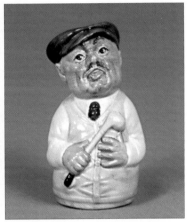

(D6740) Major Green the Golfer

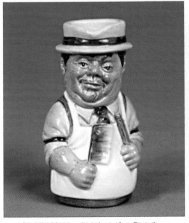

(D6743) Mr. Brisket the Butcher

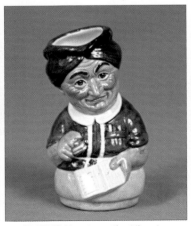

(D6715) Mrs. Loan the Librarian

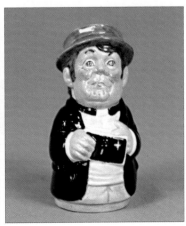

(D6702) Rev. Cassock the Clergyman

Prototypes

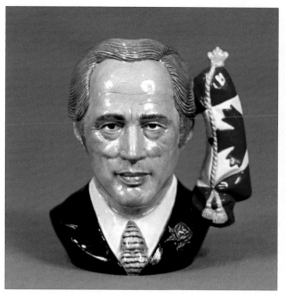

Pierre Elliot Trudeau

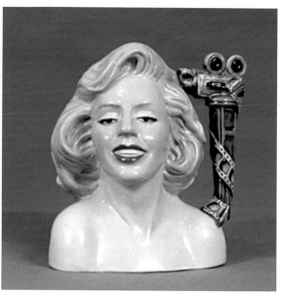

Marilyn Monroe

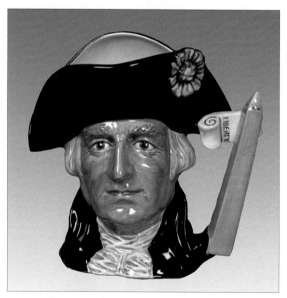

George Washington Prototype (Style Two)

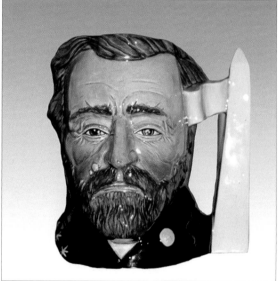

Ulysses S. Grant

Prototypes / Regular Issues

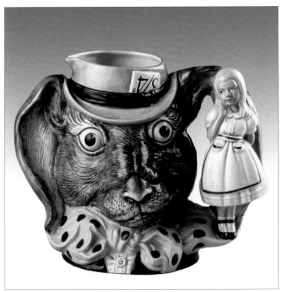

The March Hare (Prototype)

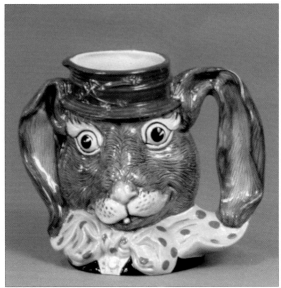

The March Hare (Regular Issue)

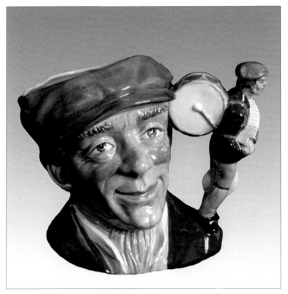

The Busker (Prototype)

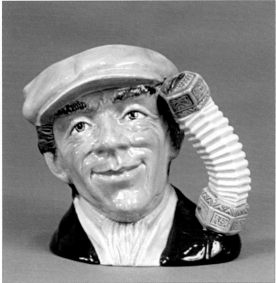

The Busker (Regular Issue)

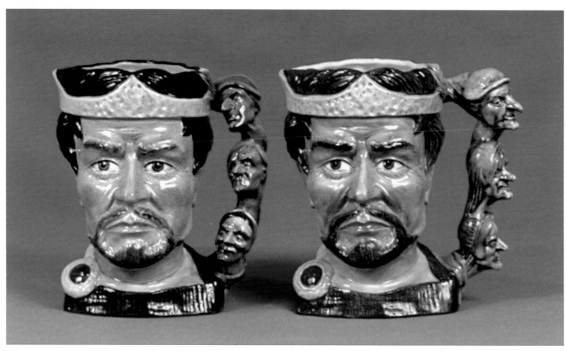

MacBeth (Regular Issue, left; Prototype, right)

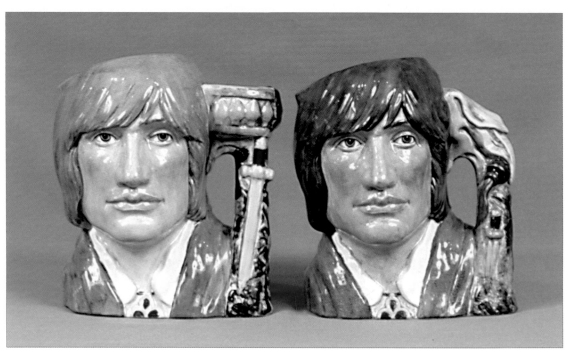

Romeo (Regular Issue, left; Prototype, right)

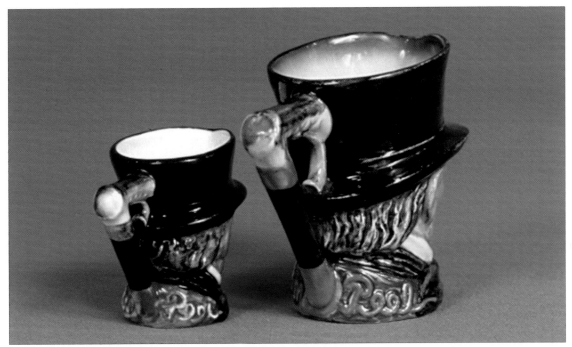

John Peel Handles

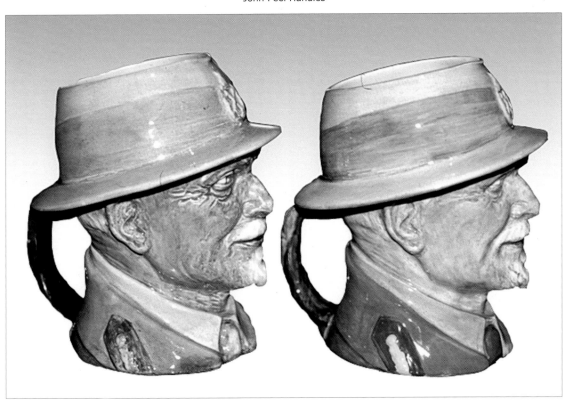

Smuts (Var. No. 1 left; Var. No. 2 right)

Journey Through Britain

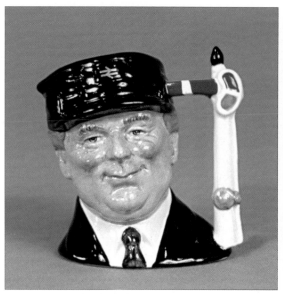

(D6823) The Engine Driver

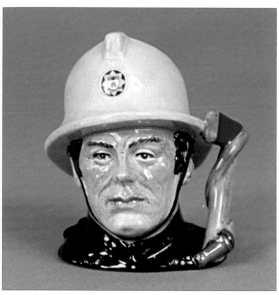

(D6839) The Fireman (Style Two)

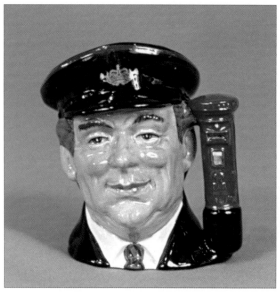

(D6801) The Postman

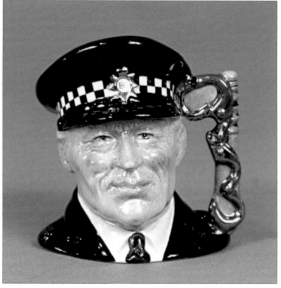

(D6852) The Policeman

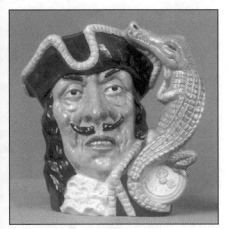

Captain Hook, Style One

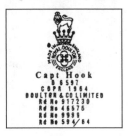

CAPT HOOK

Captain Hook is the nemesis of Peter Pan in J. M. Barrie's famous story. Peter Pan cut off Hook's hand and fed it to a crocodile, who liked it so much he followed the Captain around in hopes of eating the rest of him. Hook managed to keep eluding his predator because the crocodile had accidentally swallowed a clock that ticked inside him and ruined the element of surprise.

STYLE ONE: HANDLE — CROCODILE AND CLOCK

Designer: Max Henk
David B. Biggs

Statistics:	Number	Size	Height	Issued
1.	D6597	Large	7 ¼", 18.4 cm	1965-1971
2.	D6601	Small	4", 10.1 cm	1965-1971
3.	D6605	Miniature	2 ½", 6.4 cm	1965-1971

Handle: An alligator and clock
Colourway: Blue tricorn trimmed with yellow; green coat trimmed with yellow; white ruffles at the neck
Backstamp: Doulton

Jug No.	Doulton No.	Comp.	Issued	Current Market Value U.K. £	U.S. $	Can. $
1.	Large	EW	1965-1971	350.00	550.00	750.00
		ETC	1968-1971	400.00	600.00	900.00
2.	Small	EW	1965-1971	275.00	400.00	500.00
		ETC	1968-1971	300.00	425.00	600.00
3.	Miniature	EW	1965-1971	300.00	525.00	650.00
		ETC	1968-1971	300.00	400.00	600.00

STYLE TWO: HANDLE — SILVER HOOK AND CROCODILE

Capt Hook, Style Two, was the Character Jug of the Year for 1994.

Designer: Martyn C. R. Alcock

Statistics:	Doulton Number	Size	Height	Issued
	D6947	Large	7 ½", 19.1 cm	1994-1994

Handle: Crocodile, silver hook
Colourway: Black, scarlet and grey
Backstamp: Doulton/Character Jug of the Year, 1994
Series: Character Jug of the Year

Size	Current Market Value U.K. £	U.S. $	Can. $
Large	135.00	250.00	350.00

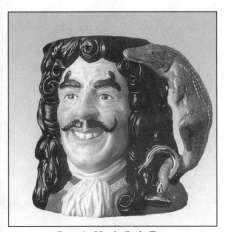

Captain Hook, Style Two

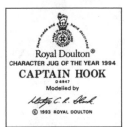

CAPTAIN JAMES COOK

In a striking tribute to the famous navigator and explorer, this character jug incorporates a first-ever feature in its handle: a working compass. This jug was issued by Lawleys By Post in a limited edition 2,500 to commemorate the life and times of Captain Cook (1728-1779).

Designer: William K. Harper

Statistics:	Doulton Number	Size	Height	Issued
	D7077	Large	6 ½", 16.5 cm	See below

Issued: 1997 in a limited edition of 2,500
Handle: Map of Australia, working compass
Colourway: Naval uniform and cap; yellow trim; gold buttons
Backstamp: Doulton

Size	Current Market Value U.K. £	U.S. $	Can. $
Large	150.00	225.00	350.00

Note: For the character jug Cook see the "Explorers Set" page 178.

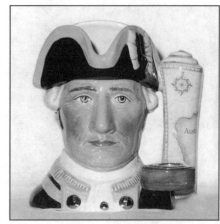

Captain James Cook

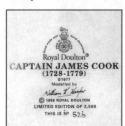

CAPTAIN SCOTT

Captain Robert Falcon Scott (1868-1912) was the leader of the ill-fated British expedition to the South Pole in 1910. Not only were they bested by Amundsen's Norwegian expedition, but also Captain Scott and his team perished and never completed the return journey.

Designer: David B. Biggs

Statistics:	Doulton Number	Size	Height	Issued
	D7116	Large	7", 17.8 cm	1998-2000

Handle: Snow, Union Jack and tent
Colourway: Cream balaclava; brown goggles
Backstamp: Doulton

Size	Current Market Value U.K. £	U.S. $	Can. $
Large	100.00	175.00	300.00

Note: For the character jug Scott see the "Explorers Set" page 178.

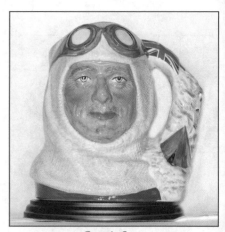

Captain Scott

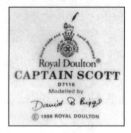

THE CARDINAL

This jug has minor colour variations in the hair. The earliest jugs had brown hair, and later jugs either grey or white hair. This jug was produced with and without pink highlighting on the raised character name.

Designer: Charles Noke

Statistics:	Doulton Number	Size	Height	Issued
1.	D5614	Large	6 ½", 16.5 cm	1936-1960
2.	D6033	Small	3 ½", 8.9 cm	1939-1960
3.	D6129	Miniature	2 ¼", 5.7 cm	1940-1960
4.	D6258	Tiny	1 ½", 3.8 cm	1947-1960

Handle: Tassel
Colourway: Scarlet robes; purple handle
Backstamp: Doulton

Jug No.	Size	Current Market Value U.K. £	U.S. $	Can. $
1.	Large	100.00	150.00	175.00
2.	Small	40.00	75.00	100.00
3.	Miniature	40.00	65.00	75.00
4.	Tiny	135.00	250.00	275.00

Note: The miniature version of The Cardinal is found in white gloss.

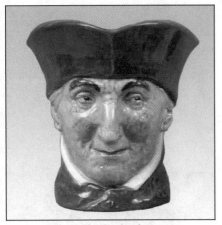

The Cardinal

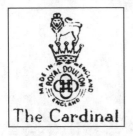

The Cardinal

THE CAROLER

This is the fifth in the Christmas Miniatures Series of jugs. Issued during 1995, the jug was commissioned and sold by Royal Doulton (U.S.A.) Limited in America, and was made available worldwide through the Royal Doulton International Collectors Club.

Designer: Martyn C. R. Alcock

Statistics:	Doulton Number	Size	Height	Issued
	D7007	Miniature	2 ½", 6.4 cm	1995-1995

Handle: Sheet music and lantern
Colourway: Black, white and blue
Backstamp: Doulton
Series: Christmas Miniatures

Size	Current Market Value U.K. £	U.S. $	Can. $
Miniature	85.00	150.00	175.00

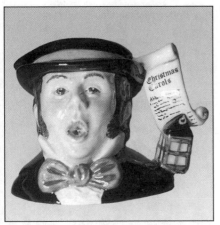

The Caroler

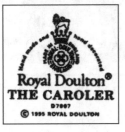

Royal Doulton®
THE CAROLER
D7007
© 1995 ROYAL DOULTON

CATHERINE OF ARAGON

Daughter of Ferdinand and Isabella of Spain, Catherine (1485-1536) was married to Arthur, Prince of Wales, in a political arrangement between the two countries. When Arthur died shortly after their wedding, she married Henry VIII to continue the arrangement. This first marriage for Henry lasted 24 years, until he became restless at the lack of a male heir and sought out Anne Boleyn. In 1527 Henry attempted to have his marriage annulled, a move that led to his excommunication by the Pope and, eventually, to the English Reformation. Catherine was banished from the royal court and lived until the age of 50, unhappy and lonely.

PROTOTYPES

STYLE ONE: HANDLE — A SCROLL

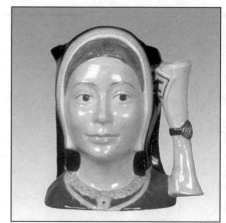

Designer: Alan Maslankowski

Statistics:

Doulton Number	Size	Height	Issued
D —	Large	6 ½", 17.8 cm	See below

Modelled: 1974
Issued: Not put into production
Handle: A scroll
Colourway: Red, gold, black, white and yellow
Backstamp: Doulton

Size	Current Market Value		
	U.K. £	U.S. $	Can. $
Large	Sold November 21, 1999 Phillips, New Bond Street London, England, £4,500.00		

Prototype, Style One, Scroll Handle

Note: A similar jug was sold at the June 24, 1999, Phillips auction for £3,200.00.

STYLE TWO: HANDLE — A TRUMPET

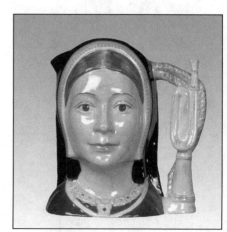

Designer: Alan Maslankowski

Statistics:

Doulton Number	Size	Height	Issued
D—	Large	6 ½", 17.8 cm	See below

Modelled: 1974
Issued: Not put into production
Handle: A trumpet
Colourway: Red, gold, black, white and yellow
Backstamp: Doulton

Size	Current Market Value		
	U.K. £	U.S. $	Can. $
Large	Sold November 21, 1999 Phillips, New Bond Street London, England, £8,500.00		

Prototype, Style Two, Trumpet Handle

CATHERINE OF ARAGON

REGULAR ISSUE

STYLE ONE: HANDLE — A TOWER

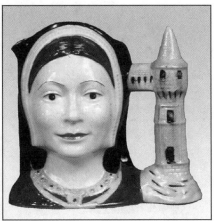

Catherine of Aragon, Regular Issue, Style One

Designer: Alan Maslankowski

	Doulton			
Statistics:	**Number**	**Size**	**Height**	**Issued**
1.	D6643	Large	7", 17.8 cm	1975-1989
2.	D6657	Small	4", 10.1 cm	1981-1989
3.	D6658	Miniature	2 ½", 6.4 cm	1981-1989

Handle: A tower
Colourway: Red, gold, black and white
Backstamp: Doulton
Series: Henry VIII and His Six Wives

Jug.		**Current Market Value**		
No.	**Size**	**U.K. £**	**U.S. $**	**Can. $**
1.	Large	75.00	150.00	175.00
2.	Small	85.00	165.00	175.00
3.	Miniature	75.00	150.00	175.00

Note: For Catherine of Aragon, Style Two, see "The Six Wives of Henry VIII" page 364.

CATHERINE HOWARD

Niece to the Duke of Norfolk, Catherine Howard (1521-1542) became Henry VIII's fifth wife on July 28, 1540, in a marriage arranged by her family. In 1541 Henry accused her of adultery and had her beheaded at the Tower of London.

STYLE ONE: HANDLE — AN AXE

Designer: Peter Gee

	Doulton			
Statistics:	**Number**	**Size**	**Height**	**Issued**
1.	D6645	Large	7", 17.8 cm	1978-1989
2.	D6692	Small	4", 10.1 cm	1984-1989
3.	D6693	Miniature	2 ½", 6.4 cm	1984-1989

Handle: An axe
Colourway: Brown, gold and white
Backstamp: Doulton
Series: Henry VIII and His Six Wives

Jug		**Current Market Value**		
No.	**Size**	**U.K. £**	**U.S. $**	**Can. $**
1.	Large	125.00	225.00	250.00
2.	Small	125.00	225.00	250.00
3.	Miniature	125.00	225.00	250.00

Note: For Catherine Howard, Style Two, see "The Six Wives of Henry VIII" page 364.

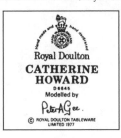

Catherine Howard, Style One

Royal Doulton
**CATHERINE
HOWARD**
D6645
Modelled by
Peter A Gee.
© ROYAL DOULTON TABLEWARE
LIMITED 1977

CATHERINE PARR

Catherine Parr (1512-1548) became Henry VIII's last wife on July 12, 1543, after being twice widowed. She came to wield considerable power in the royal court, serving for a time as Queen regent in 1544 and overseeing the start of Edward VI's reign. After Henry's death in 1547, she married Baron Seymour of Sudeley, but died during childbirth the following year.

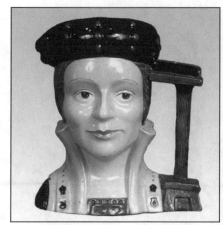

Catherine Parr, Style One

STYLE ONE: HANDLE — A BIBLE AND PULPIT

Designer: Michael Abberley

Statistics:	Doulton Number	Size	Height	Issued
1.	D6664	Large	6 ¾", 17.2 cm	1981-1989
2.	D6751	Small	4", 10.1 cm	1987-1989
3.	D6752	Miniature	2 ½", 6.4 cm	1987-1989

Handle: Bible and pulpit
Colourway: Black, brown and gold
Backstamp: Doulton
Series: Henry VIII and His Six Wives

Jug No.	Size	Current Market Value U.K. £	U.S. $	Can. $
1.	Large	125.00	250.00	350.00
2.	Small	150.00	300.00	350.00
3.	Miniature	150.00	275.00	300.00

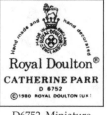

D6752, Miniature

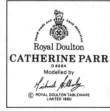

D6664, Large

Note: For Catherine Parr, Style Two, see "The Six Wives of Henry VIII" page 364.

THE CAVALIER

The cavaliers were Royalist soldiers who fought for Charles I during the English Civil War. They became known for their gallantry and haughtiness, an attitude still described as "cavalier."

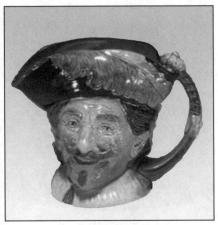

The Cavalier, Style One

STYLE ONE: CAVALIER WITH GOATEE

Designer: Harry Fenton

Statistics:	Doulton Number	Size	Height	Issued
	D6114	Large	7", 17.8 cm	1940-1950

Handle: Handle of a sword
Colourway: Green hat; white ruff
Backstamp: Doulton

	Current Market Value		
Size	U.K. £	U.S. $	Can. $
Large	2,000.00	4,000.00	5,000.00

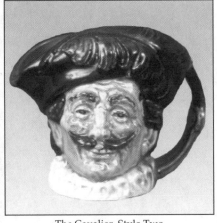

The Cavalier, Style Two

STYLE TWO: CAVALIER WITHOUT GOATEE

This jug was originally listed in Royal Doulton's product guide as the Laughing Cavalier, presumably after the famous Frans Hals painting

Slight colour changes, along with alterations to the ruff and removal of the goatee, occurred in 1950.

Designer: Harry Fenton

Statistics:	Doulton Number	Size	Height	Issued
1.	D6114	Large	7", 17.8 cm	1950-1960
2.	D6173	Small	3 ¼", 8.3 cm	1941-1960

Handle: Handle of a sword
Colourway: Green hat; white ruff
Backstamp: Doulton

Dug		Current Market Value		
No.	Size	U.K. £	U.S. $	Can. $
1.	Large	90.00	135.00	150.00
2.	Small	50.00	65.00	75.00

Note: Style Two large and small jugs are found in white gloss.

CELTIC (FOOTBALL CLUB)

Designer: Stanley J. Taylor

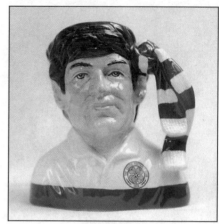

	Doulton			
Statistics:	**Number**	**Size**	**Height**	**Issued**
	D6925	Small	5", 12.7 cm	1992-1999

Handle: Team coloured scarf
Colourway: Green and white uniform
Backstamp: Doulton
Series: The Football Supporters

	Current Market Value		
Size	**U.K. £**	**U.S. $**	**Can. $**
Small	65.00	125.00	150.00

Celtic (Football Club)

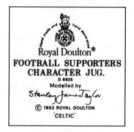

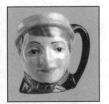

Artful Dodger

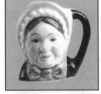

Betsy Trotwood

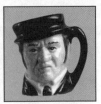

Bill Sykes

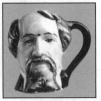

Charles Dickens

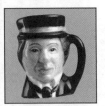

David Copperfield

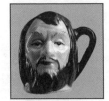

Fagin

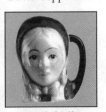

Little Nell

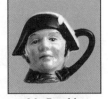

Mr. Bumble

Mrs.Bardell

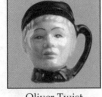

Oliver Twist

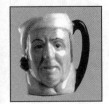

Scrooge

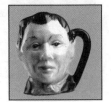

Uriah Heep

CHARLES DICKENS
COMMEMORATIVE SET

The 12 jugs in this set were issued to commemorate the 170th anniversary of the birth of Charles Dickens, and each one comes with a certificate of authenticity. A mahogany display shelf completes the set. The set was first sold by Lawleys By Post in the U.K. from 1982 to 1988, and from 1985 in North America and Australia.

STYLE ONE: CHARLES DICKENS - HANDLE PLAIN

Designers:	Artful Dodger, Charles Dickens — Eric Griffiths Betsy Trotwood, Bill Sykes, David Copperfield, Little Nell, Scrooge — Michael Abberley Fagin, Mr. Bumble, Mrs. Bardell, Oliver Twist, Uriah Heep — Robert Tabbenor
Height:	1 ½", 3.8 cm
Size:	Tiny
Issued:	1982-1989
Handle:	Plain
Colourways:	See below
Backstamp:	Doulton

Doulton Number	Name / Colourways	Current Market Value U.K. £	U.S. $	Can. $
D6678	**Artful Dodger** / Grey and black	25.00	45.00	50.00
D6685	**Betsy Trotwood** / Yellow, white and black	25.00	45.00	60.00
D6684	**Bill Sykes** / Green/dark blue	25.00	45.00	60.00
D6676	**Charles Dickens**, Style One / Grey and black	45.00	125.00	140.00
D6680	**David Copperfield** / Dark blue and black	30.00	75.00	75.00
D6679	**Fagin** / Orange and brown	30.00	75.00	75.00
D6681	**Little Nell** / Yellow/black	30.00	55.00	65.00
D6686	**Mr. Bumble** / Yellow/dark blue/green	30.00	50.00	60.00
D6687	**Mrs. Bardell** / Yellow/green	30.00	50.00	60.00
D6677	**Oliver Twist** / Dark/light blue	30.00	50.00	60.00
D6683	**Scrooge** / Yellow/brown	30.00	50.00	60.00
D6682	**Uriah Heep** / Grey and green	30.00	45.00	60.00
	Display stand for 12 tinies	55.00	40.00	40.00
	Complete Set	400.00	600.00	700.00

CHARLES DICKENS

STYLE TWO: HANDLE — QUILL PEN AND INK POT

The Charles Dickens, Style One jug was commissioned by the Royal Doulton International Collectors Club in a limited edition of 7,500 pieces.

Designer: William K. Harper

Statistics:	Doulton Number	Size	Height	Issued
	D6901	Small	4", 10.1 cm	See below

Issued: 1991 in a limited edition of 7,500
Handle: Quill pen and ink pot, the book "The Old Curiosity Shop"
Colourway: Black and olive green
Backstamp: Doulton/RDICC
Series: RDICC

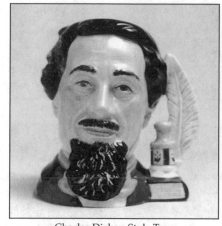

Charles Dickes, Style Two

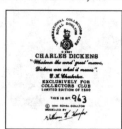

Size	Current Market Value		
	U.K. £	U.S. $	Can. $
Small	95.00	160.00	175.00

STYLE THREE: TWO-HANDLED JUG

The 125th anniversary of the death of Charles Dickens was commemorated in 1995 with a two-handled jug of Dickens, in a limited edition of 2,500.

Designer: William K. Harper

Statistics:	Doulton Number	Size	Height	Issued
	D6939	Large	7", 17.8 cm	See below

Issued: 1995 in a limited edition of 2,500
Handle: Six of Dickens characters:
Oliver Twist, Sairey Gamp, Ebenezer Scrooge, Little Nell, Mr. Pickwick and Little Dorritt
Colourway: Green, black, yellow and brown
Backstamp: Doulton

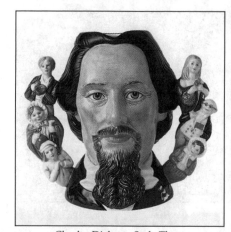

Charles Dickens, Style Three

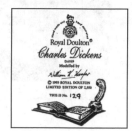

Size	Current Market Value		
	U.K. £	U.S. $	Can. $
Large	250.00	525.00	675.00

Note: For the toby jug Charles Dickens see page 43.

CHARLIE CHAPLIN

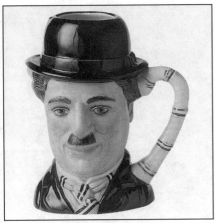

Charlie Chaplin, Style One

STYLE ONE: HANDLE — WALKING CANE

Issued in 1993 in a limited edition of 5,000, this jug was available through Lawleys By Post.

Designer: William K. Harper

	Doulton			
Statistics:	**Number**	**Size**	**Height**	**Issued**
	D6949	Large	7 ¼", 18.4 cm	See below

Issued: 1993 in a limited edition of 5,000
Handle: Cane
Colourway: Black hat and jacket; green, white and black striped tie
Backstamp: Doulton

	Current Market Value		
Size	**U.K. £**	**U.S. $**	**Can. $**
Large	135.00	250.00	300.00

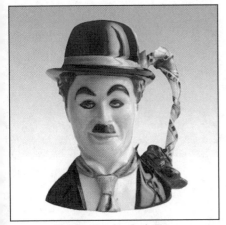

Charlie Chaplin, Style Two

STYLE TWO: HANDLE — FILM STRIP AND SHOES

Style Two was issued by Lawleys By Post, in 1999, in a limited edition of 3,500.

Designer: Robert Tabbenor

	Doulton			
Statistics:	**Number**	**Size**	**Height**	**Issued**
	D7145	Mid	4 ½", 11.9 cm	See below

Issued: 1999 in a limited edition of 3,500
Handle: Movie film wrpped around walking cane;
pair of shoes at bottom
Colourway: Black, grey and white
Backstamp: Doulton

	Current Market Value		
Size	**U.K. £**	**U.S. $**	**Can. $**
Mid	75.00	125.00	—

Note: For the toby jug Charlie see page 43.

THE CHEF

Designer: David B. Biggs

Statistics:

Doulton Number	Size	Height	Issued
D7103	Mid	6", 15.0 cm	1998 to the present

Handle: Wooden spoons, onions, striped tea towel
Colourway: White chef's jacket and hat; red neckerchief
Backstamp: Doulton

Size	Current Market Value		
	U.K. £	U.S. $	Can. $
Mid	55.00	145.00	295.00

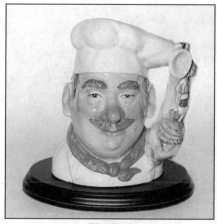

The Chef

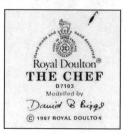

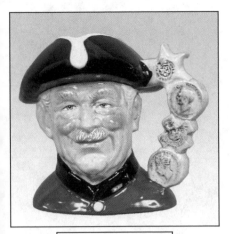

CHELSEA PENSIONER

Charles II founded the Royal Hospital for "worthy old soldiers broken in the wars." It was built by Christopher Wren and completed in 1692. Each year on Founders Day, the opening of the hospital is celebrated by the soldiers in full dress uniform, as worn by the gentleman depicted on this jug.

Designer:	Stanley J. Taylor

	Doulton			
Statistics:	**Number**	**Size**	**Height**	**Issued**
	See below	Large	6 ½", 16.5 cm	See below

Handle: Medals of honour
Colourway: Black tricorn trimmed with gold; scarlet tunic; black collar
Issued: 1A. Large — 1989-1991
 1B. Large — 1988 in a limited edition of 250
 1C. Large — 1988 in a limited edition of 250
 1D. Large — 1988 in a limited edition of 250
 1E. Large — 1988 in a limited edition of 250
Backstamp: A. Doulton: For general issue, 1989,
 B. Doulton / Joseph Hornes / To commemorate the First Anniversary of the opening of the Royal Doulton Room Joseph Horne's, Pittsburgh, Pennsylvania, U.S.A.
 C. Doulton / D. H. Holmes / To commemorate the First Anniversary of the opening of the Royal Doulton Room D. H. Holme's, New Orleans, Louisianna, U.S.A.
 D. Doulton / Higbee Company / To commemorate the Third Anniversary of the opening of the Royal Doulton Room The Higbee Company, Cleveland, Ohio, U.S.A.
 E. Doulton / Strawbridge and Clothier / To commemorate the Second Anniversary of the opening of the Royal Doulton Room Strawbridge and Clothier, Philadelphia, Pennsylvania, U.S.A.
Series: 1A. The London Collection

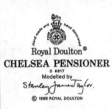

Backstamp A - Doulton

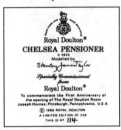

Backstamp B - Hornes

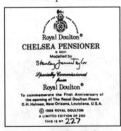

Backstamp C - Holmes

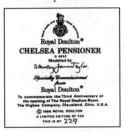

Backstamp D - Higbee

Jug No.	Doulton Number	Size	Current Market Value		
			U.K. £	**U.S. $**	**Can. $**
1A.	D6817	Large	100.00	175.00	250.00
1B.	D6830		150.00	225.00	275.00
1C.	D6831		150.00	225.00	275.00
1D.	D6832		150.00	225.00	275.00
1E.	D6833		150.00	225.00	275.00

CHIEF SITTING BULL
GEORGE ARMSTRONG CUSTER

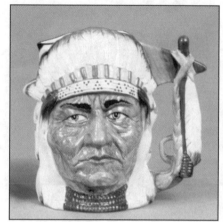

Chief Sitting Bull (1831-1890) of the Sioux Indians spent his life working for the right of his people to own and control their land. He was shot by the Indian police on a questionable charge of resisting arrest.

George Armstrong Custer (1839-1876) was the youngest general in the U.S. Army. He first saw action in the Civil War and was later stationed in the Dakota Territory during the gold rush on Sioux Land. In 1876 he led an attack against an Indian encampment at Little Big Horn. Sitting Bull and his men outnumbered Custer's regiment and easily defeated them, leaving no survivors.

This jug was issued in a limited edition of 9,500 pieces.

Designer: Michael Abberley

	Doulton			
Statistics:	**Number**	**Size**	**Height**	**Issued**
	D6712	Large	7", 17.8 cm	See below

Chief Sitting Bull, Variation No. 1

Issued: 1984 in a limited edition of 9,500
Handle: Sitting Bull — tomahawk
Custer — pistol
Backstamp: Doulton
Series: The Antagonists' Collection (Two-faced jug)

VARIATION No. 1: Colourway — Multi-coloured; Sitting Bull has grey eyes.

Colourway: Multi-coloured; Sitting Bull has grey eyes

		Current Market Value		
Size	**Variation**	**U.K. £**	**U.S. $**	**Can. $**
Large	Var. 1	150.00	250.00	300.00

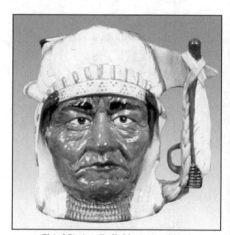

Chief Sitting Bull, Variation No. 2

VARIATION No. 2: Colourway — Multi-coloured; Sitting Bull has brown eyes

Colourway: Multi-coloured; Sitting Bull has brown eyes

		Current Market Value		
Size	**Variation**	**U.K. £**	**U.S. $**	**Can. $**
Large	Var. 2	150.00	225.00	275.00

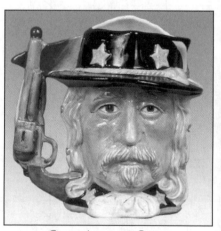

George Armstrong Custer

CHOPIN

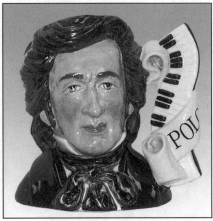

Chopin

Designer: Stanley J. Taylor

Statistics:	**Doulton Number**	**Size**	**Height**	**Issued**
	D7030	Large	7", 17.8 cm	1996-2000

Handle: Piano keyboard and scroll
Colourway: Dark blue, black, brown, white and yellow
Backstamp: Doulton
Series: Great Composers

	Current Market Value		
Size	**U.K. £**	**U.S. $**	**Can. $**
Large	100.00	200.00	300.00

CHRISTOPHER COLUMBUS

STYLE ONE: HANDLE — MAP OF THE NEW WORLD

This jug was issued in 1991 to commemorate the 500th anniversary of the discovery of the New World.

Designer: Stanley J. Taylor

Statistics:	**Doulton** Number	Size	Height	Issued
	D6891	Large	7", 17.8 cm	1991-1997

Handle: Map of the New World
Colourway: Dark blue and white
Backstamp: Doulton

Size	Current Market Value		
	U.K. £	U.S. $	Can. $
Large	75.00	125.00	200.00

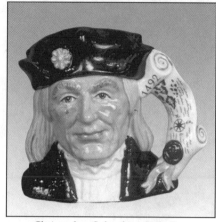

Christopher Columbus, Style One

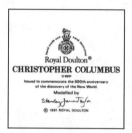

STYLE TWO: HANDLE — THE SHIP *SANTA MARIA*

This jug was issued to recognize the 500th anniversary of Columbus's voyage to America in 1492. It was created exclusively for the Royal Doulton International Collectors Club and was issued in a limited edition of 7,500. The jug was exhibited in the British Pavillion at Expo '92 in Seville, Spain.

Designer: Stanley J. Taylor

Statistics:	**Doulton** Number	Size	Height	Issued
	D6911	Small	3 ½", 8.9 cm	See below

Issued: 1992 in a limited edition of 7,500
Handle: The ship *Santa Maria*
Colourway: Brown, light brown, grey and cream
Backstamp: Doulton / RDICC / Christopher Columbus
"Admiral of the Oceans." Exclusively For Collectors Club The Discovery Edition of 7,500
Series: RDICC

Size	Current Market Value		
	U.K. £	U.S. $	Can. $
Small	85.00	150.00	175.00

Note: For Columbus see the "Explorers Set" page 178.

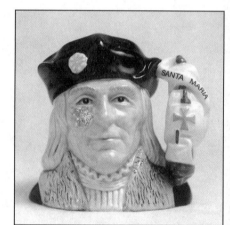

Christopher Columbus, Style Two

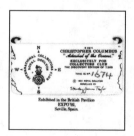

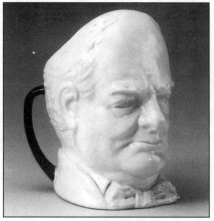

Variation No. 1

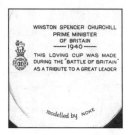

CHURCHILL

Sir Winston Leonard Spencer Churchill (1874-1965) was first lord of the Admiralty, Home Secretary and Prime Minister on three occasions. As Prime Minister during World War II, he led Britain to victory and captured the spirit of the Allies with his famous radio broadcasts. He was awarded the Nobel Prize for Literature in 1953.

Designer: Charles Noke

	Doulton			
Statistics:	**Number**	**Size**	**Height**	**Issued**
	D6170	Large	6 ½", 16.5 cm	See below

Handle: Plain
Backstamp: Doulton

VARIATION No. 1: With an inscription on the base
Colourway — Cream with two black handles

Issued: 1940-1941
Colourway: Cream; two black handles
Inscription: This loving cup was made during the "Battle of Britain" as a tribute to a great leader

		Current Market Value		
Size	**Variation**	**U.K. £**	**U.S. $**	**Can. $**
Large	Var. 1	5,000.00	9,000.00	11,000.00

VARIATION No. 2: Modelling portrays a young Churchill
Colourway — Very lightly coloured overall, with two grey handles;
Without inscription on base;
green Doulton backstamp

Issued: Unknown
Colourway: Very lightly coloured overall; two grey handles
Inscription: None

		Current Market Value		
Size	**Variation**	**U.K. £**	**U.S. $**	**Can. $**
Large	Var. 2		Extremely rare	

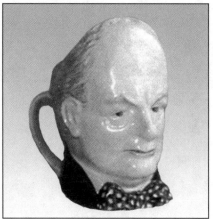

Variation No. 2

CHURCHILL (cont.)

VARIATION No. 3: Modelling portrays a young Churchill
Colourway — Fully decorated in natural
colours, with two dark brown handles
No inscription on base

Issued: Unknown
Colourway: Fully decorated in natural colours; two dark
brown handles
Inscription: None

| Size | Variation | Current Market Value | | |
		U.K. £	U.S. $	Can. $
Large	Var. 3	Extremely rare		

Note: For the Sir Winston Churchill character jug, see page 363.
For the Winston Churchill character jug, see page 397 and
for the Winston Churchill toby jug, see page 85.

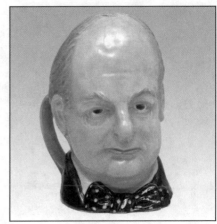

Variation No. 3

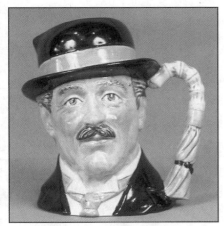

City Gent

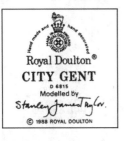

CITY GENT

Designer:	Stanley J. Taylor			

Statistics:	**Doulton**			
	Number	**Size**	**Height**	**Issued**
	D6815	Large	7", 17.8 cm	1988-1991

Handle:	Umbrella handle
Colourway:	Black and grey hat; black coat; white shirt; grey tie
Backstamp:	Doulton
Series:	The London Collection

	Current Market Value		
Size	**U.K. £**	**U.S. $**	**Can. $**
Large	75.00	150.00	175.00

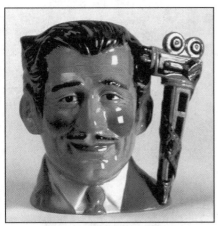

Clark Gable

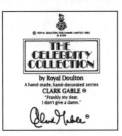

CLARK GABLE

An Ohio native, Clark Gable (1901-1960) worked in a tyre factory and as a lumberjack before he took up acting. He began his career in 1930 and appeared in over seventy films. He won an Academy Award in 1934 for his performance in *It Happened One Night,* but is perhaps best remembered as Rhett Butler in *Gone With the Wind*.

This jug was issued in the U.S.A. prior to approval from the Gable estate and had to be withdrawn when permission was denied. A small number of jugs are known to exist.

Designer:	Stanley J. Taylor			

Statistics:	**Doulton**			
	Number	**Size**	**Height**	**Issued**
	D6709	Large	7", 17.8 cm	1984-1984

Handle:	Movie camera entwined in film
Colourway:	Brown; light brown suit; tan tie
Backstamp:	Doulton
Series:	The Celebrity Collection

	Current Market Value		
Size	**U.K. £**	**U.S. $**	**Can. $**
Large	2,500.00	4,800.00	6,000.00

THE CLOWN

There are four recognised variations of The Clown without hat, those with red, brown, white or black hair.

STYLE ONE: CLOWN WITHOUT HAT

Designer: Harry Fenton
Backstamp: Doulton

Statistics:

Doulton Number	Size	Height	Issued
See below	Large	7 ½", 19.1 cm	See below

VARIATION No. 1: **Colourway** — Red hair
Handle — Multi-coloured

Issued: 1937-1942
Handle: Multi-coloured
Colourway: Red hair

Doulton Number	Variation	Colour	Current Market Value U.K. £	U.S. $	Can. $
D5610	Var. 1	Red hair	2,250.00	4,500.00	6,000.00

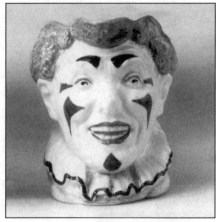

The Clown, Style One, Variation No. 1

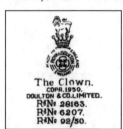

VARIATION No. 2: **Colourway** — Brown hair
Handle — Plain brown

Issued: c.1937-1942
Handle: Brown
Colourway: Brown hair

Doulton Number	Variation	Colour	Current Market Value U.K. £	U.S. $	Can. $
D5610	Var. 2	Brown hair	2,250.00	4,500.00	6,000.00

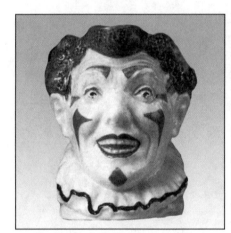

The Clown, Style One, Variation No. 2

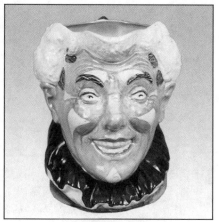

The Clown, Style One, Variation No. 3

STYLE ONE (cont.)

VARIATION No. 3: **Colourway** — White hair
Handle — Multi-coloured

Issued: 1951-1955
Handle: Multi-coloured
Colourway: White hair

Doulton Number	Variation	Colour	Current Market Value		
			U.K. £	U.S. $	Can. $
D6322	Var. 3	White hair	750.00	1,500.00	1,850.00

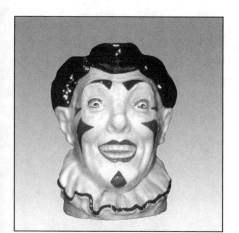

The Clown, Style One, Variation No. 4

VARIATION No. 4: **Colourway** — Black hair
Handle — Multi-coloured

Issued: c.1940s
Handle: Multi-coloured
Colourway: Black hair

Doulton Number	Variation	Colour	Current Market Value		
			U.K. £	U.S. $	Can. $
D6322	Var. 4	Black hair	Only one known to exist.		

THE CLOWN

STYLE TWO: CLOWN WITH HAT

Designer: Stanley J. Taylor

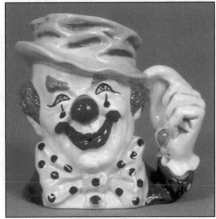

The Clown, Style Two

Statistics:

Doulton Number	Size	Height	Issued
D6834	Large	6 ½", 16.5 cm	1989-1995

Handle: Gloved hand touching cap
Colourway: Green cap; yellow bow tie with black spots; red nose and mouth
Backstamp: Doulton
Series: The Circus Performers

Size	Current Market Value		
	U.K. £	U.S. $	Can. $
Large	85.00	250.00	300.00

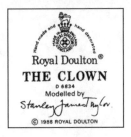

THE COLLECTOR

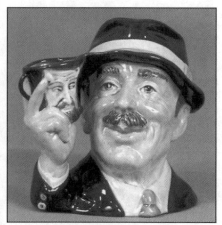

The Collector, Variation One

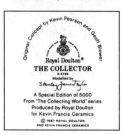

These jugs were commissioned by Kevin Francis Ceramics Ltd. The large size was issued in 1988 in a special edition of 5,000 pieces, and the small size was issued in 1991 in a special edition of 1,500 pieces. Note the Kevin Francis characteristic of the left-handed jug.

Designer: Geoff Blower
Modeller: Stanley J. Taylor

Statistics:	Doulton Number	Size	Height	Issued
1.	D6796	Large	7", 17.8 cm	See below
2.	D6906	Small	4", 10.1 cm	See below

Handle: A hand holding a Mephistopheles jug
Colourway: Black hat; dark green jacket; tan shirt
Backstamp: Doulton/Kevin Francis Ceramics
Series: The Collecting World

VARIATION No. 1: Colourway — Black hat; dark green jacket; tan shirt

Issued: 1. Large — 1988 in a special edition of 5,000
2. Small — 1991 in a special edition of 1,500
Colourway: Black hat; dark green jacket; tan shirt

Jug No.	Size	Current Market Value U.K. £	U.S. $	Can. $
1.	Large	100.00	225.00	300.00
2.	Small	85.00	175.00	225.00

VARIATION No. 2: Colourway — Creamy-blue hat; dark grey jacket; cream shirt; pale blue tie

Issued: Not put into production
Colourway: Creamy-blue hat; dark grey jacket; cream shirt; pale blue tie

Size	Current Market Value U.K. £	U.S. $	Can. $
Large	Sold November 21, 1999 Phillips, New Bond Street London, England, £1,400.00		

VARIATION No. 3: Colourway — Green hat; light green jacket; pale shirt; cream tie

Issued: Not put into production
Colourway: Green hat; light green jacket; pale shirt; cream tie

Size	Current Market Value U.K. £	U.S. $	Can. $
Large	Sold November 21, 1999 Phillips, New Bond Street London, England, £1,300.00		

CONFUCIUS

Issued in a limited edition of 1,750, this is the second jug to be decorated in flambé.

Designer: Robert I. Tabbenor

	Doulton			
Statistics:	**Number**	**Size**	**Height**	**Issued**
	D7003	Large	7", 17.8 cm	See below

Issued: 1995 in a limited edition of 1,750
Handle: Yin and Yang symbol and book of his teachings, "The Analects"
Colourway: Flambé
Backstamp: Doulton
Series: Flambé

	Current Market Value		
Size	**U.K. £**	**U.S. $**	**Can. $**
Large	250.00	550.00	750.00

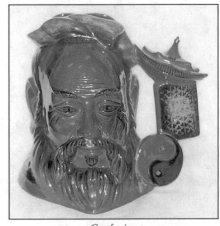

Confucius

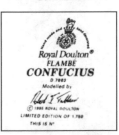

THE COOK AND THE CHESHIRE CAT

These are two characters from Lewis Carroll's *Alice's Adventures in Wonderland*.

Designer: William K. Harper

	Doulton			
Statistics:	**Number**	**Size**	**Height**	**Issued**
	D6842	Large	7", 17.8 cm	1990-1991

Handle: A Cheshire cat
Colourway: White mob cap trimmed with a blue bow
Backstamp: Doulton
Series: Alice In Wonderland

	Current Market Value		
Size	**U.K. £**	**U.S. $**	**Can. $**
Large	200.00	375.00	450.00

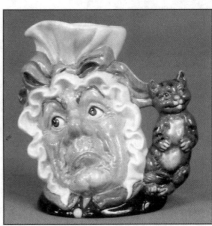

The Cook and The Cheshire Cat

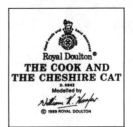

COUNT DRACULA

Count Dracula was the Character Jug of the Year for 1997.

Designer: David B. Biggs

	Doulton			
Statistics:	**Number**	**Size**	**Height**	**Issued**
	D7053	Large	7 ¼", 18.4 cm	1997-1997

Handle: Garlic, open window and a cross
Colourway: Black, red and brown
Backstamp: Doulton/Character Jug of the Year, 1997/
Sir Henry Doulton 1897-1997
Series: Character Jug of the Year

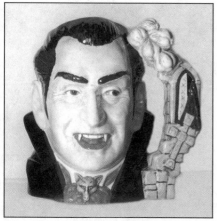

Count Dracula

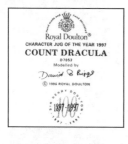

	Current Market Value		
Size	**U.K. £**	**U.S. $**	**Can. $**
Large	100.00	250.00	300.00

CYRANO DE BERGERAC

Designer: David B. Biggs

	Doulton			
Statistics:	**Number**	**Size**	**Height**	**Issued**
	D7004	Large	7", 17.8 cm	1995-1997

Handle: Sword, quill and letter
Colourway: Maroon jacket; white collar; black hat; white plume
Backstamp: Doulton

	Current Market Value		
Size	**U.K. £**	**U.S. $**	**Can. $**
Large	75.00	200.00	300.00

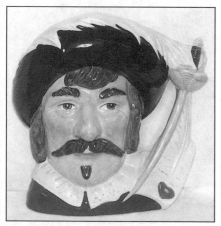

Cyrano De Bergerac

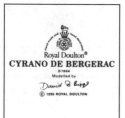

DaGAMA

For the character jug DaGama see the "Explorers Set" page 178.

D'ARTAGNAN

PROTOTYPE

Designer: Michael Abberley

Statistics:

	Doulton Number	Size	Height	Issued
	D —	Large	Unknown	See below

Modelled: 1981
Issued: Not put into production
Handle: Sword
Colourway: Black hat trimmed with yellow band and white feather; mustard tunic
Backstamp: Doulton

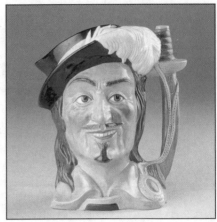

D'Artagnan, Prototype

Size	Description	Current Market Value U.K. £	U.S. $	Can. $
Large	Prototype		Extremely rare	

REGULAR ISSUE

A character in Alexandre Dumas' lively 19th-century fiction, D'Artagnan came to Paris to join the celebrated band of Three Musketeers and share their adventures.

Designer: Stanley J. Taylor

Statistics:

	Doulton Number	Size	Height	Issued
1.	D6691	Large	7 ½", 19.1 cm	1982-1995
2.	D6764	Small	4", 10.1 cm	1987-1995
3.	D6765	Miniature	2 ½", 6.4 cm	1987-1991

Handle: An extension of the feathers with a fleur-de-lis and sword at the base
Colourway: Black hat trimmed with white feathers; white lace collar
Backstamp: Doulton
Series: 1. The Three Musketeers
2. Characters From Literature

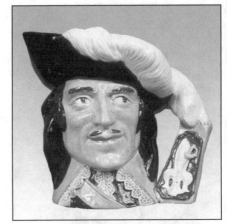

D'Artagnan, Regular Issue

Jug No.	Size	Current Market Value U.K. £	U.S. $	Can. $
1.	Large	100.00	150.00	225.00
2.	Small	75.00	150.00	200.00
3.	Miniature	75.00	150.00	200.00

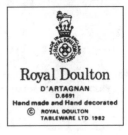

Royal Doulton
D'ARTAGNAN
D.6691
Hand made and Hand decorated
© ROYAL DOULTON
TABLEWARE LTD. 1982

DAVID COPPERFIELD

For the character jug David Copperfield see the "Charles Dickens Commemorative Set" page 143.

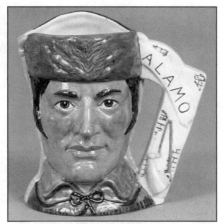

Davy Crockett

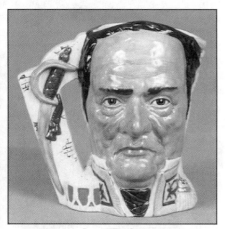

Antonio Lopez De Santa Anna

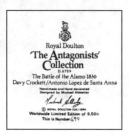

DAVY CROCKETT AND
ANTONIO LOPEZ DE SANTA ANNA

Davy Crockett (1786-1836) was a hunter and expert marksman, as well as a gregarious drinker. Antonio Lopez de Santa Anna (1795-1876) was a Mexican general who led troops on many missions into the U.S. He was finally defeated in Texas in 1837 and jailed for a year.

This jug was issued in 1985 in a limited edition of 9,500 pieces.

Designer: Michael Abberley

Statistics:	Doulton Number	Size	Height	Issued
	D6729	Large	7", 17.8 cm	See below

Issued: 1985 in a limited edition of 9,500
Handle: Crockett — Alamo, a horn, mission wall
Santa Anna — Sword, mission wall
Colourway: Yellow and brown
Backstamp: Doulton
Series: The Antagonists' Collection (Two-faced jug)

Size	Current Market Value		
	U.K. £	U.S. $	Can. $
Large	100.00	150.00	225.00

DENIS COMPTON C.B.E.

This jug was issued to commemorate Denis Charles Scott Compton, C.B.E., contribution to the sport of cricket during the 1940s and 1950s. This limited edition (9,500) character jug, commissioned by Lawleys By Post, joins the other great cricketers, Grace, Hutton, Bird and Johnston.

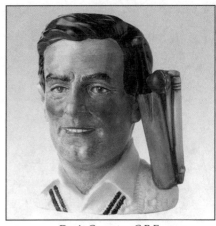

Designer: Stanley J. Taylor

Statistics:	Doulton Number	Size	Height	Issued
	D7076	Small	4 ½", 11.9 cm	See below

Issued: 1997 in a limited edition of 9,500
Handle: Cricket bat, ball and wicket
Colourway: Black, white and red
Backstamp: Doulton

Denis Compton C.B.E.

Size	Current Market Value		
	U.K. £	U.S. $	Can. $
Small	50.00	125.00	150.00

DENNIS AND GNASHER

Dennis the Menace is a cartoon character from the U.K. comic magazine, *The Beano*. To celebrate the 60th anniversary of *The Beano* comic in 1998 a special anniversary logo appeared on the base of the large and small jugs for that year.

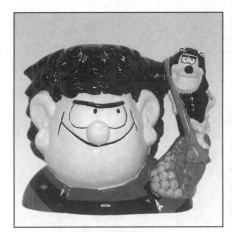

Designer: Simon Ward

Statistics:	Doulton Number	Size	Height	Issued
1.	D7005	Large	7", 17.8 cm	1995-1999
2.	D7033	Small	4", 10.1 cm	1996-1999

Handle: A bag of peas, pea shooter, Gnasher the dog
Colourway: Red, black and green
Backstamp: A. Doulton/© D.C. Thomson & Co., Ltd.
B. 60th Anniversary logo
Series: Characters from *The Beano* and *The Dandy*

Dennis and Gnasher

Jug No.	Size	Issued	Current Market Value		
			U.K. £	U.S. $	Can. $
1A.	Large	1995-1999	100.00	200.00	300.00
1B.		1998-1998	100.00	200.00	300.00
2A.	Small	1996-1999	60.00	125.00	175.00
2B.		1998-1998	60.00	125.00	175.00

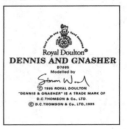

Royal Doulton®
DENNIS AND GNASHER
D7005
Modelled by
Simon Ward
© 1995 ROYAL DOULTON
"DENNIS & GNASHER" IS A TRADE MARK OF
D.C.THOMSON & Co. LTD.
© D.C.THOMSON & Co. LTD. 1995

DESPERATE DAN

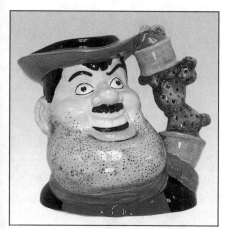

Desperate Dan

Desperate Dan is a cartoon character from the U.K. comic *The Dandy*. To celebrate the 60th anniversary of *The Dandy* comic in 1998 a special anniversary logo appeared on the base of the large and small jugs for that year.

Designer: Simon Ward

Statistics:	Doulton Number	Size	Height	Issued
1.	D7006	Large	7", 17.8 cm	1995-1999
2.	D7034	Small	4", 10.1 cm	1996-1999

Handle: A cow pie, cactus and jug of Owl Hoot juice
Colourway: Red shirt; black vest; blue scarf; brown and black hat
Backstamp: A. Doulton/© D.C. Thomson & Co., Ltd.
B. 60th Anniversary logo
Series: Characters from *The Beano* and *The Dandy*

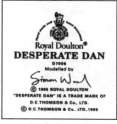

Backstamp A

Jug No.	Size	Issued	Current Market Value U.K. £	U.S. $	Can. $
1A.	Large	1995-1999	100.00	150.00	200.00
1B.		1998-1998	100.00	150.00	200.00
2A.	Small	1996-1999	60.00	90.00	125.00
2B.		1998-1998	60.00	90.00	125.00

DIAMOND ANNIVERSARY SET

This set was issued in 1994 to commemorate the Diamond Anniversary of the revival of the traditional Staffordshire jugs by Charles Noke in 1934. It was issued in a limited edition of 2,500 and came with a diamond shaped wall stand.

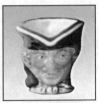

Dick Turpin

Designer: William K. Harper

Statistics:	**Doulton Number**	**Size**	**Height**	**Issued**
	See below	Tiny	1 ½", 3.8 cm	See below

Issued: 1994 in a limited edition of 2,500
Handle: As original model
Colourway:
1. **Dick Turpin** — Brown, grey and green
2. **John Barleycorn** — Browns
3. **Jester** — Brown, green and yellow
4. **Granny** — Grey and white
5. **Parson Brown** — Grey and white
6. **Simon the Cellarer** — Maroon and white

Backstamp: Doulton

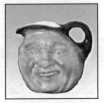

John Barleycorn

Jug No.	Doulton Number	Name	Current Market Value U.K. £	U.S. $	Can. $
1.	D6951	Dick Turpin	45.00	75.00	100.00
2.	D6952	John Barleycorn	45.00	75.00	100.00
3.	D6953	Jester	45.00	75.00	100.00
4.	D6954	Granny	45.00	75.00	100.00
5.	D6955	Parson Brown	45.00	75.00	100.00
6.	D6956	Simon the Cellarer	45.00	75.00	100.00
		Complete set / stand	250.00	425.00	575.00

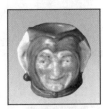

Jester

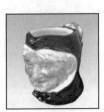

Granny

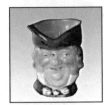

Parson Brown

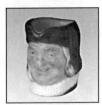

Simon the Cellarer

DICK TURPIN

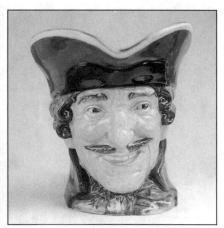

Dick Turpin, Style One

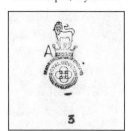

Dick Turpin (1705-1739) joined forces with fellow highwayman Tom King, whom he accidentally shot. Before he died, King betrayed him. Dick Turpin was hanged in 1739 for the murder of an Epping Forest gamekeeper.

The first style of the Dick Turpin jug has the mask up on the brim of the tricorn, and a pistol forms the handle. All of the sizes should have "R.T." inscribed on the pistol grip; however, it may be more obvious on certain jugs due to the casting variations. There is no premium value whether or not the "R.T." inscription is visible.

STYLE ONE: HANDLE — A PISTOL

Designer: Charles Noke
Harry Fenton

Statistics:	Doulton Number	Size	Height	Issued
1.	D5485	Large	6 ½", 16.5 cm	1935-1960
2.	D5618	Small	3 ½", 8.9 cm	1936-1960
3.	D6128	Miniature	2 ¼", 5.7 cm	1940-1960

Handle: Pistol
Colourway: Brown hat; black mask up; green coat; white cravat
Backstamps: A. Doulton
B. Doulton / Bentalls / Souvenir From Bentalls 1936

Jug No.	Size	Issued	Current Market Value		
			U.K. £	U.S. $	Can. $
1A.	Large	1935-1960	100.00	175.00	225.00
2A.	Small	1936-1960	50.00	70.00	90.00
2B.	Small	1936-1936	450.00	750.00	1,000.00
3A.	Miniature	1940-1960	40.00	50.00	65.00

Dick Turpin Derivative

Item: MATCH STAND/ASHTRAY
Height: 2 ¾", 7.0 cm
Issued: 1936-1960

Doulton Number	Item	Current Market Value		
		U.K. £	U.S. $	Can. $
D5601	Match Stand/Ashtray	85.00	150.00	200.00

Note: 1. All three sizes of Dick Turpin, Style One are found in white gloss.
2. For tiny version of the Dick Turpin character jug see the "Diamond Anniversary Set" page 164.

DICK TURPIN

This second style of Dick Turpin has the mask covering the eyes, and the handle depicts a horse's head and neck.

STYLE TWO: HANDLE — NECK AND HEAD OF HORSE

Designer: David B. Biggs

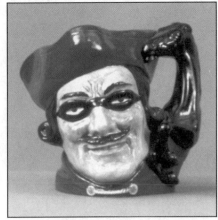

Dick Turpin, Style Two

Statistics:	Doulton Number	Size	Height	Issued
1.	D6528	Large	7", 17.8 cm	1960-1981
2.	D6535	Small	3 ¾", 9.5 cm	1960-1981
3.	D6542	Miniature	2 ¼", 5.7 cm	1960-1981

Handle: Head and neck of a horse
Colourway: Green tricorn; black mask over the eyes; red jacket
Backstamp: Doulton

Jug No.	Size	Comp.	Issued	Current Market Value U.K. £	U.S. $	Can. $
1.	Large	EW	1960-1981	65.00	100.00	135.00
		ETC	1968-1971	125.00	180.00	200.00
2.	Small	EW	1960-1981	40.00	80.00	100.00
		ETC	1968-1971	75.00	125.00	150.00
3.	Miniature	EW	1960-1981	40.00	75.00	100.00
		ETC	1968-1971	60.00	100.00	125.00

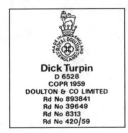

Dick Turpin
D 6528
COPR 1959
DOULTON & CO LIMITED
Rd No 893841
Rd No 39649
Rd No 8313
Rd No 420/59

Note: The large size jug Dick Turpin, Style Two is found in white gloss.

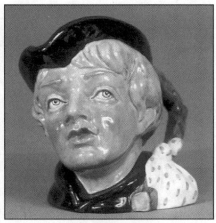

Dick Whittington

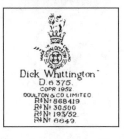

DICK WHITTINGTON

The first Dick Whittington jug was styled on the character of a poor orphan boy who was employed in a London kitchen, as described in a play dated 1605. He gave his cat to his employer to sell to earn money, but then ran away to escape his evil employer's cook who mistreated him. The Bow Bells rang as he fled and seemed to say, "Turn back, Whittington, Lord Mayor of London." He obeyed and found that his cat had fetched a huge sum, making him a wealthy man.

Designer: Geoff Blower

Statistics:	Doulton Number	Size	Height	Issued
	D6375	Large	6 ½", 16.5 cm	1953-1960

Handle: A stick and handkerchief
Colourway: Dark green cap and robes
Backstamp: Doulton

	Current Market Value		
Size	U.K. £	U.S. $	Can. $
Large	275.00	550.00	700.00

DICK WHITTINGTON
LORD MAYOR OF LONDON

Richard Whittington (1358-1423), in actual fact, made his fortune as a textile dealer. He entered London politics as a councilman and rose to become the Lord Mayor of London in 1397, an office he held three times.

This jug was commissioned by The Guild of Specialist China and Glass Retailers and issued in 1989 in a special edition of 5,000 pieces.

Designer: William K. Harper

Statistics:	Doulton Number	Size	Height	Issued
	D6846	Large	7 ½", 19.1 cm	See below

Issued: 1989 in a special edition of 5,000
Handle: Handle is of a signpost to London, the Bow Bells are above the signpost and a sack of gold is at the base
Colourway: Blue tricorn hat trimmed with white feathers; blue coat trimmed with white fur; yellow chain of office
Backstamp: Doulton/Guild of Specialist China and Glass Retailers

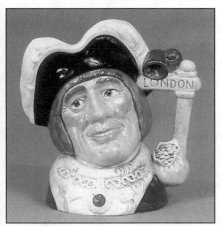

Dick Whittington, Lord Mayor of London

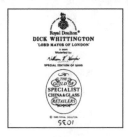

	Current Market Value		
Size	U.K. £	U.S. $	Can. $
Large	85.00	200.00	225.00

DOC HOLLIDAY

The son of a lawyer, John Henry Holliday (1852-1887) worked as a dentist in Baltimore, Maryland. At the age of 20 he learned he had tuberculosis and moved west to a warmer climate to prolong his life. He became adept at using firearms and the bowie knife and became known for his wild gambling, brawls and shootouts. He survived the famous gunfight at the O.K. Corral, but died in a sanatorium at age 35.

Designer: Stanley J. Taylor

Statistics:	Doulton Number	Size	Height	Issued
	D6731	Mid	5 ½", 14.0 cm	1985-1989

Handle: Pistol in a holster and dice
Colourway: Black and grey hat; black coat
Backstamp: Doulton
Series: The Wild West Collection

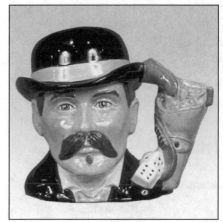

Doc Holliday

	Current Market Value		
Size	U.K. £	U.S. $	Can. $
Mid	85.00	150.00	175.00

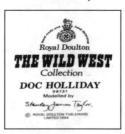

DON QUIXOTE

Don Quixote is the hero of the novel by Cervantes, a satirical parody of the chivalrous knight. Don Quixote leads a life of adventure, capturing many hearts along the way.

The helmet colour of the jugs varies from dark grey to light grey, with no difference in value.

Designer: Geoff Blower

Statistics:		Doulton Number	Size	Height	Issued
	1.	D6455	Large	7 ¼", 18.4 cm	1957-1991
	2.	D6460	Small	3 ¼", 8.3 cm	1957-1991
	3.	D6511	Miniature	2 ½", 6.4 cm	1960-1991

Issued: See below
Handle: A feather with a shield at the base
Colourway: Blue-grey helmet; dark green robes
Backstamp: Doulton
Series: Characters From Literature

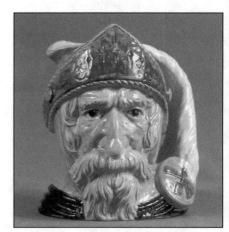

Don Quixote

Jug No.	Size	Comp.	Issued	Current Market Value		
				U.K. £	U.S. $	Can. $
1.	Large	EW	1957-1991	85.00	125.00	150.00
		ETC	1968-1971	125.00	200.00	225.00
2.	Small	EW	1957-1991	50.00	70.00	80.00
		ETC	1968-1971	65.00	100.00	125.00
3.	Miniature	EW	1960-1991	40.00	65.00	85.00
		ETC	1968-1971	65.00	100.00	125.00

DR LIVINGSTONE

For the character jug Dr Livingstone see the "Explorers Set" page 178.

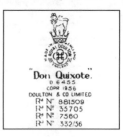

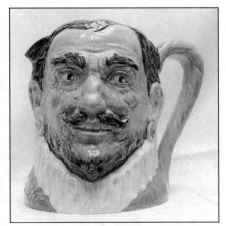

Drake, Style One, Variation No. 1

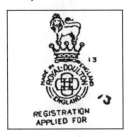

DRAKE

Sir Francis Drake (1540-1596) was an English navigator and admiral. He was Queen Elizabeth I's right hand against the Spanish, going on many plundering expeditions in the Spanish West Indies. On one of these voyages, between 1577 and 1580, Drake became the first Englishman to sail around the world. He also repelled the Spanish Armada sent to invade England.

STYLE ONE: WITHOUT HAT

Designer: Harry Fenton

Statistics:	Doulton Number	Size	Height	Issued
	D6115	Large	5 ¾", 14.6 cm	1940-1941

Handle: Plain
Backstamp: Doulton

VARIATION No. 1: Colourway — White ruff; red-brown collar
The raised lettering "Sir Francis Drake" on the back of the coat is painted over.

Colourway: White ruff; red-brown collar

Size	Variation	Current Market Value		
		U.K. £	U.S. $	Can. $
Large	Var. 1	2,250.00	5,000.00	6,500.00

VARIATION No. 2: Colourway — White ruff; green collar
The raised lettering "Sir Francis Drake" on the back of the coat is painted white, highlighting the name.

Colourway: White ruff; green collar

Size	Variation	Current Market Value		
		U.K. £	U.S. $	Can. $
Large	Var. 2	Sold at Phillips Auction, London England, October 29, 1998, £4,850.00		

Note: Drake, Style One, is found in white gloss.

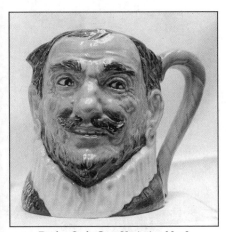

Drake, Style One, Variation No. 2

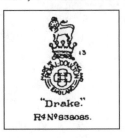

DRAKE (cont.)

STYLE TWO: WITH HAT

Designer: Harry Fenton

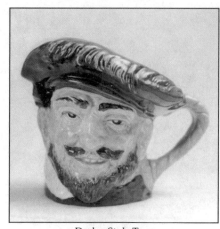

	Doulton			
Statistics:	**Number**	**Size**	**Height**	**Issued**
1.	D6115	Large	5 ¾", 14.6 cm	1940-1960
2.	D6174	Small	3 ¼", 8.3 cm	1941-1960

Handle: Rope
Colourway: Brown hat; green robes; white ruff; brown drum at back of handle along side ruff
Backstamp: Doulton

Jug		Current Market Value		
No.	**Size**	**U.K. £**	**U.S. $**	**Can. $**
1.	Large	100.00	175.00	225.00
2.	Small	55.00	80.00	100.00

Drake, Style Two

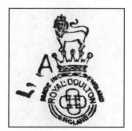

Note: 1. Drake, Style Two large and small jugs are found in white gloss.
2. For the toby jug Sir Francis Drake see page 80, and for the character jug Sir Francis Drake see page 357.

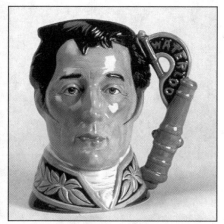

Duke of Wellington

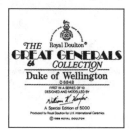

DUKE OF WELLINGTON

Arthur Wellesley (1769-1852), first Duke of Wellington, was a British general and statesman. He led the British forces in the defeat of Napoleon at Waterloo in 1815 and also served as Prime Minister from 1828 to 1830.

This jug was commissioned by UK International Ceramics Ltd., in a special edition of 5,000.

Designer: William K. Harper

	Doulton			
Statistics:	**Number**	**Size**	**Height**	**Issued**
	D6848	Large	7 ¼", 18.4 cm	See below

Issued: 1989 in a special edition of 5,000
Handle: Cannon above a banner reading "Waterloo"
Colourway: Blue and gold
Backstamp: Doulton
Series: The Great Generals Collection

	Current Market Value		
Size	**U.K. £**	**U.S. $**	**Can. $**
Large	100.00	150.00	200.00

Note: For the character jug Wellington see "Napoleon and Wellington" page 287.

EARL MOUNTBATTEN OF BURMA

A British naval and military leader, Louis Francis Albert Victor Nicholas Mountbatten (1900-1979) was the last Viceroy of India. Mountbatten was Governor-General of the Dominion of India from 1947 to 1948, relinquishing power to native rule in 1948. Upon his retirement from the navy in 1959, he became the principal military adviser to the Ministry of Defence. He was killed when a bomb exploded his fishing boat off the coast of Ireland.

This jug was commissioned by Lawleys By Post. It was issued in 1989 as one of a set of three, in a limited edition of 9,500 pieces.

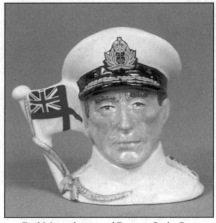

Earl Mountbatten of Burma, Style One

STYLE ONE: HANDLE — NAVAL ENSIGN

Designer: Stanley J. Taylor

Statistics:

Doulton Number	Size	Height	Issued
D6851	Small	3 ¼", 8.3 cm	See below

Issued: 1990 in a limited edition of 9,500
Handle: Naval ensign
Colourway: White naval uniform trimmed with gold
Backstamp: Doulton
Series: Heroic Leaders

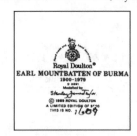

	Current Market Value		
Size	U.K. £	U.S. $	Can. $
Small	125.00	150.00	200.00

STYLE TWO: HANDLE — ANCHOR AND INTERTWINED ROPE

This was the first large-size character jug to be commissioned by the Royal Doulton International Collectors Club and was issued in a limited edition of 5,000 jugs.

Designer: Stanley J. Taylor

Statistics:

Doulton Number	Size	Height	Issued
D6944	Large	7", 17.8 cm	See below

Issued: 1993 in a limited edition of 5,000
Handle: Anchor and intertwined rope
Colourway: Yellow, black and white
Backstamp: Doulton/RDICC
Series: RDICC

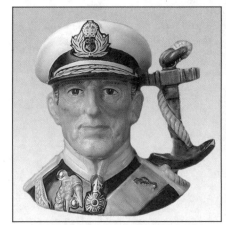

Earl Mountbatten of Burma, Style Two

	Current Market Value		
Size	U.K. £	U.S. $	Can. $
Large	150.00	275.00	300.00

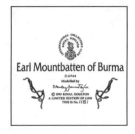

EDWARD VII

Edward VII ascended to the throne after the death of his mother, Queen Victoria, in 1901. That same year, he granted his Royal Warrant and allowed the name "Royal Doulton" to be used.

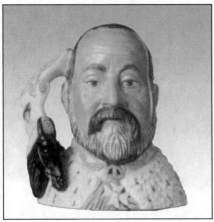

Edward VII

STYLE TWO: HANDLE — PORTRAIT OF LILY LANGTRY; THE HEAD OF A HORSE

Designer: Robert Tabbenor

	Doulton			
Statistics:	**Number**	**Size**	**Height**	**Issued**
	D7154	Large	7 ½", 19.1 cm	See below

Issued: 2001 in a limited edition of 1,000
Handle: Portrait of Lily Langtree; the head of a horse
Colourway: Gold, cream, black and brown
Backstamp: Doulton

	Current Market Value		
Size	U.K. £	U.S. $	Can. $
Large	150.00	310.00	—

Note: For King Edward VII see page 246, for Edward VII, Style One, see the "Kings and Queens of the Realm" page 247.

THE ELEPHANT TRAINER

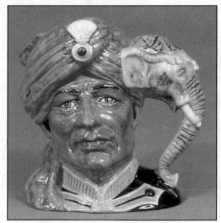

The Elephant Trainer

Designer: Stanley J. Taylor

Statistics:

	Doulton Number	Size	Height	Issued
1A.	D6841	Large	7", 17.8 cm	1990-1993
1B.	D6856	Large	7", 17.8 cm	1989 Ltd. ed.
1C.	D6857	Large	7", 17.8 cm	1989 Ltd. ed.

Issued: A. 1990-1993
B. 1989 in a limited edition of 250
C. 1989 in a limited edition of 250

Handle: Head of an elephant

Colourway: Orange turban; black coat trimmed with green and yellow

Backstamps: A. Doulton
General issue, 1990.
B. Doulton/The Higbee Company/To commemorate the Fourth Anniversary of the opening of The Royal Doulton Room The Higbee Company, Cleveland, Ohio, U.S.A. Commissioned by the Higbee Company, Cleveland, Ohio. Issued in 1989 in a limited edition of 250 pieces.
C. Doulton/Royal Doulton Rooms USA Strawbridge and Clothier, Hornes, Holmes/To commemorate the anniversary of the opening of the Royal Doulton Rooms in the United States of America. Issued in a limited edition of 250.

Series: The Circus Performers

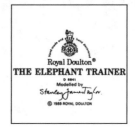

Jug. No	Doulton Number	Backstamp	Current Market Value U.K. £	U.S. $	Can. $
1A.	D6841	Doulton	125.00	275.00	300.00
1B.	D6856	Higbee	250.00	325.00	350.00
1C.	D6857	Strawbridge	250.00	325.00	350.00

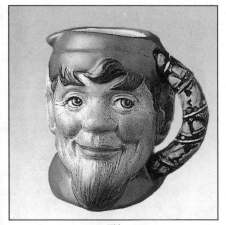

Elf

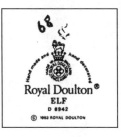

ELF

The Elf miniature character jug was specially commissioned for the U.S. market. It was designed to complement the miniature Caroler (D7007), Christmas Angel (D7051), Mrs. Claus (D6922), Santa Claus (D6900) and Snowman (D6972). Although commissioned for the U.S. market, the jug was also available in other countries through the Royal Doulton International Collectors Club.

Designer: William K. Harper

Statistics:	Doulton Number	Size	Height	Issued
	D6942	Miniature	2 ¾", 7.0 cm	1993-1993

Handle: Holly wreath
Colourway: Green
Backstamp: Doulton
Series: Christmas Miniatures

	Current Market Value		
Size	U.K. £	U.S. $	Can. $
Miniature	75.00	135.00	165.00

ELGAR

The Elgar jug completes the eight-piece Great Composers collection. One of England's greatest composers, Edward Elgar (1857-1934) is especially remembered for his Pomp and Circumstance marches, especially *Land of Hope and Glory*, which is traditionally part of the fitting climax to the Promenade Concerts *Last Night of the Proms*.

Designer: Stanley J. Taylor

Statistics:	Doulton Number	Size	Height	Issued
	D7118	Large	7", 17.8 cm	1998-2001

Handle: Organ pipes, *Land of Hope and Glory*
Colourway: Black, white, brown and cream
Backstamp: Doulton
Series: Great Composers

	Current Market Value		
Size	U.K. £	U.S. $	Can. $
Large	100.00	175.00	300.00

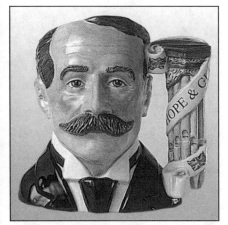

Elgar

ELVIS PRESLEY

PROTOTYPE

Elvis Aaron Presley (1935-1977), the "King of Rock 'n' Roll," was the most popular artist in the history of American rock music. After his debut in 1955, he appeared in 33 films, as well as on numerous albums. This jug was not issued due to copyright problems, and while at least two prototypes are known to exist, none are known to be in private collections.

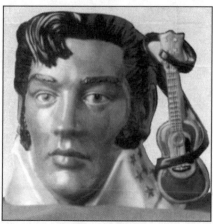

Elvis Presley

Designer:	Stanley J. Taylor			
	Doulton			
Statistics:	**Number**	**Size**	**Height**	**Issued**
	D6730	Large	7 ¼", 18.4 cm	See below

Modelled:	1985
Issued:	Not put into production
Handle:	Guitar and strap
Colourway:	Black hair; white shirt with gold trim
Backstamp:	Doulton
Series:	The Celebrity Collection

	Current Market Value		
Size	U.K. £	U.S. $	Can. $
Large	Only two known to exist		

THE ENGINE DRIVER

Each jug in the Journey Through Britain series was given a specially designed backstamp relating to the subject of the jug. The backstamp on the Engine Driver has the wording within the outline of a locomotive engine. It was issued through Lawleys By Post in a limited edition of 5,000 pieces.

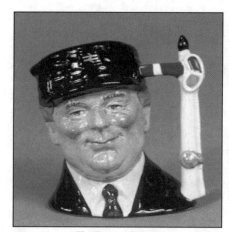

The Engine Driver

Designer:	Stanley J. Taylor			
	Doulton			
Statistics:	**Number**	**Size**	**Height**	**Issued**
	D6823	Small	4", 10.1 cm	See below

Issued:	1988 in a limited edition of 5,000
Handle:	A railway signal
Colourway:	Black cap and coat; white shirt
Backstamp:	Doulton
Series:	Journey Through Britain

	Current Market Value		
Size	U.K. £	U.S. $	Can. $
Small	100.00	150.00	200.00

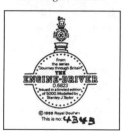

ERIC KNOWLES

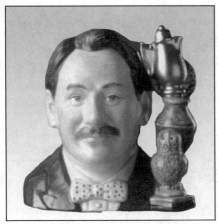

Eric Knowles

Eric Knowles is a director of the Bonham Auction House and is well known for his appearances on the U.K. television programme, the *Antiques Road Show*.

This jug was issued by Lawleys By Post in a limited edition of 1,500.

Designer: David B. Biggs

Statistics:	Doulton Number	Size	Height	Issued
	D7130	Small	4", 10.1 cm	See below

Issued: 1999 in a limited edition of 1,500
Handle: Owl jar, silver coffee pot, vase, blue and white plate
Colourway: Black jacket; yellow dotted bow tie
Backstamp: Doulton

	Current Market Value		
Size	U.K. £	U.S. $	Can. $
Small	80.00	132.00	—

EVERTON (FOOTBALL CLUB)

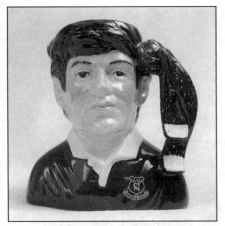

Everton (Football Club)

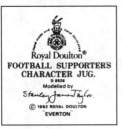

Designer: Stanley J. Taylor

Statistics:	Doulton Number	Size	Height	Issued
	D6926	Small	5", 12.7 cm	1992-1999

Handle: Team coloured scarf
Colourway: Blue and white uniform
Backstamp: Doulton
Series: The Football Supporters

	Current Market Value		
Size	U.K. £	U.S. $	Can. $
Small	50.00	100.00	125.00

EXPLORERS

The Explorers collection present six tiny character jugs modelled after the great explorers who ushered in a new era in world history. Each set, issued in a limited edition of 2,500, comes complete with a wooden wall mount display stand.

Designer: Stanley J. Taylor

Statistics:

	Doulton Number	Size	Height	Issued
	See below	Tiny	1 ½", 3.8 cm	See below

Issued: 1997 in limited edition of 2,500
Handle: Globe and navigation chart showing each man's area of exploration
Colourway:
1. **Columbus** — Red, grey, blue and tan
2. **Scott** — Browns
3. **DaGama** — Green, grey and brown
4. **Marco Polo** — Red, brown, green and grey
5. **Dr. Livingstone** — Yellow, browm and green
6. **Cook** — Dark blue, yellow, white and tan

Backstamp: Doulton

Jug No.	Doulton Number	Name	Current Market Value U.K. £	U.S. $	Can. $
1.	D7081	Columbus	50.00	80.00	100.00
2.	D7082	Scott	50.00	80.00	100.00
3.	D7083	DaGama	50.00	80.00	100.00
4.	D7084	Marco Polo	50.00	80.00	100.00
5.	D7085	Dr. Livingstone	50.00	80.00	100.00
6.	D7086	Cook	50.00	80.00	100.00
		Complete Set	275.00	450.00	550.00

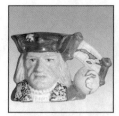

Columbus

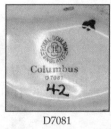

D7081

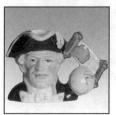

Cook

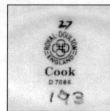

D7086

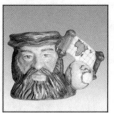

DaGama

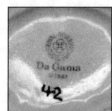

D7083

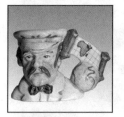

Dr. Livingstone

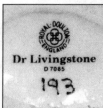

D7085

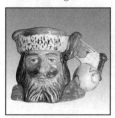

Marco Polo

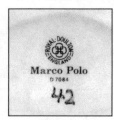

D7084

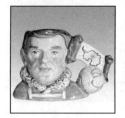

Scott

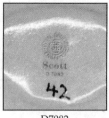

D7082

FAGIN

For the character jug Fagin see the "Charles Dickens Commemorative Set" page 143.

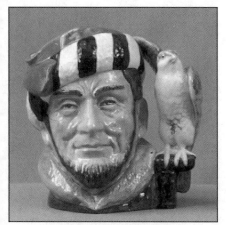

The Falconer, Variation No. 1

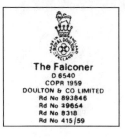

The Falconer
D 6540
COPR 1959
DOULTON & CO LIMITED
Rd No 893846
Rd No 39654
Rd No 8318
Rd No 415/59

THE FALCONER

Once called the sport of kings, falconry is the art of training birds of prey for the hunt. The sport began in China more than 3,000 years ago and still enjoys popularity in Europe and North America.

Designer: Max Henk
Handle: A falcon

VARIATION No. 1: Colourway — Green with black and white striped fur hat; green coat; grey and white falcon

Statistics:	Doulton Number	Size	Height	Issued
1.	D6533	Large	7 ½", 19.1 cm	1960-1991
2.	D6540	Small	3 ¾", 9.5 cm	1960-1991
3.	D6547	Miniature	2 ¾", 7.0 cm	1960-1991

Colourway: Green with black and white striped fur hat; green coat; grey and white falcon
Backstamp: Doulton

Jug No.	Size	Comp.	Issued	Current Market Value U.K. £	U.S. $	Can. $
1.	Large	EW	1960-1991	75.00	100.00	125.00
		ETC	1968-1971	100.00	175.00	200.00
2.	Small	EW	1960-1991	50.00	70.00	90.00
		ETC	1968-1971	75.00	100.00	125.00
3.	Miniature	EW	1960-1991	45.00	60.00	80.00
		ETC	1968-1971	55.00	80.00	100.00

VARIATION No. 2: Colourway — Dark green and brown striped fur hat; dark brown coat; ginger beard; brown falcon

Statistics:	Doulton Number	Size	Height	Issued
	D6798	Large	7 ½", 19.1 cm	See below

Issued: 1987 in a limited edition of 250
Colourway: Dark green and brown striped fur hat; dark brown coat; ginger beard; brown falcon
Backstamp: Doulton/Joseph Horne Company / Celebrating the opening of The Royal Doulton Room, Hornes, Pittsburgh, Pennsylvania, U.S.A. Specially commissioned from Royal Doulton by the Joseph Horne Company, Pittsburgh, Pennsylvania, U.S.A. Issued in 1987 in a limited edition of 250 pieces.

Size	Variation	Current Market Value U.K. £	U.S. $	Can. $
Large	Var. 2	175.00	275.00	325.00

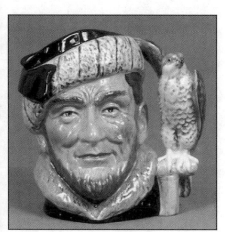

The Falconer, Variation No. 2

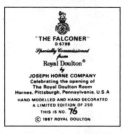

"THE FALCONER"
D 6798
Specially Commissioned from
Royal Doulton®
by
JOSEPH HORNE COMPANY
Celebrating the opening of
The Royal Doulton Room
Hornes, Pittsburgh, Pennsylvania, U.S.A
HAND MODELLED AND HAND DECORATED
A LIMITED EDITION OF 250
THIS IS NO. 76
© 1987 ROYAL DOULTON

THE FALCONER (cont.)

VARIATION No. 3: Colourway — Black with maroon and white striped fur hat; red-brown coat; brown falcon

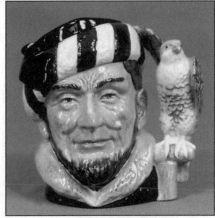

Statistics:	Doulton Number	Size	Height	Issued
	D6800	Large	7 ½", 19.1 cm	See below

Issued: 1987 in a special edition of 1000
Colourway: Black with maroon and white striped fur hat; red-brown coat; brown falcon
Backstamp: Doulton / Peter Jones China Ltd / New Colourway 1987 Special Commission 1000 Peter Jones Collection Leeds and Wakefield Commissioned by Peter Jones China Ltd, Leeds and Wakefield, England. Issued in 1987 in a special edition of 1,000 pieces.

The Falconer, Variation No. 3

		Current Market Value		
Size	Variation	U.K. £	U.S. $	Can. $
Large	Var. 3	125.00	225.00	300.00

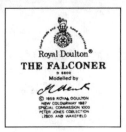

FALSTAFF

A trial piece exists in a red and dark green colourway, but it was not released for sale.

Designer: Harry Fenton
Handle: Plain

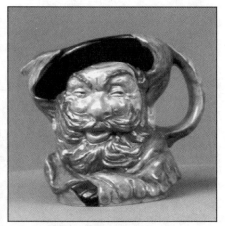

Falstaff, Variation No. 1

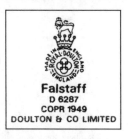

VARIATION No. 1: **Colourway** — Rose tunic; black hat, rose plumes; grey beard

Statistics:	Doulton Number	Size	Height	Issued
1.	D6287	Large	6", 15.0 cm	1950-1995
2.	D6385	Small	3 ½", 8.9 cm	1950-1995
3.	D6519	Miniature	2 ½", 6.4 cm	1960-1991

Issued: See below
Colourway: Rose tunic; black hat, rose plumes; grey beard
Backstamp: Doulton
Series: Characters From Literature

Jug No.	Size	Comp.	Issued	Current Market Value		
				U.K. £	U.S. $	Can. $
1.	Large	EW	1950-1995	75.00	125.00	150.00
		ETC	1968-1971	125.00	175.00	200.00
2.	Small	EW	1950-1995	40.00	55.00	65.00
		ETC	1968-1971	55.00	85.00	95.00
3.	Miniature	EW	1960-1991	45.00	65.00	80.00
		ETC	1968-1971	60.00	90.00	100.00

VARIATION No. 2: **Colourway** — Yellow tunic; black hat, yellow plumes; brown beard

Statistics:	Doulton Number	Size	Height	Issued
	D6795	Large	6", 15.0 cm	See below

Issued: 1987 in a sepcial edition of 1,500
Colourway: Yellow tunic; black hat with yellow plumes; brown beard
Backstamp: Doulton/U.K. Fairs Ltd.
Produced exclusively for U.K. Fairs Ltd. in a special edition of 1,500.

Size	Variation	Current Market Value		
		U.K. £	U.S. $	Can. $
Large	Var. 2	55.00	150.00	200.00

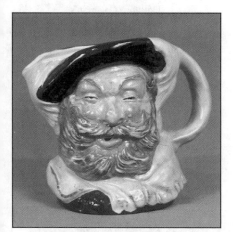

Falstaff, Variation No. 2

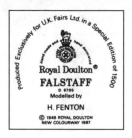

Falstaff Derivatives

Item:	TABLE LIGHTER	**Item:**	TEAPOT
Height:	3 ½", 8.9 cm	**Height:**	Unknown
Issued:	1958-1973	**Issued:**	1989-1991

Doulton Number	Item	Current Market Value		
		U.K. £	U.S. $	Can. $
D6385	Table Lighter	125.00	175.00	250.00
D6854	Teapot	125.00	200.00	250.00

Note: For the toby jug Falstaff see page 49.

FARMER JOHN

STYLE ONE: HANDLE — INSIDE JUG

Designer: Charles Noke

Statistics:	**Doulton Number**	**Size**	**Height**	**Issued**
1.	D5788	Large	6 ½", 16.5 cm	1938-Unk.
2.	D5789	Small	3 ¼", 8.3 cm	1938-Unk.

Handle: Brown handle set within the neck of the jug
Colourway: Browns
Backstamps: A. Doulton
B. Doulton/Coleman's/Coleman's Compliment

Jug			Current Market Value		
No.	Size	Issued	U.K. £	U.S. $	Can. $
1A.	Large	1938-Unknown	100.00	225.00	200.00
1B.		1938-1938	1,100.00	2,000.00	2,500.00
2A.	Small	1938-Unknown	50.00	90.00	125.00

Note: Both the large and small size jugs of Farmer John, Style One, are found in white gloss.

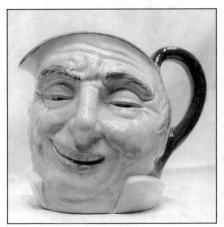

Farmer John, Style One

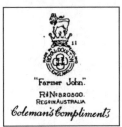

Backstamp B -
Doulton/Coleman's

STYLE TWO: HANDLE — OUTSIDE JUG

Designer: Charles Noke

Statistics:	**Doulton Number**	**Size**	**Height**	**Issued**
1.	D5788	Large	6 ½", 16.5 cm	Unk.-1960
2.	D5789	Small	3 ¼", 8.3 cm	Unk.-1960

Handle: Brown handle set at the top of the neck.
Colourway: Brown
Backstamp: Doulton

Jug			Current Market Value		
No.	Size	Issued	U.K. £	U.S. $	Can. $
1.	Large	Unknown-1960	100.00	150.00	175.00
2.	Small	Unknown-1960	50.00	75.00	100.00

Note: The large size, Farmer John, Style Two, is found in white gloss.

Farmer John Derivative

Item: ASH BOWL
Height: 3", 7.6 cm
Issued: 1939-1960

Doulton		Current Market Value		
Number	Item	U.K. £	U.S. $	Can. $
D6007	Ash Bowl	125.00	165.00	200.00

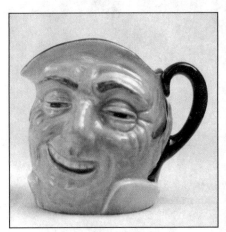

Farmer John, Style Two

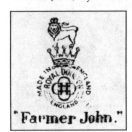

FAT BOY

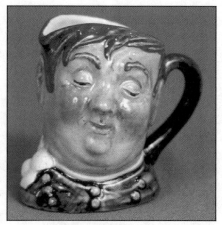

Fat Boy

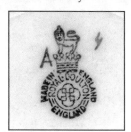

Another wonderful Dickens character, Joe, the Fat Boy, was the lazy glutton who worked as servant to Mr. Wardle in *The Pickwick Papers*.

Designer:	Leslie Harradine
	Harry Fenton

	Doulton			
Statistics:	**Number**	**Size**	**Height**	**Issued**
1.	D5840	Mid	4", 10.1 cm	1938-1948
2.	D5840	Small	3 ¼", 8.3 cm	1948-1960
3.	D6139	Miniature	2 ½", 6.4 cm	1940-1960
4.	D6142	Tiny	1 ½", 3.8 cm	1940-1960

Handle:	Plain
Colourway:	Blue shirt; white scarf
Backstamp:	Doulton

Jug		**Current Market Value**		
No.	**Size**	**U.K. £**	**U.S. $**	**Can. $**
1.	Mid	150.00	225.00	275.00
2.	Small	75.00	150.00	175.00
3.	Miniature	50.00	85.00	100.00
4.	Tiny	50.00	85.00	100.00

Fat Boy Derivatives

Item:	NAPKIN RING	**Item:**	TOOTHPICK HOLDER
Height:	3 ½", 8.9 cm	**Height:**	2 ¼", 5.7 cm
Issued:	1935-1939	**Issued:**	Unknown

Doulton		**Current Market Value**		
Number	**Item**	**U.K. £**	**U.S. $**	**Can. $**
M59	Napkin Ring	300.00	575.00	750.00
—	Toothpick Holder	600.00	900.00	1,000.00

Note: 1. The miniature Fat Boy jug is found in white gloss.

2. For the toby jug Fat Boy see page 50.

FIELD MARSHAL MONTGOMERY

Issued for the 50th anniversary of Montgomery's victory over Rommel in North Africa in 1942, this jug was produced in a limited edition of 2,500 pieces worldwide.

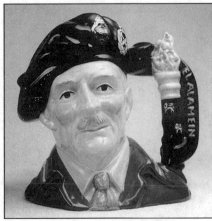

Designer: Stanley J. Taylor

	Doulton			
Statistics:	**Number**	**Size**	**Height**	**Issued**
	D6908	Large	6 ½", 16.5 cm	See below

Issued: 1992 in a limited edition of 2,500
Handle: Baton, oak leaves, "El Alamein"
Colourway: Black beret; khaki uniform; purple and cream baton
Backstamp: Doulton

	Current Market Value		
Size	**U.K. £**	**U.S. $**	**Can. $**
Large	125.00	250.00	300.00

Field Marshal Montgomery

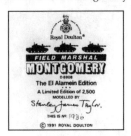

Note: For the character jug Monty see page 278, and for the character jug Viscount Montgomery of Alamein see page 390.

THE FIGURE COLLECTOR

Designer: Robert Tabbenor

	Doulton			
Statistics:	**Number**	**Size**	**Height**	**Issued**
	D7156	Small	4 ¾", 12.1 cm	2001-2001

Handle: A figure collector's book illustrating Amy, the inaugural Figure of the Year launched in 1990; RDICC logo
Colourway: Dark blue jacket; light blue shirt
Backstamp: Doulton
Series: RDICC

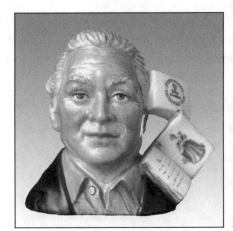

	Current Market Value		
Size	**U.K. £**	**U.S. $**	**Can. $**
Small	85.00	145.00	195.00

The Figure Collector

THE FIREMAN

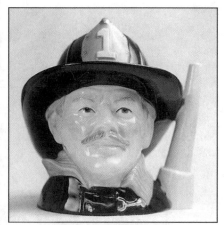

The Fireman, Style One

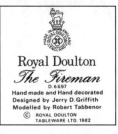

Launched exclusively by Griffith Pottery House in 1983, The Fireman jug was then released into the general range in 1984. Varieties of the handle exist, with the nozzle ranging from dark orange to light yellow, but there is no premium value for these colourway variations.

An error in this jug exists. The red background of the helmet badge was not applied during painting, resulting in a white badge. This curiosity piece has very little premium value.

STYLE ONE: HANDLE — NOZZLE OF FIRE HOSE

Designer: Jerry D. Griffith
Modeller: Robert I. Tabbenor

Statistics:	**Doulton Number**	**Size**	**Height**	**Issued**
	D6697	Large	7 ¼", 18.4 cm	See below

Handle: Nozzle of fire hose
Colourway: Black, brown and red helmet badge
Backstamps: **A.** Doulton/Hand made and hand decorated. No credits
 B. Doulton/Hand made and Hand decorated Modelled by Robert Tabbenor
 C. Doulton/Hand made and Hand decorated Designed by Jerry D. Griffith/Modelled by Robert Tabbenor

Jug No.	Size	Issued	Current Market Value		
			U.K. £	**U.S. $**	**Can. $**
1A.	Large	1984-1991	100.00	200.00	225.00
1B.		1984-1991	100.00	200.00	225.00
1C.		1983-1991	100.00	200.00	225.00

STYLE TWO: HANDLE — AXE AND FIRE HOSE

As with the other pieces in this series, the wording of the backstamp is contained within a design connected to the subject. This design is a coiled hose. Issued through Lawleys By Post in 1988, this jug was produced in a limited edition of 5,000 pieces.

Designer: Stanley J. Taylor

Statistics:	**Doulton Number**	**Size**	**Height**	**Issued**
	D6839	Small	4 ¼", 10.8 cm	See below

Issued: 1989 in a limited edition of 5,000
Handle: An axe and fire hose
Colourway: Yellow helmet; dark blue jacket
Backstamp: Doulton
Series: Journey Through Britain

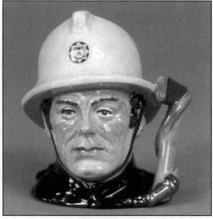

The Fireman, Style Two

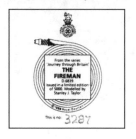

Size	Current Market Value		
	U.K. £	**U.S. $**	**Can. $**
Small	100.00	175.00	200.00

FISHERMAN

PROTOTYPE

Designer: David B. Biggs
Height: Unknown
Modelled: 1968
Issued: Not put into production
Handle: Lighthouse, fishing nets
Colourway: Black coat and hat; grey lighthouse
Backstamp: Doulton

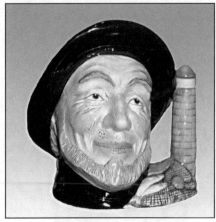

Fisherman, Prototype

Doulton Number	Description	Current Market Value U.K. £	U.S. $	Can. $
—	Prototype	Extremely rare		

THE FORTUNE TELLER

STYLE ONE: HANDLE — SIGNS OF THE ZODIAC

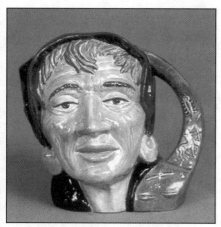

The Fortune Teller, Style One

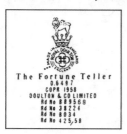

Designer: Garry Sharpe

Statistics:	Doulton Number	Size	Height	Issued
1.	D6497	Large	6 ¾", 17.2 cm	1959-1967
2.	D6503	Small	3 ¾", 9.5 cm	1959-1967
3.	D6523	Miniature	2 ½", 6.4 cm	1960-1967

Handle: Zodiac design
Colourway: Green scarf around head; black shawl; purple handle
Backstamp: Doulton

Jug No.	Size	Current Market Value		
		U.K. £	U.S. $	Can. $
1.	Large	400.00	650.00	850.00
2.	Small	225.00	400.00	500.00
3.	Miniature	250.00	400.00	500.00

STYLE TWO: HANDLE — TAROT CARDS

Beginning in 1991, one jug was selected as the Character Jug of the Year, produced for one year only and issued with a certificate of authenticity. The Fortune Teller was the Character Jug of the Year for 1991.

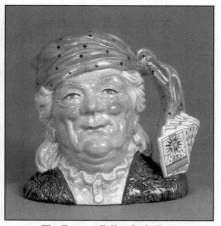

The Fortune Teller, Style Two

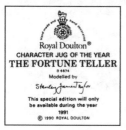

Designer: Stanley J. Taylor

Statistics:	Doulton Number	Size	Height	Issued
	D6874	Large	7", 17.8 cm	1991-1991

Handle: Bandana and tarot cards
Colourway: Orange polka-dot bandana; light blue shirt
Backstamp: Doulton/Character Jug of the Year, 1991
Series: Character Jug of the Year

Size	Current Market Value		
	U.K. £	U.S. $	Can. $
Large	175.00	325.00	350.00

FRANCIS ROSSI and RICK PARFITT (STATUS QUO)

Produced in a limited edition of 2,500, the Francis Rossi jug was issued in conjunction with the Rick Parfitt jug, commemorating the U.K. band, Status Quo. The Parfitt jug handle is on the left, and the Rossi handle is on the right, so they can be displayed as a pair.

Designer: Martyn C. R. Alcock

	Doulton			
Statistics:	**Number**	**Size**	**Height**	**Issued**
1.	D6961	Mid	5", 12.7 cm	See below
2.	D6962	Mid	5", 12.7 cm	See below

Issued: 1993 in a limited edition of 2,500
Handle: Cream and brown guitar
Colourway: Blue and brown
Backstamp: Doulton / © Phantom Music Ltd.

Jug No.	Doulton Number	Name	Current Market Value U.K. £	U.S. $	Can. $
1.	D6961	Francis Rossi	50.00	85.00	125.00
2.	D6962	Rick Parfitt	50.00	85.00	125.00
		Pair	100.00	175.00	225.00

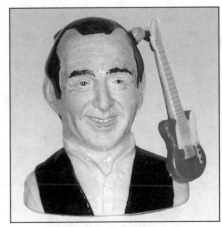

Francis Rossi

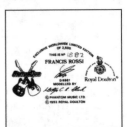

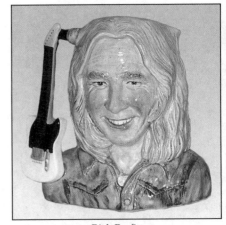

Rick Parfitt

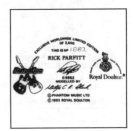

FRANKENSTEIN'S MONSTER

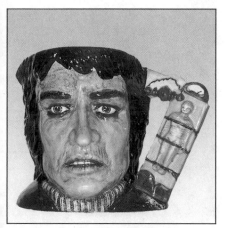

Frankenstein's Monster

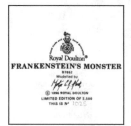

The Frankenstein character first appeared in a 19th century book written by Mary Shelley. The Hollywood film of 1931 starring Boris Karloff as Frankenstein creating his "monster" on the electric operating table carried the legend to new heights.

This jug was issued by Lawleys By Post in a limited edition of 2,500.

Designer: Martyn C. R. Alcock

Statistics:	Doulton Number	Size	Height	Issued
	D7052	Large	6 ½", 16.5 cm	See below

Issued: 1996 in a limited edition of 2,500
Handle: The monster on the electric table
Colourway: Black, brown and grey
Backstamp: Doulton

	Current Market Value		
Size	U.K. £	U.S. $	Can. $
Large	125.00	250.00	300.00

FREDDIE TRUEMAN O.B.E.

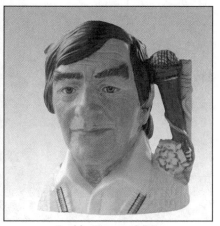

Freddie Truman O.B.E.

This jug was issued by Lawleys By Post in a limited edition of 9,500.

Designer: Stanley J. Taylor

Statistics:	Doulton Number	Size	Height	Issued
	D7090	Small	4 ¼", 10.8 cm	See below

Issued: 1997 in a limited edition of 9,500
Handle: Microphone, cricket stump and rosette
Colourway: Cream, black and brown
Backstamp: Doulton
Series: Cricketers

	Current Market Value		
Size	U.K. £	U.S. $	Can. $
Large	50.00	85.00	125.00

FRIAR TUCK

Fat and jolly and fond of drink, Friar Tuck joined the legendary Robin Hood and his band of rogues in Sherwood Forest as they robbed the rich to feed the poor in rural England.

Designer: Harry Fenton

Statistics:	**Doulton** **Number**	**Size**	**Height**	**Issued**
	D6321	Large	7", 17.8 cm	1951-1960

Handle: Tree trunk
Colourway: Light and dark brown robes; green oak leaves
Backstamp: Doulton

	Current Market Value		
Size	**U.K. £**	**U.S. $**	**Can. $**
Large	300.00	550.00	700.00

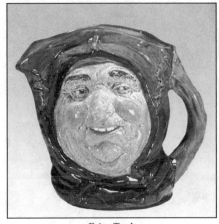

Friar Tuck

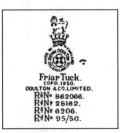

GAOLER

Designer: David B. Biggs

Statistics:	**Doulton** **Number**	**Size**	**Height**	**Issued**
1.	D6570	Large	7", 17.8 cm	1963-1983
2.	D6577	Small	3 ¾", 9.5 cm	1963-1983
3.	D6584	Miniature	2 ¾", 7.0 cm	1963-1983

Handle: Two keys
Colourway: Black tricorn; white shirt; red vest
Backstamp: Doulton
Series: Characters From Williamsburg

Jug **No.**	**Size**	**Comp.**	**Issued**	**Current Market Value** **U.K. £**	**U.S. $**	**Can. $**
1.	Large	EW	1963-1983	100.00	150.00	175.00
		ETC	1968-1971	125.00	200.00	250.00
2.	Small	EW	1963-1983	50.00	85.00	100.00
		ETC	1968-1971	85.00	125.00	150.00
3.	Miniature	EW	1963-1983	50.00	85.00	100.00
		ETC	1968-1971	85.00	125.00	150.00

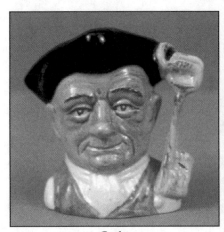

Gaoler

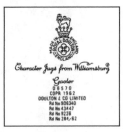

THE GARDENER

STYLE ONE: HANDLE — A SPADE AND VEGETABLES

Designer: David B. Biggs

Handle: A spade with carrots and a marrow at the base
Backstamp: Doulton

VARIATION No. 1: **Colourway** — Red scarf; red striped shirt; brown hat

	Doulton			
Statistics:	**Number**	**Size**	**Height**	**Issued**
1.	D6630	Large	7 ¾", 19.7 cm	1971-1971

Colourway: Red scarf; red striped shirt; brown hat

Jug			Current Market Value		
No.	**Size**	**Variation**	**U.K. £**	**U.S. $**	**Can. $**
1.	Large	Var. 1		Rare	

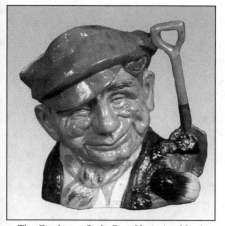

VARIATION No. 2: **Colourway** — Yellow scarf; white shirt; light brown hat

	Doulton			
Statistics:	**Number**	**Size**	**Height**	**Issued**
1.	D6630	Large	7 ¾", 19.7 cm	1973-1981
2.	D6634	Small	4", 10.1 cm	1973-1981
3.	D6638	Miniature	2 ¾", 7.0 cm	1973-1981

Colourway: Yellow scarf; white shirt; light brown hat

Jug			Current Market Value		
No.	**Size**	**Variation**	**U.K. £**	**U.S. $**	**Can. $**
1.	Large	Var. 2	125.00	175.00	200.00
2.	Small	Var. 2	65.00	95.00	120.00
3.	Miniature	Var. 2	75.00	110.00	150.00

The Gardener, Style One, Variation No. 2

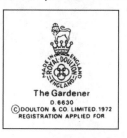

The Gardener
D.6630
©DOULTON & CO. LIMITED. 1972
REGISTRATION APPLIED FOR

THE GARDENER

STYLE TWO: HANDLE — A RED FLOWERING
POTTED PLANT

Designer: Stanley J. Taylor
Handle: A potted plant
Colourway: Beige hat; green sweater; beige shirt
Backstamp: Doulton
Series: Characters From Life

VARIATION No. 1:   **Mould** — Younger face with hair in front

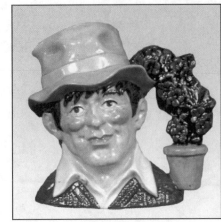

Statistics:	Doulton Number	Size	Height	Issued
	D6867	Large	7 ¼", 18.4 cm	1990-1991

		Current Market Value		
Size	Variation	U.K. £	U.S. $	Can. $
Large	Var. 1	100.00	175.00	225.00

The Gardener, Style Two, Variation No. 1

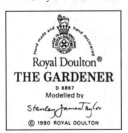

VARIATION No. 2:   **Mould** — Older face without hair in front

Statistics:	Doulton Number	Size	Height	Issued
	D6868	Small	4", 10.1 cm	1990-1995

		Current Market Value		
Size	Variation	U.K. £	U.S. $	Can. $
Small	Var. 2	40.00	85.00	110.00

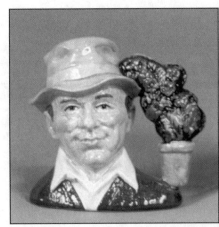

The Gardener, Style Two, Variation No. 2

GENERAL CUSTER

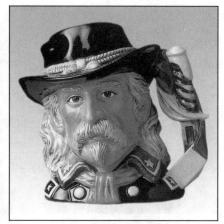

General Custer

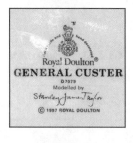

Designer:	Stanley J. Taylor	

	Doulton			
Statistics:	**Number**	**Size**	**Height**	**Issued**
	D7079	Large	7", 17.8 cm	1997-1999

Handle:	A sword and flag
Colourway:	Black, yellow and red
Backstamp:	Doulton

	Current Market Value		
Size	U.K. £	U.S. $	Can. $
Large	175.00	300.00	450.00

GENERAL EISENHOWER

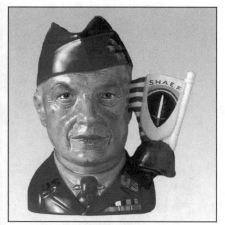

General Eisenhower

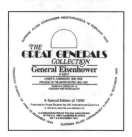

This jug was commissioned by U.K. International Ceramics in a special edition of 1,000. It commemorates the 50th anniversary of the U.S. Army's landing in Africa on November 7 and 8, 1942.

Designer:	William K. Harper	

	Doulton			
Statistics:	**Number**	**Size**	**Height**	**Issued**
	D6937	Large	7", 17.8 cm	See below

Issued:	1993 in a special edition of 1,000
Handle:	Face — Shield "S.H.A.E.F."
	Back — U.S. flag
	Both rest on tin helmet
Colourway:	Brown uniform; cream shield;
	red and white stars and stripes
Backstamp:	Doulton
Series:	Great Generals

	Current Market Value		
Size	U.K. £	U.S. $	Can. $
Large	225.00	375.00	425.00

GENERAL GORDON

Charles George Gordon (1833-1885) was known as "Chinese Gordon" after he commanded the Chinese forces against Taiping rebels in 1863. As Governor-General of the Sudan, he was instrumental in closing down the slave trade. In 1884 he was ordered to rescue the Egyptian garrison at Khartoum; instead he was besieged in Khartoum and killed.

The jug was commissioned by U.K. International Ceramics and issued in 1991 in a special edition of 1,500 pieces.

Designer: William K. Harper

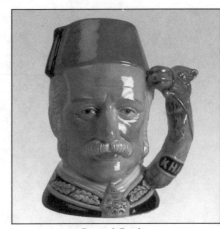

General Gordon

Statistics:

Doulton Number	Size	Height	Issued
D6869	Large	7 ¼", 18.4 cm	See below

Issued: 1991 in a special edition of 1,500
Handle: Camel's head and neck with Khartoum ensign
Colourway: Red, blue and gold
Backstamp: Doulton
Series: Great Generals

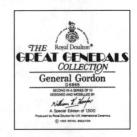

Size	Current Market Value		
	U.K. £	U.S. $	Can. $
Large	125.00	225.00	250.00

GENERAL PATTON

This jug was commissioned in 1996 to commemorate the 50th anniversary of VE-Day, May 8th, 1945, by UKI Ceramics in a special edition of 1,000.

Designer: Warren Platt

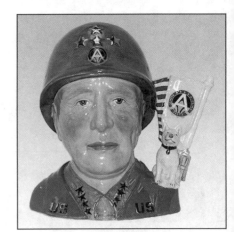

General Patton

Statistics:

Doulton Number	Size	Height	Issued
D7026	Large	7", 17.8 cm	See below

Issued: 1995 in a special edition of 1,000
Handle: Revolver, bulldog and flags
Colourways: Brown, khaki and green
Backstamp: Doulton
Series: Great Generals

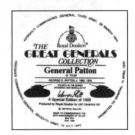

Size	Current Market Value		
	U.K. £	U.S. $	Can. $
Large	225.00	375.00	425.00

THE GENIE

PROTOTYPE

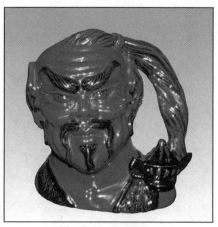

The Genie, Prototype

Designer: Stanley J. Taylor

	Doulton			
Statistics:	**Number**	**Size**	**Height**	**Issued**
	D —	Large	7", 17.8 cm	See below

Modelled: Unknown
Issued: Not put into production
Handle: Lamp and hair
Colourway: Flambé
Backstamp: Doulton

		Current Market Value		
Size	Description	U.K. £	U.S. $	Can. $
Large	Prototype		Extremely rare	

REGULAR ISSUE

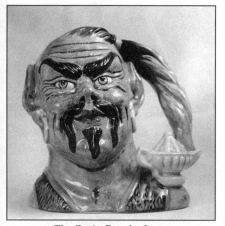

The Genie, Regular Issue

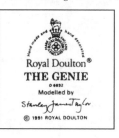

Royal Doulton®
THE GENIE
D 6892
Modelled by
Stanley James Taylor
© 1991 ROYAL DOULTON

Popularized through legend, the genie is said to reside in a magic lantern and to become the servant of whoever frees him.

Designer: Stanley J. Taylor

	Doulton			
Statistics:	**Number**	**Size**	**Height**	**Issued**
	D6892	Large	7", 17.8 cm	1991-1991

Handle: Lamp and hair
Colourway: Grey, black, red and yellow
Backstamp: Doulton
Series: Mystical Characters

	Current Market Value		
Size	U.K. £	U.S. $	Can. $
Large	150.00	300.00	350.00

GEOFFREY CHAUCER
LOVING CUP

This jug was issued in 1996 in a limited edition of 1,500.

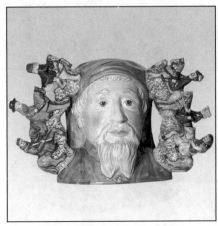

Designer: Robert I. Tabbenor

Statistics:	**Doulton Number**	**Size**	**Height**	**Issued**
	D7029	Large	7 ½", 19.1 cm	See below

Issued: 1996 in a limited edition of 1,500
Handle: Three mounted riders on either side
Colourway: Browns
Backstamp: Doulton

Size	Current Market Value		
	U.K. £	**U.S. $**	**Can. $**
Large	300.00	800.00	1,000.00

Geoffrey Chaucer Loving Cup

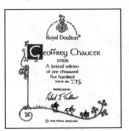

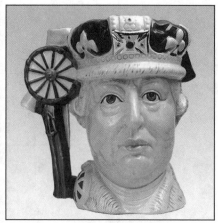

George III

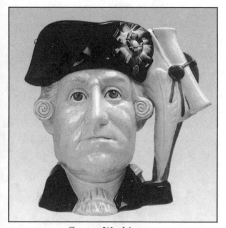

George Washington

GEORGE III AND GEORGE WASHINGTON

George Washington (1732-1799), as commander-in-chief of the American States, led the U.S. to victory in the War of Independence. In 1789 he became the first president of the United States, governing for two terms until 1797.

King George III (1738-1820) ruled Great Britain from 1760 until his death. He led his country in the war against the American States, which he lost in 1776.

This jug was issued in 1986 in a limited edition of 9,500.

Designer: Michael Abberley

	Doulton			
Statistics:	**Number**	**Size**	**Height**	**Issued**
	D6749	Large	7 ¼", 18.4 cm	See below

Issued: 1986 in a limited edition of 9,500.
Handle: George Washington — Declaration of Independence
George III — A cannon
Colourway: Red crown; black hat
Backstamp: Doulton
Series: The Antagonists' Collection (Two-faced jug)

	Current Market Value		
Size	**U.K. £**	**U.S. $**	**Can. $**
Large	100.00	175.00	200.00

GEORGE HARRISON

One of the members of the legendary rock band, the Beatles, George Harrison was born in 1943 in Liverpool, England. He is a guitar player and song writer, and since the break-up of the Beatles in 1970, Harrison has pursued a solo career.

Designer: Stanley J. Taylor

Statistics:

Doulton Number	Size	Height	Issued
D6727	Mid	5 ½", 14.0 cm	1984-1991

Handle: Plain
Colourway: Green tunic; orange collar and epaulettes
Backstamp: Doulton
Series: The Beatles

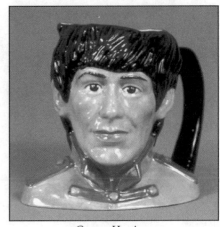

George Harrison

	Current Market Value		
Size	U.K. £	U.S. $	Can. $
Mid	175.00	300.00	400.00

GEORGE STEPHENSON

Created to mark the 150th anniversary of the death of George Stephenson, this character jug highlights his achievements. Inventor of the Rocket steam locomotive, George Stephenson is considered the father of the Railway Age that made such a change in the economic and social life of the country. This jug was issued in a limited edition of 1,848 by Lawleys By Post.

Designer: William K. Harper

Statistics:

Doulton Number	Size	Height	Issued
D7093	Large	7", 17.8 cm	See below

Issued: 1997 in a limited edition of 1,848
Handle: Metal model of the Rocket steam locomotive bridge structure dated 1830
Colourway: Black, maroon, white and tan
Backstamp: Doulton

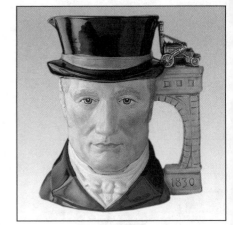

George Stephenson

	Current Market Value		
Size	U.K. £	U.S. $	Can. $
Large	100.00	200.00	300.00

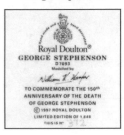

Royal Doulton®
GEORGE STEPHENSON
D7093
Modelled by

TO COMMEMORATE THE 150th
ANNIVERSARY OF THE DEATH
OF GEORGE STEPHENSON
© 1997 ROYAL DOULTON
LIMITED EDITION OF 1,848
THIS IS N°

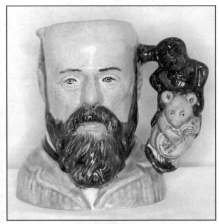

George Tinworth

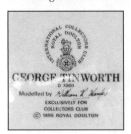

GEORGE TINWORTH

This jug was created exclusively for the Royal Doulton International Collectors Club.

Designer: William K. Harper

Statistics:

Doulton Number	Size	Height	Issued
D7000	Small	4 ¼", 10.8 cm	1995-1996

Handle: Tinworth sculptures
Colourway: Browns, black and grey
Backstamp: Doulton/RDICC
Series: RDICC

Size	Current Market Value		
	U.K. £	U.S. $	Can. $
Small	75.00	125.00	150.00

GEORGE WASHINGTON

PROTOTYPES

STYLE ONE: HANDLE — STARS AND STRIPES FLAG, "LIBERTY" SCROLL

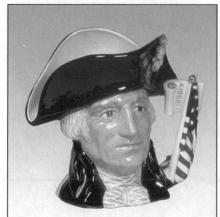

George Washington, Prototype, Style One

Designer: Stanley J. Taylor

Statistics:

Doulton Number	Size	Height	Issued
D6669	Large	7 ½", 19.1 cm	See below

Modelled: Unknown
Issued: Not put into production
Handle: Stars and Stripes flag, "Liberty" scroll
Colourway: Black tricorn hat; black coat; white shirt
Backstamp: Doulton

Size	Current Market Value		
	U.K. £	U.S. $	Can. $
Large	Sold November 21, 1999 Phillips, New Bond Street London, England, £10,500.00		

STYLE TWO: HANDLE — MONUMENT, "LIBERTY" SCROLL

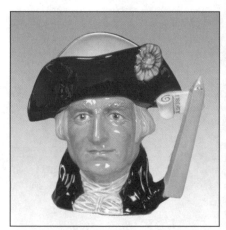

George Washington, Prototype, Style Two

Designer: Stanley J. Taylor

Statistics:

Doulton Number	Size	Height	Issued
D6669	Large	7 ½", 19.1 cm	See below

Modelled: Unknown
Issued: Not put into production
Handle: Washington Monument, "Liberty" scroll
Colourway: Black tricorn hat; black coat; white shirt
Backstamp: Doulton

Size	Current Market Value		
	U.K. £	U.S. $	Can. $
Large	Sold November 21, 1999 Phillips, New Bond Street London, England, £9,000.00		

GEORGE WASHINGTON

REGULAR ISSUE

As commander-in-chief of the American States, George Washington (1732-1799) led them to victory in the War of Independence. In 1789 he became the first President of the United States, governing for two terms until 1797. This jug was issued to celebrate the 250th anniversary of Washington's birth.

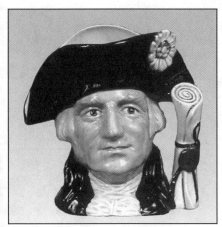

George Washington, Style One

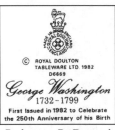

Backstamp B - Dates of Birth

STYLE ONE: HANDLE — DECLARATION OF INDEPENDENCE

Designer: Stanley J. Taylor

	Doulton			
Statistics:	**Number**	**Size**	**Height**	**Issued**
1.	D6669	Large	7 ½", 19.1 cm	1982-1994
2.	D6824	Small	4", 10.1 cm	1989-1991
3.	D6825	Miniature	2 ½", 6.4 cm	1989-1994

Handle: Declaration of Independence
Colourway: Black hat and coat; beige shirt
Backstamps: A. Doulton
  B. Doulton/George Washington 1732-1799/First Issued in 1982 to Celebrate the 250th Anniversary of his Birth
  C. Doulton/George Washington/To Commemorate the 200th Anniversary of the Election of the First President of the United States of America

Jug			Current Market Value		
No.	Size	Issued	U.K. £	U.S. $	Can. $
1A.	Large	1982-1994	100.00	175.00	200.00
1B.		1989-1989	125.00	200.00	225.00
2A.	Small	1989-1991	50.00	100.00	125.00
2B.		1989-1989	55.00	80.00	100.00
2C.		1989-1991	75.00	100.00	125.00
3A.	Miniature	1989-1994	50.00	125.00	150.00
3C.		1989-1991	100.00	150.00	175.00

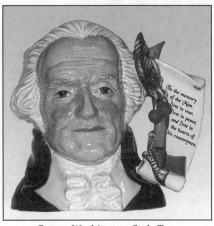

George Washington, Style Two

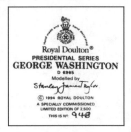

STYLE TWO: HANDLE — AXE, CHERRIES, LEAVES AND SCROLL

Designer: Stanley J. Taylor

	Doulton			
Statistics:	**Number**	**Size**	**Height**	**Issued**
	D6965	Large	7", 17.8 cm	See below

Issued: 1995 in a limited edition of 2,500
Handle: Axe, cherries and leaves with scroll reading "To the memory of the man, first in war, first in peace, first in the hearts of his countrymen"
Colourway: Green, cream and red
Backstamp: Doulton
Series: Presidents of the United States

	Current Market Value		
Size	U.K. £	U.S. $	Can. $
Large	175.00	300.00	350.00

GERONIMO

Geronimo (1829-1909) was the last leader of the Apache Indians while they were still independent of American colonial rule. Although he fought many battles to protect the freedom of his people, in 1886 he surrendered to General Nelson Miles, and Apache territory became the state of Arizona.

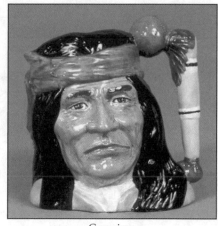

Geronimo

Designer: Stanley J. Taylor

Statistics:	Doulton Number	Size	Height	Issued
	D6733	Mid	5 ½", 14.0 cm	1985-1989

Handle: Indian game pieces
Colourway: Black, red and white
Backstamp: Doulton
Series: The Wild West Collection

Size	Current Market Value		
	U.K. £	U.S. $	Can. $
Mid	125.00	200.00	250.00

GLADIATOR

From about 246 B.C., gladiatorial games were a popular form of entertainment for Roman audiences. The gladiators were most often slaves or prisoners condemned to fight, which they did to the death using sword, spear or trident. The most famous gladiator of the period was Spartacus, a slave who led an unsuccessful rebellion against Rome. Emperor Honorius banned the brutal games in 404 A.D.

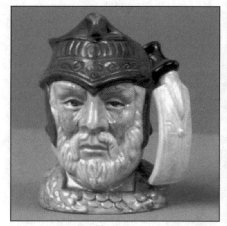

Gladiator

Designer: Max Henk

Statistics:	Doulton Number	Size	Height	Issued
1.	D6550	Large	7 ¾", 19.7 cm	1961-1967
2.	D6553	Small	4 ¼", 10.8 cm	1961-1967
3.	D6556	Miniature	2 ¾", 7.0 cm	1961-1967

Handle: A dagger and shield
Colourway: Brown helmet; grey armour
Backstamp: Doulton

Jug No.	Size	Current Market Value		
		U.K. £	U.S. $	Can. $
1.	Large	400.00	750.00	900.00
2.	Small	275.00	450.00	550.00
3.	Miniature	275.00	450.00	550.00

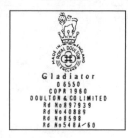

Gladiator
D 6550
COPR 1960
DOULTON & CO LIMITED
Rd No 897939
Rd No 40889
Rd No 8593
Rd No 548 A-60

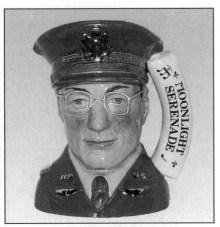

Glenn Miller

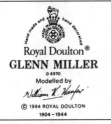

Backstamp A - With
Dates

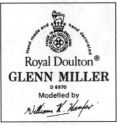

Backstamp B - Without
Dates

GLENN MILLER

This jug commemorates the 50th anniversary of the disappearance of Glenn Miller in an airplane over the Bay of Biscay in 1944. Glenn wears his uniform and a pair of metal glasses. The backstamp includes his date of birth and death on the jugs issued in 1994.

Designer: William K. Harper

	Doulton			
Statistics:	**Number**	**Size**	**Height**	**Issued**
1.	D6970	Large	7 ½", 19.1 cm	1994-1998

Handle: Song sheet for "Moonlight Serenade"
Colourway: Browns and beige
Backstamps: **A.** Doulton/Dates of Miller's birth and death included
      B. Doulton/Without dates

Jug			Current Market Value		
No.	**Size**	**Issued**	**U.K. £**	**U.S. $**	**Can. $**
1A.	Large	1994-1994	125.00	275.00	375.00
1B.		1995-1998	100.00	250.00	325.00

GOLFER

STYLE ONE: HANDLE — GOLD BAG AND CLUBS

This Golfer character jug was modelled in the likeness of W. J. Carey, the former chairman of Doulton U.S.A.

Designer: David B. Biggs
Handle: A golf bag and clubs

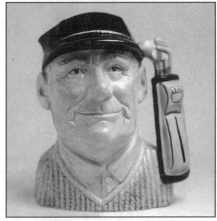

Golfer, Style One, Variation No. 1

VARIATION No. 1: **Colourway** — Blue cap; brown sweater; brown golf bag

Statistics:	Doulton Number	Size	Height	Issued
1.	D6623	Large	7", 17.8 cm	1971-1995
2.	D6756	Small	4 ½", 11.9 cm	1987-1990
3.	D6757	Miniature	2 ½", 6.4 cm	1987-1991

Colourway: Blue cap; brown sweater; brown golf bag
Backstamp: Doulton

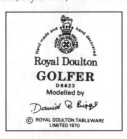

Jug No.	Size	Variation	Current Market Value		
			U.K. £	U.S. $	Can. $
1.	Large	Var. 1	65.00	100.00	125.00
2.	Small		50.00	70.00	90.00
3.	Miniature		50.00	80.00	100.00

VARIATION No. 2: **Colourway** — Dark blue cap; blue striped sweater; light brown golf bag

Statistics:	Doulton Number	Size	Height	Issued
	D6784	Large	7", 17.8 cm	See below

Issued: 1987 in a limited edition of 1,000
Colourway: Dark blue cap; blue striped sweater; light brown golf bag
Backstamp: Doulton / Commissioned by John Sinclair, Sheffield, England. Issued in 1987 in a limited edition of 1,000 pieces.

Size	Variation	Current Market Value		
		U.K. £	U.S. $	Can. $
Large	Var. 2	100.00	250.00	250.00

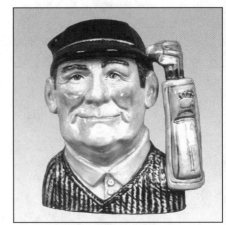

Golfer, Style One, Variation No. 2

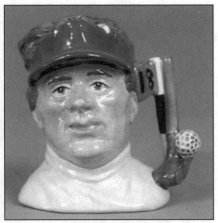

The Golfer, Style Two

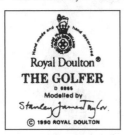

THE GOLFER / THE MODERN GOLFER

STYLE TWO: HANDLE — 18TH-HOLE FLAG, BALL,
TEE AND GOLF CLUB

In the United States, the Royal Doulton product list carried this jug as "The Modern Golfer."

Designer: Stanley J. Taylor

Statistics:	Doulton Number	Size	Height	Issued
	D6865	Small	4", 10.1 cm	1990-1995

Handle: Golf club, 18th-hole flag, ball and tee
Colourway: Yellow sweater; green sun visor
Backstamp: Doulton
Series: Characters From Life

	Current Market Value		
Size	U.K. £	U.S. $	Can. $
Small	45.00	100.00	125.00

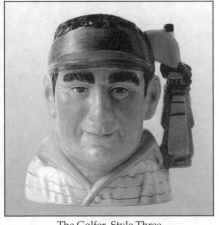

The Golfer, Style Three

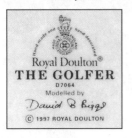

STYLE THREE: HANDLE — GOLF BAG, CLUBS, FLAG

Designer: David B. Biggs

Statistics:	Doulton Number	Size	Height	Issued
	D7064	Small	4 ¾", 12.1 cm	1997-1999

Handle: Golf bag, clubs and flag
Colourway: Yellow shirt; white collar; blue visor
Backstamp: Doulton

	Current Market Value		
Size	U.K. £	U.S. $	Can. $
Small	60.00	150.00	250.00

GONDOLIER

The shallow, long craft the gondolier pilots through Venetian canals must be painted all black, according to ancient law. When not ferrying or serenading lovers on moonlight rides, the gondolier moors his gondola to a brightly striped pole by the waterside.

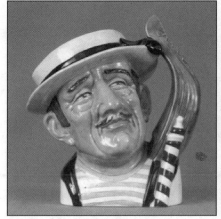

Gondolier

Designer: David B. Biggs

Statistics:	Doulton Number	Size	Height	Issued
1.	D6589	Large	8", 20.3 cm	1964-1969
2.	D6592	Small	4", 10.1 cm	1964-1969
3.	D6595	Miniature	2 ½", 6.4 cm	1964-1969

Handle: Gondola
Colourway: Yellow hat; blue and white t-shirt; maroon and white pole
Backstamp: Doulton

Jug No.	Size	Current Market Value U.K. £	U.S. $	Can. $
1.	Large	400.00	700.00	850.00
2.	Small	300.00	475.00	600.00
3.	Miniature	275.00	450.00	500.00

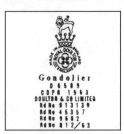

GONE AWAY

This very British huntsman looks ready to give the traditional call signalling the loss of the quarry. His prey, the fox, has won this round!

Designer: Garry Sharpe

Statistics:	Doulton Number	Size	Height	Issued
1.	D6531	Large	7 ¼", 18.4 cm	1960-1982
2.	D6538	Small	3 ¾", 9.5 cm	1960-1982
3.	D6545	Miniature	2 ½", 6.4 cm	1960-1982

Handle: A fox
Colourway: Red jacket; black cap
Backstamp: Doulton

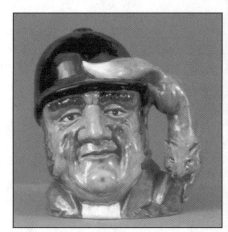

Gone Away

Jug No.	Size	Comp.	Issued	Current Market Value U.K. £	U.S. $	Can. $
1.	Large	EW	1960-1982	75.00	125.00	150.00
		ETC	1968-1971	125.00	200.00	250.00
2.	Small	EW	1960-1982	50.00	75.00	100.00
		ETC	1968-1971	80.00	110.00	150.00
3.	Miniature	EW	1960-1982	45.00	75.00	80.00
		ETC	1968-1971	70.00	100.00	125.00

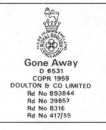

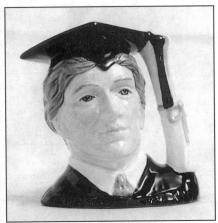

The Graduate (Male)

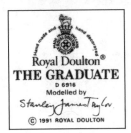

THE GRADUATE (MALE)

Designer: Stanley J. Taylor

	Doulton			
Statistics:	**Number**	**Size**	**Height**	**Issued**
	D6916	Small	3 ½", 8.9 cm	1991-1995

Handle: Diploma
Colourway: Black and white
Backstamp: Doulton

	Current Market Value		
Size	**U.K. £**	**U.S. $**	**Can. $**
Small	45.00	100.00	150.00

GRANNY

PROTOTYPE

This early coloured prototype of the toothless Grannny proved too expensive to produce. Only one copy is known to exist.

Designer: Harry Fenton

Statistics:

	Doulton Number	Size	Height	Issued
	D5521	Large	6 ¼", 15.9 cm	See below

Modelled: 1935
Issued: Not put into production
Handle: Plain
Colourway: Yellows
Backstamp: Doulton

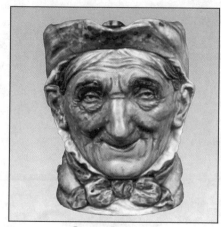

Granny, Prototype

Size	Description	Current Market Value		
		U.K. £	U.S. $	Can. $
Large	Prototype		Unique	

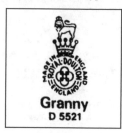

GRANNY

REGULAR ISSUE

STYLE ONE: TOOTHLESS GRANNY

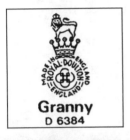

Granny, Style One

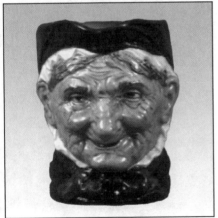

The wimple on this style does not show between the hat and the hair at the front of the head. There is no tooth showing between the lips.

Designer: Harry Fenton

Statistics:	Doulton Number	Size	Height	Issued
1.	D5521	Large	6 ¼", 15.9 cm	1935-1941
2.	D6384	Small	3 ¼", 8.3 cm	1935-Unk.

Handle: Pink, blue, green and cream tied yarn
Colourway: Dark green and white
Backstamp: Doulton

Jug No.	Size	Issued	Current Market Value		
			U.K. £	U.S. $	Can. $
1.	Large	1935-1941	500.00	950.00	1,200.00
2.	Small	1935-Unknown	Extremely rare		

STYLE TWO: GRANNY WITH ONE TOOTH SHOWING

The wimple on Style Two jugs is in waves under most of the hat.

Designer: Large — Harry Fenton
Small and Miniature — Max Henk

Statistics:	Doulton Number	Size	Height	Issued
1.	D5521	Large	6 ¼", 15.9 cm	1941-1983
2.	D6384	Small	3 ¼", 8.3 cm	1953-1983
3.	D6520	Miniature	2 ¼", 5.7 cm	1960-1983

Handle: Pink, blue, green and cream tied yarn
Colourway: Dark grey and white
Backstamp: Doulton

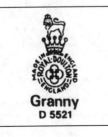

Granny, Style Two

Jug No.	Size	Comp.	Issued	Current Market Value		
				U.K. £	U.S. $	Can. $
1.	Large	EW	1941-1983	60.00	100.00	125.00
		ETC	1968-1971	100.00	150.00	175.00
2.	Small	EW	1953-1983	45.00	65.00	80.00
		ETC	1968-1971	65.00	100.00	125.00
3.	Miniature	EW	1960-1983	50.00	85.00	100.00
		ETC	1968-1971	65.00	100.00	125.00

GRANNY (cont.)

Granny Derivative

Item:	TABLE LIGHTER	**Item:**	MUSICAL JUG
Height:	3 ½", 8.9 cm	**Height:**	7 ½", 19.1 cm
Issued:	Unknown	**Issued:**	Unknown

Doulton		Current Market Value		
Number	Item	U.K. £	U.S. $	Can. $
D —	Table Lighter	Extremely rare		
D —	Musical Jug	Only one known to exist		

Note: For the tiny version of the Granny character jug see the "Diamond Anniversary Set" page 164.

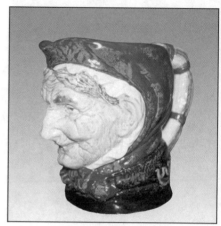

Granny 'Musical Jug'

GREAT BRITAIN'S BRITANNIA

The Romans gave the name Britannia to England. Here she is depicted in shades of blues representing a distinguished naval history. This jug was commissioned by Travers Stanley Collections in a limited edition of 1,997.

Designer: William K. Harper

	Doulton			
Statistics:	**Number**	**Size**	**Height**	**Issued**
	D7107	Small	4 ¼", 10.8 cm	See below

Issued: 1997 in a limited edition of 1,997
Handle: Crest of helmet
Colourway: Blues
Backstamp: Doulton / Travers Stanley

	Current Market Value		
Size	U.K. £	U.S. $	Can. $
Small	60.00	120.00	175.00

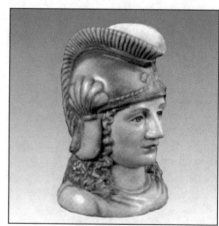

Great Britain's Britannia

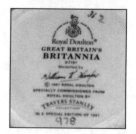

GROUCHO MARX

PROTOTYPE

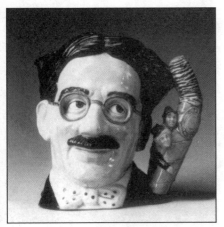

Groucho Marx, Prototype

This design, with two of the Marx Brothers peering out from behind the cigar, was never put into production due to the complicated handle. Possibly only one is known to exist.

Designer: Stanley J. Taylor

Statistics:	Doulton Number	Size	Height	Issued
	D6710	Large	7", 17.8 cm	See below

Modelled: c.1984
Issued: Not put into production
Handle: Cigar with two other Marx Brothers
Colourway: Plain jacket; spotted bow tie
Backstamp: Doulton

Size	Description	Current Market Value U.K. £	U.S. $	Can. $
Large	Prototype	Extremely rare Last sold March 12, 1997 Sotheby's Arcade Auction New York, $8,050.00		

REGULAR ISSUE

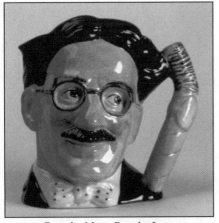

Groucho Marx, Regular Issue

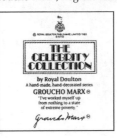

Julius Marx (1895-1977) was one of four brothers who became stars of American comedy. The Marx Brothers were known for their crazy slapstick antics and hilarious puns. Groucho led the gang, always smoking his trademark cigar.

Designer: Stanley J. Taylor

Statistics:	Doulton Number	Size	Height	Issued
	D6710	Large	7", 17.8 cm	1984-1988

Handle: Cigar
Colourway: Plain jacket; spotted bow tie
Backstamp: Doulton
Series: The Celebrity Collection

Size	Description	Current Market Value U.K. £	U.S. $	Can. $
Large	Regular issue	100.00	175.00	200.00

GUARDSMAN

STYLE ONE: TRICORN HAT WITH PIKE

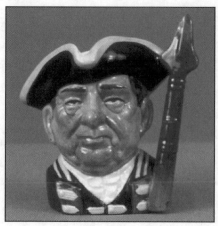

Designer: Max Henk

Statistics:	Doulton Number	Size	Height	Issued
1.	D6568	Large	6 ¾", 17.2 cm	1963-1983
2.	D6575	Small	4 ¼", 10.8 cm	1963-1983
3.	D6582	Miniature	2 ½", 6.4 cm	1963-1983

Handle: Pike
Colourway: Dark blue and yellow hat and jacket
Backstamp: Doulton
Series: Characters From Williamsburg

Guardsman, Style One

Jug No.	Size	Comp.	Issued	Current Market Value U.K. £	U.S. $	Can. $
1.	Large	EW	1963-1983	90.00	150.00	175.00
		ETC	1968-1971	125.00	200.00	225.00
2.	Small	EW	1963-1983	60.00	100.00	115.00
		ETC	1968-1971	75.00	125.00	150.00
3.	Miniature	EW	1963-1983	55.00	100.00	100.00
		ETC	1968-1971	75.00	125.00	150.00

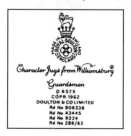

Character Jugs from Williamsburg
Guardsman
D 6575
COPR 1962
DOULTON & CO LIMITED
Rd No 906338
Rd No 43445
Rd No 9224
Rd No 286/62

THE GUARDSMAN

STYLE TWO: BEARSKIN HAT WITH SWORD

PROTOTYPE

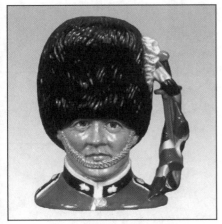

The Guardsman, Prototype

This was the original design of The Guardsman jug, a prototype with the Union Jack.

Designer: Stanley J. Taylor

Statistics:	**Doulton Number**	**Size**	**Height**	**Issued**
	D —	Large	8", 20.3 cm	See below

Issued: Not put into production
Handle: A sword draped with the Union Jack
Colourway: Red tunic; black bearskin hat
Backstamp: Doulton

		Current Market Value		
Size	Description	U.K. £	U.S. $	Can. $
Large	Prototype		Extremely rare	

REGULAR ISSUE

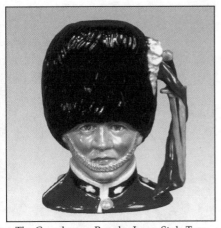

The Guardsman, Regular Issue, Style Two

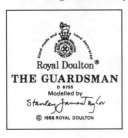

Long a fixture in London, the guardsman is easily identified by his tall bearskin hat and scarlet uniform. Today he still stands outside Buckingham Palace to protect the Queen. Guardsman models exist with white (gloss) tunics.

Designer: Stanley J. Taylor

Statistics:	**Doulton Number**	**Size**	**Height**	**Issued**
1.	D6755	Large	8", 20.3 cm	1986-1999
2.	D6771	Small	4", 10.1 cm	1987-1999
3.	D6772	Miniature	2 ½", 6.4 cm	1987-1991

Handle: Sword with draped brown flag
Colourway: Red tunic; black bearskin hat
Backstamp: Doulton
Series: The London Collection

Jug No.	Size	Current Market Value		
		U.K. £	U.S. $	Can. $
1.	Large	70.00	145.00	200.00
2.	Small	40.00	80.00	115.00
3.	Miniature	50.00	100.00	125.00

GULLIVER

Jonathon Swift satirized society's leading men and institutions in his book, *Gulliver's Travels*, published in 1726. In it Gulliver the traveller sails to foreign lands, surviving shipwrecks, giants and the tiny people of Lilliput.

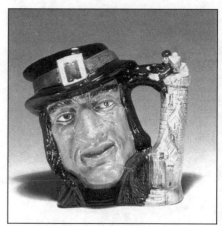

Gulliver

Designer: David B. Biggs

Statistics:	Doulton Number	Size	Height	Issued
1.	D6560	Large	7 ½", 19.1 cm	1962-1967
2.	D6563	Small	4", 10.1 cm	1962-1967
3.	D6566	Miniature	2 ½", 6.4 cm	1962-1967

Handle: Castle tower with two Lilliputians in the turret
Colourway: Dark blue and grey hat; blue jacket; grey handle
Backstamp: Doulton

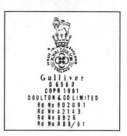

Jug No.	Size	Comp.	Issued	Current Market Value U.K. £	U.S. $	Can. $
1.	Large	EW	1962-1967	500.00	900.00	1,000.00
2.	Small	EW	1962-1967	350.00	500.00	600.00
3.	Miniature	EW	1962-1967	300.00	475.00	550.00
3.		ETC	1968-1971	Rare		

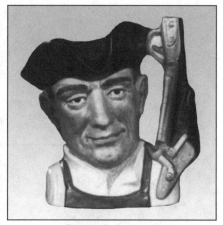

Gunsmith, Prototype

GUNSMITH

PROTOTYPE

This prototype has a different hat, hair style and handle from the design that was issued. Only one jug is known to exist.

Designer: David B. Biggs

Statistics:	**Doulton Number**	**Size**	**Height**	**Issued**
	D —	Large	7 ¼", 18.4 cm	See below

Modelled: c.1963
Issued: Not put into production
Handle: Stock of a musket and flintlock
Colourway: Black hat; cream shirt; light brown apron
Backstamp: Doulton

		Current Market Value		
Size	**Description**	**U.K. £**	**U.S. $**	**Can. $**
Large	Prototype		Unique	

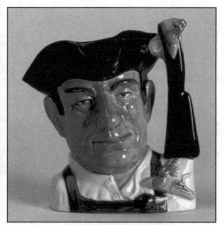

Gunsmith, Regular Issue

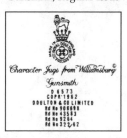

REGULAR ISSUE

Designer: David B. Biggs

Statistics:	**Doulton Number**	**Size**	**Height**	**Issued**
1.	D6573	Large	7 ¼", 18.4 cm	1963-1983
2.	D6580	Small	3 ½", 8.9 cm	1963-1983
3.	D6587	Miniature	2 ½", 6.4 cm	1963-1983

Handle: Stock of a musket
Colourway: Black hat; cream shirt; light brown apron
Backstamp: Doulton
Series: Characters From Williamsburg

Jug No.	Size	Comp.	Issued	**Current Market Value**		
				U.K. £	**U.S. $**	**Can. $**
1.	Large	EW	1963-1983	80.00	125.00	165.00
		ETC	1968-1971	100.00	165.00	195.00
2.	Small	EW	1963-1983	60.00	80.00	100.00
		ETC	1968-1971	65.00	100.00	135.00
3.	Miniature	EW	1963-1983	50.00	80.00	100.00
		ETC	1968-1971	65.00	100.00	135.00

GUY FAWKES

Guy Fawkes (1570-1606) was part of the infamous "Gunpowder Plot," a plan by Catholic rebels to blow up the British Houses of Parliament and King James I on November 5, 1605. The conspiracy was leaked by a letter to Lord Monteagle, and Guy Fawkes was arrested and hanged. Every year on November 5, Guy Fawkes Day is celebrated with fireworks and the burning of Fawkes in effigy.

Designer: William K. Harper
Handle: A lantern above a barrel of gunpowder

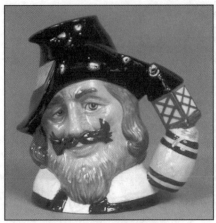

Guy Fawkes, Variation No. 1

VARIATION No. 1: Colourway — Black hat; red band; white collar on black coat

Statistics:	Doulton Number	Size	Height	Issued
	D6861	Large	7", 17.8 cm	1990-1996

Colourway: Black hat; red band; white collar; black coat
Backstamp: Doulton

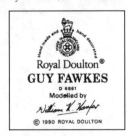

Size	Backstamp	Current Market Value		
		U.K. £	U.S. $	Can. $
Large	Doulton	75.00	150.00	175.00

VARIATION No. 2: Colourway — Black hat; orange band; white collar on black coat

Statistics:	Doulton Number	Size	Height	Issued
	D6861	Large	7", 17.8 cm	See below

Issued: 1990 in a limited edition of 750
Colourway: Black hat; orange band; white collar; black coat
Backstamp: Doulton / Canadian Art and Collectables Show
Pre-release was limited to 750 for Annual Canadian Doulton Show and the Third Sale in conjuction with the 1990 Canadian Collectables Showcase, May 5 and 6, 1990, Durham, Ontario.

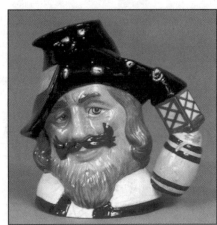

Guy Fawkes, Variation No. 2

Size	Backstamp	Current Market Value		
		U.K. £	U.S. $	Can. $
Large	Doulton/Canadian Art	125.00	175.00	200.00

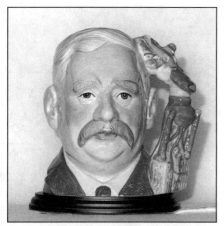

H. G. Wells

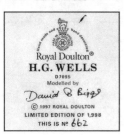

H. G. WELLS

Not just prolific in his output, H. G. Wells was a futuristic writer, one of the earliest science fiction novelists. His character jug marks the centenary of the publication of the *War of the Worlds*, one of his best-known and celebrated works. This jug was issued in a limited edition of 1,998.

Designer:	David B. Biggs			

Statistics:	**Doulton Number**	**Size**	**Height**	**Issued**
	D7095	Large	6 ¾", 17.2 cm	See below

Issued:	1998 in a limited edition of 1,998
Handle:	Martian fighting machine and an aeroplane
Colourway:	Green jacket; yellow shirt; maroon tie
Backstamp:	Doulton

Size	Current Market Value		
	U.K. £	**U.S. $**	**Can. $**
Large	100.00	175.00	350.00

HAMLET

Probably Shakespeare's most famous play, *Hamlet, Prince of Denmark,* was first performed between 1599 and 1602. Hamlet became the quintessential tragic hero, driven by conscience and familial obligation to avenge his father's murder.

Designer: Michael Abberley
Handle: A dagger and skull join the feather of the cap

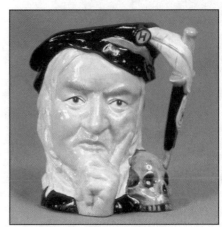

Hamlet, Variation No. 1

Statistics:	**Doulton** **Number**	**Size**	**Height**	**Issued**
	D6672	Large	7 ¼", 18.4 cm	See below

VARIATION No. 1: Colourway — Black cap and robes

Issued: 1982-1989
Colourway: Black cap and robes; blond hair; grey feather
Backstamp: Doulton
Series: The Shakespearean Collection

		Current Market Value		
Size	**Variation**	**U.K. £**	**U.S. $**	**Can. $**
Large	Var. 1	100.00	150.00	175.00

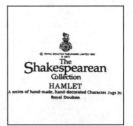

VARIATION No. 2: Colourway — Black cap, yellow robes

Issued: Not put into production
Colourway: Black cap; yellow robes
Backstamp: Doulton

		Current Market Value		
Size	**Variation**	**U.K. £**	**U.S. $**	**Can. $**
Large	Var. 2	Sold November 21, 1999 Phillips, New Bond Street London, England, £1,300.00		

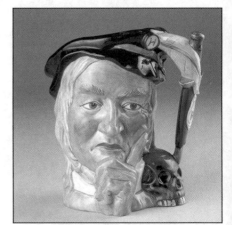

Hamlet, Variation No. 2

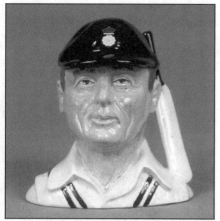

The Hampshire Cricketer

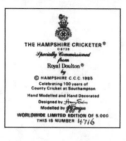

THE HAMPSHIRE CRICKETER

The Hampshire Cricketer jug was developed and sold by the Hampshire Cricket Club to celebrate the centenary of the Hampshire cricket grounds. It was issued in 1985 in a limited edition of 5,000 pieces.

Designer: Harry Sales
Modeller: Graham Tongue

Statistics:	Doulton Number	Size	Height	Issued
	D6739	Small	5", 12.7 cm	See below

Issued: 1985 in a limited edition of 5,000
Handle: Cricket bat
Colourway: Navy blue cap; cream sweater with navy/yellow stripes
Backstamp: Doulton/© Hampshire C. C. C. 1985
Series: Cricketers

Size	Current Market Value		
	U.K. £	U.S. $	Can. $
Small	65.00	100.00	140.00

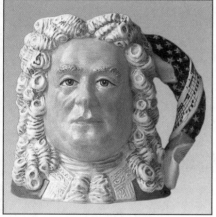

Handel

HANDEL

The great composer George Frederick Handel (1685-1759) resided in England for a great portion of his adult life, though he was born in Germany. The music score which forms part of the handle is from Handel's famous *Fireworks* composition.

Designer: Stanley J. Taylor

Statistics:	Doulton Number	Size	Height	Issued
	D7080	Large	7", 17.8 cm	1997-2001

Handle: Music score, multi-coloured stars representing fireworks
Colourway: Green and gold jacket; blue-grey cravat; grey wig
Backstamp: Doulton
Series: Great Composers

Size	Current Market Value		
	U.K. £	U.S. $	Can. $
Large	90.00	200.00	300.00

HAROLD DENNIS "DICKIE BIRD" M.B.E.

Commissioned by Lawleys By Post in a limited edition of 9,500. This character jug pays homage to Dickie Bird who, for over a quarter century, was the top test match umpire in England.

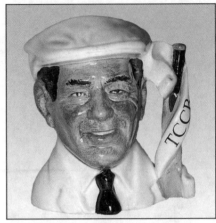

Harold Dennis "Dickie Bird" M.B.E.

Designer: Stanley J. Taylor

Statistics:	Doulton Number	Size	Height	Issued
	D7068	Small	4 ½", 11.9 cm	See below

Issued: 1996 in a limited edition of 9,500
Handle: Cricket bat and TCCB banner (Test and County Cricket Board)
Colourway: White and black
Backstamp: Doulton

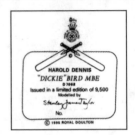

Size	Current Market Value		
	U.K. £	U.S. $	Can. $
Small	60.00	125.00	150.00

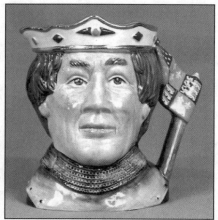

Henry V, Style One, Variation No. 1

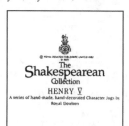

HENRY V

King Henry V (1387-1422) renewed the Hundred Years' War against France, and at the Battle of Agincourt in 1415, he won one of the most famous victories in English history. Henry married the daughter of King Charles VI of France and by the Treaty of Troyes became heir to the French throne.

STYLE ONE: LARGE SIZE: HANDLE — ROYAL ENSIGN

Designer: Robert Tabbenor

Statistics:	**Doulton Number**	**Size**	**Height**	**Issued**
	D6671	Large	7 ¼", 18.4 cm	See below

Handle: Royal Ensign
Backstamp: Doulton
Series: The Shakespearean Collection

VARIATION No. 1: Handle — Embossed
Colourway — Yellow crown with gold, turquoise and red design

Issued: 1982-c.1984
Colourway: Yellow crown with gold, turquoise and red design

Size	Variation	Current Market Value		
		U.K. £	**U.S. $**	**Can. $**
Large	Var. 1	150.00	250.00	275.00

VARIATION No. 2: Handle — Embossed
Colourway — Yellow crown; some blue colouring; no red or gold

This jug is actually a factory second, marked and sold as such. One of the steps used when firing and painting the jugs was missed. Hundreds are known to exist.

Issued: Unknown
Colourway: Yellow crown with blue colouring

Size	Variation	Current Market Value		
		U.K. £	**U.S. $**	**Can. $**
Large	Var. 2	1,000.00	1,750.00	2,000.00

VARIATION No. 3: Handle — Decorated with a decal
Colourway — Yellow crown with gold, blue and red design

Issued: c.1984-1989
Colourway: Yellow crown with gold, turquoise and red design

Size	Variation	Current Market Value		
		U.K. £	**U.S. $**	**Can. $**
Large	Var. 3	90.00	150.00	175.00

Note: For the charaacter jug Henry V (Style Two) see "Kings and Queens of the Realm" page 247, for the bookend Henry V, see page 405.

HENRY VIII

Henry VIII (1491-1547) was king of Great Britain from 1509 to 1547, during which time his infamous private life changed the course of history. Attempting to produce a male heir to the throne, he married six times, was excommunicated by the Pope for divorce and founded the Church of England.

STYLE ONE: LARGE SIZE: HANDLE — TOWER

Designer: Eric Griffiths

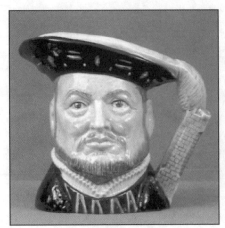

Henry VIII, Style One

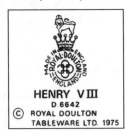

	Doulton			
Statistics:	**Number**	**Size**	**Height**	**Issued**
1.	D6642	Large	6 ½", 16.5 cm	1975-2000
2.	D6647	Small	3 ¾", 9.5 cm	1979-1999
3.	D6648	Miniature	2 ¾", 7.0 cm	1979-1991

Handle: A tower joins the feather in the hat
Colourway: Black and gold hat; white plume; brown and maroon tunic
Backstamp: Doulton
Series: Henry VIII and His Six Wives

Jug		**Current Market Value**		
No.	**Size**	**U.K. £**	**U.S. $**	**Can. $**
1.	Large	60.00	150.00	200.00
2.	Small	35.00	80.00	115.00
3.	Miniature	50.00	110.00	135.00

Note: For the character jugs Henry VIII (Style Two) see the "Kings and Queens of the Realm Set" page 247, for King Henry VIII, see page 246, and for the toby jug King Henry VIII see page 65.

HENRY COOPER

Henry Cooper, OBE, became British heavyweight champion in 1959 and held the title until 1971. During that time he won three Lonsdale belts in defence of his crown.

This jug was commissioned by Lawleys By Post in a limited edition of 9,500.

Designer: Stanley J. Taylor

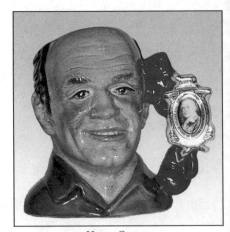

Henry Cooper

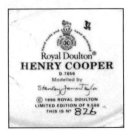

	Doulton			
Statistics:	**Number**	**Size**	**Height**	**Issued**
	D7050	Small	4", 10.1 cm	See below

Issued: 1996 in a limited edition of 9,500
Handle: Lonsdale belt and boxing gloves
Colourway: Blue, white, brown and gold
Backstamp: Doulton

	Current Market Value		
Size	**U.K. £**	**U.S. $**	**Can. $**
Small	60.00	125.00	150.00

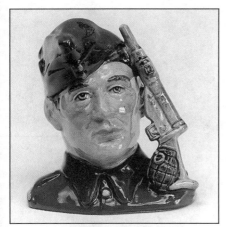

Home Guard

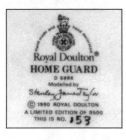

HOME GUARD

In the early part of World War II, young and old joined the Home Guard to protect the country from what was perceived as an imminent invasion by the German army, allowing the regular army to be used elsewhere. The Heroes of the Blitz series was available only from Lawleys By Post, in a limited edition of 9,500.

Designer: Stanley J. Taylor

Statistics:	**Doulton Number**	**Size**	**Height**	**Issued**
	D6886	Small	4", 10.1 cm	See below

Issued: 1991 in a limited edition of 9,500
Handle: Sten gun with hand grenade
Colourway: Khaki uniform and cap
Backstamp: Doulton
Series: Heroes of the Blitz

Size	Current Market Value		
	U.K. £	**U.S. $**	**Can. $**
Small	125.00	225.00	275.00

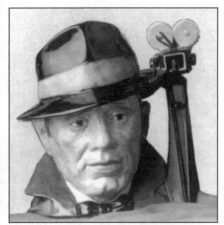

Humphrey Bogart, Prototype

HUMPHREY BOGART

PROTOTYPE

Humphrey DeForest Bogart began his acting career in 1920 and enjoyed a prolific career, winning an Academy Award in 1952 for his performance in *The African Queen*. His best-known role, however, was that of Rick in *Casablanca*. The jug could not be issued due to copyright problems and is not known to be in private collections.

Designer: Eric Griffiths

Statistics:	**Model Number**	**Size**	**Height**	**Issued**
	2656	Large	7", 17.8 cm	See below

Modelled: 1979
Issued: Not put into production
Handle: Movie camera pointing right
Colourway: Black hat; brown coat; black bow tie
Backstamp: Doulton
Series: The Celebrity Collection

Size	Description	Current Market Value		
		U.K. £	**U.S. $**	**Can. $**
Large	Prototype	Extremely rare		

IAN BOTHAM O.B.E.

This jug, of one of England's most famous all-round cricketers, was issued by Lawleys By Post in a limited edition of 9,500.

Designer: David B. Biggs

	Doulton			
Statistics:	**Number**	**Size**	**Height**	**Issued**
	D7091	Small	4 ½", 11.9 cm	See below

Issued: 1998 in a limited edition of 9,500
Handle: Shin pad and cricket ball
Colourway: White sweater with red, yellow and navy stripes
Backstamp: Doulton
Series: Cricketers

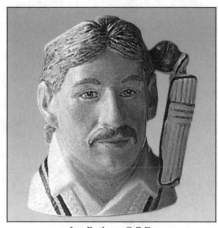

Ian Botham O.B.E.

Size	Current Market Value		
	U.K. £	**U.S. $**	**Can. $**
Small	55.00	80.00	125.00

IZAAK WALTON

The English writer Izaak Walton (1593-1683) is best known for his book *The Compleat Angler, or Contemplative Man's Recreation*. First published in 1653, this work became the most famous book written on the sport of fishing.

Designer: Geoff Blower

	Doulton			
Statistics:	**Number**	**Size**	**Height**	**Issued**
1.	D6404	Large	7", 17.8 cm	1953-1982

Handle: A fishing rod resting on a tree trunk
Colourway: Brown hat and coat; white collar
Backstamps: A. Doulton
  B. Doulton/City of Stoke-on-Trent Jubilee Year
  1959-1960 With the compliments of Lord Mayor
  and Lady Mayoress Alderman Harold Clowes,
  O.B.E., J.P. and Miss Christine Clowes

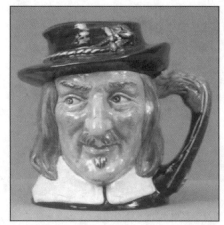

Izaak Walton

Jug				Current Market Value		
No.	**Size**	**Comp.**	**Issued**	**U.K. £**	**U.S. $**	**Can. $**
1A.	Large	EW	1953-1982	75.00	110.00	135.00
1A.		ETC	1968-1971	150.00	225.00	250.00
1B.		EW	1959-1960	5,000.00	7,500.00	10,000.00

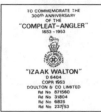

Backstamp A - Doulton

Backstamp B - City of Stoke-on-Trent

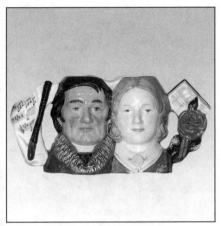

Jane Eyre and Mr Rochester

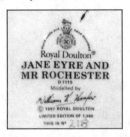

JANE EYRE AND MR ROCHESTER

The Charlotte Bronte characters from her 1847 *Jane Eyre* form the second in the double character jug series. This jug was issued by Lawleys By Post in a limited edition of 1,500 pieces.

Designer: William K. Harper

Statistics:

	Doulton Number	Size	Height	Issued
	D7115	Small	4 ¾", 12.1 cm	See below

Issued: 1998 in a limited edition of 1,500
Handle: Jane Eyre — A book, rose and paint brushes
Mr Rochester — Musical score and riding crop
Colourway: Jane Eyre — Grey dress; white collar; yellow brooch
Mr Rochester — Maroon smoking jacket; brown collar
Backstamp: Doulton
Series: Double Character Jugs

Size	Current Market Value		
	U.K. £	U.S. $	Can. $
Small	125.00	200.00	300.00

JANE SEYMOUR

While serving as lady-in-waiting to both Catherine of Aragon and Anne Boleyn, Jane Seymour (1509-1537) attracted the attention of Henry VIII. She refused any proposal from the King except marriage, a factor leading to the trial of Anne. Two weeks after Anne Boleyn was beheaded, Jane Seymour became the third wife of Henry VIII, and the only one to bear him a male heir. She died shortly after Edward was born, and was the only wife to be buried at Henry's side.

STYLE ONE: HANDLE: A MANDOLIN

Designer: Large size — Michael Abberley
Small and miniature sizes — Peter Gee

Statistics:

	Doulton Number	Size	Height	Issued
1.	D6646	Large	7 ¼", 18.4 cm	1979-1990
2.	D6746	Small	4 ¼", 10.8 cm	1986-1990
3.	D6747	Miniature	2 ¾", 7.0 cm	1986-1990

Handle: A mandolin
Colourway: Black and gold
Backstamp: Doulton
Series: Henry VIII and His Six Wives

Jug No.	Size	Current Market Value		
		U.K. £	U.S. $	Can. $
1.	Large	100.00	175.00	200.00
2.	Small	100.00	175.00	200.00
3.	Miniature	115.00	190.00	200.00

Note: For Jane Seymour, Style Two, see the "Six Wives of Henry VIII" page 364.

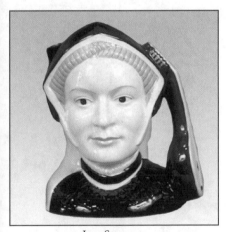

Jane Seymour

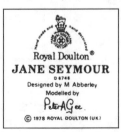

JARGE

Jarge, the colloquial version of George, is a typical country bumpkin, with his polka-dot scarf and the piece of straw in his teeth.

Designer: Harry Fenton

Statistics:

	Doulton Number	Size	Height	Issued
1.	D6288	Large	6 ½", 16.5 cm	1950-1960
2.	D6295	Small	3 ½", 8.9 cm	1950-1960

Handle: The scarf extends upwards to the cap
Colourway: Green cap; white scarf with red polka-dots
Backstamp: Doulton

Jug No.	Size	Current Market Value U.K. £	U.S. $	Can. $
1.	Large	250.00	375.00	450.00
2.	Small	150.00	250.00	375.00

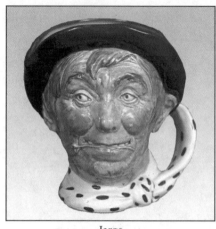

Jarge

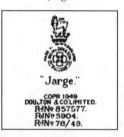

JESSE OWENS

This jug was issued as the Character Jug of the Year for 1996, to commemorate both the Summer Olympic Games in Atlanta, Georgia, and the first African-American to win a gold medal in the Olympic Games. Owens won four gold medals in Berlin during the 1936 Summer Games.

Designer: Stanley J. Taylor

Statistics:

	Doulton Number	Size	Height	Issued
	D7019	Large	7", 17.8 cm	1996-1996

Handle: U.S. flag and olympic torch
Colourway: Black, brown and white
Backstamp: Doulton/Character Jug of the Year, 1996
© The Jesse Owens Trust
Series: Character Jug of the Year

Size	Current Market Value U.K. £	U.S. $	Can. $
Large	125.00	200.00	225.00

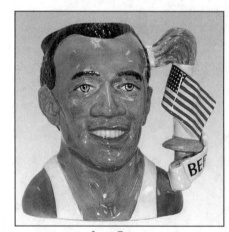

Jesse Owens

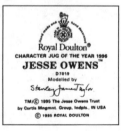

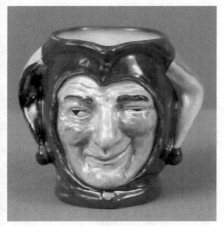

Jester

JESTER

The green and yellow colouring on either side of the hat may be reversed as a preference of the painter. Minor variations of this nature do not command a price differential.

Designer: Charles Noke

Statistics:	Doulton Number	Size	Height	Issued
1.	D5556	Small	3 ¼", 8.3 cm	1936-1960

Handle: Plain
Colourway: Brown, green and yellow
Backstamps: A. Doulton
B. Doulton/Bentalls/Souvenir From Bentalls. 1936. Commissioned by Bentalls as an advertising piece.
C. Doulton/Darley/Souvenir from Darley & Son, Sheffield & Rotherham

Jug No.	Size	Issued	Current Market Value		
			U.K. £	U.S. $	Can. $
1A.	Small	1936-1960	65.00	110.00	135.00
1B.		1936-1936	450.00	675.00	850.00
1C.		1936-1936	450.00	675.00	850.00

Jester Derivative

Item: WALL POCKET
Size: 7 ¼", 18.4 cm
Issued: 1940-1941

Doulton Number	Item	Current Market Value		
		U.K. £	U.S. $	Can. $
D6111	Wall Pocket	900.00	1,400.00	1,750.00

Note: For the tiny version of the Jester character jug see the "Diamond Anniversary Set" page 164.

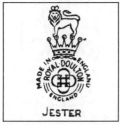

Backstamp A - Doulton

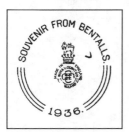

Backstamp B - Bentalls

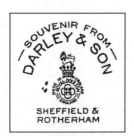

Backstamp C - Darley & Son

JIMMY DURANTE

James Francis Durante (1893-1980) began his entertaining career playing the piano, but it was his singing and clowning that brought him fame in Vaudeville theatre, night clubs, films, radio and television. Using his large nose as the object of jokes, Durante earned his nickname "Schnozzle."

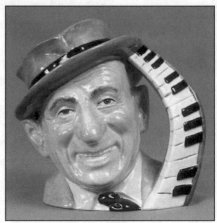

Jimmy Durante

Designer: David B. Biggs

Statistics:

	Doulton Number	Size	Height	Issued
	D6708	Large	7 ½", 19.1 cm	1985-1988

Handle: A piano keyboard
Colourway: Grey and black cap; yellow jacket; cream shirt
Backstamp: Doulton
Series: The Celebrity Collection

Size	Current Market Value		
	U.K. £	U.S. $	Can. $
Large	100.00	200.00	250.00

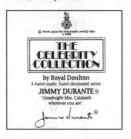

JOCKEY

Small and miniature sized jugs of the Jockey were test piloted but not produced. A small pilot jug is known to exist.

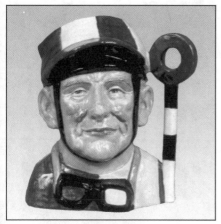

Jockey, Style One

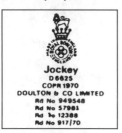

STYLE ONE: GOGGLES RESTING ON HIS CHEST
HANDLE — WINNING POLE

Designer: David B. Biggs

Statistics:	Doulton Number	Size	Height	Issued
1.	D6625	Large	7 ¾", 19.7 cm	1971-1975
2.	D6629	Small	4", 10.1 cm	1974-1974

Handle: The winning pole
Colourway: Red and yellow striped cap and racing jersey
Backstamp: Doulton

Jug No.	Size	Current Market Value U.K. £	U.S. $	Can. $
1.	Large	250.00	425.00	575.00
2.	Small		Unique	

STYLE TWO: GOGGLES RESTING ON CAP
HANDLE — WINNING POLE AND
HORSE HEAD

Designer: Stanley J. Taylor

Statistics:	Doulton Number	Size	Height	Issued
	D6877	Small	4", 10.1 cm	1991-1995

Handle: Head of a horse and the winning pole
Colourway: Beige riding cap; yellow and black racing jersey
Backstamp: Doulton
Series: Characters From Life

Size	Current Market Value U.K. £	U.S. $	Can. $
Small	45.00	90.00	125.00

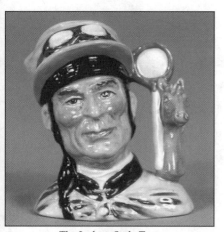

The Jockey, Style Two

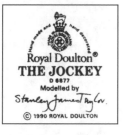

JOHANN STRAUSS II

Famous for his waltzes, especially the *Blue Danube* composition featured on the handle of this jug, Johann Strauss II (1825-1899) is known as the Waltz King.

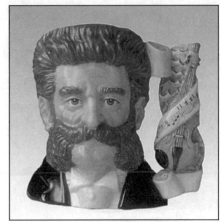

Designer: Stanley J. Taylor

Statistics:	Doulton Number	Size	Height	Issued
	D7097	Large	7", 17.8 cm	1998-2001

Handle: Violin, waves, Blue Danube score
Colourway: Brown, black and yellow
Backstamp: Doulton
Series: Great Composers

	Current Market Value		
Size	U.K. £	U.S. $	Can. $
Large	100.00	200.00	325.00

Johann Stauss II

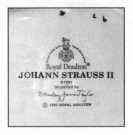

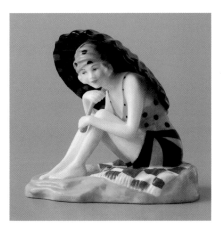
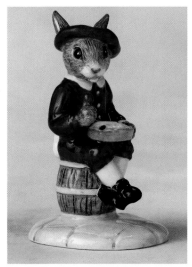
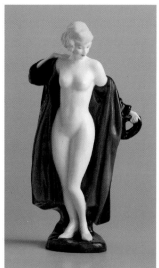

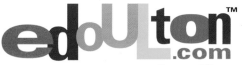

JOHN BARLEYCORN

John Barleycorn is the personification of barley, the grain source of malt liquor. This character jug was the first design created by Charles Noke in 1934.

STYLE ONE: HANDLE — INSIDE JUG, 1934 TO 1939

Designer: Charles Noke

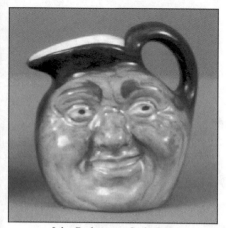

John Barleycorn, Style One

Statistics:	Doulton Number	Size	Height	Issued
1.	D5327	Large	6 ½", 16.5 cm	1934-1939
2.	D5735	Small	3 ½", 8.9 cm	1937-1939
3.	D6041	Miniature	2 ½", 6.4 cm	Unknown

Handle: Plain brown
Colourway: Brown rim with light brown body
Backstamps: **A.** Doulton
B. Doulton/Coleman's/
Coleman's Compliments
This large-size jug was commissioned by Coleman's as an advertising piece.
C. Doulton/Salt River Cement Works/
With Compliments From Salt River Cement Works
This large-size jug was commissioned by Salt River Cement Works as an advertising piece.

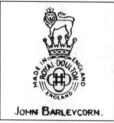

Backstamp A - Doulton

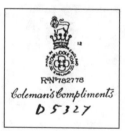

Backstamp B - Coleman's

Jug No.	Size	Issued	Current Market Value		
			U.K. £	U.S. $	Can. $
1A.	Large	1934-1939	125.00	200.00	225.00
1B.		1938-1939	1,000.00	2,000.00	2,250.00
1C.		Unknown	1,500.00	2,500.00	3,000.00
2A.	Small	1937-1939	60.00	85.00	110.00
3A.	Miniature	Unknown	60.00	85.00	110.00

Note: John Barleycorn, Style One, large, miniature and small jugs are found in white gloss.

JOHN BARLEYCORN

STYLE TWO: HANDLE — OUTSIDE JUG, 1939 TO 1982

VARIATION No. 1: **Handle** — Brown shading

Designer: Charles Noke

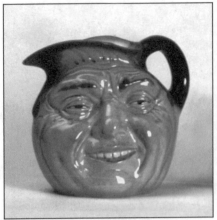

Statistics:	Doulton Number	Size	Height	Issued
1.	D5327	Large	6 ½", 16.5 cm	1939-1960
2.	D5735	Small	3 ½", 8.9 cm	1939-1960
3.	D6041	Miniature	2 ½", 6.4 cm	1939-1960

Handle: Plain, brown shading
Colourway: Brown rim; light brown face
Backstamp: Doulton

Jug No.	Size	Current Market Value U.K. £	U.S. $	Can. $
1.	Large	75.00	150.00	175.00
2.	Small	50.00	85.00	132.00
3.	Miniature	45.00	85.00	125.00

John Barleycorn, Style Two, Variation No. 1

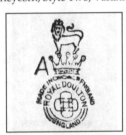

Note: 1. John Barleycorn, Style Two, small size jugs are found in white gloss.
2. For the tiny version of John Barleycorn character jug see the "Diamond Anniversary Set" page 164.

VARIATION No. 2: **Handle** — Black shading

Issued from 1978 to 1982, this jug was similar to the previous variation, but a new mould had to be made because the original was not available. This special exhibition jug was sold at Royal Doulton events.

Designer: Charles Noke   **Modeller:** Michael Abberley

Statistics:	Doulton Number	Size	Height	Issued
	D5327	Large	6", 15.0 cm	See below

Issued: 1978 in a limited edition of 7,500
Handle: Plain, black shading
Colourway: Brown rim; light brown face
Backstamp: Doulton/Special Exhibition Reproduction Limited to 7,500 Pieces

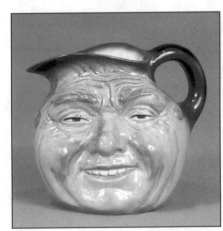

Size	Backstamp	Current Market Value U.K. £	U.S. $	Can. $
Large	Doulton/Special	125.00	175.00	200.00

John Barleycorn, Style Two, Variation No. 2

John Barleycorn Derivatives

Item:	ASH BOWL	Item:	ASH TRAY
Height:	4", 10.1 cm	Height:	2 ¾", 7.0 cm
Issued:	1936-1960	Issued:	1936-1960

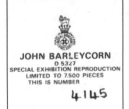

JOHN BARLEYCORN
D 5327
SPECIAL EXHIBITION REPRODUCTION
LIMITED TO 7,500 PIECES
THIS IS NUMBER
4145

Doulton Number	Item	Current Market Value U.K. £	U.S. $	Can. $
D5602	Ash Bowl	95.00	135.00	175.00
D —	Ash Tray	95.00	135.00	175.00

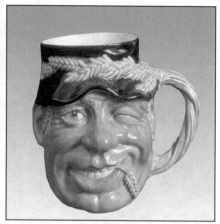

John Barleycorn, Style Three, Prototype

JOHN BARLEYCORN TANKARD

STYLE THREE: HAT WITH BARLEY EARS

PROTOTYPE

Designer: Stanley J. Taylor

	Doulton			
Statistics:	**Number**	**Size**	**Height**	**Issued**
	D6780	Mid	5 ½", 14.0 cm	See below

Modelled: Unknown
Issued: Not put into production
Handle: Twisted barley stalk
Colourway: Black cap; golden brown barley ears
Backstamp: Doulton

		Current Market Value		
Size	**Description**	**U.K. £**	**U.S. $**	**Can. $**
Mid	Prototype		Extremely rare	

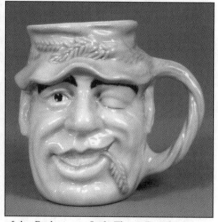

John Barleycorn, Style Three, Regular Issue

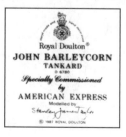

REGULAR ISSUE

Commissioned by American Express to form part of a 12-tankard set from various manufacturers, John Barleycorn was sold to between 500 and 600 card members.

This jug was issued only in English Translucent China.

Designer: Stanley J. Taylor

	Doulton			
Statistics:	**Number**	**Size**	**Height**	**Issued**
	D6780	Mid	5 ½", 14.0 cm	See below

Issued: 1988 in a special edition
Handle: Twisted barley stalk
Colourway: Pale blue cap; light brown barley ears
Backstamp: Doulton/American Express

		Current Market Value		
Size	**Composition**	**U.K. £**	**U.S. $**	**Can. $**
Mid	ETC	175.00	275.00	375.00

JOHN DOULTON

John Doulton (1793-1873) served a seven-year apprenticeship in the pottery industry as a thrower before fortune smiled on him and he was able to buy into a pottery partnership. In 1815 he bought a one-third share of a stoneware pot-house in Vauxhall Walk, Lambeth, and the company of Doulton and Watts was born.

To honour John Doulton, the Royal Doulton International Collectors Club made this jug available to all their original charter members in 1980.

This first varation of this jug has the time shown on "Big Ben" as eight o'clock.

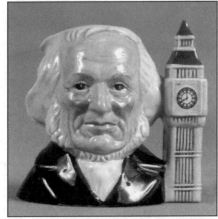

John Doulton, Variation No. 1

Designer: Eric Griffiths

Statistics:

Doulton Number	Size	Height	Issued
D6656	Small	4 ¼", 10.8 cm	See below

Handle: The tower of Big Ben
Backstamp: Doulton/RDICC
Series: RDICC

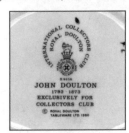

VARIATION No. 1: TIME SHOWN ON BIG BEN IS EIGHT O'CLOCK

Issued: 1980-c.1982
Colourway: Black coat with purple collar; lemon cravat; Big Ben is light brown

Size	Variation	Current Market Value U.K. £	U.S. $	Can. $
Small	Var. 1	65.00	120.00	135.00

VARIATION No. 2: TIME SHOWN ON BIG BEN IS TWO O'CLOCK

Starting in 1981 each new member joining the Royal Doulton International Collectors Club had the opportunity of purchasing the John Doulton jug; however, the time now shown on Big Ben is two o'clock.

Issued: 1981-1994
Colourway: Black coat with purple collar; yellow cravat; Big Ben is dark brown

Size	Variation	Current Market Value U.K. £	U.S. $	Can. $
Small	Var. 2	45.00	75.00	90.00

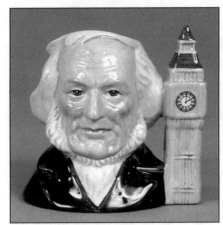

John Doulton, Variation No. 2

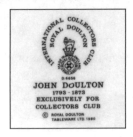

JOHN GILPIN

PROTOTYPE

"The Diverting History of John Gilpin" is an 18th-century poem by Cowper. In it Gilpin, a "linen draper bold," and his wife go to Edmonton to celebrate their 20th wedding anniversary. His horse runs out of control, however, and John careens ten miles beyond Edmonton and back again.

STYLE ONE: OLDER, COMICAL FACE

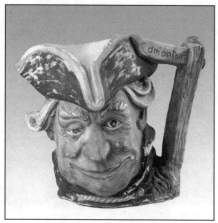

John Gilpin, Prototype, Style One

Designer:	Unknown
Height:	Unknown
Size:	Large
Issued:	Not put into production
Handle:	Brown wood sign post reading "Edmonton"
Colourway:	Maroon hat with gold trim; purple coat; grey hair
Backstamp:	Doulton

Doulton Number	Current Market Value		
	U.K. £	**U.S. $**	**Can. $**
D —	Extremely rare. Only two known.		

PROTOTYPE

STYLE TWO: YOUNGER, SAD FACE

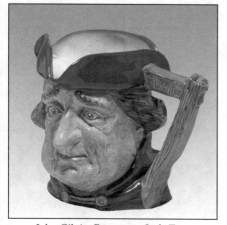

John Gilpin, Prototype, Style Two

Designer:	David B. Biggs
Height:	7", 17.8 cm
Size:	Large
Issued:	Not put into production
Handle:	Brown wood sign post reading "Edmonton"
Colourway:	Dark green hat; maroon coat; brown hair
Backstamp:	Doulton

Doulton Number	Current Market Value		
	U.K. £	**U.S. $**	**Can. $**
D —	Extremely rare.		

JOHN LENNON

John Winston Lennon (1940-1980) played guitar and wrote songs for the Beatles until the group disbanded in 1970. With his wife Yoko Ono, Lennon pursued a successful solo career until his tragic assassination in 1980.

Designer: Stanley J. Taylor
Handle: Plain

| Statistics: | **Doulton**
Number
See below | **Size**
Mid | **Height**
5 ½", 14.0 cm | **Issued**
See below |

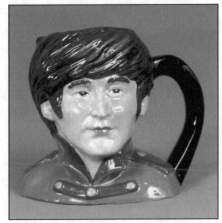

John Lennon, Variation No. 1

VARIATION No. 1: **Colourway** — Turquoise jacket with maroon collar and epaulettes

Issued: 1984-1991
Colourway: Turquoise jacket with maroon collar and epaulettes
Backstamp: Doulton
Series: The Beatles

Doulton		Current Market Value		
Number	Variation	U.K. £	U.S. $	Can. $
D6725	Var. 1	125.00	300.00	350.00

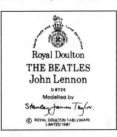

VARIATION No. 2: **Colourway** — Red jacket with yellow collar and epaulettes

Issued: 1987 in a limited edition of 1,000
Colourway: Red jacket with yellow collar and epaulettes
Backstamp: Doulton/John Sinclair
New Colourway 1987 Special Edition of 1000 for John Sinclair, Sheffield.

Doulton		Current Market Value		
Number	Variation	U.K. £	U.S. $	Can. $
D6797	Var. 2	200.00	400.00	450.00

VARIATION No. 3 **Colourway** — Maroon jacket with amber collar and epaulettes
Handle — Blue

Modelled: c.1983
Issued: Not put into production
Colourway: Maroon jacket with amber collar and epaulettes
Backstamp: Doulton

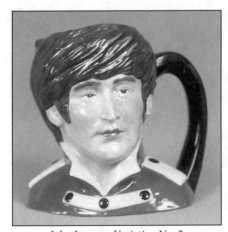

John Lennon, Variation No. 2

Doulton		Current Market Value		
Number	Variation	U.K. £	U.S. $	Can. $
D —	Var. 3	Sold March 27, 2001 Phillips, New Bond Street London, England, £2,400.00		

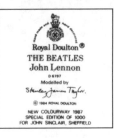

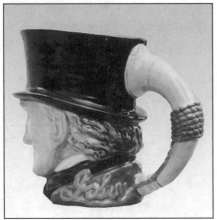

John Peel, Prototype

JOHN PEEL

John Peel (1776-1854) was a famous English huntsman, known for his enthusiasm, skill and hospitality. Fond of drink, he hosted large, popular post-hunt celebrations. Peel has been immortalized in the song "D'ye ken John Peel," written by John Woodcock Graves.

PROTOTYPE

Designer: Harry Fenton

Statistics:	Doulton Number	Size	Height	Issued
	—	Large	6 ½"	Unknown

Modelled: Unknown
Issued: Not put into production
Backstamp: Doulton
Handle: Yellow hunting horn
Colourway: Dark grey hat; maroon coat; dark blue bow tie
Backstamp: Doulton

Size	Description	Current Market Value		
		U.K. £	U.S. $	Can. $
Large	Prototype		Extremely rare	

JOHN PEEL

REGULAR ISSUE

Designer: Harry Fenton
Handle: Riding crop, with hunting horn forming inner section of upper handle
Backstamp: Doulton

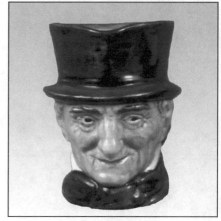

John Peel, Regular Issue

VARIATION No. 1: Colourway — Grey handle

Statistics:	Doulton Number	Size	Height	Issued
1.	D5612	Large	6 ½", 16.5 cm	1936-1960
2.	D5731	Small	3 ½", 8.9 cm	1937-1960
3.	D6130	Miniature	2 ¼", 5.7 cm	1940-1960
4.	D6259	Tiny	1 ¼", 3.1 cm	1947-1960

Colourway: Dark grey hat; maroon coat; dark blue bow tie; grey handle

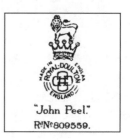

"John Peel."
R^dN^o809559.

Jug No.	Size	Current Market Value U.K. £	U.S. $	Can. $
1.	Large	100.00	175.00	200.00
2.	Small	45.00	70.00	90.00
3.	Miniature	45.00	65.00	85.00
4.	Tiny	125.00	225.00	250.00

VARIATION No. 2: Colourway — Black and orange handle

Statistics:	Doulton Number	Size	Height	Issued
1.	D5612	Large	6 ½", 16.5 cm	Unknown
2.	D5731	Small	3 ½", 8.9 cm	c.1942-Unk.
3.	D6130	Miniature	2 ¼", 5.7 cm	c.1942-Unk.

Colourway: Dark grey hat; maroon coat; dark blue bow tie; black and orange handle

Jug No.	Size	Current Market Value U.K. £	U.S. $	Can. $
1.	Large	125.00	200.00	225.00
2.	Small	50.00	75.00	100.00
3.	Miniature	50.00	75.00	100.00

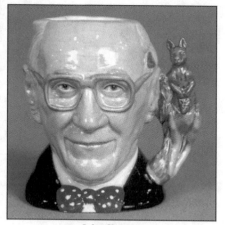

John Shorter

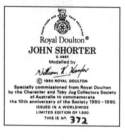

JOHN SHORTER

Commissioned by the Character and Toby Jug Collectors Society of Australia, this depiction of Australian retailer John Shorter was released in 1991 in a limited edition of 1,500 pieces.

Designer: William K. Harper

	Doulton			
Statistics:	**Number**	**Size**	**Height**	**Issued**
	D6880	Small	4 ¼", 10.8 cm	See below

Issued: 1991 in a limited edition of 1,500
Handle: A kangaroo and joey
Colourway: Grey hair; black jacket; maroon and white polka-dot bow tie
Backstamp: Doulton/CJCSA

	Current Market Value		
Size	**U.K. £**	**U.S. $**	**Can. $**
Small	125.00	200.00	225.00

"JOHNNERS" BRIAN JOHNSTON

Brian "Johnners" Johnston, 1912-1994, was a famous radio broadcaster. He was well liked for his test match commentaries. This jug was released by Lawleys by Post in a limited edition of 9,500.

Designer: Stanley J. Taylor

	Doulton			
Statistics:	**Number**	**Size**	**Height**	**Issued**
	D7018	Small	4", 10.1 cm	See below

Issued: 1996 in a limited edition of 9,500
Handle: Microphone, cricket ball and bail
Colourway: White, blue, red and black
Backstamp: Doulton

	Current Market Value		
Size	**U.K. £**	**U.S. $**	**Can. $**
Small	50.00	125 .00	150.00

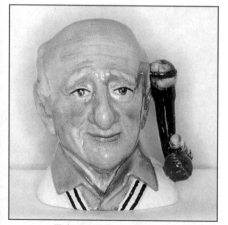

"Johnners" Brian Johnston

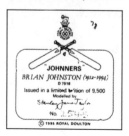

JOHNNY APPLESEED

John Chapman (1774-1845) was an American pioneer who sold and gave saplings and apple seeds to colonizing families. He travelled the eastern U.S., sowing apple orchards and tending his trees. After his death, Chapman became the hero of many legends.

Designer: Harry Fenton

Statistics:

Doulton Number	Size	Height	Issued
D6372	Large	6", 15.0 cm	1953-1969

Handle: An apple tree and knapsack
Colourway: Maroon and grey cap; brown robes
Backstamp: Doulton

Size	Current Market Value		
	U.K. £	U.S. $	Can. $
Large	250.00	425.00	500.00

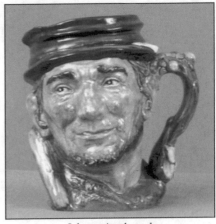

Johnny Appleseed

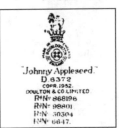

THE JUG COLLECTOR

Designer: Robert Tabbenor

Statistics:

Doulton Number	Size	Height	Issued
D7147	Small	4 ¾", 12.1 cm	2000-2000

Handle: The Maori, RDICC 20th Anniversary logo
Colourway: White shirt; rose sweater
Backstamp: Doulton/RDICC 20th Anniversary
Series: RDICC

Size	Current Market Value		
	U.K. £	U.S. $	Can. $
Small	75.00	175.00	250.00

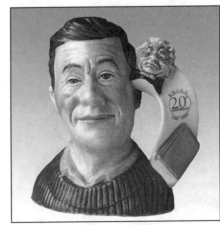

The Jug Collector

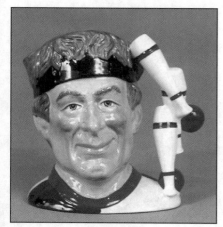

The Juggler

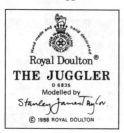

THE JUGGLER

Designer:	Stanley J. Taylor			
	Doulton			
Statistics:	**Number**	**Size**	**Height**	**Issued**
	D6835	Large	6 ½", 16.5 cm	1989-1991

Handle: Skittles and balls
Colourway: Brown hair; yellow, blue and red tunic; dark green head band
Backstamp: Doulton
Series: The Circus Performers

	Current Market Value		
Size	**U.K. £**	**U.S. $**	**Can. $**
Large	85.00	200.00	225.00

KING ARTHUR and GUINEVERE

Arthur is the legendary fifth-century King of Britain, known for his courage and honesty. His 12 knights, with whom he ruled and planned his campaigns, sat at a round table, so that none had precedence. His best friend, the knight Lancelot, betrayed him by falling in love with his beautiful wife Guinevere. Arthur died at Camelford in a battle against his usurping nephew Mordred.

This jug was issued in 1989 in a limited edition of 9,500.

Designer: Stanley J. Taylor

Statistics:	Doulton Number	Size	Height	Issued
	D6836	Large	6 ½", 16.5 cm	See below

Issued: 1989 in a limited edition of 9,500
Handle: King Arthur — Sword
Guinevere — Chalice
Colourway: Blue-grey, yellow and white
Backstamp: Doulton
Series: The Star-Crossed Lovers Collection (Two-faced jug)

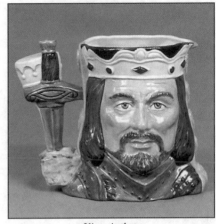

King Arthur

	Current Market Value		
Size	U.K. £	U.S. $	Can. $
Large	100.00	200.00	225.00

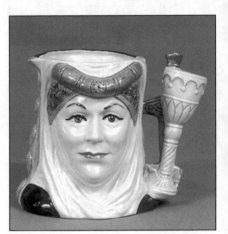

Guinevere

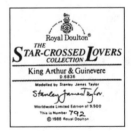

KING ARTHUR and MERLIN

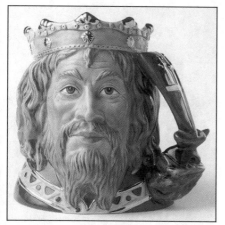

King Arthur

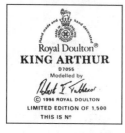

The companion jugs King Arthur, released in 1997, and Merlin in 1998, were issued in a limited edition of 1,500 each.

STYLE TWO: MERLIN: HANDLE — DRAGON AND SWORD

Designer: Robert Tabbenor

Statistics:	Doulton Number	Size	Height	Issued
1.	D7055	Large	7 ¼", 18.4 cm	See below
2.	D7117	Large	7", 17.8 cm	See below

Issued: 1. King Arthur — 1997 in a limited edition of 1,500
2. Merlin — 1999 in a limited edition of 1,500
Handle: 1. King Arthur — A shield and an anvil
2. Merlin — A dragon and sword Excalibur
Colourway: 1. King Arthur — Red, brown, black and gold
2. Merlin — White, red, gold and purple, platinum highlights
Backstamp: Doulton

Jug No.	Doulton Number	Name	Current Market Value		
			U.K. £	U.S. $	Can. $
1.	D7055	King Arthur	150.00	325.00	500.00
2.	D7117	Merlin	150.00	325.00	500.00

Note: For the character jug Merlin (Style One) see page 274.

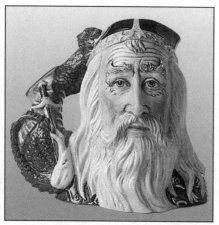

Merlin

KING CHARLES I

This jug was issued in a limited edition of 2,500 to commemorate the 350th anniversary of the English Civil War in 1642. It is unusual in the sense that it is the first three-handled character jug ever produced by Doulton. On Charles's left Oliver Cromwell forms the handle, on his right, Queen Henrietta. The third handle, at the King's back and not seen in the photograph, is a plume.

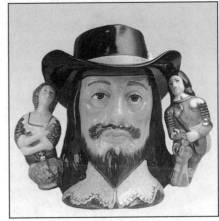

King Charles I, Style One

STYLE ONE: THREE-HANDLED JUG

Designer: William K. Harper

Statistics:	Doulton Number	Size	Height	Issued
	D6917	Large	7", 17.8 cm	See below

Issued: 1992 in a limited edition of 2,500
Handle: Three handles (see above)
Colourway: Black, yellow and red
Backstamp: Doulton

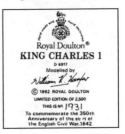

Size	Current Market Value		
	U.K. £	U.S. $	Can. $
Large	250.00	400.00	450.00

Note: For Charles I see the "Kings and Queens of the Realm" page 247.

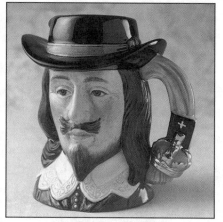

King Charles I, Style Two

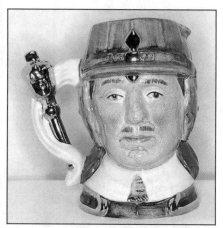

Oliver Cromwell, Style Two

KING CHARLES I
and
OLIVER CROMWELL

Commissioned by Lawleys By Post, Charles I (1600-1649) and his companion jug, Oliver Cromwell (1599-1659), form a pair which were issued in a limited edition of 2,500.

STYLE TWO: **CHARLES I** — HANDLE IS CROWN, BIBLE AND SASH

STYLE TWO: **OLIVER CROMWELL** — HANDLE IS SILVER MACE AND SASH

Designer: William K. Harper

Statistics:

	Doulton Number	Size	Height	Issued
1.	D6985	Small	4 ½", 11.9 cm	See below
2.	D6986	Small	4 ½", 11.9 cm	See below

Issued: 1994 in a limited edition of 2,500
Handle: 1. King Charles I — Crown and bible against a red sash
2. Oliver Cromwell — Silver mace; sash
Colourway: 1. King Charles I — Black hat; maroon and purple jacket; cream collar
2. Oliver Cromwell — Grey and white with silver details
Backstamp: Doulton

Jug No.	Doulton Number	Name	Current Market Value		
			U.K. £	U.S. $	Can. $
1.	D6985	King Charles I	125.00	175.00	225.00
2.	D6986	Cromwell	125.00	175.00	225.00
		Pair	200.00	325.00	425.00

Note: 1. For Charles I, see the "Kings and Queens of the Realm" page 247, and for King Charles I (Style One) see page 244.
2. For Oliver Cromwell (Style One) see page 297.

KING EDWARD VII

In this jug, King Edward VII is shown wearing a crown and all his finery. The handle comprises the traditional Royal Doulton backstamp of the crown and lion. This piece had a limited edition of 2,500 and was issued exclusively for the Royal Doulton International Collectors Club.

Designer: William K. Harper

Statistics:	Doulton Number	Size	Height	Issued
	D6923	Mid	5 ½", 14.0 cm	See below

Issued: 1992 in a limited edition of 2,500
Handle: Lion and crown of the Doulton backstamp
Colourway: Red, gold, and white
Backstamp: Doulton/RDICC
Series: RDICC

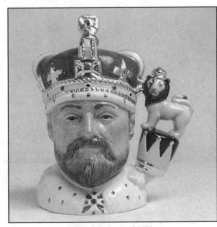

King Edward VII

Size	Current Market Value		
	U.K. £	U.S. $	Can. $
Mid	150.00	250.00	300.00

Note: For the Edward VIII (Style One) see "Kings and Queens of the Realm" page 247, and for Edward VII (Style Two) see page 173.

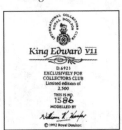

KING HENRY VIII

This is a two-handled jug and, strictly speaking, should be classified as a loving cup. It was issued in 1991 in a limited edition of 1,991 to commemorate the 500th anniversary of the birth of Henry VIII.

Designer: William K. Harper

Statistics:	Doulton Number	Size	Height	Issued
	D6888	Large	7", 17.8 cm	See below

Issued: 1991 in a limited edition of 1,991
Handle: Double handle, three wives on either side
Colourway: White and black with gold trim
Backstamp: Doulton

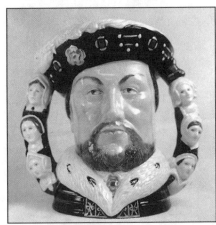

King Henry VIII

Size	Current Market Value		
	U.K. £	U.S. $	Can. $
Large	650.00	1,000.00	1,250.00

Note: For Henry VIII (Style One), see page 222; for Henry VIII, (Style Two) see the "Kings and Queens of the Realm" page 247, and for the toby jug King Henry VIII, see page 65.

KING JOHN

For the character jug King John see page 323.

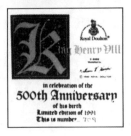

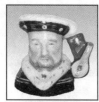

Henry VIII (D6990)

Queen Victoria
(D6991)

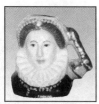

Elizabeth I (D6992)

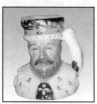

Edward VII(D6993)

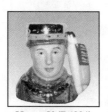

Henry V (D6994)

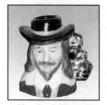

Charles I (D6995)

KINGS AND QUEENS OF THE REALM

This set of six tinies was issued by Lawleys By Post in a limited edition of 2,500 sets. Each set came with a wooden display stand and a certificate of authenticity.

Designer: William K. Harper
Height: 1 ½", 3.8 cm
Issued: 1994 in a limited edition of 2,500
Handles: 1. **Henry VIII** (Style Two) — Bible and lute
2. **Victoria** — Gold lion and crown
3. **Elizabeth I** — Orb and sceptre
4. **Edward VII** (Style One) — Scroll reading "Entente Cordiale"
5. **Henry V** (Style Two) — Royal standard
6. **Charles I** — Crown and sceptre
Colourways: 1. **Henry VIII** — Black, white and gold
2. **Victoria** — Yellow, brown and silver
3. **Elizabeth I** — Green, yellow and brown
4. **Edward VII** — Gold, white and yellow
5. **Henry V** — Gold, maroon and yellow
6. **Charles I** — Black, yellow and red
Backstamp: Doulton

Jug No.	Doulton No.	Name	U.K. £	U.S. $	Can. $
1.	D6990	Henry VIII (Style Two)	50.00	80.00	100.00
2.	D6991	Victoria	50.00	80.00	100.00
3.	D6992	Elizabeth I	50.00	80.00	100.00
4.	D6993	Edward VII (Style One)	50.00	80.00	100.00
5.	D6994	Henry V (Style Two)	50.00	80.00	100.00
6.	D6995	Charles I	50.00	80.00	100.00
		Complete set with stand	275.00	450.00	550.00

Note: Models exist without the gold highlights.

LAUREL AND HARDY

The Laurel and Hardy jugs were commissioned by Lawleys By Post and issued as a pair in a limited edition of 3,500.

Designer: William K. Harper

Statistics:

	Doulton Number	Size	Height	Issued
1.	D7008	Small	4", 10.1 cm	See below
2.	D7009	Small	4", 10.1 cm	See below

Issued: 1995 in a limited edition of 3,500
Handles: Early movie camera
Colourway: Browns, black, white and red
Backstamp: Doulton

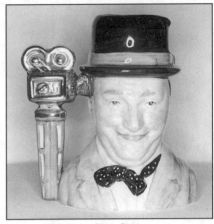

Laurel

Jug No.	Doulton Number	Size	Name	Current Market Value U.K. £	U.S. $	Can. $
1.	D7008	Small	Laurel	75.00	120.00	150.00
2.	D7009	Small	Hardy	75.00	120.00	150.00
	Pair			150.00	240.00	300.00

Note: For the Laurel and Hardey bookends see page 407.

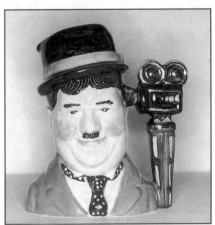

Hardy

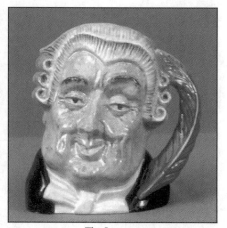

The Lawyer

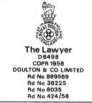

Backstamp - Large
Size Jug

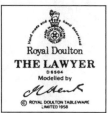

Backstamp - Small
Size Jug

THE LAWYER

Designer: Max Henk

Statistics:	Doulton Number	Size	Height	Issued
1.	D6498	Large	7", 17.8 cm	1959-1996
2.	D6504	Small	4", 10.1 cm	1959-1996
3.	D6524	Miniature	2 ½", 6.4 cm	1960-1991

Handle: Green feather quill
Colourway: Grey wig; black robes; white shirt
Backstamp: Doulton

Jug No.	Size	Comp.	Issued	Current Market Value U.K. £	U.S. $	Can. $
1.	Large	EW	1959-1996	60.00	100.00	125.00
		ETC	1968-1971	100.00	150.00	175.00
2.	Small	EW	1959-1996	35.00	65.00	80.00
		ETC	1968-1971	65.00	100.00	125.00
3.	Miniature	EW	1960-1991	35.00	70.00	80.00
		ETC	1968-1971	65.00	100.00	125.00

The Lawyer Derivative

Item: TABLE LIGHTER
Height: 3 ½", 8.9 cm
Issued: 1962-1974

Doulton Number	Item	Current Market Value U.K. £	U.S. $	Can. $
D6504	Table Lighter	175.00	275.00	350.00

LEEDS UNITED (FOOTBALL CLUB)

Designer: Stanley J. Taylor

Statistics:	Doulton Number	Size	Height	Issued
	D6928	Small	5", 12.7 cm	1992-1999

Handle: Team coloured scarf
Colourway: White, blue and yellow uniform
Backstamp: Doulton
Series: The Football Supporters

Size	Current Market Value U.K. £	U.S. $	Can. $
Small	50.00	110.00	125.00

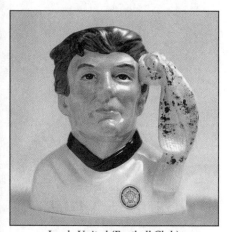

Leeds United (Football Club)

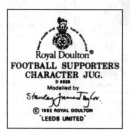

LEN HUTTON

Sir Leonard Hutton played for the Yorkshire County Cricket Club. The ribbon bearing the number 364, which is intertwined around the handle of the jug, represents his famous record innings against Australia at the Oval cricket grounds in 1938, a record which still stands in England today. The jug was commissioned by Lawleys By Post and was issued in a limited edition of 9,500. The first jug was presented to Her Royal Highness, the Duchess of Kent, who is patron of the Len Hutton 364 Appeal.

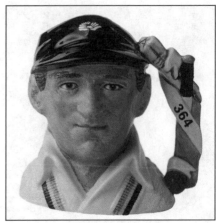

Len Hutton

Designer: Stanley J. Taylor

Statistics:	**Doulton Number**	**Size**	**Height**	**Issued**
	D6945	Small	4", 10.1 cm	See below

Issued: 1993 in a limited edition of 9,500
Handle: Cricket bat, stumps and ball
Colourway: White shirt and sweater; black cap
Backstamp: Doulton
Series: Cricketers

	Current Market Value		
Size	U.K. £	U.S. $	Can. $
Small	65.00	150.00	175.00

LEPRECHAUN

This wizened little elf is a legendary Irish sprite with a mischievous nature. The Irish believed that leprechauns guarded hoards of treasure hidden at the end of rainbows.

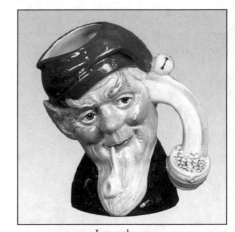

Leprechaun

Designer: William K. Harper

Statistics:	**Doulton Number**	**Size**	**Height**	**Issued**
1.	D6847	Large	7 ½", 19.1 cm	1990-1996
2.	D6899	Small	4 ½", 11.9 cm	1991-1996

Handle: Rainbow with a sack of gold at the base
Colourway: Green cap; brown coat
Backstamps: A. Doulton
For general release:
Large size — 1991, Small size — 1992
B. Doulton/The Site of the Green
Large size commissioned by the Site of the Green and issued in 1990 in a special edition of 500 pieces.
C. Doulton/The Site of the Green
Small size commissioned by the Site of the Green and issued in 1991 in a special edition of 500 pieces.

Jug No.	Size	Issued	Current Market Value		
			U.K. £	U.S. $	Can. $
1A.	Large	1991-1996	65.00	100.00	125.00
1B.		1990	65.00	100.00	125.00
2A.	Small	1992-1996	40.00	65.00	85.00
2C.		1991	45.00	65.00	85.00

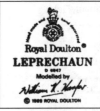

Backstamp A - Doulton

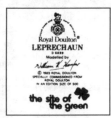

Backstamp B - Site of the Green

LEWIS CARROLL

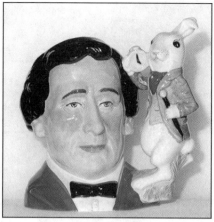

Lewis Carroll

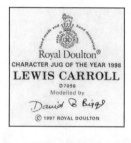

One hundred years after the death of Lewis Carroll, creator of *Alice's Adventures in Wonderland*, he is celebrated with this Character Jug of The Year for 1998.

Designer: David B. Biggs

	Doulton			
Statistics:	**Number**	**Size**	**Height**	**Issued**
	D7096	Large	8", 20.3 cm	1998-1998

Handle: A white rabbit and a clock
Colourway: Maroon jacket; white shirt; black bow tie
Backstamp: Doulton/Character Jug of the Year, 1998
Series: Character Jug of the Year

	Current Market Value		
Size	**U.K. £**	**U.S. $**	**Can. $**
Large	100.00	175.00	25.00

Note: For the toby jug Lewis Carroll see page 66.

LITTLE MESTER MUSEUM PIECE

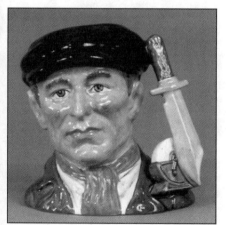

Little Mester Museum Piece

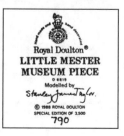

This jug was modelled on the likeness of Grinder Rowland Swindon, a grinder from Sheffield, England. It was commissioned by John Sinclair of Sheffield and issued in 1988 in a limited edition of 3,500 pieces. One thousand jugs were bought by the World Student Games to help launch the games in Sheffield.

Designer: Stanley J. Taylor

	Doulton			
Statistics:	**Number**	**Size**	**Height**	**Issued**
	D6819	Large	6 ¾", 17.2 cm	See below

Issued: 1988 in a special edition of 3,500
Handle: Bowie knife and grinder
Colourway: Black cap; blue jacket; white shirt; red scarf
Backstamp: Doulton

	Current Market Value		
Size	**U.K. £**	**U.S. $**	**Can. $**
Large	100.00	200.00	250.00

LITTLE NELL

For the character jug Little Nell see the "Charles Dickens Commemorative Set" page 143.

LIVERPOOL (FOOTBALL CLUB)

Designer: Stanley J. Taylor

Statistics:	**Doulton Number**	**Size**	**Height**	**Issued**
	D6930	Small	5", 12.7 cm	1992-1999

Handle: Team coloured scarf
Colourway: Red and white uniform
Backstamp: Doulton
Series: The Football Supporters

	Current Market Value		
Size	**U.K. £**	**U.S. $**	**Can. $**
Small	50.00	110.00	125.00

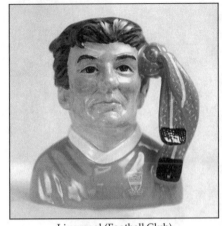

Liverpool (Football Club)

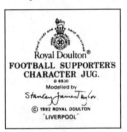

LIVERPOOL CENTENARY JUG (BILL SHANKLY)

Issued to commemorate the 100th anniversary of the Liverpool Football Club in 1992, this jug is a limited edition of 5,500.

Designer: William K. Harper

Statistics:	**Doulton Number**	**Size**	**Height**	**Issued**
	D6914	Small	5", 12.7 cm	See below

Issued: 1992 in a limited edition of 5,500
Handle: Two footballs and flag
Colourway: Red jersey; white collar; grey hair
Backstamp: Doulton/Liverpool F.C.

	Current Market Value		
Size	**U.K. £**	**U.S. $**	**Can. $**
Small	75.00	150.00	175.00

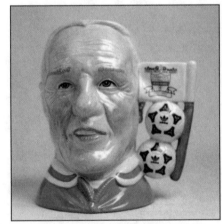

Liverpool Centenary Jug (Bill Shankly)

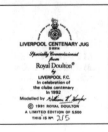

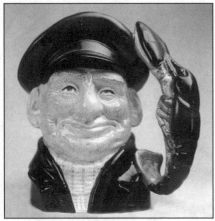

Lobster Man

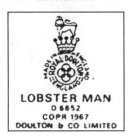

LOBSTER MAN
D 6652
COPR 1967
DOULTON & CO LIMITED

LOBSTER MAN

Designer: David B. Biggs
Handle: Lobster
Backstamp: Doulton

VARIATION No. 1: **Colourway** — Dark blue jacket and cap; white fisherman's jersey

Statistics:	Doulton Number	Size	Height	Issued
1.	D6617	Large	7 ½", 19.1 cm	1968-1991
2.	D6620	Small	3 ¾", 9.5 cm	1968-1991
3.	D6652	Miniature	2 ¾", 7.0 cm	1980-1991

Colourway: Dark blue jacket and cap; white fisherman's jersey

Jug. No.	Size	Comp.	Issued	Current Market Value U.K. £	U.S. $	Can. $
1.	Large	EW	1968-1991	60.00	85.00	100.00
		ETC	1968-1971	65.00	100.00	150.00
2.	Small	EW	1968-1991	40.00	70.00	80.00
		ETC	1968-1971	60.00	90.00	125.00
3.	Miniature	EW	1980-1991	40.00	50.00	60.00

VARIATION No. 2: **Colourway** — Dark blue jacket and cap; blue-grey fisherman's jersey

Statistics:	Doulton Number	Size	Height	Issued
	D6783	Large	8", 20.3 cm	1987-1989

Colourway: Dark blue jacket and cap; blue fisherman's jersey

Size	Issued	Current Market Value U.K. £	U.S. $	Can. $
Large	1987-1989	75.00	200.00	250.00

VARIATION No. 3: **Colourway** — Light blue jacket

Statistics:	Doulton Number	Size	Height	Issued
	D —	Small	3 ¾", 9.5 cm	1987-Unk.

Colourway: Light blue jacket

Size	Issued	Current Market Value U.K. £	U.S. $	Can. $
Small	1987- Unknown	85.00	150.00	185.00

THE LONDON 'BOBBY'

Designer: Stanley J. Taylor
Handle: Tower of Big Ben and a whistle
Backstamp: Doulton

Statistics:	Doulton Number	Size	Height	Issued
1.	D6744	Large	7", 17.8 cm	1986-2001
2.	D6762	Small	3 ½", 8.9 cm	1987-Current
3.	D6763	Miniature	2 ½", 6.4 cm	1987-1991

Colourway: Black uniform; white and black helmet badge (see variations); grey whistle
Series: The London Collection

Variation No. 1: Hat badge embossed and hand painted

Jug No.	Size	Issued	Current Market Value U.K. £	U.S. $	Can. $
1.	Large	1986-1987	175.00	275.00	300.00
2.	Small	1987-1987	125.00	200.00	225.00
3.	Miniature	1987-1987	125.00	225.00	250.00

Variation No. 2: Hat badge decal decorated

Jug No.	Size	Issued	Current Market Value U.K. £	U.S. $	Can. $
1.	Large	1987-2001	90.00	150.00	200.00
2.	Small	1987-Current	55.00	90.00	120.00
3.	Miniature	1987-1991	50.00	100.00	130.00

Variation No. 3: Silver hat badge and whistle

This model is marked "For Approval Trial No. 2 Doulton Burslem."

Statistics:	Doulton Number	Size	Height	Issued
	D —	Large	7", 17.8 cm	See below

Modelled: c.1985
Issued: Not put into production
Handle: Tower of Big Ben and whistle
Colourway: Black uniform; silver badge and whistle
Backstamp: Doulton

Size	Current Market Value U.K. £	U.S. $	Can. $
Large	Sold June 24, 1999 Phillips, New Bond Street London, England, £1,400.00		

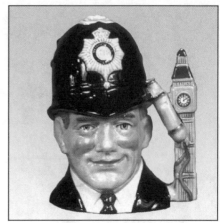

The London 'Bobby', Regular Issue

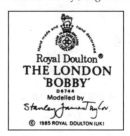

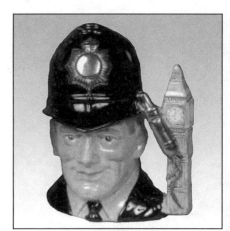

The London 'Bobby', Variation No. 3

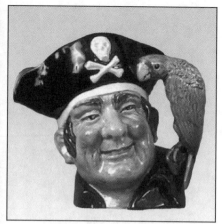

Long John Silver, Variation No. 1

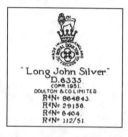

LONG JOHN SILVER

This scoundrel and pirate from Robert Louis Stevenson's *Treasure Island* had a wooden leg and a parrot companion. Together with the boy-hero Jim Hawkins, he set sail in a hair-raising search for buried treasure.

Designer: Max Henk
Handle: A parrot
Backstamp: Doulton

VARIATION No. 1:   **Colourway** — Maroon shirt; green and grey parrot

Statistics:	Doulton Number	Size	Height	Issued
1.	D6335	Large	7", 17.8 cm	1952-1998
2.	D6386	Small	4", 10.1 cm	1952-1998
3.	D6512	Miniature	2 ½", 6.4 cm	1960-1991

Colourway: Maroon shirt; green and grey parrot
Series: Characters From Literature

Jug No.	Size	Comp.	Issued	Current Market Value U.K. £	U.S. $	Can. $
1.	Large	EW	1952-1998	85.00	150.00	200.00
		ETC	1968-1971	125.00	200.00	250.00
2.	Small	EW	1952-1998	50.00	75.00	110.00
		ETC	1968-1971	80.00	125.00	165.00
3.	Miniature	EW	1960-1991	40.00	55.00	65.00
		ETC	1968-1971	50.00	75.00	90.00

VARIATION No. 2:   **Colourway** — Yellow shirt; yellow-green parrot

Statistics:	Doulton Number	Size	Height	Issued
	D6799	Large	7", 17.8 cm	See below

Issued: 1987 in a limited edition of 250
Backstamp: Doulton/D. H. Holmes/Specially Commissioned from Royal Doulton by D. H. Holmes Company Ltd./ Celebrating the opening of The Royal Doulton Room D. H. Holmes, New Orleans, Louisiana, U.S.A. Commissioned by D. H. Holmes Company Ltd. and issued in 1987 in a limited edition of 250 pieces.

Size	Variation	Current Market Value U.K. £	U.S. $	Can. $
Large	Var. 2	225.00	400.00	475.00

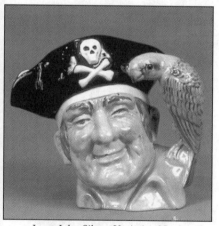

Long John Silver, Variation No. 2

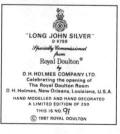

LONG JOHN SILVER (cont.)

VARIATION No. 3:   Colourway — Dark brown shirt; crimson hat; green parrot

This special colourway of the small size Long John Silver jug was available only at the Michael Doulton Treasure Chest Events held during 1999. An incorrect backstamp reads 'We want that silver and we'll have it" on the first jugs issued. This was later corrected to read "We want that treasure and we'll have it" that now appears on the jug.

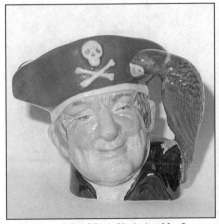

Long John Silver, Variation No. 3

Statistics:

Doulton Number	Size	Height	Issued
D7138	Small	4", 10.1 cm	1999-2000

Backstamp: Doulton/Michael Doulton Treasure Chest
Exclusive colourway for Treasure Chest Events

Jug No.	Backstamp	Issued	Current Market Value		
			U.K. £	U.S. $	Can. $
A.	'Silver'	1999-1999	100.00	150.00	175.00
B.	'Treasure'	1999-2000	50.00	85.00	125.00

Long John Silver Derivatives

Item:	TABLE LIGHTER	**Item:**	TEAPOT
Height:	3 ½", 8.9 cm	**Height:**	7", 17.8 cm
Issued:	1958-1973	**Issued:**	1990-1991

Doulton Number	Item	Current Market Value		
		U.K. £	U.S. $	Can. $
D6386	Lighter	150.00	250.00	275.00
D6853	Teapot	175.00	275.00	350.00

Incorrect Bankstamp

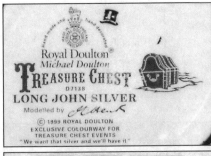

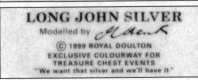

"We want that silver and we'll have it"

Correct Backstamp

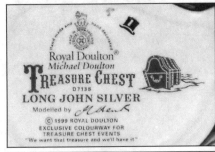

"We want that treasure and we'll have it"

LORD BADEN-POWELL

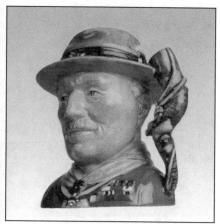

Lord Baden-Powell

Commissioned by Travers Stanley Collections, and with permission from the Scout Association, this character jug, issued in a limited edition of 2,500, portrays the founder of the Boy Scout movement. A certificate of authenticity accompanies this jug.

Designer: William K. Harper

Statistics:

	Doulton Number	Size	Height	Issued
	D7144	Small	4 ¼", 10.8 cm	See below

Issued: 1999 in a limited edition of 2,500
Handle: Kudu horn and Wood Badge
Colourway: Browns, black and red
Backstamp: Doulton / Travers Stanley Collections

Size	Current Market Value		
	U.K. £	U.S. $	Can. $
Small	60.00	125.00	175.00

LORD KITCHENER

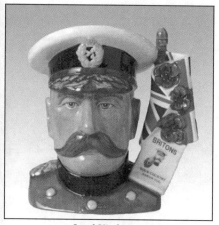

Lord Kitchener

Lord Horatio Kitchener was renowned for his war efforts. This model was issued to commemorate the 150th anniversary of Lord Kitchener's death.

Designer: David B. Biggs

Statistics:

	Doulton Number	Size	Height	Issued
	D7148	Large	7 ¼", 18.4 cm	See below

Issued: 2000 in a limited edition of 1,500
Handle: Union Jack, poppies, WWI poster "Britons Your Country Needs You"
Colourway: Khaki uniform with black collar; white and brown cap
Backstamp: Doulton

Size	Current Market Value		
	U.K. £	U.S. $	Can. $
Large	150.00	310.00	—

LORD MAYOR OF LONDON

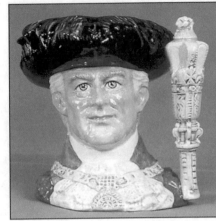

Designer: Stanley J. Taylor

Statistics:

Doulton Number	Size	Height	Issued
D6864	Large	7 ¼", 18.4 cm	1990-1991

Handle: Sceptre of office
Colourway: Black plume hat; red cloak; yellow chain of office
Backstamp: Doulton
Series: The London Collection

Size	Current Market Value		
	U.K. £	U.S. $	Can. $
Large	100.00	175.00	200.00

Lord Mayor of London

LORD NELSON

Horatio Nelson (1758-1805), a member of the navy since the age of 12, was made commander-in-chief of his own fleet in 1803. He saw action in the West Indies and in Canada, but is best remembered for his defeat of the French and Spanish navies at the Battle of Trafalgar in 1805. Nelson died during the battle.

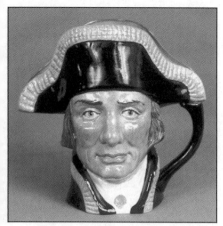

Lord Nelson

Designer:	Geoff Blower			

	Doulton			
Statistics:	**Number**	**Size**	**Height**	**Issued**
	D6336	Large	7", 17.8 cm	See below

Handle: Plain
Colourway: Blue tricorn and jacket with gold trim; white cravat
Backstamps: **A.** Doulton
B. Doulton/Battle of Trafalgar/
Commemorating the 150th Anniversary of the Battle of Trafalgar 21st October 1955
Commissioned for the Admiralty to commemorate the 150th anniversary of Nelson's victory at Trafalgar, October 21, 1955.
C. Three of the jugs carry an added line to the backstamp, either "First Lord," "First Sea Lord" or "Secretary," the intention being that these three jugs would be held in perpetuity at the respective offices. However one of the elected officials left office with a jug, which later appeared on the market.

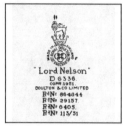

Backstamp A - Doulton

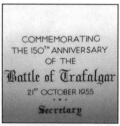

Backstamp C "Secretary"

Jug No.	Issued	Current Market Value		
		U.K. £	**U.S. $**	**Can. $**
A.	1952-1969	250.00	500.00	600.00
B.	1955-1955	Rare		
C.	1955-1955	Extremely rare, only three issued and each with a different backstamp		

Note: For the character jug Nelson see page 287 and for the character jug Vice-Admiral Nelson see page 388.

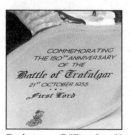

Backstamp C "First Lord"

LORD NELSON AND LADY HAMILTON

Lord Nelson led England to victory in the Battle of Trafalgar, but lost his own life. Lady Emma Hamilton secured supplies to Malta during its French occupation. Nelson and Lady Hamilton had a daughter, Horatia, born in 1801.

This jug was issued by Lawleys By Post in a limited edition of 1,500 pieces.

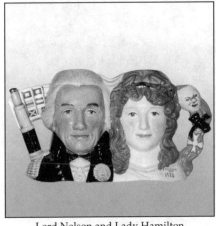

Designer: William K. Harper

Statistics:	**Doulton Number**	**Size**	**Height**	**Issued**
	D7092	Small	4", 10.1 cm	See below

Issued:	1997 in a limited edition of 1,500
Handle:	Nelson — Admiralty flags and a telescope
	Lady Hamilton — Theatrical mask and a Maltese Cross
Colourway:	Nelson — Naval uniform, grey hair
	Lady Hamilton — White dress, auburn hair
Backstamp:	Doulton
Series:	Double Character Jugs

Lord Nelson and Lady Hamilton

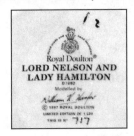

	Current Market Value		
Size	**U.K. £**	**U.S. $**	**Can. $**
Small	120.00	175.00	250.00

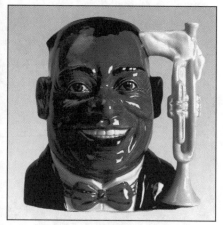

Louis Armstrong, Variation No. 1

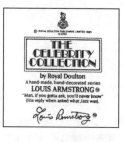

LOUIS ARMSTRONG

Daniel Louis "Satchmo" Armstrong (1900-1971) evolved from a self-taught cornet player to the first internationally famous soloist in jazz. He was well known for both his brilliant technique on the trumpet and for his deep throaty singing. Appearing in many live shows, Broadway musicals and films, Armstrong's music had a lasting influence on jazz.

Designer: David B. Biggs
Handle: Trumpet and handkerchief
Backstamp: Doulton

Statistics:	Doulton Number	Size	Height	Issued
	D6707	Large	7 ½", 19.1 cm	See below

Variation No. 1: **Colourway** — Yellow trumpet

Issued: 1984-1988
Colourway: Dark brown, black, pink and white
Series: The Celebrity Collection

		Current Market Value		
Size	Variation	U.K. £	U.S. $	Can. $
Large	Var. 1	125.00	300.00	350.00

Variation No. 2: **Colourway** — Gold trumpet

Issued: Not put into production
Colourway: Light brown, black, pink and white

		Current Market Value		
Size	Variation	U.K. £	U.S. $	Can. $
Large	Var. 2		Extremely rare	

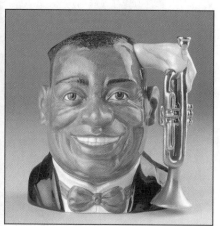

Louis Armstrong, Variation No. 2

LUMBERJACK

The Lumberjack is one of three jugs that received a special backstamp in 1967. The other two, the North American Indian and the Trapper, complete the three-jug Canadian Centennial Series. A small quantity of miniature Lumberjack prototypes are known to exist.

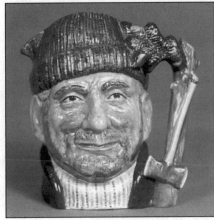

Lumberjack

Designer: Max Henk

Statistics:

	Doulton Number	Size	Height	Issued
1.	D6610	Large	7 ¼", 18.4 cm	1967-1982
2.	D6613	Small	3 ½", 8.9 cm	1967-1982
3.	D —	Miniature	2 ½", 6.4 cm	Unknown

Handle: Tree trunk and axe
Colourway: Red cap; green jacket; pink sweater
Backstamps: A. Doulton
  B. Doulton/Canadian Centenary/Canadian Centennial Series 1867-1967 Available in North America during 1967 only.
Series: Canadian Centennial Series, 1867-1967

Jug No.	Size	Comp.	Issued	Current Market Value U.K. £	U.S. $	Can. $
1A.	Large	EW	1967-1982	85.00	125.00	150.00
1A.		ETC	1968-1971	125.00	200.00	225.00
1B.	Large	EW	1967-1967	150.00	250.00	275.00
2A.	Small	EW	1967-1982	45.00	70.00	90.00
2A.		ETC	1968-1971	65.00	100.00	125.00
3.	Miniature	EW	Unknown	1,750.00	3,000.00	4,000.00

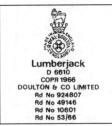

Backstamp A - Doulton

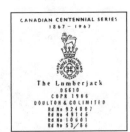

Backstamp B -
Doulton/Canadian
Centennial Series

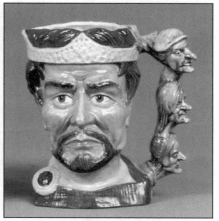

Macbeth, Style One

MACBETH

First performed in 1606, this Shakespearean tragedy was based on Scottish history. With the help of his wife, Macbeth plots to usurp the throne. Three witches prophesy that he will succeed, but that the heirs of his enemy Banquo will one day rule the kingdom. In a series of grisly events, their dark predictions are fulfilled.

STYLE ONE: HANDLE — WITCHES FACING OUTWARD

The faces of the three witches on the outer side of the handle face outward (noses out). Only after the jug was in the initial stages of production did Doulton realize that the possibility of the handle being damaged during shipping was great, and thus the moulds were quickly modified resulting in the production of Style Two.

Designer: Michael Abberley

Statistics:	**Doulton** **Number**	**Size**	**Height**	**Issued**
	D6667	Large	7 ¼", 18.4 cm	1981

Issued: Not put into production
Handle: Three witches facing to the right
Colourway: Brown, yellow and green
Backstamp: Doulton

Size	Description	Current Market Value U.K. £	U.S. $	Can. $
Large	Style One	Extremely rare Sold November 21, 1999. Phillips, New Bond Street, London, England, £3,000.00.		

STYLE TWO: HANDLE — WITCHES FACING INWARD

Designer: Michael Abberley

Statistics:	**Doulton** **Number**	**Size**	**Height**	**Issued**
	D6667	Large	7 ¼", 18.4 cm	1982-1989

Handle: The faces of the three witches are on the front of the handle facing forwards
Colourway: Brown, yellow and grey
Backstamp: Doulton
Series: The Shakespearean Collection

Size	Description	Current Market Value U.K. £	U.S. $	Can. $
Large	Style Two	100.00	150.00	175.00

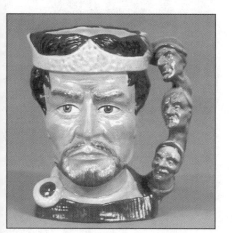

Macbeth, Style Two

MAD HATTER

A character from Lewis Carroll's *Alice's Adventures in Wonderland*, the Mad Hatter wears a watch that tells time in months, rather than in hours.

Designer: Max Henk
Handle: A dormouse above a pocket watch

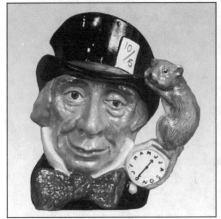

Mad Hatter, Variation No. 1

VARIATION No. 1: Colourway — Black hat; dark red bow tie

Statistics:	Doulton Number	Size	Height	Issued
1.	D6598	Large	7 ¼", 18.4 cm	1965-1983
2.	D6602	Small	3 ¾", 9.5 cm	1965-1983
3.	D6606	Miniature	2 ½", 6.4 cm	1965-1983

Colourway: Black hat; dark red bow tie
Backstamp: Doulton
Series: Alice In Wonderland

Jug No.	Size	Comp.	Issued	Current Market Value U.K. £	U.S. $	Can. $
1.	Large	EW	1965-1983	100.00	225.00	275.00
		ETC	1968-1971	200.00	300.00	350.00
2.	Small	EW	1965-1983	80.00	150.00	175.00
		ETC	1968-1971	125.00	175.00	225.00
3.	Miniature	EW	1965-1983	75.00	125.00	145.00
		ETC	1968-1971	100.00	150.00	185.00

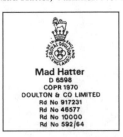

Mad Hatter
D 6598
COPR 1970
DOULTON & CO LIMITED
Rd No 917231
Rd No 46577
Rd No 10000
Rd No 592/64

VARIATION No. 2: Colourway — Black hat; yellow bow tie

Statistics:	Doulton Number	Size	Height	Issued
1.	D6748	Large	7", 17.8 cm	See below
2.	D6790	Small	3 ¼", 8.3 cm	See below

Issued: 1. Large — 1985 in a limited edition of 250
2. Small — 1987 in a limited edition of 500
Colourway: Black hat; yellow bow tie
Backstamp: A. Doulton / Higbee's
The large-size jug was commissioned by the Higbee Company to celebrate the opening of the first Royal Doulton Room. Issued on October 28, 1985, in a limited edition of 250 pieces.
B. Doulton/Higbee's
The small-size jug was commissioned by the Higbee Department Store to celebrate the second anniversary of the opening of the Royal Doulton Room. Issued in 1987 in a limited edition of 500 pieces.

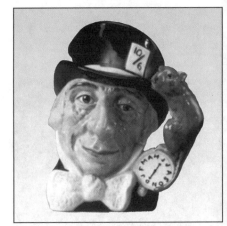

Mad Hatter, Variation No. 2

Jug No.	Size	Variation	Current Market Value U.K. £	U.S. $	Can. $
1A.	Large	Var. 2	500.00	900.00	1,000.00
2B.	Small	Var. 2	200.00	275.00	325.00

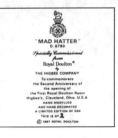

"MAD HATTER"
D.6790
Specially Commissioned from
Royal Doulton®
by
THE HIGBEE COMPANY
To commemorate
the Second Anniversary of
the opening of
the First Royal Doulton Room
Higbee's, Cleveland, Ohio, U.S.A.
HAND MODELLED
AND HAND DECORATED
A LIMITED EDITION OF 500
THIS IS № 2
© 1987 ROYAL DOULTON

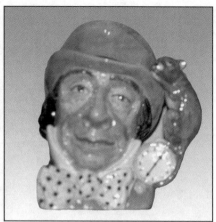

Mad Hatter, Variation No. 3

MAD HATTER (cont.)

VARIATION No. 3: **Colourway** — Pale blue and coat; yellow bow tie with red dots

	Doulton			
Statistics:	**Number**	**Size**	**Height**	**Issued**
	D —	Large	7", 17.8 cm	See below

Issued: Not put into production
Colourway: Pale blue hat and coat; yellow bow tie with red dots
Backstamp: Doulton

		Current Market Value		
Size	**Variation**	**U.K. £**	**U.S. $**	**Can. $**
Large	Var. 3	Extremely rare		

MAE WEST

PROTOTYPE

Designer: David B. Biggs

	Doulton			
Statistics:	**Number**	**Size**	**Height**	**Issued**
	—	Large	Unknown	See below

Modelled: Unknown
Issued: Not put into production
Handle: Pink umbrella
Colourway: Dark blue hat with a green feather; blonde hair; grey fur collar
Backstamps: Doulton

		Current Market Value		
Size	**Description**	**U.K. £**	**U.S. $**	**Can. $**
Large	Prototype		Extremely rare	

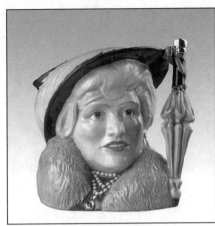

Mae West, Prototype

REGULAR ISSUE

From her screen debut in 1932, Mae West (1892-1980) became an instant hit. She is best known for portraying tough, sophisticated characters who loved luxury and men. The public adored her and her witty quips, the most famous of which appears on the base of the jug: "When I'm good, I'm very good. But when I'm bad, I'm better."

Designer: Colin M. Davidson

	Doulton			
Statistics:	**Number**	**Size**	**Height**	**Issued**
	D6688	Large	7", 17.8 cm	1983-1986

Handle: Umbrella with a bow tied around the handle
Colourway: Yellow hair; white feather dress
Backstamps: A. Doulton / General issue, 1983.
B. Doulton/American Express/Premier Edition for American Express. This series was first introduced in the U.S.A. as a promotional jug for the American Express Company. Approximately 500 jugs were given the special backstamp and were available only to the North American market.
Series: The Celebrity Collection

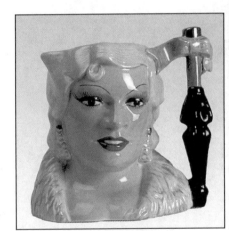

Mae West, Regular Issue

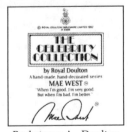

Backstamp A - Doulton

Jug			**Current Market Value**		
No.	**Size**	**Issued**	**U.K. £**	**U.S. $**	**Can. $**
1A.	Large	1983-1986	100.00	175.00	225.00
1B.		1983-1983	275.00	425.00	525.00

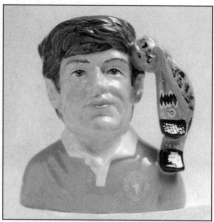

Manchester United (Football Club)

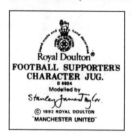

MANCHESTER UNITED
(FOOTBALL CLUB)

Designer: Stanley J. Taylor

Statistics:	Doulton Number	Size	Height	Issued
	D6924	Small	5", 12.7 cm	1992-1999

Handle: Team coloured scarf
Colourway: Red, white and black uniform
Backstamp: Doulton
Series: The Football Supporters

Size	Current Market Value		
	U.K. £	U.S. $	Can. $
Small	50.00	110.00	125.00

MAORI

The Maori people of Polynesian descent were the first inhabitants of present-day New Zealand. Beginning as hunters and fishermen, the Maori later turned to agriculture and woodworking.

STYLE ONE: BLUE-GREY HAIR, FRIENDLY EXPRESSION

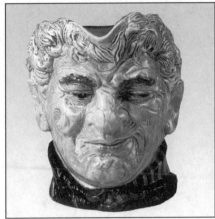

Maori, Style One

Designer: Unknown

Statistics:	Doulton Number	Size	Height	Issued
	D6080	Large	7", 17.8 cm	1939-1939

Handle: Plain with plaque of Maori
Colourway: Brown and grey
Backstamp: Doulton

	Current Market Value		
Size	U.K. £	U.S. $	Can. $
Large	Extremely rare. Only three known. Last sold May 1998. Phillips, New Bond Street London, England, £21,850.00		

STYLE TWO: DARK HAIR, TWO WHITE-TIPPED FEATHERS IN HAIR, SERIOUS EXPRESSION

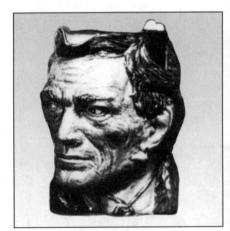

Maori, Style Two

Designer: Unknown

Statistics:	Doulton Number	Size	Height	Issued
	D6080	Large	7", 17.8 cm	1939-1939

Handle: Plain with plaque of Maori
Colourway: Brown and grey
Backstamp: Doulton

	Current Market Value		
Size	U.K. £	U.S. $	Can. $
Large	Extremely rare		

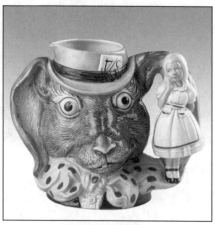

The March Hare, Prototype

THE MARCH HARE

PROTOTYPE

Designer: William K. Harper

	Doulton			
Statistics:	**Number**	**Size**	**Height**	**Issued**
	D —	Large	6", 15.0 cm	See below

Issued: Not put into production
Handle: Alice in Wonderland rests on the rabbit's ear
Colourway: Blue hat with dark blue band; yellow bow tie with red dots; Alice wears white
Backstamp: Doulton

		Current Market Value		
Size	**Description**	**U.K. £**	**U.S. $**	**Can. $**
Large	Prototype		Extremely rare	

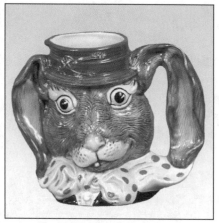

The March Hare, Regular Issue

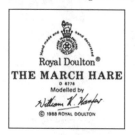

THE MARCH HARE

REGULAR ISSUE

At the March Hare's home in Wonderland it is always six o'clock and time for tea. Not having a moment to tidy up, he and his friends, the Mad Hatter and the dormouse, sit at a table laid for a great number and change seats as they dirty the dishes. Alice makes herself unpopular by asking what they do when they arrive back at the beginning.

Designer: William K. Harper

	Doulton			
Statistics:	**Number**	**Size**	**Height**	**Issued**
	D6776	Large	6", 15.0 cm	1989-1991

Handle: One of the Hare's ears
Colourways: Green hat; yellow bow tie with blue dots
Backstamp: Doulton
Series: Alice in Wonderland

	Current Market Value		
Size	**U.K. £**	**U.S. $**	**Can. $**
Large	175.00	325.00	400.00

MARCO POLO

For the character jug Marco Polo see the "Explorers Set" page 178.

MARILYN MONROE

PROTOTYPE

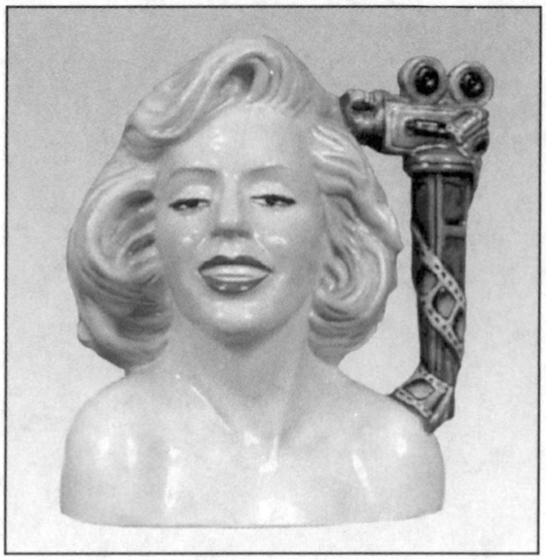

Norma Jean Baker (1926-1962) made her screen debut in 1948, and as Marilyn Monroe, her beauty and charisma established her as an international sex symbol. She died at the age of 36.

There are only two of these jugs known to exist. One is in the Doulton Museum, Stoke-on-Trent. The other came to auction in 1992 in Toronto and fetched $17,500.00. The jug was not issued due to copyright problems.

Marilyn Monroe

Designer: Eric Griffiths

Statistics:	Doulton Number	Size	Height	Issued
	D6719	Large	7 ¼", 18.4 cm	See below

Modelled: 1983
Issued: Not put into production
Handle: A cine-camera encircled by a roll of film
Colourway: Yellow, white and grey
Backstamp: Doulton
Series: The Celebrity Collection

		Current Market Value		
Size	Description	U.K. £	U.S. $	Can. $
Large	Prototype			Extremely rare
				Last sold September 1992
				Britannia Fair, Toronto,
				Canada $17,500.00

MARK TWAIN

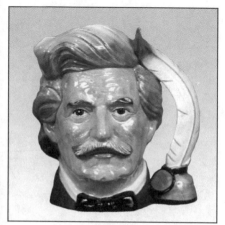

Mark Twain

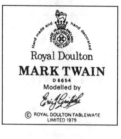

Born Samuel Langhorne Clemens (1835-1910), Mark Twain was an American writer and humourist. He was best loved for his classic adventure stories, *Tom Sawyer* (1876) and *The Adventures of Huckleberry Finn* (1884), which told of life in his native Mississippi.

The small jug was modelled for "The Queen's Table," Royal Doulton's exhibit at the United Kingdom Showcase at Walt Disney's Epcot Center in Orlando, Florida. The jug was sold exclusively to Epcot tourists visiting the exhibition during 1982.

Designer: Eric Griffiths

	Doulton			
Statistics:	Number	Size	Height	Issued
1.	D6654	Large	7 ½", 19.1 cm	1980-1990
2.	D6694	Small	4", 10.1 cm	1983-1990
3.	D6758	Miniature	2 ½", 6.4 cm	1986-1990

Handle: Quill and ink pot
Colourway: Black coat and bow tie; grey hair
Backstamp: Doulton

Jug		Current Market Value		
No.	Size	U.K. £	U.S. $	Can. $
1.	Large	90.00	150.00	175.00
2.	Small	60.00	90.00	110.00
3.	Miniature	75.00	125.00	150.00

MARLEY'S GHOST

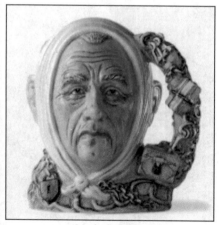

Marley's Ghost

Depicting the ghost of Jacob Marley, who visits Scrooge in Charles Dickens' *A Christmas Carol*, this character jug was available through Lawleys By Post in a limited edition of 2,500.

Designer: David B. Biggs

	Doulton			
Statistics:	Number	Size	Height	Issued
	D7142	Large	7 ½", 19.1 cm	See below

Issued: 1999 in a limited edition of 2,500
Handle: Chain of keys, padlocks and heavy purses
Colourway: Grey, white and tan
Backstamp: Doulton

	Current Market Value		
Size	U.K. £	U.S. $	Can. $
Large	120.00	200.00	—

THE MASTER / EQUESTRIAN

This piece was released in the U.K. as The Master, and in North America as The Equestrian.

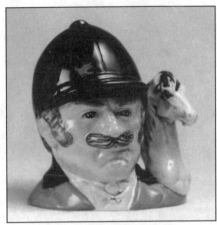

Designer: Stanley J. Taylor

	Doulton			
Statistics:	**Number**	**Size**	**Height**	**Issued**
	D6898	Small	4", 10.1 cm	1991-1995

Handle: Horse head
Colourway: Dark blue, red and white
Backstamp: Doulton

	Current Market Value		
Size	**U.K. £**	**U.S. $**	**Can. $**
Small	50.00	100.00	150.00

The Master / Equestrian

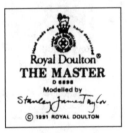

McCALLUM

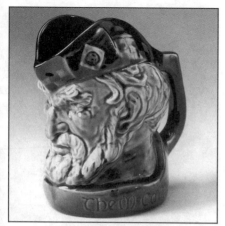

McCallum, Variation No. 1

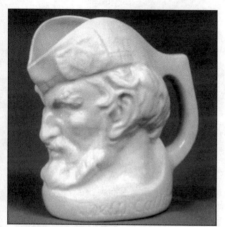

McCallum, Variation No. 2

Produced as a promotional item for the D & J McCallum Distillery, Scotland, this jug exists in three different colour varieties, all in very limited quantities. This jug was also produced by other manufacturers from an almost identical design. The colourways and size are extremely close to the jug produced by Doulton. The backstamp is the best way to tell the difference.

Designer: McCallum

	Doulton			
Statistics:	**Number**	**Size**	**Height**	**Issued**
	D —	Large	7", 17.8 cm	1930-Unk.

Handle: Plain
Colourway: See below
Backstamp: Doulton

Variation No. 1: Kingsware
Colourway — Light and dark browns
Approximately 1,000 to 1,500 pieces are thought to have been made

		Current Market Value		
Size	**Variation**	**U.K. £**	**U.S. $**	**Can. $**
Large	Var. 1	1,250.00	2,500.00	3,500.00

Variation No. 2: Colourway — Ivory glaze
Approximately 1,000 pieces were produced

		Current Market Value		
Size	**Variation**	**U.K. £**	**U.S. $**	**Can. $**
Large	Var. 2	1,250.00	2,500.00	3,000.00

MEPHISTOPHELES

First found in 16th-century German legend, Mephistopheles became best known in Johann von Goethe's drama, *Faust* (1808). In it he is portrayed as an evil spirit or devil to whom Faust sells his soul in return for services.

Designer: Charles Noke
Harry Fenton

	Doulton			
Statistics:	**Number**	**Size**	**Height**	**Issued**
1.	D5757	Large	7", 17.8 cm	1937-1948
2.	D5758	Small	3 ¾", 9.5 cm	1937-1948

Handle: Plain
Colourway: Red and brown
Backstamps: A. Doulton — With verse
B. Doulton — Without verse

Jug		Current Market Value		
No.	**Size**	**U.K. £**	**U.S. $**	**Can. $**
1A.	Large	1,200.00	2,500.00	3,000.00
1B.		1,100.00	2,000.00	2,500.00
2A.	Small	800.00	1,300.00	1,650.00
2N.		700.00	1,000.00	1,350.00

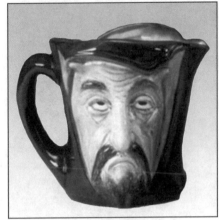

Mephistopheles

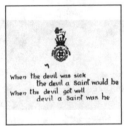

When the devil was sick
the devil a saint would be
when the devil got well
devil a saint was he

Backstamp A - With
Verse

MERLIN

STYLE ONE: HANDLE — AN OWL

Designer: Garry Sharpe

	Doulton			
Statistics:	**Number**	**Size**	**Height**	**Issued**
1.	D6529	Large	7 ¼", 18.4 cm	1960-1998
2.	D6536	Small	3 ¾", 9.5 cm	1960-1998
3.	D6543	Miniature	2 ¾", 7.0 cm	1960-1991

Handle: An owl
Colourway: Black, grey and brown
Backstamp: Doulton
Series: Characters From Literature

Jug				Current Market Value		
No.	**Size**	**Comp.**	**Issued**	**U.K. £**	**U.S. $**	**Can. $**
1.	Large	EW	1960-1998	75.00	125.00	175.00
		ETC	1968-1971	125.00	200.00	250.00
2.	Small	EW	1960-1998	45.00	75.00	110.00
		ETC	1968-1971	80.00	125.00	150.00
3.	Miniature	EW	1960-1991	40.00	60.00	70.00
		ETC	1968-1971	60.00	85.00	110.00

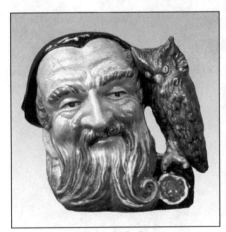

Merlin, Style One

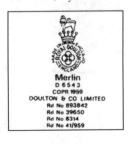

Merlin
D 6543
COPR 1959
DOULTON & CO LIMITED
Rd No 893842
Rd No 39650
Rd No 8314
Rd No 41/959

Note: For Merlin (Style Two) see, King Arthur and Merlin, page 243.

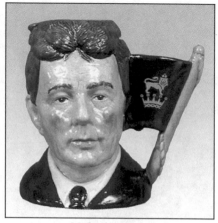

Michael Doulton

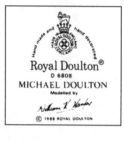

MICHAEL DOULTON

This jug was manufactured in an edition of 9,500 pieces. It was only available for sale at retail locations where and when Michael Doulton was present.

Designer: William K. Harper

Statistics:

	Doulton Number	Size	Height	Issued
	D6808	Small	4 ¼", 10.8 cm	See below

Issued: 1988 in a limited edition of 9,500
Handle: Flag bearing the Royal Doulton logo
Colourway: Black, brown and blue
Backstamp: Doulton

Size	Current Market Value		
	U.K. £	U.S. $	Can. $
Small	40.00	50.00	65.00

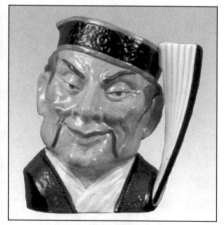

The Mikado

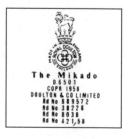

THE MIKADO

"Mikado" is the ancient title for the emperor of Japan, beginning with the reign of the Mikado Jimmu in 660 B.C. Believed by many to have descended from the all-powerful Sun Goddess, the same family line has been traced through 124 reigns. The mikado is popularly known through the Gilbert and Sullivan operetta (1885) of the same name.

Designer: Max Henk

Statistics:

	Doulton Number	Size	Height	Issued
1.	D6501	Large	6 ½", 16.5 cm	1959-1969
2.	D6507	Small	3 ¾", 9.5 cm	1959-1969
3.	D6525	Miniature	2 ½", 6.4 cm	1960-1969

Handle: A fan
Colourway: Black and turquoise hat; green and white robes
Backstamp: Doulton

Jug No.	Size	Comp.	Issued	Current Market Value		
				U.K. £	U.S. $	Can. $
1.	Large	EW	1959-1969	450.00	800.00	950.00
		ETC	1968-1971	550.00	900.00	1,150.00
2.	Small	EW	1959-1969	275.00	400.00	575.00
		ETC	1968-1971	300.00	500.00	650.00
3.	Miniature	EW	1960-1969	275.00	450.00	600.00
		ETC	1968-1971	325.00	425.00	675.00

THE MILLER

PROTOTYPE

From the proposed series 'The Canterbury Tales."

STYLE ONE: HANDLE — BAGPIPES

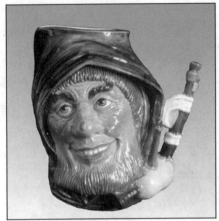

The Miller, Style One

Designer: William K. Harper

	Doulton			
Statistics:	**Number**	**Size**	**Height**	**Issued**
	D6779	Mid	5 ½", 14 cm	See below

Modelled: 1987
Issued: Not put into production
Handle: Bagpipes
Colourway: Blue-hooded cloak
Backstamp: Doulton

	Current Market Value		
Size	U.K. £	U.S. $	Can. $
Mid	Sold November 21, 1999 Phillips, New Bond Street London, England, £3,800.00		

STYLE TWO: HANDLE — SACK OF CORN AND WATERWHEEL

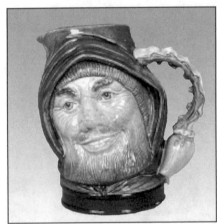

The Miller, Style Two

Designer: William K. Harper

	Model			
Statistics:	**Number**	**Size**	**Height**	**Issued**
	3099	Mid	5 ½", 14 cm	See below

Modelled: 1987
Issued: Not put into production
Handle: A waterwheel and a sack or corn
Colourway: Blue-hooded cloak
Backstamp: Doulton

	Current Market Value		
Size	U.K. £	U.S. $	Can. $
Mid	Sold November 21, 1999 Phillips, New Bond Street London, England, £6,000.00		

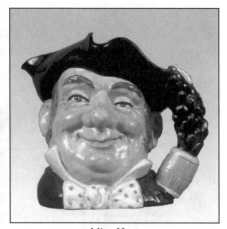

Mine Host

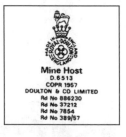

MINE HOST

The forerunner of today's English publican, this cheerful man would hang a pine bough on the door of his home to let travellers know that refreshments were available. As the handle shows, these often ran to a good pint of strong ale!

Designer: Max Henk

Statistics:	Doulton Number	Size	Height	Issued
1.	D6468	Large	7", 17.8 cm	1958-1982
2.	D6470	Small	3 ½", 8.9 cm	1958-1982
3.	D6513	Miniature	2 ½", 6.4 cm	1960-1982

Handle: Evergreen bough and barrel
Colourway: Black tricorn; red coat; white bow tie with gold spots
Backstamp: Doulton

Jug No.	Size	Comp.	Issued	Current Market Value U.K. £	U.S. $	Can. $
1.	Large	EW	1958-1982	80.00	125.00	150.00
		ETC	1968-1971	100.00	175.00	200.00
2.	Small	EW	1958-1982	50.00	70.00	85.00
		ETC	1968-1971	65.00	100.00	125.00
3.	Miniature	EW	1960-1982	50.00	70.00	85.00
		ETC	1968-1971	65.00	85.00	100.00

MINNIE THE MINX

To celebrate the 60th anniversary of the Dandy and Beano comics in 1998, a special anniversary logo appeared on the base of the jug for that year.

Designer: Simon Ward

Statistics:	Doulton Number	Size	Height	Issued
	D7036	Small	4 ½", 11.9 cm	1996-1999

Handle: Cat, sling shot and apples
Colourway: Black, red and brown
Backstamp: A. Doulton/© D.C. Thomson & Co. Ltd.
B. 60th Anniversary logo
Series: Characters from *The Dandy* and *The Beano*

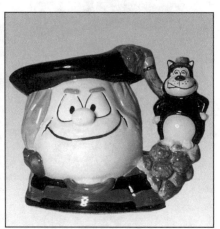

Minnie the Minx

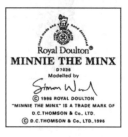

Jug No.	Backstamp	Issued	Current Market Value U.K. £	U.S. $	Can. $
1A.	Doulton/Thomson	1996-1999	55.00	95.00	125.00
1B.	60th Anniversary logo	1998-1998	55.00	95.00	125.00

MONET

Claude Monet (1840-1926) was one of the pioneers of Impressionism, a painting style which used short brushstrokes of bright colours in immediate juxtaposition to represent the effect of light on objects.

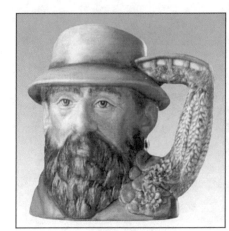

Monet

Designer: David B. Biggs

Statistics:

Doulton Number	Size	Height	Issued
D7150	Large	7 ¼", 18.4 cm	2000 to the present

Handle: Bridge, yellow flowers and water lilies
Colourway: Tan hat; blue shirt
Backstamp: Doulton
Series: Famous Artists

Size	Current Market Value		
	U.K. £	U.S. $	Can. $
Large	120.00	205.00	—

Note: Available only from Royal Doulton Outlets worldwide.

MONTY

Bernard Law Montgomery (1887-1976), first Viscount Montgomery of Alamein, was referred to familiarly as Monty. The highlights of his long and distinguished military career include the first Allied victory of World War II in North Africa in 1942 and the acceptance of the German surrender at Luneburg Heath in 1945. He was Deputy Supreme Commander of the Allied Powers in Europe from 1951 to 1958.

In 1954 a minor colourway change occurred when the yellow highlighting on the cap badge was dropped.

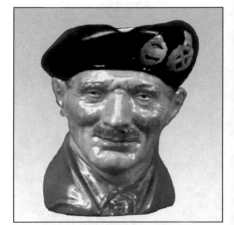

Monty

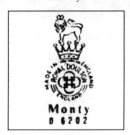

Designer: Harry Fenton

Statistics:

Doulton Number	Size	Height	Issued
D6202	Large	5 ¾", 14.6 cm	1946-1991

Handle: Plain
Colourway: Brown beret; khaki uniform
　　　　　　　A. Cap badge with yellow highlights
　　　　　　　B. Cap badge without highlights
Backstamp: Doulton

Jug No.	Size	Comp.	Current Market Value			
			Issued	U.K. £	U.S. $	Can. $
1A.	Large	EW	1946-1954	90.00	125.00	150.00
1B.		EW	1954-1991	65.00	100.00	125.00
1B.		ETC	1968-1971	100.00	150.00	175.00

Note: For the character jug Field Marshall Montgomery, see page 184, and for the character jug Viscount Montgomery of Alamein, see page 390.

MOZART

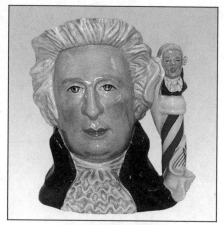

Mozart

	Designer:	Stanley J. Taylor			
		Doulton			
	Statistics:	**Number**	**Size**	**Height**	**Issued**
		D7031	Large	7", 17.8 cm	1996-2001

Handle: Barber of Seville, bar of music and barber pole
Colourway: Black, white and red
Backstamp: Doulton
Series: Great Composers

Size	Current Market Value		
	U.K. £	U.S. $	Can. $
Large	95.00	225.00	275.00

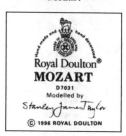

Royal Doulton®
MOZART
D7031
Modelled by
Stanley James Taylor
© 1996 ROYAL DOULTON

MR. BUMBLE

For the character jug Mr. Bumble see the "Charles Dickens Commemorative Set" page 143.

MR. MICAWBER

In Charles Dickens' classic, *David Copperfield*, Wilkins Micawber is Copperfield's landlord and friend. A sanguine idler, Micawber unmasks Uriah Heep as a villain and is rewarded with passage to Australia, where he settles happily in a prominent neighbourhood.

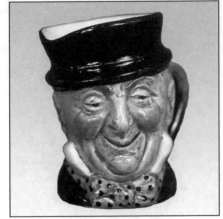

Mr. Micawber, Style One

STYLE ONE: HANDLE — PLAIN

Designer: Leslie Harradine
Harry Fenton

Statistics:	Doulton Number	Size	Height	Issued
1.	D5843	Mid	4 ¼", 10.8 cm	1938-1948
2.	D5843	Small	3 ¼", 8.3 cm	1948-1960
3.	D6138	Miniature	2 ¼", 5.7 cm	1940-1960
4.	D6143	Tiny	1 ¼", 3.1 cm	1940-1960

Handle: Plain
Colourway: Black hat; green coat; blue polka-dot bow tie
Backstamp: Doulton

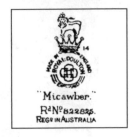

"Micawber."
Rᵈ Nº 822825.
Regᵈ in Australia

Jug No.	Size	Current Market Value U.K. £	U.S. $	Can. $
1.	Mid	125.00	200.00	250.00
2.	Small	65.00	100.00	125.00
3.	Miniature	40.00	55.00	60.00
4.	Tiny	60.00	80.00	100.00

Mr. Micawber Derivatives

Item	Doulton Number	Height	Issued
Bookend	HN1615	4", 10.1 cm	1934-c.1939
Bust	D6050	2 ¼", 5.7 cm	1939-1960
Napkin ring	M58	3 ½", 8.9 cm	c.1935-1939
Table lighter	D5843	3 ½", 8.9 cm	1958-1959

Doulton Number	Item	Current Market Value U.K. £	U.S. $	Can. $
D5843	Table Lighter	200.00	350.00	450.00
D6050	Bust	80.00	100.00	120.00
HN1615	Bookend	1,000.00	1,600.00	2,250.00
M58	Napkin Ring	300.00	600.00	850.00

Note: 1. Mr. Micawber (Style One) mid and miniature size jugs are found in white gloss.
2. For the toby jug Mr. Micawber see page 72.

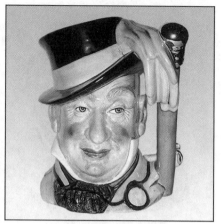

Mr. Micawber, Style Two

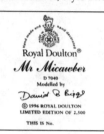

MR. MICAWBER

This jug was commissioned by Lawleys By Post in a limited edition of 2,500 and comes with a certificate of authenticity.

STYLE TWO: HANDLE — WALKING STICK AND GLOVES

Designer: David B. Biggs

Statistics:	**Doulton Number**	**Size**	**Height**	**Issued**
	D7040	Large	7 ½", 19.1 cm	See below

Issued: 1996 in a limited edition of 2,500
Handle: Walking stick and gloves
Colourway: Mustard jacket; blue cravat; white shirt points; black hat with grey band
Backstamp: Doulton

Size	Current Market Value		
	U.K. £	**U.S. $**	**Can. $**
Large	150.00	300.00	400.00

MR. PICKWICK

Founder and chairman of the Pickwick Club, this gentleman is the elegant and genial hero of Charles Dickens' *The Posthumous Papers of the Pickwick Club*, first published in 1837.

STYLE ONE: HANDLE — PLAIN

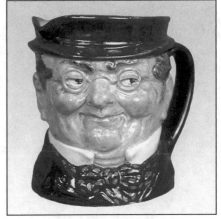

Mr. Pickwick, Style One

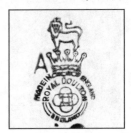

Designer: Leslie Harradine
Harry Fenton

Statistics:	Doulton Number	Size	Height	Issued
1.	D6060	Large	7", 17.8 cm	1940-1960
2.	D5839	Mid	5 ½", 14.0 cm	1938-1948
3.	D5839	Small	3 ½", 8.9 cm	1948-1960
4.	D6254	Miniature	2 ¼", 5.7 cm	1947-1960
5.	D6260	Tiny	1 ¼", 3.1 cm	1947-1960

Handle: Plain
Colourway: Green hat and coat; maroon bow tie
Backstamp: Doulton

Jug No.	Size	Current Market Value		
		U.K. £	U.S. $	Can. $
1.	Large	135.00	200.00	225.00
2.	Mid	150.00	225.00	250.00
3.	Small	65.00	90.00	100.00
4.	Miniature	55.00	80.00	90.00
5.	Tiny	125.00	225.00	250.00

Mr. Pickwick Derivatives

Item	Doulton Number	Height	Issued
Bookend	HN1623	4", 10.1 cm	1934-c.1939
Bust	D6049	3 ½", 8.9 cm	1939-1960
Napkin ring	M57	3 ½", 8.9 cm	c.1935-1939
Table lighter	D5839	3 ½", 8.9 cm	1958-1961

Doulton Number	Item	Current Market Value		
		U.K. £	U.S. $	Can. $
D5839	Table Lighter	250.00	400.00	450.00
D6049	Bust	80.00	95.00	110.00
HN1623	Bookend	1,000.00	1,800.00	2,500.00
M57	Napkin Ring	300.00	600.00	800.00

Note: 1. Mr. Pickwick (Style One) large and mid size jugs are found in white gloss.
2. For the toby jug Mr. Pickwick see page 73.

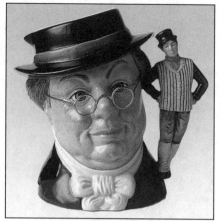

Mr. Pickwick, Style Two

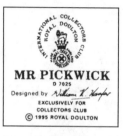

MR PICKWICK

The large version of this jug was sold by Lawleys By Post in a limited edition of 2,500 pieces and the small version was released through the Royal Doulton International Collectors Club in a limited edition of 2,500. The Mr. Pickwick jugs were issued with metal spectacles, as was the Glenn Miller jug.

STYLE TWO: HANDLE — FIGURE OF SAM WELLER

Designer: William K. Harper

Statistics:	Doulton Number	Size	Height	Issued
1.	D6959	Large	7", 17.8 cm	See below
2.	D7025	Small	4", 10.1 cm	See below

Issued: 1. Large — 1994 in a limited edition of 2,500
2. Small — 1996 in a limited edition of 2,500
Handle: The figure of Sam Weller
Colourway: Blue, black, green and cream
Backstamp: A. Large — Doulton
B. Small — Doulton/RDICC

Jug No.	Size	Backstamp	Current Market Value U.K. £	U.S. $	Can. $
1A.	Large	Doulton	150.00	275.00	300.00
2B.	Small	Doulton/RDICC	65.00	125.00	150.00

MR QUAKER

These jugs were made as an advertising piece for the internal use of Quaker Oats Limited, and a few were sold to members of the Royal Doulton International Collectors Club. They were issued with a certificate signed by Sir Richard Bailey and Michael Doulton.

Mr. Quaker was commissioned by Quaker Oats Limited and issued in 1985 in a limited edition of 3,500 pieces.

Designer: Harry Sales
Modeller: Graham Tongue

Statistics:	Doulton Number	Size	Height	Issued
	D6738	Large	7 ½", 19.1 cm	See below

Issued: 1985 in a limited edition of 3,500
Handle: A sheaf of wheat
Colourway: Black, white and yellow
Backstamp: Doulton/Quaker Oats Ltd

Size	Current Market Value U.K. £	U.S. $	Can. $
Large	475.00	1,000.00	1,250.00

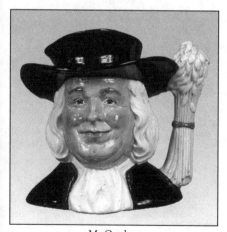

Mr Quaker

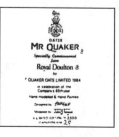

MRS. BARDELL

For the character jug Mrs. Bardell see the "Charles Dickens Commemorative Set" page 143.

MRS. CLAUS

Commissioned for the North American market, Mrs. Claus has her handle to the left so she can be paired with her husband Santa Claus (D6900), whose handle points in the opposite direction.

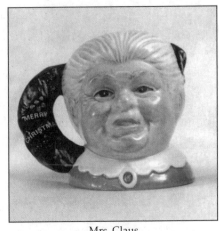

Mrs. Claus

Designer: Stanley J. Taylor

Statistics:	Doulton Number	Size	Height	Issued
	D6922	Miniature	2 ½", 6.4 cm	See below

Issued: 1992 in a special edition
Handle: Holly wreath
Colourway: Red, cream and green
Backstamp: Doulton
Series: Christmas Miniatures

Size	Current Market Value U.K. £	U.S. $	Can. $
Miniature	75.00	150.00	175.00

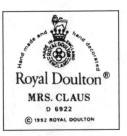

Royal Doulton®
MRS. CLAUS
D 6922
© 1992 ROYAL DOULTON

MURRAY WALKER O.B.E.

Murray Walker was famous for his enthusiastic lap-by-lap commentary of Formular One motor racing. This jug, commisioned by Lawleys By Post, was issued in a limited edition of 2,500 pieces.

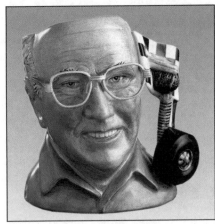

Murray Walker O.B.E.

Designer: Stanley J. Taylor

Statistics:	Doulton Number	Size	Height	Issued
	D7094	Small	4", 10.1 cm	See below

Issued: 1997 in a limited edition of 2,500
Handle: A checkered flag, microphone and racing tyre
Colourway: Tan, mustard, black and white
Backstamp: Doulton

Size	Current Market Value U.K. £	U.S. $	Can. $
Small	65.00	110.00	150.00

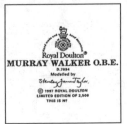

Royal Doulton®
MURRAY WALKER O.B.E.
D.7094
Modelled by
Stanley James Taylor
© 1997 ROYAL DOULTON
LIMITED EDITION OF 2,500
THIS IS N?

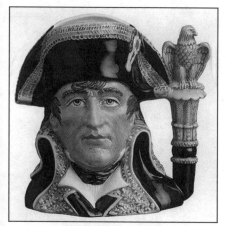

Napoleon, (Style One)

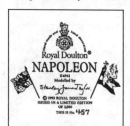

NAPOLEON

Issued in a limited edition of 2,000 pieces, the Napoleon jug bears a special backstamp and comes with a certificate of authenticity.

STYLE ONE: HANDLE — AN EAGLE

Designer: Stanley J. Taylor

Statistics:	Doulton Number	Size	Height	Issued
	D6941	Large	7", 17.8 cm	See below

Issued: 1993 in a limited edition of 2,000
Handle: An eagle
Colourway: Black and gold
Backstamp: Doulton

Size	Current Market Value		
	U.K. £	U.S. $	Can. $
Large	150.00	325.00	400.00

NAPOLEON AND JOSEPHINE

Napoleon (1769-1821) stood only 5 feet 2 inches tall, but he was a military genius who amassed an empire that covered most of western and central Europe. Josephine (1763-1814) married him in 1796, after her first husband, the Vicomte de Beauharnais, was killed during the French Revolution. Unable to produce an heir, Napoleon divorced Josephine in 1809 to marry a younger woman.

This jug was issued in 1986 in a limited edition of 9,500 pieces.

Designer: Michael Abberley

Statistics:	Doulton Number	Size	Height	Issued
	D6750	Large	7", 17.8 cm	See below

Issued: 1986 in a limited edition of 9,500
Handle: Napoleon — French Flag
Josephine — A fan and mirror
Colourway: Black, white, yellow and brown
Backstamp: Doulton
Series: Star-Crossed Lovers (Two-faced jug)

Size	Current Market Value		
	U.K. £	U.S. $	Can. $
Large	100.00	150.00	175.00

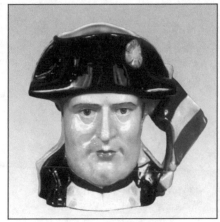

Napoleon

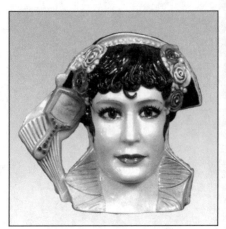

Josephine

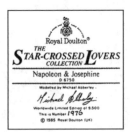

NAPOLEON AND WELLINGTON

These jugs were issued to commemorate the 180th anniversary of the Battle of Waterloo. The pair were commissioned by Lawleys By Post and issued in a limited edition of 2,500 sets.

STYLE TWO: NAPOLEON: HANDLE — CROWN AND SCROLLS

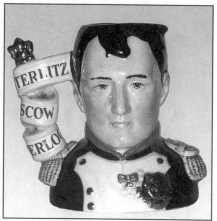

Napoleon, Style Two

Designer: William K. Harper

Statistics:	Doulton Number	Size	Height	Issued
1.	D7001	Small	4", 10.1 cm	See below
2.	D7002	Small	4", 10.1 cm	See below

Issued: 1995 in a limited edition of 2,500
Handles: Gold emblazoned crown atop scrolls showing the names of famous battles
Colourway: 1. Napoleon — Blue and white uniform; yellow and white handle
2. Wellington — Red and gold uniform; yellow and white handle
Backstamp: Doulton

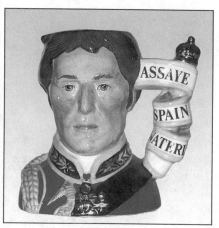

Wellington

Jug No.	Doulton Number	Name	Current Market Value U.K. £	U.S. $	Can. $
1.	D7001	Napoleon	100.00	200.00	250.00
2.	D7002	Wellington	100.00	200.00	250.00
		Pair	200.00	400.00	500.00

Note: For the character jug Duke of Wellington see page 171.

NELSON

Issued by the Royal Doulton International Collectors Club, the Nelson jug was available only to their members from 1994 to March 1995.

Designer: Warren Platt

Statistics:	Doulton Number	Size	Height	Issued
	D6963	Small	4 ½", 11.9 cm	1994-1995

Handle: The naval ensign
Colourway: Black, white, red and gold
Backstamp: Doulton/RDICC
Series: RDICC

Size	Current Market Value U.K. £	U.S. $	Can. $
Small	85.00	175.00	200.00

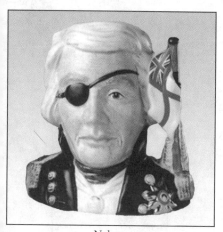

Nelson

Note: For the character jugs Lord Nelson see page 259, and for Vice-Admiral Lord Nelson see page 388.

NEPTUNE

PROTOTYPE

Designer: Max Henk

Statistics:	Doulton Number	Size	Height	Issued
	D —	Large	6 ½", 16.5 cm	See below

Issued: Not put into production
Handle: Trident and fish
Colourway: Flambé
Backstamp: Doulton

Doulton Number	Description	Current Market Value		
		U.K. £	U.S. $	Can. $
—	Prototype		Extremely rare	

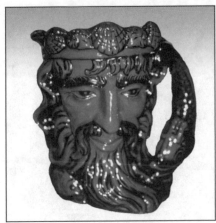

Neptune, Prototype

REGULAR ISSUE

In Roman mythology, Neptune is the god of the sea. According to legend Neptune married the sea nymph Amphitrite and together they had a son named Triton, who was half man and half fish.

Designer: Max Henk

Statistics:	Doulton Number	Size	Height	Issued
1.	D6548	Large	6 ½", 16.5 cm	1961-1991
2.	D6552	Small	3 ¾", 9.5 cm	1961-1991
3.	D6555	Miniature	2 ½", 6.4 cm	1961-1991

Handle: Trident and fish
Colourway: Blue, grey and green
Backstamp: Doulton

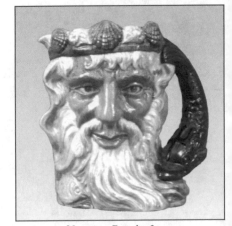

Neptune, Regular Issue

Jug No.	Size	Comp.	Issued	Current Market Value		
				U.K. £	U.S. $	Can. $
1.	Large	EW	1961-1991	75.00	110.00	125.00
		ETC	1968-1971	100.00	165.00	195.00
2.	Small	EW	1961-1991	50.00	75.00	100.00
		ETC	1968-1971	65.00	100.00	145.00
3.	Miniature	EW	1961-1991	45.00	60.00	75.00
		ETC	1968-1971	65.00	100.00	115.00

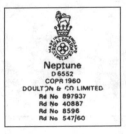

Neptune
D 6552
COPR 1960
DOULTON & CO LIMITED
Rd No 897937
Rd No 40887
Rd No 8596
Rd No 547/60

NIGHT WATCHMAN

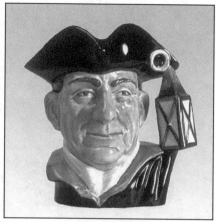

Night Watchman

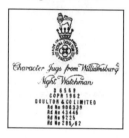

Statistics:	Doulton Number	Size	Height	Issued
Designer: Max Henk				
1.	D6569	Large	7", 17.8 cm	1963-1983
2.	D6576	Small	3 ½", 8.9 cm	1963-1983
3.	D6583	Miniature	2 ½", 6.4 cm	1963-1983

Handle: Lantern
Colourway: Black-purple tricorn and cloak
Backstamp: Doulton
Series: Character From Williamsburg

Jug No.	Size	Comp.	Issued	Current Market Value U.K. £	U.S. $	Can. $
1.	Large	EW	1963-1983	100.00	150.00	175.00
		ETC	1968-1971	125.00	225.00	250.00
2.	Small	EW	1963-1983	65.00	100.00	125.00
		ETC	1968-1971	90.00	150.00	185.00
3.	Miniature	EW	1963-1983	50.00	85.00	100.00
		ETC	1968-1971	75.00	125.00	150.00

NOAH

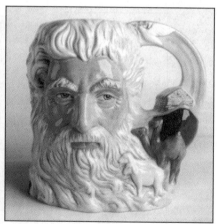

Noah

Designer: David B. Biggs

Statistics:	Doulton Number	Size	Height	Issued
	D7165	Large	7 ¼", 18.4 cm	See below

Issued: 2001 in a limited edition of 1,000
Handle: A rainbow with a dove at top and the ark and camels below
Colourway: White, grey, browns, red, yellow, green and blue
Backstamp: Doulton

Size	Current Market Value U.K. £	U.S. $	Can. $
Large	—	295.00	—

Note: Exlusive to the U.S.A. market.

NORTH AMERICAN INDIAN

The North American Indian is one of three jugs which received a special backstamp in 1967. The other two, the Lumberjack and the Trapper form a three-jug Canadian Centennial Series.

Designer: Max Henk
Handle: A totem pole

VARIATION No. 1: Colourway — Red, white and black feathers; yellow and white band; green robes; dark brown handle

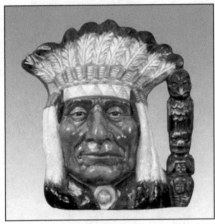

North American Indian, Variation No. 1

	Doulton			
Statistics:	Number	Size	Height	Issued
1.	D6611	Large	7 ¾", 19.7 cm	1967-1991
2.	D6614	Small	4 ¼", 10.8 cm	1967-1991
3.	D6665	Miniature	2 ¾", 7.0 cm	1981-1991

Colourway: Red, white and black feathers; yellow and white band; green robes; dark brown handle

Backstamps: A. Doulton
B. Doulton/Canadian Centenary/Canadian Centennial Series 1867-1967
Available only in North America during 1967
C. Doulton/Okoboji 75 Anniversary 1973
Issued for the 75th anniversary of the Okoboji Trap Shooting Club. 180 jugs were presented at the annual pow-wow.

Series: B. Canadian Centennial Series, 1867-1967

Jug				Current Market Value		
No.	Size	Comp.	Issued	U.K. £	U.S. $	Can. $
1A.	Large	EW	1967-1991	80.00	125.00	150.00
1A.		ETC	1968-1971	125.00	200.00	225.00
1B.		EW	1967-1967	150.00	250.00	275.00
1C.		EW	1973-1973	1,000.00	2,000.00	2,750.00
2A.	Small	EW	1967-1991	45.00	75.00	100.00
2A.		ETC	1968-1971	80.00	125.00	150.00
3A.	Miniature	EW	1981-1991	40.00	65.00	75.00
3A.		ETC	1968-1971	70.00	100.00	125.00

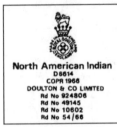

Backstamp A - Doulton

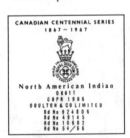

Backstamp B - Canadian Centennial Series

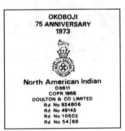

Backstamp C - Okoboji

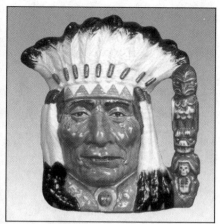

North American Indian, Variation No. 2

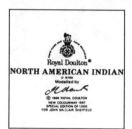

NORTH AMERICAN INDIAN *(cont.)*

VARIATION No. 2: **Colourway** —Yellow, blue, white and black feathers; green and white band; orange robes; light brown handle

Statistics:	Doulton Number	Size	Height	Issued
1.	D6786	Large	7 ¾", 19.7 cm	1987
2.	D —	Small	4 ¼", 10.8 cm	1987-1987
3.	D —	Miniature	2 ¾", 7.0 cm	1987-1987

    Issued: 1987 in a special edition of 1,000
Colourway: Yellow, blue, white and black feathers; green and white band; orange robes; light brown handle
Backstamp: Doulton/John Sinclair
Commissioned by John Sinclair, Sheffield, England. Issued in 1987 in a special edition of 1,000 pieces

Jug No.	Size	Current Market Value		
		U.K. £	**U.S. $**	**Can. $**
1.	Large	125.00	250.00	325.00
2.	Small		Extremely rare	
3.	Miniature		Extremely rare	

Note: The small and miniature North American Indian jugs were sold at Sotheby's Arcade Auction, New York, on March 12, 1997. These two jugs carried the standard Royal Doulton backstamp plus the words "The property of Royal Doulton Tableware Ltd. Not produced for sale."

OLD CHARLEY

"Ten o'clock and all's well" was the familiar call of the Charlies, watchmen who originated during the reign of Charles II and were named after him. They enjoyed a history of almost two hundred years, before being replaced in the early 1800s by a version of the present-day policeman.

Designer: Charles Noke
Handle: Plain

VARIATION No. 1: Colourway — Brown hat; dark green coat; blue polka-dot bow tie

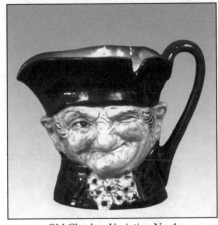

Old Charley, Variation No. 1

	Doulton			
Statistics:	Number	Size	Height	Issued
1.	D5420	Large	5 ½", 14.0 cm	1934-1983
2.	D5527	Small	3 ¼", 8.3 cm	1935-1983
3.	D6046	Miniature	2 ¼", 5.7 cm	1939-1983
4.	D6144	Tiny	1 ¼", 3.1 cm	1940-1960

Colourway: Brown hat; dark green coat; blue polka-dot bow tie
Backstamps: A. Doulton
B. Doulton/Bentalls/Souvenir from Bentalls. Jubilee Year, 1935. Bentalls Ltd. is a London department store.
C. Doulton/Bentalls/Souvenir from Bentalls. 1936.

Jug				Current Market Value		
No.	Size	Comp.	Issued	U.K. £	U.S. $	Can. $
1A.	Large	EW	1934-1983	65.00	100.00	110.00
		ETC	1968-1971	90.00	145.00	165.00
2A.	Small	EW	1935-1983	40.00	60.00	85.00
2A.		ETC	1968-1971	60.00	90.00	110.00
2B.		EW	1935-1935	475.00	750.00	1,000.00
2C.		EW	1936-1936	475.00	750.00	1,000.00
3A.	Miniature	EW	1939-1983	30.00	55.00	65.00
		ETC	1968-1971	60.00	90.00	100.00
4A.	Tiny	EW	1940-1960	65.00	90.00	100.00

Note: 1. Jugs exist without the polka-dots on the bow tie (colouring omission).
2. Old Charley large and mid size jugs are found in white gloss.

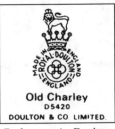

Old Charley
D5420
DOULTON & CO. LIMITED.

Backstamp A - Doulton

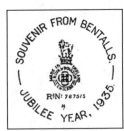

Backstamp B - Bentalls
1935

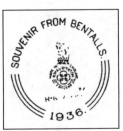

Backstamp C - Bentalls
1936

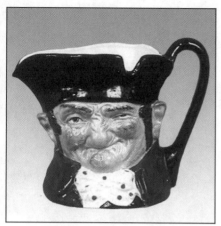

Old Charley, Variation No. 2

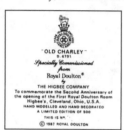

OLD CHARLEY (cont.)

VARIATION No. 2: **Colourway** — Black hat; maroon coat; black polka-dot bow tie

	Doulton			
Statistics:	**Number**	**Size**	**Height**	**Issued**
1.	D6761	Large	5 ½", 14.0 cm	1986-1986
2.	D6791	Small	3 ¼", 8.3 cm	1987-1987

Backstamps: **A.** Doulton/Higbee/Specially Commissioned from Royal Doulton by The Higbee Company To Commemorate the First Anniversary of the Opening of the First Royal Doulton Room Higbee's, Cleveland, Ohio, U.S.A. Commissioned by the Higbee Department Store in 1985. Issued in 1986 in a limited edition of 250 pieces.

B. Doulton/Higbee/Specially Commissioned from Royal Doulton by The Higbee Company To Commemorate the Second Anniversary of the Opening of the First Royal Doulton Room Higbee's, Cleveland, Ohio, U.S.A. Commissioned by the Higbee Department Store and issued in a limited edition of 500 pieces.

Jug			Current Market Value		
No.	Size	Variation	U.K. £	U.S. $	Can. $
1A.	Large	Var. 2	325.00	350.00	400.00
2B.	Small		200.00	250.00	300.00

Old Charley Derivatives

	Doulton		
Item	Number	Height	Issued
Ash Bowl	D5925	3", 7.6 cm	1939-1960
Ash Tray	D5599	2 ¾", 7.0 cm	1936-1960
Musical Jug	D5858	5 ½", 14.0 cm	1938-1939
Sugar Bowl	D6012	2 ½", 6.4 cm	1939-1960
Table lighter	D5227	3 ½", 8.9 cm	1959-1973
Tea Pot	D6017	7", 17.8 cm	1939-1960
Tobacco Jar	D5844	5 ½", 14.0 cm	1937-1960
Toothpick Holder	D6152	2 ¼", 5.7 cm	1940-1960
Wall Pocket	D6110	7 ¼", 18.4 cm	1940-1960

	Doulton	Current Market Value		
Item	Number	U.K. £	U.S. $	Can. $
Ash Bowl	D5925	75.00	125.00	175.00
Ashtray	D5599	75.00	125.00	175.00
Musical Jug	D5858	575.00	1,000.00	1,200.00
Sugar Bowl	D6012	400.00	700.00	800.00
Table Lighter	D5227	150.00	175.00	225.00
Teapot	D6017	850.00	1,500.00	2,000.00
Tobacco Jar	D5844	1,000.00	1,850.00	2,250.00
Toothpick Holder	D6152	475.00	800.00	1,100.00
Wall Pocket	D6110	850.00	1,500.00	2,000.00

Note: The tune played on the musical jug is "Here's a Health Unto His Majesty."

OLD KING COLE

"Old King Cole was a Merry Old Soul" are the words of the nursery rhyme that inspired the design of this jug. The collar frill was remodelled around 1939 and Variation Two can be found with both deep and shallow white ruff modellings.

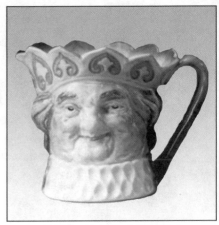

Designer: Harry Fenton
Handle: Plain

VARIATION No. 1: **Colourway** — Yellow crown; frills in the white ruff are deep and pronounced

Statistics:	Doulton Number	Size	Height	Issued
1.	D6036	Large	5 ½", 14.0 cm	1938-1939
2.	D6037	Small	3 ½", 8.9 cm	1938-1939

Old King Cole, Variation No. 1

Colourway: Yellow crown; frills in the white ruff are deep and pronounced
Backstamp: Doulton

Jug No.	Size	Variation	Current Market Value U.K. £	U.S. $	Can. $
1.	Large	Var. 1	2,000.00	5,000.00	6,000.00
2.	Small		1,500.00	3,500.00	4,000.00

VARIATION No. 2: **Colourway** — Brown crown

Statistics:	Doulton Number	Size	Height	Issued
1.	D6036	Large	5 ¾", 14.6 cm	1939-1960
2.	D6037	Small	3 ½", 8.9 cm	1939-1960
3.	D6871	Tiny	1 ½", 3.8 cm	1990-1990

Colourway: Brown crown
Backstamps: **A.** Doulton
B. Doulton/Royal Doulton International Collectors Club
Series: Tiny — RDICC

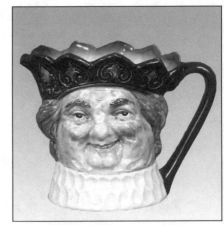

Jug No.	Size	Variation	Current Market Value U.K. £	U.S. $	Can. $
1A.	Large	Var. 2	175.00	275.00	300.00
2A.	Small		90.00	125.00	175.00
3B.	Tiny		100.00	150.00	175.00

Old King Cole, Variation No. 2

Old King Cole Derivatives

Item: Musical Jug
Height: 7 ½", 19.1 cm
Issued: 1939-1939
Colourways: See below

Doulton Number	Variation 3	Current Market Value U.K. £	U.S. $	Can. $
D —	Yellow crown	1,750.00	3,750.00	4,000.00
D6014	Brown crown	1,000.00	2,250.00	2,500.00

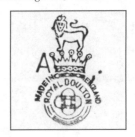

Note: The tune played on the musical jugs is "Old King Cole was a Merry Old Soul."

OLD SALT

When the miniature Old Salt jug was launched in 1984, it had a hollow crook in the mermaid's arm. Later that year, because of production problems, the arm was moulded to the body. The first version of this miniature has attained near pilot status and commands a large premium over the general issue.

Designer: Large and small — Gary Sharpe
Miniature — Peter Gee
Handle: A mermaid
Backstamp: Doulton

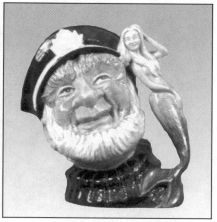

Old Salt, Variation No. 1

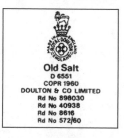

Old Salt
D 6551
COPR 1960
DOULTON & CO LIMITED
Rd No 898030
Rd No 40938
Rd No 8616
Rd No 572/60

VARIATION No. 1: **Colourway** — Dark blue fisherman's jersey
Handle — Mermaid has blue tail

Statistics:	Doulton Number	Size	Height	Issued
1.	D6551	Large	7 ½", 19.1 cm	1961-2001
2.	D6554	Small	4", 10.1 cm	1961-2001
3.	D6557	Miniature	2 ½", 6.4 cm	1984-1991

Colourway: Dark blue fisherman's jersey; mermaid has blue tail

Jug No.	Size	Comp.	Issued	Current Market Value U.K. £	U.S. $	Can. $
1.	Large	EW	1961-2001	75.00	150.00	200.00
		ETC	1968-1971	125.00	225.00	250.00
2.	Small	EW	1961-2001	40.00	85.00	115.00
		ETC	1968-1971	80.00	125.00	150.00
3A.	Miniature	Open arm	1984-1984	700.00	1,250.00	1,500.00
3B.	Miniature	Closed arm	1984-1991	45.00	70.00	80.00

VARIATION No. 2: **Colourway** — Light and dark blue fisherman's jersey
Handle — Mermaid has yellow and black tail

Statistics:	Doulton Number	Size	Height	Issued
	D6782	Large	8", 20.3 cm	1987-1990

Colourway: Light and dark blue fisherman's jersey; mermaid has yellow and black tail

Size	Variation	Current Market Value U.K. £	U.S. $	Can. $
Large	Var. 2	125.00	225.00	300.00

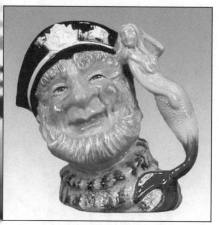

Old Salt, Variation No. 2

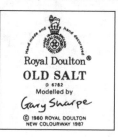

Royal Doulton®
OLD SALT
D 6782
Modelled by
Gary Sharpe
© 1960 ROYAL DOULTON
NEW COLOURWAY 1987

OLD SALT (cont.)

VARIATION No. 3: Colourway — Black cap with gold detail; cream fisherman's jersey
Handle — Mermaid has bright blue tail

	Doulton			
Statistics:	**Number**	**Size**	**Height**	**Issued**
	D7153	Small	4 ¼", 10.8 cm	2001-2001

Colourway: Black cap with gold detail; cream fisherman's jersey; mermaid has bright blue tail
Backstamp: Doulton
Series: Michael Doulton Events

		Current Market Value		
Size	**Variation**	**U.K. £**	**U.S. $**	**Can. $**
Small	Var. 3	65.00	110.00	—

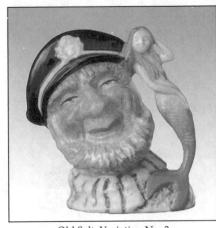

Old Salt, Variation No. 3

Old Salt Derivative

Item: TEAPOT
Height: 6 ¼", 15.9 cm
Issued: 1989-1989

Doulton		**Current Market Value**		
Number	**Item**	**U.K. £**	**U.S. $**	**Can. $**
D6818	Teapot	135.00	275.00	300.00

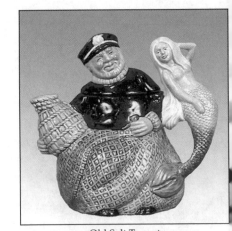

Old Salt Teapot

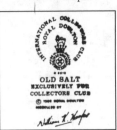

OLIVER CROMWELL

This is a two-handled jug, with Colonel Fairfax and Charles I forming the handles. It was issued in a limited edition of 2,500 to celebrate the 350th Anniversary of the Battle of Marston Moor in 1644.

STYLE ONE: LARGE-SIZE, TWO-HANDLED JUG

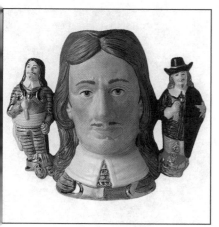

Oliver Cromwell, Style One

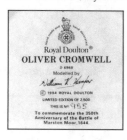

Designer: William K. Harper

Statistics:	Doulton Number	Size	Height	Issued
	D6968	Large	7", 17.8 cm	See below

Issued: 1994 in a limited edition of 2,500
Handle: Colonel Fairfax and Charles I
Colourways: Brown, cream, blue and black
Backstamp: Doulton

Size	Current Market Value		
	U.K. £	U.S. $	Can. $
Large	225.00	400.00	475.00

Note: For the character jug Oliver Cromwell (Style Two) see King Charles I and Oliver Cromwell page 245.

OLIVER TWIST

For the character jug Oliver Twist see the "Charles Dickens Commemorative Set" page 143.

OSCAR WILDE

Issued to commemorate the 100th anniversary of his death (November 1900).

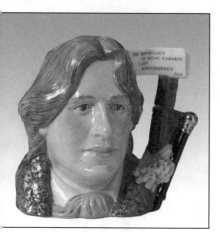

Oscar Wilde

Designer: David B. Briggs

Statistics:	Doulton Number	Size	Height	Issued
	D7146	Large	7", 17.8 cm	2000-2000

Handle: Gloves, cane and carnation; "The Importance of Being Earnest / Lady Windermere's Fan"
Colourway: Brown, tan and green
Backstamp: Doulton
Series: Character Jug of the Year

Size	Current Market Value		
	U.K. £	U.S. $	Can. $
Large	125.00	225.00	300.00

OTHELLO

In Shakespeare's tragic play of 1604, Othello is a successful Venetian soldier who marries the attractive Desdemona. Out of spite and jealousy, his subordinate Iago convinces Othello that Desdemona has been unfaithful. Outraged, Othello kills her, then commits suicide.

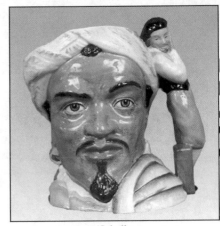

Othello

Designer: Michael Abberley

Statistics:	Doulton Number	Size	Height	Issued
	D6673	Large	7 ¼", 18.4 cm	1982-1989

Handle: A figure of Iago
Colourway: Yellow turban; green, yellow and white robes
Backstamp: Doulton
Series: The Shakespearean Collection

	Current Market Value		
Size	U.K. £	U.S. $	Can. $
Large	100.00	150.00	175.00

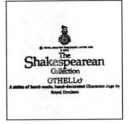

PADDY

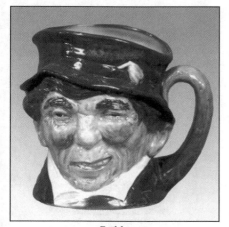

Paddy

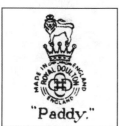

"Paddy."

Paddy, a colloquial term for an Irishman, is derived from St. Patrick, the country's patron saint. This gent is dressed in traditional green for St. Patrick's Day.

Designer: Harry Fenton

Statistics:	Doulton Number	Size	Height	Issued
1.	D5753	Large	6", 15.0 cm	1937-1960
2.	D5768	Small	3 ¼", 8.3 cm	1937-1960
3.	D6042	Miniature	2 ¼", 5.7 cm	1939-1960
4.	D6145	Tiny	1 ¼", 3.1 cm	1940-1960

Handle: Plain
Colourway: Brown hat; green coat; yellow and red scarf
Backstamp: Doulton

Jug No.	Size	Current Market Value		
		U.K. £	U.S. $	Can. $
1.	Large	75.00	100.00	125.00
2.	Small	40.00	65.00	85.00
3.	Miniature	40.00	55.00	65.00
4.	Tiny	65.00	85.00	100.00

Paddy Derivatives

Item:	TOBACCO JAR	**Item:**	MUSICAL JUG
Height:	5 ½", 14.0 cm	**Height:**	7", 17.8 cm
Issued:	1939-1942	**Issued:**	1938-c.1939
Backstamp:	A. Doulton		
	B. Salt River		
	C. Coleman's		

Item:	ASH BOWL	**Item:**	TOOTHPICK HOLDER
Height:	3", 7.6 cm	**Height:**	2 ¼", 5.7 cm
Issued:	1938-1960	**Issued:**	1940-1941

Doulton Number	Item	Backstamp	Current Market Value		
			U.K. £	U.S. $	Can. $
D5845	Tobacco Jar	Doulton	900.00	1,500.00	1,800.00
D5845	Tobacco Jar	Salt River	1,000.00	1,750.00	2,000.00
D5845	Tobacco Jar	Coleman's	900.00	1,500.00	1,800.00
D5887	Musical Jug	Doulton	500.00	900.00	1,000.00
D5926	Ash Bowl	Doulton	90.00	135.00	160.00
D6151	Toothpick Holder	Doulton	400.00	650.00	900.00

Note: 1. The tune played on the musical jug is an Irish jig.
2. Paddy small and miniature jugs are found in white gloss.

PARSON BROWN

For the tiny version of Parson Brown see the "Diamond Anniversary Set" page 214.

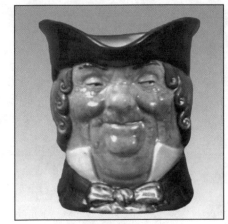

Parson Brown

Designer: Charles Noke

Statistics:	Doulton Number	Size	Height	Issued
1.	D5486	Large	6 ½", 16.5 cm	1935-1960
2.	D5529	Small	3 ½", 8.9 cm	1935-1960

Issued: See below

Handle: Plain
Colourway: Dark grey
Backstamps: A. Doulton
B. Doulton/Commissioned by Bentalls to celebrate Bentalls Jubilee Year 1935
C. Doulton/Bentalls/Souvenir from the silver jubilee of King George V
D. Doulton/Bentalls/Souvenir from Bentalls. 1936.
E. Doulton/Darley/Souvenir from Darley & Son Sheffield & Rotherham

Jug No.	Size	Issued	Current Market Value U.K. £	U.S. $	Can. $
1A.	Large	1935-1960	100.00	175.00	225.00
2A.	Small	1935-1960	50.00	80.00	110.00
2B.		1935-1935	400.00	650.00	900.00
2C.		1936-1936	400.00	650.00	900.00
2D.		1936-1936	400.00	650.00	900.00
2E		1936-1936	400.00	650.00	900.00

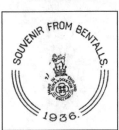

Backstamp D - Bentalls
1936

Note: A large size jug featuring a hallmarked silver rim, colourway green and grey, sold at BBR Auctions for £1,400.00.

Parson Brown Derivatives

Item:	ASH TRAY	Item:	ASH BOWL
Height:	2 ¾", 7.0 cm	Height:	3", 7.6 cm
Issued:	1936-1960	Issued:	1939-1960

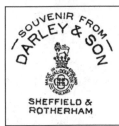

Backstamp E - Darley & Son

Doulton Number	Item	Current Market Value U.K. £	U.S. $	Can. $
D5600	Ashtray	100.00	150.00	175.00
D6008	Ash Bowl	100.00	150.00	175.00

PAUL McCARTNEY

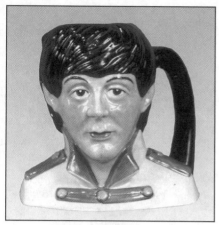

Paul McCartney

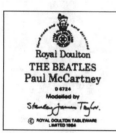

Paul McCartney (b. 1942) was a singer, songwriter and the bass player with the Beatles, until they disbanded in 1970. He then performed with his own band, Wings, until 1981, and since then has remained active in the music field. This jug was issued only in Great Britain, due to copyright reasons.

Designer: Stanley J. Taylor

Statistics:	Doulton Number	Size	Height	Issued
	D6724	Mid	5 ½", 14.0 cm	1984-1991

Handle: Plain
Colourway: Yellow tunic; blue collar and epaulettes
Backstamp: Doulton
Series: The Beatles

Size	Current Market Value		
	U.K. £	U.S. $	Can. $
Mid	125.00	250.00	275.00

PEARLY BOY

The Pearly Boy is a coster or costermonger, one who sells fruits and vegetables from a barrow in the streets of London. His finest attire consists of clothes covered in pearl buttons. 'Arry (page 104) is a costermonger without his buttons.

Designer: Harry Fenton
Handle: Plain

Statistics:

	Doulton Number	Size	Height	Issued
1.	D —	Large	6 ½", 16.5 cm	See below
2.	D —	Small	3 ½", 8.9 cm	See below
3.	D —	Miniature	2 ½", 6.4 cm	See below

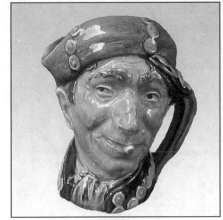

Pearly Boy, Variation No. 1

VARIATION No. 1: Colourway — Brown hat with blue peak; blue coat; pearl buttons

Issued: 1947-Unknown
Colourway: Brown hat with blue peak; blue coat; white buttons.
Backstamps: A. Doulton/Crown and lion
B. Doulton/'Arry and crown and lion

Jug No.	Size	Variation	Current Market Value U.K. £	U.S. $	Can. $
1.	Large	Var. 1	4,000.00	6,500.00	8,500.00
2.	Small	Var. 1	2,500.00	4,500.00	5,500.00
3.	Miniature	Var. 1	Extremely rare		

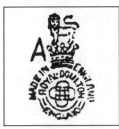

Backstamp A

VARIATION No. 2: Colourway — Brown hat and coat; pearl buttons

Issued: 1947-Unknown
Colourways: Brown hat and coat; pearl buttons
Backstamp: Doulton

Jug No.	Size	Variation	Current Market Value U.K. £	U.S. $	Can. $
1.	Large	Var. 2	Extremely rare		
2.	Small	Var. 2	2,000.00	4,000.00	5,000.00
3.	Miniature	Var. 2	2,000.00	4,000.00	5,000.00

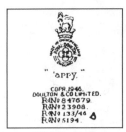

Backstamp B

Note: For the character jug 'Arry see page 104.

PEARLY BOY (cont.)

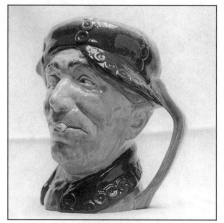

Pearly Boy, Variation No. 3

VARIATION No. 3:   **Colourway** — Brown hat and coat; brown buttons

Issued: 1947-1947
Colourways: Brown hat and coat; brown buttons
Backstamp: Doulton

Jug No.	Size	Variation	Current Market Value U.K. £	U.S. $	Can. $
1.	Large	Var. 3	1,250.00	2,500.00	2,750.00
2.	Small	Var. 3	550.00	1,200.00	1,400.00
3.	Miniature	Var. 3	450.00	1,000.00	1,200.00

VARIATION No. 4:   **Colourway** — Beige hat; brown coat; pearl buttons

Issued: 1947-Unknown
Colourways: Beige hat; brown coat; pearl buttons
Backstamp: Doulton

Jug No.	Size	Variation	Current Market Value U.K. £	U.S. $	Can. $
1.	Large	Var. 4	Extremely rare		
2.	Small	Var. 4	2,000.00	4,000.00	5,000.00
3.	Miniature	Var. 4	2,000.00	4,000.00	5,000.00

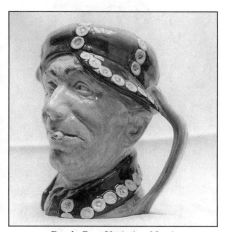

Pearly Boy, Variation No. 4

VARIATION No. 5:   **Colourway** — White glaze

Issued: 1947-Unknown
Colourways: White glaze
Backstamp: Doulton

Jug No.	Size	Variation	Current Market Value U.K. £	U.S. $	Can. $
2.	Small	Var. 5	Sold October 26, 2000. Phillips, New Bond Street, London, England, £3,400.00.		

Note: Variation No. 5 which sold at auction had a small concealed chip to handle.

PEARLY GIRL

Pearly Girl is the female counterpart of Pearly Boy. She was a costermonger who sold her produce in the streets of London. Pearly Girl is 'Arriet (page 104) dressed in her finest.

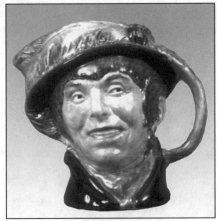

Pearly Girl, Variation 1

Designer: Harry Fenton
Handle: Hat feather

Statistics:	Doulton Number	Size	Height	Issued
1.	D —	Large	6 ½", 16.5 cm	1946-Unk.
2.	D —	Small	3 ¼", 8.3 cm	1946-Unk.
3.	D —	Miniature	2 ½", 6.4 cm	1946-Unk.

VARIATION No. 1: Colourway — Blue jacket; lime-green feather; maroon hat and button

Colourway: Blue jacket; lime-green feather; maroon hat and button
Backstamp: A. Doulton/Crown and lion
B. Doulton/'Arriet and crown and lion

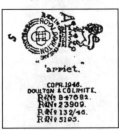

Backstamp B

Jug No.	Size	Variation	Current Market Value U.K. £	U.S. $	Can. $
1.	Large	Var. 1	5,000.00	10,000.00	10,000.00
2.	Small	Var. 1	2,500.00	4,750.00	5,000.00
3.	Miniature	Var. 1	Extremely rare		

VARIATION No. 2: Colourway — Dark brown jacket; lime-green feather; pink hat and button

Colourways: Dark brown jacket; lime-green feather; pink hat and button
Backstamp: Doulton

Jug No.	Size	Variation	Current Market Value U.K. £	U.S. $	Can. $
1.	Large	Var. 2	Extremely rare		
2.	Small	Var. 2	Extremely rare		

Note: For the character jug 'Arry see page 104.

PEARLY KING

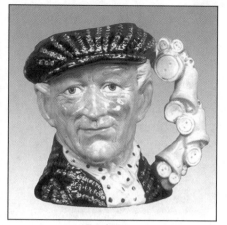

Pearly King

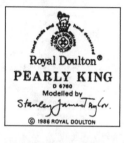

The Pearly King is the head spokesman for the street-market costers of London. Over a hundred years ago, his chief mandate was as a go-between for the costers and the London police. Today the Pearlies have turned their energy to raising money for charity.

Designer: Stanley J. Taylor

Statistics:	Doulton Number	Size	Height	Issued
1.	D6760	Large	6 ¾", 17.2 cm	1987-1991
2.	D6844	Small	3 ½", 8.9 cm	1987-1991

Handle: The Bow Bells; pearl buttons
Colourway: Black cap and jacket with silver buttons; yellow scarf with red polka dots
Backstamp: Doulton
Series: The London Collection

Jug No.	Size	Current Market Value		
		U.K. £	U.S. $	Can. $
1.	Large	100.00	175.00	200.00
2.	Small	60.00	100.00	125.00

PEARLY QUEEN

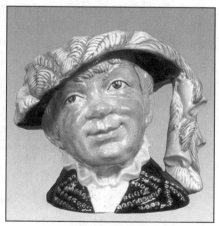

Pearly Queen

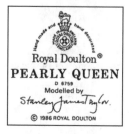

The Pearly Queen, like the Pearly King, is the chief spokesperson for the street-market costers of London. The office is both hereditary and elected.

Designer: Stanley J. Taylor

Statistics:	Doulton Number	Size	Height	Issued
1.	D6759	Large	7", 17.8 cm	1987-1991
2.	D6843	Small	3 ½", 8.9 cm	1987-1991

Handle: The Bow Bells and pink and blue feathers
Colourway: Black coat with silver buttons; black hat with white, pink and blue feathers
Backstamp: Doulton
Series: The London Collection

Jug No.	Size	Current Market Value		
		U.K. £	U.S. $	Can. $
1.	Large	100.00	175.00	200.00
2.	Small	60.00	100.00	125.00

THE PENDLE WITCH

This jug was the first and only jug issued in the proposed series, Myths, Fantasies and Legends. It was commissioned and distributed by Kevin Francis Ceramics in 1989 in a special edition of 5,000 pieces.

Designer: Stanley J. Taylor

Statistics:

Doulton Number	Size	Height	Issued
D6826	Large	7 ¼", 18.4 cm	See below

Issued: 1989 in a special edition of 5,000
Handle: A hound
Colourway: Grey hair; black dress
Backstamp: Doulton

Size	Current Market Value		
	U.K. £	U.S. $	Can. $
Large	200.00	300.00	425.00

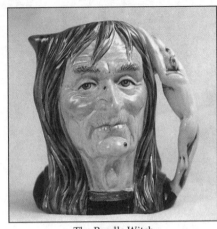

The Pendle Witch

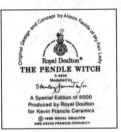

THE PHANTOM OF THE OPERA

Commissioned by Lawleys By Post to commemorate Gaston Leroux's 1910 novel *Le fantome de L'Opera*, this jug was issued in a limited edition of 2,500.

Designer: David B. Biggs

Statistics:

Doulton Number	Size	Height	Issued
D7017	Large	7", 17.8 cm	See below

Issued: 1995 in a limited edition of 2,500
Handle: A stage curtain and lantern
Colourway: Black, white, red and blue
Backstamp: Doulton

Size	Current Market Value		
	U.K. £	U.S. $	Can. $
Large	175.00	350.00	400.00

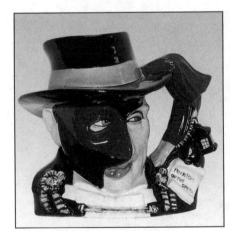

The Phantom of the Opera

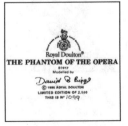

THE PHARAOH

This was the last flambé character jug to be produced by Royal Doulton at Stoke. The jug was issued by Lawleys By Post in 1996 in a limited edition of 1,500.

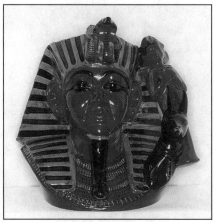

The Pharaoh

Designer: Robert I. Tabbenor

Statistics:	Doulton Number	Size	Height	Issued
	D7028	Large	8", 20.3 cm	See below

Issued: 1996 in a limited edition of 1,500
Handle: The symbol ankh; Shawabtwy (funerary figure); Head of Anubis (jackal-god of mummification)
Colourway: Flambé
Backstamp: Doulton
Series: Flambé

	Current Market Value		
Size	U.K. £	U.S. $	Can. $
Large	400.00	800.00	900.00

PIED PIPER

PROTOTYPE

Designer: Geoff Blower

	Doulton			
Statistics:	**Number**	**Size**	**Height**	**Issued**
	D6403	Large	7", 17.8 cm	Unknown

Handle: White rat at the top of a dark brown flute
Colourway: Maroon cap; maroon and yellow tunic, white collar; blonde hair
Backstamp: Doulton

		Current Market Value		
Size	**Description**	**U.K. £**	**U.S. $**	**Can. $**
Large	Prototype		Unique	

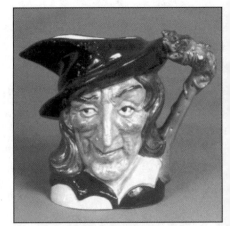

Pied Piper, Prototype

REGULAR ISSUE

In German legend, a stranger came to the town of Hamelin and told the mayor he would rid the village of rats for a sum of money. The Pied Piper walked through town playing a flute, and the rats followed him to the Weser River, where they drowned. When the mayor refused to pay him, the Pied Piper played his flute again, and this time the village children followed him into a cave, never to be seen again.

Designer: Geoff Blower

	Doulton			
Statistics:	**Number**	**Size**	**Height**	**Issued**
1.	D6403	Large	7", 17.8 cm	1954-1981
2.	D6462	Small	3 ¾", 9.5 cm	1957-1981
3.	D6514	Miniature	2 ½", 6.4 cm	1960-1981

Handle: Three brown rats atop a flute
Colourway: Green cap; maroon and yellow tunic; brown hair
Backstamp: Doulton

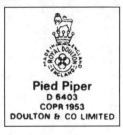

Pied Piper, Regular Issue

Jug				**Current Market Value**		
No.	**Size**	**Comp.**	**Issued**	**U.K. £**	**U.S. $**	**Can. $**
1.	Large	EW	1954-1981	80.00	125.00	150.00
		ETC	1968-1971	100.00	200.00	250.00
2.	Small	EW	1957-1981	50.00	85.00	100.00
		ETC	1968-1971	80.00	125.00	150.00
3.	Miniature	EW	1960-1981	50.00	80.00	100.00
		ETC	1968-1971	60.00	100.00	115.00

Pied Piper
D 6403
COPR 1953
DOULTON & CO LIMITED

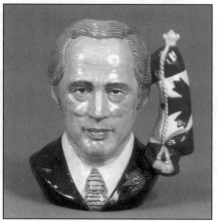

Pierre Elliot Trudeau, Prototype

PIERRE ELLIOT TRUDEAU

PROTOTYPE

Joseph Philippe Pierre Yves Elliott Trudeau (1919-2000) became Canada's Minister of Justice and Attorney General in 1967. He was elected Prime Minister from 1968 to 1979 and from 1980 to 1984.

Doulton was unable to obtain permission to issue this jug.

Designer: William K. Harper

Statistics:	Model Number	Size	Height	Issued
	2952	Large	7", 17.8 cm	See below

Modelled: 1986
Issued: Not put into production
Handle: The Canadian flag
Colourway: Black and grey
Backstamp: Doulton

	Current Market Value		
Size	U.K. £	U.S. $	Can. $
Large		Unique	

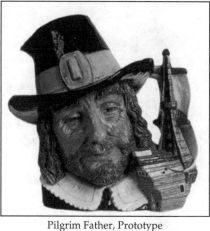

Pilgrim Father, Prototype

PILGRIM FATHER

PROTOTYPE

Designer: David B. Biggs

Statistics:	Doulton Number	Size	Height	Issued
	D —	Large	7 ¾", 19.7 cm	See below

Modelled: 1969
Issued: Not put into production
Handle: The Mayflower
Colourway: Black suit; white collar; brown and white ship
Backstamp: None

	Current Market Value		
Size	U.K. £	U.S. $	Can. $
Large		Sold March 27, 2001 Phillips, New Bond Street London, England, £10,000.00	

THE PIPER

The Piper jug was issued in a limited edition of 2,500 pieces.

Designer: Stanley J. Taylor

	Doulton			
Statistics:	**Number**	**Size**	**Height**	**Issued**
	D6918	Large	8 ¼", 21.0 cm	See below

Issued: 1992 in a limited edition of 2,500
Handle: Bagpipes
Colourway: Black, red, white and yellow
Backstamp: Doulton

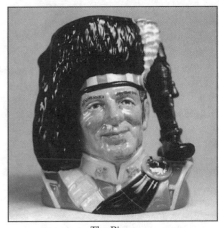
The Piper

	Current Market Value		
Size	**U.K. £**	**U.S. $**	**Can. $**
Large	200.00	400.00	450.00

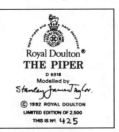

PLUG OF THE BASH STREET KIDS

To celebrate the 60th anniversary of the Dandy and Beano comics in 1998, a special anniversary logo appeared on the base of the jug for that year.

Designer: Simon Ward

	Doulton			
Statistics:	**Number**	**Size**	**Height**	**Issued**
1.	D7035	Small	4 ½", 11.9 cm	1996-1999

Handle: Banana, arrows and quiver
Colourways: Red, yellow and brown
Backstamp: **A.** Doulton/© D.C. Thomson & Co., Ltd.
B. 60th Anniversary logo
Series: Characters from *The Beano* and *The Dandy*

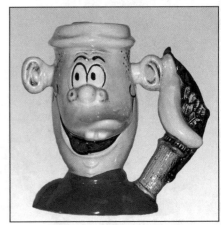
Plug of the Bash Street Kids

Jug			Current Market Value		
No.	**Size**	**Issued**	**U.K. £**	**U.S. $**	**Can. $**
1A.	Small	1996-1999	55.00	125.00	150.00
1B.		1998-1998	55.00	125.00	150.00

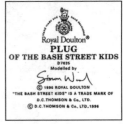
Backstamp A

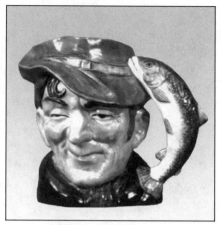

The Poacher, Variation No. 1

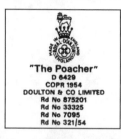

"The Poacher"
D 6429
COPR 1954
DOULTON & CO LIMITED
Rd No 875201
Rd No 33325
Rd No 7095
Rd No 321/54

THE POACHER

Designer: Max Henk
Handle: A salmon
Backstamp: Doulton

VARIATION No. 1: **Colourway** — Green coat; red scarf; light brown hat

Statistics:	Doulton Number	Size	Height	Issued
1.	D6429	Large	7", 17.8 cm	1955-1995
2.	D6464	Small	4", 10.1 cm	1957-1995
3.	D6515	Miniature	2 ½", 6.4 cm	1960-1991

Colourway: Green coat; red scarf; light brown hat

Jug No.	Size	Comp.	Issued	Current Market Value U.K. £	U.S. $	Can. $
1.	Large	EW	1955-1995	60.00	100.00	125.00
		ETC	1968-1971	75.00	125.00	150.00
2.	Small	EW	1957-1995	40.00	60.00	80.00
		ETC	1968-1971	45.00	65.00	100.00
3.	Miniature	EW	1960-1991	40.00	50.00	60.00
		ETC	1968-1971	45.00	60.00	90.00

VARIATION No 2: **Colourway** — Maroon coat; yellow striped scarf; black hat

Statistics:	Doulton Number	Size	Height	Issued
	D6781	Large	7", 17.8 cm	1987-1989

Colourway: Green coat; red scarf; light brown hat

Size	Variation	Current Market Value U.K. £	U.S. $	Can. $
Large	Var. 2	150.00	225.00	275.00

The Poacher Derivative

Item: TABLE LIGHTER
Height: 4 ¾", 12.1 cm
Issued: c.1960-1973

Doulton Number	Item	Current Market Value U.K. £	U.S. $	Can. $
D6464	Table Lighter	150.00	225.00	275.00

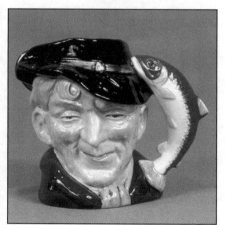

The Poacher, Variation No. 2

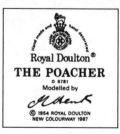

Royal Doulton®
THE POACHER
D 6781
Modelled by
© 1954 ROYAL DOULTON
NEW COLOURWAY 1987

THE POLICEMAN

The Policeman was commissioned by Lawleys By Post and issued in 1989 in a limited edition of 5,000 pieces. The Doulton backstamp is set within the design of a policeman's badge.

Designer: Stanley J. Taylor

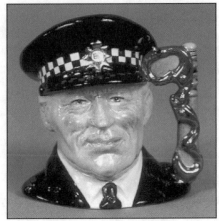

Statistics:

	Doulton Number	Size	Height	Issued
	D6852	Small	4", 10.1 cm	See below

Issued: 1989 in a limited edition of 5,000
Handle: Handcuffs and truncheon
Colourway: Black and white
Backstamp: Doulton
Series: Journey Through Britain

	Current Market Value		
Size	U.K. £	U.S. $	Can. $
Small	125.00	275.00	350.00

The Policeman

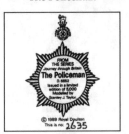

PORTHOS

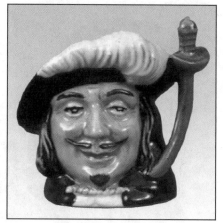

Porthos, Variation No. 1

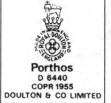

Backstamp A -
Doulton

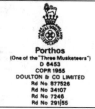

Backstamp B -
Doulton/"One of"

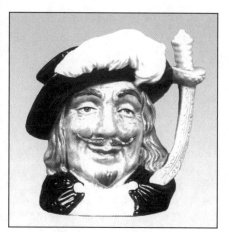

Porthos, Variation No. 2

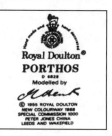

One of the much-loved three musketeers in the 1844 novel by Alexandre Dumas, Porthos roamed Europe with his merry band in search of adventure. "One of the Three Musketeers" was included in the early backstamp to indicate that Porthos was one of the famous Musketeers.

The price differential between backstamp A and B is no longer of significance.

Designer: Max Henk
Handle: A sword

VARIATION No. 1: Colourway — Black hat; red cloak; black hair and moustache

Statistics:	Doulton Number	Size	Height	Issued
1.	D6440	Large	7 ¼", 18.4 cm	1956-1991
2.	D6453	Small	4", 10.1 cm	1956-1991
3.	D6516	Miniature	2 ¾, 7.0 cm	1960-1991

Colourway: Black hat; red cloak; black hair and moustache
Backstamps: A. Doulton
 B. Doulton/(One of the "Three Musketeers")
Series: Characters From Literature / The Three Musketeers

Jug No.	Size	Comp.	Current Market Value Issued	U.K. £	U.S. $	Can. $
1.	Large	EW	1956-1991	70.00	85.00	100.00
		ETC	1968-1971	125.00	250.00	375.00
2.	Small	EW	1956-1991	50.00	65.00	80.00
		ETC	1968-1971	65.00	100.00	150.00
3.	Miniature	EW	1960-1991	40.00	60.00	70.00
		ETC	1968-1971	45.00	65.00	100.00

VARIATION No. 2: Colourway — Maroon hat; blue cloak; ginger hair and moustache

Statistics:	Doulton Number	Size	Height	Issued
	D6828	Large	7 ¼", 18.4 cm	1988-1988

Colourway: Maroon hat; blue cloak; ginger hair and moustache
Backstamp: Doulton/Peter Jones China Ltd.
 Commissioned by Peter Jones China Ltd., Sheffield, England. Issued in 1988 in a limited edition of 1,000 pcs.

Size	Current Market Value U.K. £	U.S. $	Can. $
Large	100.00	225.00	250.00

Porthos Derivative

Item: TABLE LIGHTER
Height: 3 ½", 8.9 cm
Issued: 1958-Unknown

Doulton Number	Item	Current Market Value U.K. £	U.S. $	Can. $
D6453	Table Lighter	450.00	650.00	650.00

THE POSTMAN

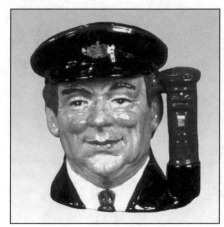

The Postman was commissioned by Lawleys By Post and issued in 1988 in a limited edition of 5,000 pieces. The Doulton backstamp is set within the design of a postage stamp.

Designer: Stanley J. Taylor

Statistics:	Doulton Number	Size	Height	Issued
	D6801	Small	4", 10.1 cm	See below

Issued: 1988 in a limited edition of 5,000
Handle: A pillar box
Colourway: Black jacket and cap; white shirt; red pillar box
Backstamp: Doulton
Series: Journey Through Britain

The Postman

	Current Market Value		
Size	U.K. £	U.S. $	Can. $
Small	150.00	325.00	375.00

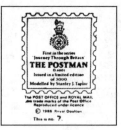

PUNCH AND JUDY

This two-faced jug was created exclusively for the Royal Doulton International Collectors Club, in a limited edition of 2,500.

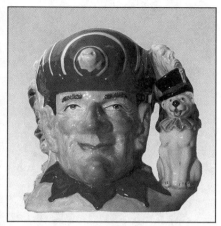

Punch

Designer: Stanley J. Taylor

Statistics:	Doulton Number	Size	Height	Issued
	D6946	Large	7", 17.8 cm	See below

Issued: 1994 in a limited edition of 2,500
Handle: Punch — dog
Judy — crocodile
Colourway: Red, yellow, blue, white and green
Backstamp: Doulton/RDICC
Series: RDICC

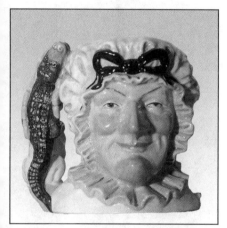

Judy

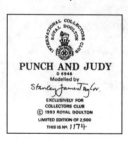

Size	Current Market Value		
	U.K. £	U.S. $	Can. $
Large	325.00	450.00	450.00

PUNCH & JUDY MAN

Coming to England in the 17th century by way of Italy and France, the Punch and Judy puppet show features Punch, the hunchbacked boastful husband, who beats his shrew-like wife Judy.

The colours on Punch's bat are occasionally reversed with no effect on the market value.

Designer: David B. Biggs

Statistics:	Doulton Number	Size	Height	Issued
1.	D6590	Large	7", 17.8 cm	1964-1969
2.	D6593	Small	3 ½", 8.9 cm	1964-1969
3.	D6596	Miniature	2 ½", 6.4 cm	1964-1969

Handle: Punch
Colourway: Brown hat; green coat; yellow scarf
Backstamp: Doulton

Jug No.	Size	Comp.	Issued	Current Market Value U.K. £	U.S. $	Can. $
1.	Large	EW	1964-1969	425.00	775.00	900.00
		ETC	1968-1971		Rare	
2.	Small	EW	1964-1969	275.00	475.00	600.00
		ETC	1968-1971	350.00	600.00	700.00
3.	Miniature	EW	1964-1969	275.00	475.00	600.00
		ETC	1968-1971	350.00	600.00	700.00

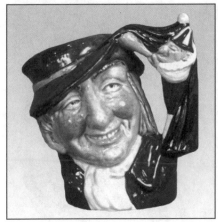

Punch & Judy Man

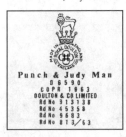

QUASIMODO

Quasimodo was the hunchback featured in Victor Hugo's 1831 novel *Notre Dame de Paris*. The handle represents the belfry of the Notre Dame Cathedral, and the bell it was his job to ring, even as his heart yearned in vain for the beautiful gypsy girl. This jug was issued by Lawleys By Post in a limited edition of 2,500 pieces.

Designer: David B. Biggs

Statistics:	Doulton Number	Size	Height	Issued
	D7108	Large	7", 17.8 cm	See below

Issued: 1998 in a limited edition of 2,500
Handle: Cathedral belfry and bell
Colourway: Green, orange and tan
Backstamp: Doulton

Size	Current Market Value U.K. £	U.S. $	Can. $
Large	100.00	250.00	350.00

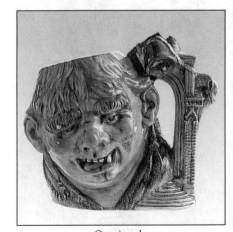

Quasimodo

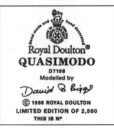

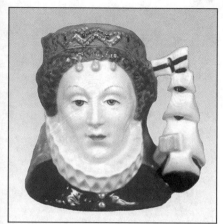

Queen Elizabeth

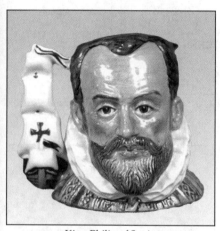

King Philip of Spain

QUEEN ELIZABETH I
and
KING PHILIP OF SPAIN

Daughter of Anne Boleyn, the second wife of Henry VIII, Elizabeth (1533-1603) enjoyed a 45-year reign. With the leadership of Sir Francis Drake, her Royal Navy defeated the Spanish Armada and Philip's attempted invasion of England. Issued by Lawleys By Post in 1988, this jug was one of a pair (with King Philip of Spain) that was produced to celebrate the 400th anniversary of the defeat of the Spanish Armada in 1588. Both jugs were issued in limited editions of 9,500 pieces.

Designer: William K. Harper

Statistics:	Doulton Number	Size	Height	Issued
1.	D6821	Small	4", 10.1 cm	See below
2.	D6822	Small	4", 10.1 cm	See below

Issued: 1988 in a limited edition of 9,500
Handle: Warship
Colourway: Grey, dark red and white
Backstamp: Doulton

Jug No.	Doulton Number	Description	Current Market Value U.K. £	U.S. $	Can. $
1.	D6821	Queen Elizabeth I	100.00	175.00	200.00
2.	D6822	King Philip of Spain	100.00	175.00	200.00
	Pair		200.00	350.00	400.00

Note: For Elizabeth I see the "Kings and Queens of the Realm Set" page 247.

QUEEN VICTORIA

Alexandrina Victoria (1819-1901) succeeded her uncle William IV to the throne on her eighteenth birthday in 1837. Reigning until her death in 1901, she had a longer rule than any other British monarch, and her reign became known as one of the most peaceful in English history.

For Victoria see the "Kings and Queens of the Realm Set" page 328.

Designer: Stanley J. Taylor
Handle: Sceptre

STYLE ONE: HANDLE — SCEPTRE

VARIATION No. 1: Colourway — Dark blue and yellow crown; beige and pink veil

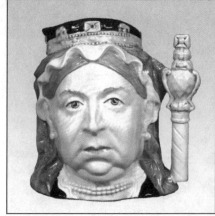

Queen Victoria, Style One, Variation One

Statistics:	Doulton Number	Size	Height	Issued
1.	D6816	Large	7 ¼", 18.4 cm	See below
2.	D6913	Small	3 ½", 8.9 cm	See below

Issued: 1. Large — 1989-1991
2. Small — 1992 in a special edition of 1,500
Colourway: Dark blue and yellow crown; beige and pink veils; yellow jewel in sceptre
Backstamps: A. Large — Doulton
B. Small — Special Limited Edition of 1,500
The small size jug was commissioned by Pascoe & Co. in a special edition of 1,500.

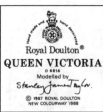

Backstamp A - Large Size Jug

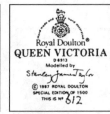

Backstamp B - Small Size Jug

Jug No.	Size	Variation	Current Market Value U.K. £	U.S. $	Can. $
1.	Large	Var. 1	100.00	200.00	250.00
2.	Small	Var. 1	75.00	150.00	200.00

VARIATION No. 2: Colourway — Purple and yellow crown; grey veil with white frills; red jewel in sceptre

Statistics:	Doulton Number	Size	Height	Issued
	D6788	Large	7 ¼", 18.4 cm	See below

Issued: 1988 in a special edition of 3,000
Colourway: Purple and yellow crown; grey veil with white frills; red jewel in sceptre
Backstamp: The Guild of Specialist China & Glass Retailers Commissioned by the Guild of Specialist China & Glass Retailers in 1988 and issued in a special edition of 3,000 pieces.

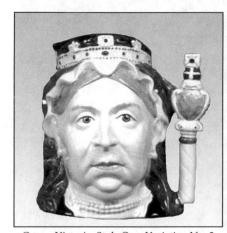

Queen Victoria, Style One, Variation No. 2

Size	Variation	Current Market Value U.K. £	U.S. $	Can. $
Large	Var. 2	100.00	200.00	250.00

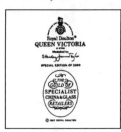

STYLE ONE (cont.)

VARIATION No. 3:   Colourway — Pale blue and yellow crown; cream veil; pale blue jewel in sceptre

	Doulton			
Statistics:	**Number**	**Size**	**Height**	**Issued**
	D6816	Large	7 ¼", 18.4 cm	See below

Issued: Not put into production
Colourway: Pale blue and yellow crown; cream veil; pale blue jewel in sceptre
Backstamp: Doulton

		Current Market Value		
Size	**Variation**	**U.K. £**	**U.S. $**	**Can. $**
Small	Var. 3	Sold November 1999 Phillips, New Bond Street London, England for £600.00		

Photograph not available at press time

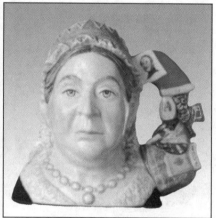

Queen Victoria, Style Three

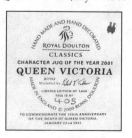

QUEEN VICTORIA

This jug was issued to commemorate the 100th anniversary of the death of Queen Victoria, the longest reigning British Monarch.

STYLE THREE: HANDLE — PORTRAIT OF PRINCE ALBERT AND THE VICTORIA CROSS

Designer: Robert Tabbenor

	Doulton			
Statistics:	**Number**	**Size**	**Height**	**Issued**
	D7152	Large	7", 17.8 cm	See below

Issued: 2001 in a limited edition of 1,000
Handle: Portrait of Prince Albert, an elephant, her pet spaniel "Dash" and the Victoria Cross
Colourway: Gold, cream and black
Backstamp: Doulton
Series: Character Jug of the Year 2001

	Current Market Value		
Size	**U.K. £**	**U.S. $**	**Can. $**
Large	150.00	245.00	—

QUEEN VICTORIA and PRINCE ALBERT

Issued in 1997 by Lawleys by Post in a limited edition of 2,500 pairs, these character jugs commemorate the marriage of Victoria and Albert in 1840.

STYLE TWO: QUEEN VICTORIA: HANDLE — UNION JACK AND CROWN

Designer: William K. Harper

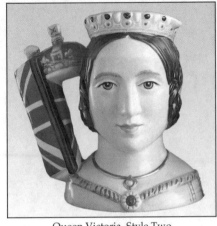

Queen Victoria, Style Two

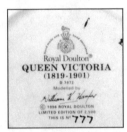

Statistics:	Doulton Number	Size	Height	Issued
1.	D7072	Small	4", 10.1 cm	See below
2.	D7073	Small	4", 10.1 cm	See beliw

Issued: 1997 in a limited edition of 2,500
Handle: 1. Victoria — Union Jack and crown
2. Albert — The Great Exhibition of 1851 banner
Colourway: 1. Victoria — Brown, red, white, blue and yellow
2. Albert — Black, red, yellow and white
Backstamp: Doulton

Jug No.	Doulton Number	Name	Current Market Value		
			U.K. £	U.S. $	Can. $
1.	D7072	Queen Victoria	65.00	175.00	200.00
2.	D7073	Prince Albert	65.00	175.00	200.00
		Pair	125.00	350.00	400.00

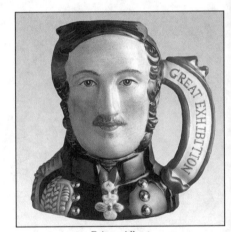

Prince Albert

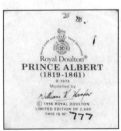

RANGERS (FOOTBALL CLUB)

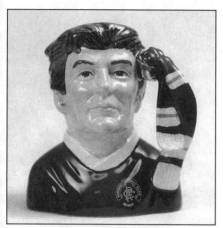

Rangers (Football Club)

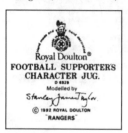

Designer: Stanley J. Taylor

Statistics:	Doulton Number	Size	Height	Issued
	D6929	Small	5", 12.7 cm	1992-1999

Handle: Team coloured scarf
Colourway: Blue, white and red uniform
Backstamp: Doulton
Series: The Football Supporters

	Current Market Value		
Size	U.K. £	U.S. $	Can. $
Small	50.00	110.00	125.00

THE RED QUEEN

A character from Lewis Carroll's *Alice's Adventures in Wonderland*, the Queen of Hearts shows her suit on the blade of an axe and cries, "Off With His Head." Issued in 1987, it was the first in the Alice in Wonderland series.

Designer: William K. Harper

Statistics:	Doulton Number	Size	Height	Issued
1.	D6777	Large	7 ¼", 18.4 cm	1987-1991
2.	D6859	Small	3", 7.6 cm	1990-1991
3.	D6860	Miniature	2", 5.0 cm	1990-1991

Handle: An axe
Colourway: Yellow, red and blue
Backstamp: Doulton
Series: Alice in Wonderland

Jug No.	Size	Current Market Value U.K. £	U.S. $	Can. $
1.	Large	100.00	175.00	225.00
2.	Small	75.00	150.00	175.00
3.	Miniature	75.00	150.00	175.00

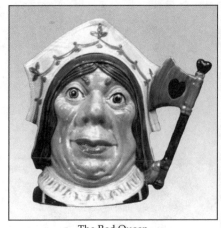

The Red Queen

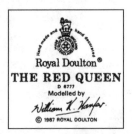

REGENCY BEAU

The regency of the Prince of Wales lasted from 1811 to 1820, when the Prince became George IV. The Regency Period, however, is a term loosely applied to the years from 1805 to 1830, when classical mythology and Greek and Roman authors were popular.

Designer: David B. Biggs

Statistics:	Doulton Number	Size	Height	Issued
1.	D6559	Large	7 ¼", 18.4 cm	1962-1967
2.	D6562	Small	4 ¼", 10.8 cm	1962-1967
3.	D6565	Miniature	2 ¾", 7.0 cm	1962-1967

Handle: Cane and handerchief
Colourway: Green coat; green and yellow hat
Backstamp: Doulton

Jug No.	Size	Current Market Value U.K. £	U.S. $	Can. $
1.	Large	650.00	1,250.00	1,500.00
2.	Small	450.00	700.00	1,000.00
3.	Miniature	550.00	1,200.00	1,400.00

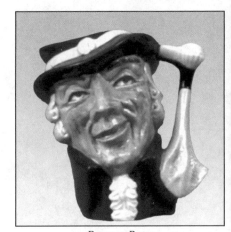

Regency Beau

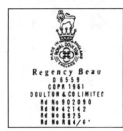

RICHARD III and KING JOHN

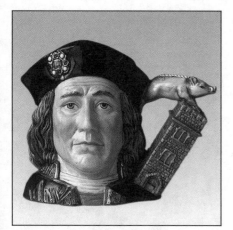

Richard III

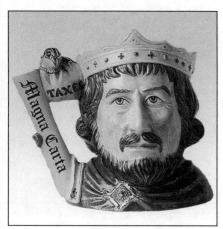

King John

These companion piece jugs, issued in a limited edition of 1,500 each, were available exclusively through the Royal Doulton International Collectors Club. Richard III was introduced in 1998, with King John being introduced in 1999.

Designer: Robert Tabbenor

Statistics:	Doulton Number	Size	Height	Issued
1.	D7099	Large	7", 17.8 cm	See below
2.	D7125	Large	7 ¼", 18.4 cm	See below

Size: Large

Issued:
1. Richard III — 1998 in a limited edition of 1,500
2. King John — 1999 in a limited edition of 1,500

Handle:
1. Richard III — Tower and boar
2. King John — Magna Carta manuscript, sack of taxes

Colourway:
1. Richard III — Navy, brown, black and red
2. King John — Brown, yellow, green, red and blue

Backstamp: Doulton/RDICC

Series: RDICC

Jug No.	Doulton Number	Description	Current Market Value		
			U.K. £	U.S. $	Can. $
1.	D7099	Richard III	150.00	300.00	400.00
2.	D7125	King John	150.00	300.00	400.00

THE RING MASTER

Designer: Stanley J. Taylor

Statistics:

Doulton Number	Size	Height	Issued
D6863	Large	7 ½", 19.1 cm	1990-1993

Handle: Horse's head and plume
Colourway: Black top hat with a light blue ribbon; red jacket; black lapel; green plume atop horses head
Backstamps: A. Doulton
For general release, 1991.
B. Doulton/The Maple Leaf Edition/ The International Royal Doulton Collectors Weekend 1990. Toronto, Ontario, Canada/ The Maple Leaf Edition. Commissioned to commemorate the International Royal Doulton Collectors Weekend, September 14, 15 and 16, 1990. The design incorporates a red maple leaf in honour of the 25th anniversary of Canada's flag. Issued with a certificate of authenticity. Pre-released in 1990 in a special edition of 750 pieces.
Series: The Circus Performers

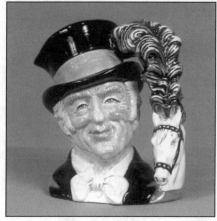

The Ring Master

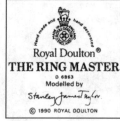

Backstamp A - Doulton

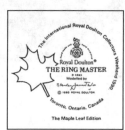

Backstamp B - Doulton/Maple Leaf

Jug No.	Size	Issued	Current Market Value U.K. £	U.S. $	Can. $
1A.	Large	1991-1993	100.00	200.00	225.00
1B.	Large	1990	175.00	250.00	275.00

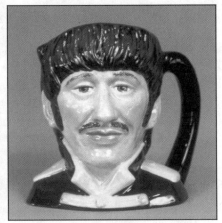

Ringo Starr

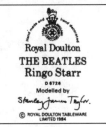

RINGO STARR

Richard Starkey (b. 1940) was the drummer for the Beatles until they disbanded in 1970.

Designer: Stanley J. Taylor

	Doulton			
Statistics:	**Number**	**Size**	**Height**	**Issued**
	D6726	Mid	5 ½", 14.0 cm	1984-1991

Handle: Plain
Colourway: Black tunic; yellow collar and epaulettes
Backstamp: Doulton
Series: The Beatles

	Current Market Value		
Size	U.K. £	U.S. $	Can. $
Mid	175.00	275.00	350.00

RIP VAN WINKLE

In 1820, the American writer Washington Irving wrote the story of Rip Van Winkle, based on legends he had heard from Dutch settlers. While walking in the Catskill Mountains of New York, Rip drinks a fairy potion, falls asleep for 20 years and wakes to find an unrecognizable world.

Designer:	Geoff Blower
Handle:	A man resting against the trunk of a tree, with a blackbird sitting atop it

VARIATION No. 1: **Colourway** — Grey-blue cap; brown robes; figure dressed in blue resting against tree

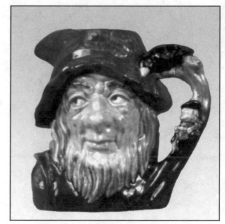

Rip Van Winkle, Variation No. 1

Statistics:	Doulton Number	Size	Height	Issued
1.	D6438	Large	6 ½", 16.5 cm	1955-1995
2.	D6463	Small	4", 10.1 cm	1957-1995
3.	D6517	Miniature	2 ½", 6.4 cm	1960-1991

Colourway:	Grey-blue cap; brown robes; figure dressed in blue resting against tree
Backstamp:	Doulton
Series:	Characters from Literature

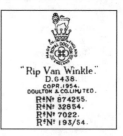

Jug No.	Size	Comp.	Issued	Current Market Value		
				U.K. £	U.S. $	Can. $
1.	Large	EW	1955-1995	65.00	100.00	125.00
		ETC	1968-1971	100.00	150.00	200.00
2.	Small	EW	1957-1995	40.00	65.00	80.00
		ETC	1968-1971	65.00	100.00	150.00
3.	Miniature	EW	1960-1991	30.00	50.00	60.00
		ETC	1968-1971	60.00	80.00	100.00

VARIATION No. 2: **Colourway** — Black cap; green robes; figure dressed in black resting against tree

Statistics:	Doulton Number	Size	Height	Issued
	D6785	Large	7", 17.8 cm	See below

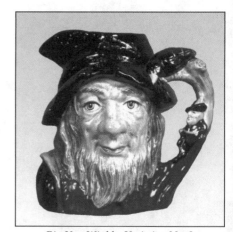

Rip Van Winkle, Variation No. 2

Issued:	1987 in a limited edition of 1,000
Colourway:	Black cap; green robes; figure dressed in black
Backstamp:	Doulton/John Sinclair
	Commissioned by John Sinclair, Sheffield, England. Issued in 1987 in a special edition of 1,000 pieces.

Size	Variation	Current Market Value		
		U.K. £	U.S. $	Can. $
Large	Var. 2	100.00	200.00	275.00

Rip Van Winkle Derivative

Item:	TABLE LIGHTER
Height:	3 ½", 8.9 cm
Issued:	1958-Unknown

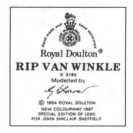

Doulton Number	Item	Current Market Value		
		U.K. £	U.S. $	Can. $
D6463	Table Lighter	500.00	850.00	1,000.00

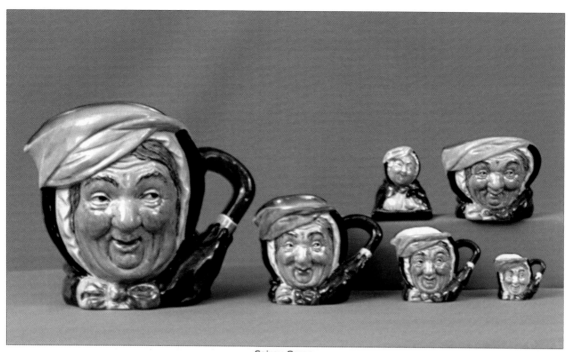

Sairey Gamp
Large, Small, Miniature and Tiny character jugs. Bust and sugar bowl.

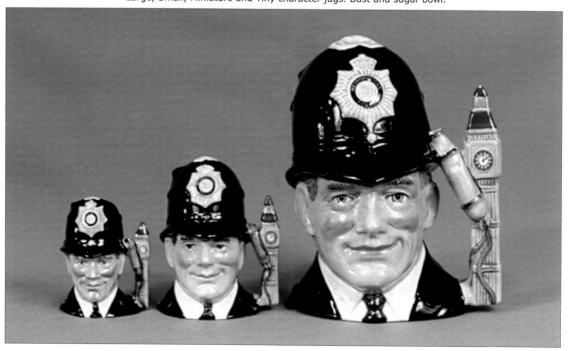

The London 'Bobby'

"The Beatles"

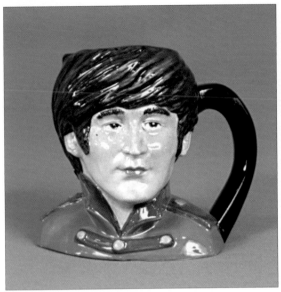

(D6725) John Lennon

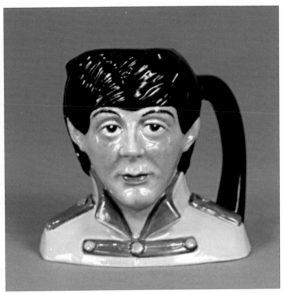

(D6724) Paul McCartney

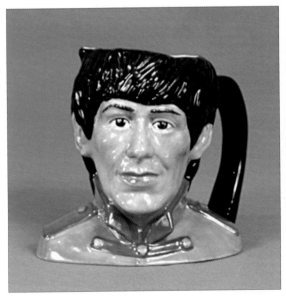

(D6727) George Harrison

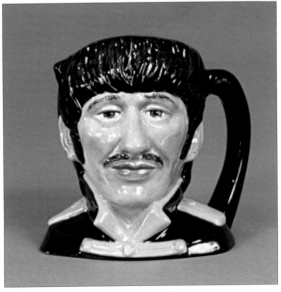

(D6726) Ringo Starr

"Santa Claus"

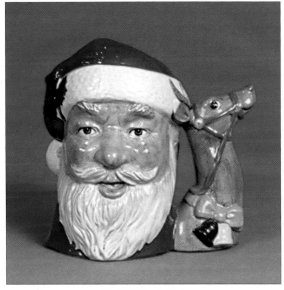

(D6675) Style Two

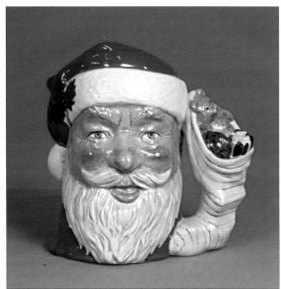

(D6690) Style Three

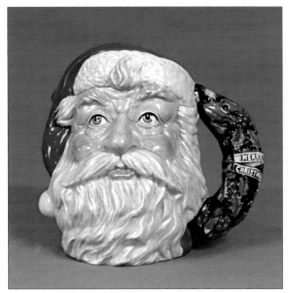

(D6794) Style Five

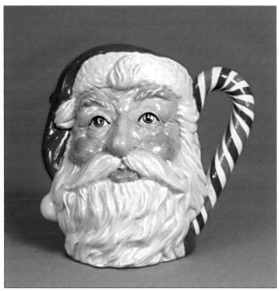

(D6840) Style Six, Var. No. 2

Colourways

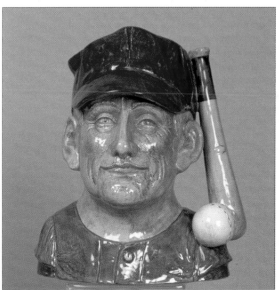

(D6624) Baseball Player, Var. No. 1

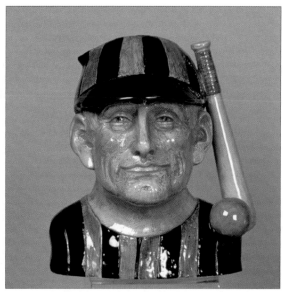

(D6624) Baseball Player, Var. No. 2

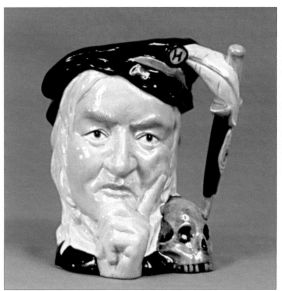

(D 6672) Hamlet, Var. No. 1

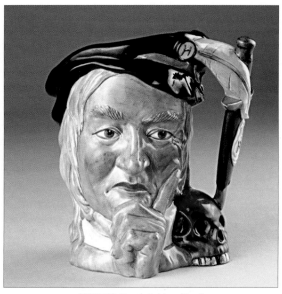

(D6672) Hamlet, Var. No. 2

Colourways

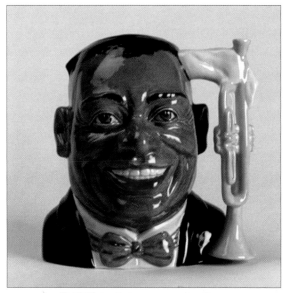

(D6707) Louis Armstrong, Var. No. 1

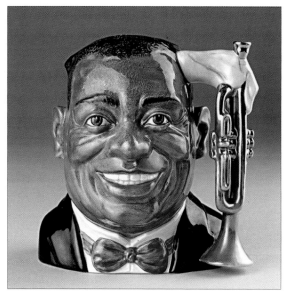

(D6707) Louis Armstrong, Var. No. 2

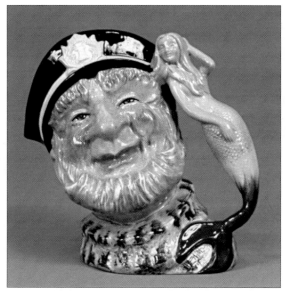

(D6782) Old Salt, Var. No. 2

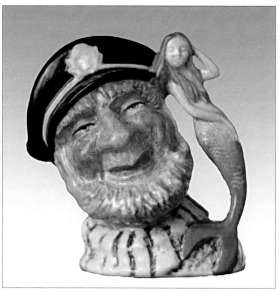

(D7153) Old Salt, Var. No. 3

Liquor Containers

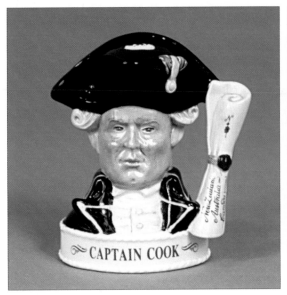

Captain Cook

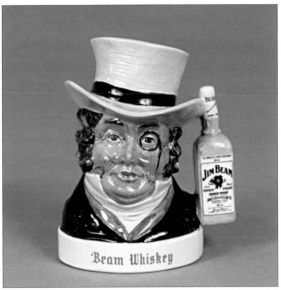

Old Mr. Turverydrop

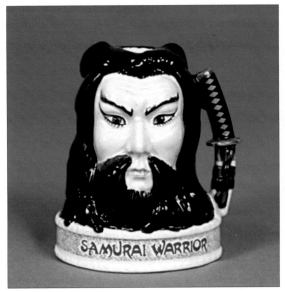

Samurai Warrior

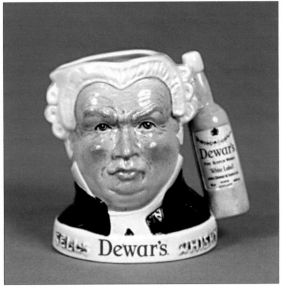

Sgt. Buz Fuz

Liquor Containers

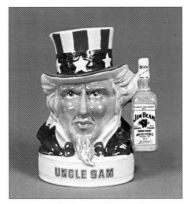

Uncle Sam (Style One)

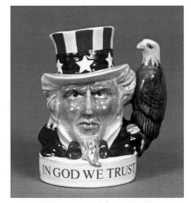

Uncle Sam (Style Two)

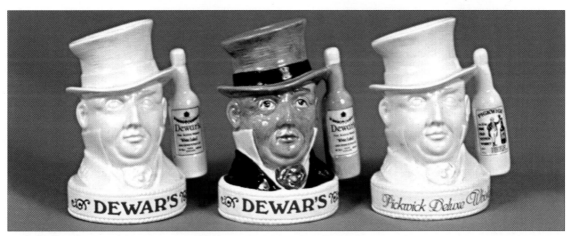

Style Two, Var. No. 2

Mr. Micawber
Style One, Var. No. 1

Style Two, Var. No. 3

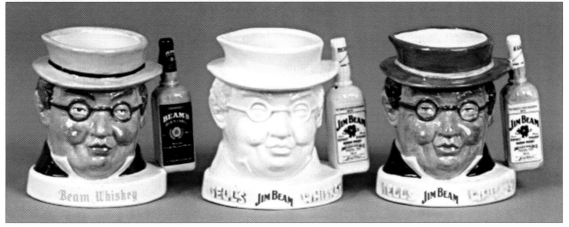

Var. No. 4

Mr. Pickwick
Var. No. 6

Var. No. 7

Loving Cups and Jugs

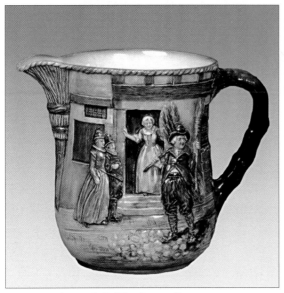

I. T. Wigg Broom Man

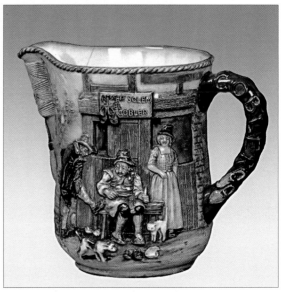

Roger Solemel, Cobbler

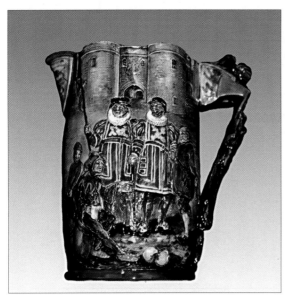

Tower of London

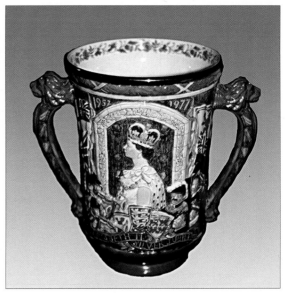

Queen Elizabeth II (Var. No. 2)

ROBIN HOOD

PROTOTYPE

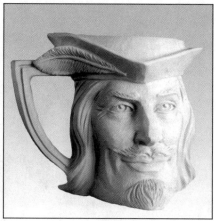

Robin Hood, Prototype

Designer: Eric Griffiths

Statistics:	Model Number	Size	Height	Issued
	3600	Large	6 ½", 16.5 cm	See below

Modelled: 1987
Issued: Not put into production
Handle: Plain
Colourway: Black, brown and green
Backstamp: Doulton

Size	Variation	Current Market Value U.K. £	U.S. $	Can. $
Large	Prototype		Unique	

REGULAR ISSUE

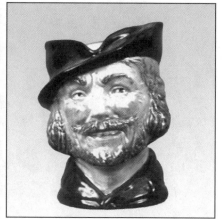

Robin Hood, Style One

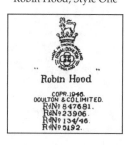

A legendary figure from the reign of Richard I in 12th-century England, Robin Hood and his group of benevolent bandits had many adventures while robbing the rich to help the poor.

STYLE ONE: HAT WITH NO FEATHER
HANDLE — PLAIN

Designer: Harry Fenton

Statistics:	Doulton Number	Size	Height	Issued
1.	D6205	Large	6 ¼", 15.9 cm	1947-1960
2.	D6234	Small	3 ¼", 8.3 cm	1947-1960
3.	D6252	Miniature	2 ¼", 5.7 cm	1947-1960

Handle: Two feathers
Colourway: Brown hat; green robes
Backstamp: Doulton

Jug No.	Size	Current Market Value U.K. £	U.S. $	Can. $
1.	Large	100.00	175.00	200.00
2.	Small	60.00	80.00	100.00
3.	Miniature	50.00	75.00	85.00

ROBIN HOOD

STYLE TWO: HAT WITH FEATHER
HANDLE — BOW, QUIVER AND ARROWS

Designer: Max Henk

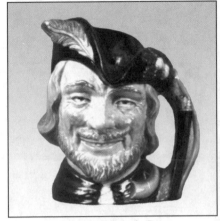

Statistics:	Doulton Number	Size	Height	Issued
1.	D6527	Large	7 ½", 19.1 cm	1960-1992
2.	D6534	Small	4", 10.1 cm	1960-1992
3.	D6541	Miniature	2 ¾", 7.0 cm	1960-1991

Handle: Bow and quiver of arrows
Colourway: Brown hat with white feather on one side and
oak leaves and acorns on the other; green robes
Backstamp: Doulton
Series: Characters From Literature

Robin Hood, Style Two

Jug No.	Size	Comp.	Issued:	Current Market Value U.K. £	U.S. $	Can. $
1.	Large	EW	1960-1992	70.00	100.00	125.00
		ETC	1968-1971	100.00	150.00	200.00
2.	Small	EW	1960-1992	40.00	70.00	90.00
		ETC	1968-1971	75.00	125.00	150.00
3.	Miniature	EW	1960-1991	35.00	60.00	70.00
		ETC	1968-1971	60.00	85.00	100.00

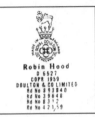

Robin Hood
D 6527
COPR 1959
DOULTON & CO LIMITED
Rd No 893840
Rd No 39646
Rd No 8372
Rd No 421,59

Backstamp - Large

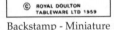

Royal Doulton
ROBIN HOOD
D 6541
© ROYAL DOULTON
TABLEWARE LTD 1959

Backstamp - Miniature

STYLE THREE: HANDLE — FIGURES OF MAID MARION,
FRIAR TUCK, LITTLE JOHN AND THE
SHERIFF OF NOTTINGHAM

Style Three was issued in a limited edition of 2,500.

Designer: William K. Harper

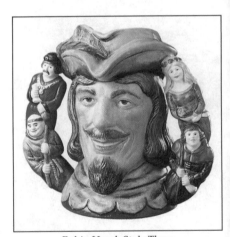

Statistics:	Doulton Number	Size	Height	Issued
	D6998	Large	7", 17.8 cm	See below

Issued: 1995 in a limited edition of 2,500
Handle: Figures of Maid Marion and Little John (right)
Friar Tuck and the Sheriff of Nottingham (left)
Colourway: Green hat and tunic collar with brown
Backstamp: Doulton

Size	Current Market Value U.K. £	U.S. $	Can. $
Large	275.00	550.00	800.00

Robin Hood, Style Three

Note: Sold (no. 1 of 2,500) November 21, 1999, Phillips, New Bond
Street, London, England, for £400.

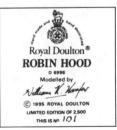

Royal Doulton®
ROBIN HOOD
D 6998
Modelled by
William K. Harper
© 1995 ROYAL DOULTON
LIMITED EDITION OF 2,500
THIS IS № 101

ROBINSON CRUSOE

In 1719, Daniel Defoe wrote *Robinson Crusoe*, based on the experiences of Alexander Selkirk, who was marooned on a deserted Pacific island for five years.

Designer: Max Henk

Statistics:	Doulton Number	Size	Height	Issued
1.	D6532	Large	7 ½", 19.1 cm	1960-1982
2.	D6539	Small	4", 10.1 cm	1960-1982
3.	D6546	Miniature	2 ¾", 7.0 cm	1960-1982

Handle: The man Friday peers from behind a palm tree
Colourway: Brown and green
Backstamp: Doulton

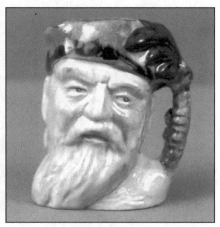

Robinson Crusoe

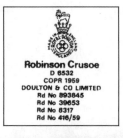

Robinson Crusoe
D 6532
COPR 1959
DOULTON & CO LIMITED
Rd No 893845
Rd No 39653
Rd No 8317
Rd No 416/59

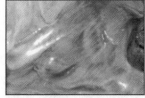

Variation No. 2 - Footprint on shoulder

VARIATION No. 1: With footprint on shoulder

Jug No.	Size	Comp.	Issued	Current Market Value U.K. £	U.S. $	Can. $
1.	Large	EW	1960-1982	100.00	150.00	175.00
2.	Small	EW	1960-1982	55.00	85.00	100.00
3.	Miniature	EW	1960-1982	50.00	80.00	100.00

VARIATION No. 2: Without footprint on shoulder

Jug No.	Size	Comp.	Issued	Current Market Value U.K. £	U.S. $	Can. $
1.	Large	EW	1960-1982	75.00	125.00	150.00
		ETC	1968-1971	100.00	175.00	200.00
2.	Small	EW	1960-1982	50.00	65.00	90.00
		ETC	1968-1971	65.00	100.00	125.00
3.	Miniature	EW	1960-1982	45.00	60.00	90.00
		ETC	1968-1971	65.00	100.00	125.00

ROMEO

The hero of Shakespeare's 1596 romantic play, Romeo falls in love with Juliet, the daughter of a Verona family feuding with his own. The lives of these two clandestine lovers end tragically and, with bitter irony, cause the reconciliation of the two families.

PROTOTYPE

STYLE ONE: HANDLE — A VIAL OF POISON SPILLS OVER A DAGGER BELOW

Designer: David B. Biggs

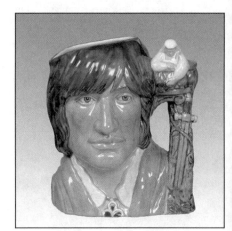

Romeo, Prototype, Style One

Statistics:

Doulton Number	Size	Height	Issued
D6670	Large	7", 17.8 cm	See below

Issued: Not put into production
Handle: A vial of poison spills over a dagger below
Colourway: Brown and white
Backstamp: Doulton

		Current Market Value		
Size	Description	U.K. £	U.S. $	Can. $
Large	Style One		Extremely rare	

STYLE TWO: HANDLE — JULIET ON BALCONY OVER A DAGGER BELOW

Designer: David B. Biggs

Statistics:

Doulton Number	Size	Height	Issued
D6670	Large	7 ½", 19.1 cm	See below

Issued: Not put into production
Handle: Juliet stands on balcony over a dagger below
Colourway: Brown, white and grey
Backstamp: Doulton

		Current Market Value		
Size	Description	U.K. £	U.S. $	Can. $
Large	Style Two		Sold November 21, 1999 Phillips, New Bond Street London, England, £10,000.00	

Romeo, Prototype, Style Two

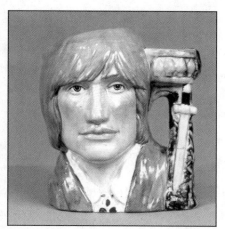

Romeo, Regular Issue

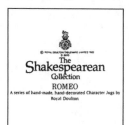

ROMEO

REGULAR ISSUE

The handle for the regular issue jug incorporates a dagger superimposed on a column supporting a balcony.

Designer: David B. Biggs

Statistics:	Doulton Number	Size	Height	Issued
	D6670	Large	7 ½", 19.1 cm	1983-1989

Handle: A dagger superimposed on the column supporting a balcony
Colourway: Brown and white
Backstamp: Doulton
Series: The Shakespearean Collection

Size	Description	Current Market Value U.K. £	U.S. $	Can. $
Large	Style Three	65.00	100.00	125.00

RONALD REAGAN

Ronald Wilson Reagan (b. 1911) began as an Iowa sports announcer, then worked as a movie actor for 30 years. In 1966 Reagan was elected governor of California, then he became President of the United States in 1980 and served two terms until 1988.

PROTOTYPE

The protoype jug has the U.S. flag tied with a green cord and has no cap.

Designer: Eric Griffiths

Statistics:	Doulton Number	Size	Height	Issued
	D6718	Large	7 ¾", 19.7 cm	See below

Modelled: 1984
Issued: Not put into production
Handle: The U.S. flag with green cord, no cap
Colourway: Blue grey suit; dark blue tie
Backstamp: Doulton

	Current Market Value		
Size	U.K. £	U.S. $	Can. $
Large		Unique	

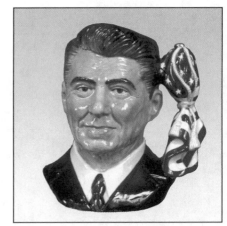

Photograph not available at press time

Ronald Reagan, Prototype

REGULAR ISSUE

This jug has the U.S. flag tied with yellow cord and a gold cap at the top.

The jug was commissioned for the Republican National Committee. Originally planned as a limited edition of 5,000 pieces, the jug did not sell well and only 2,000 pieces were said to have been produced. It was issued with a certificate and photograph of President Reagan in a decorative folio.

Designer: Eric Griffiths

Statistics:	Doulton Number	Size	Height	Issued
	D6718	Large	7 ¾", 19.7 cm	See below

Issued: 1984 in a limited edition of 2,000
Handle: The U.S. flag with yellow cord, gold cap
Colourway: Dark blue suit; white shirt; purple striped tie
Backstamp: Doulton/Reagan

	Current Market Value		
Size	U.K. £	U.S. $	Can. $
Large	425.00	850.00	1,000.00

Ronald Reagan, Regular Issue

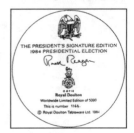

THE PRESIDENT'S SIGNATURE EDITION
1984 PRESIDENTIAL ELECTION

Ronald Reagan

Royal Doulton
Worldwide Limited Edition of 5000
This is number 1166.
© Royal Doulton Tableware Ltd. 1984

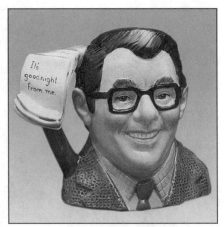

Ronnie Corbett O.B.E.

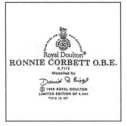

RONNIE CORBETT O.B.E.
and RONNIE BARKER O.B.E.
(THE TWO RONNIES)

Ronnie Corbett and Ronnie Barker, the comic duo whose television show, The Two Ronnies, enthralled viewers for seventeen years, gain enduring recognition in this companion pair of character jugs, issued in a limited edition of 5,000. This jug was commissioned by Lawleys By Post.

Designer: David B. Biggs

Statistics:	Doulton Number	Size	Height	Issued
1.	D7113	Small	4", 10.1 cm	See below
2.	D7114	Small	4 ½", 11.9 cm	See below

Issued: 1998 in a limited edition of 5,000 each
Handle: Scripts: Ronnie Corbett — "It's goodnight from me."
Ronnie Barker — "And it's goodnight from him."
Colourway: 1. Ronnie Corbett — Browns, red and black
2. Ronnie Barker — Grey, blue and black
Backstamp: Doulton

Jug No.	Doulton Number	Name	Current Market Value U.K. £	U.S. $	Can. $
1.	D7113	R. Corbett	125.00	200.00	300.00
2.	D7114	R. Barker		Price per pair	

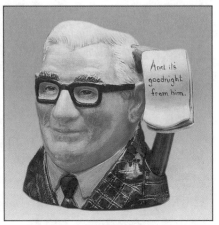

Ronnie Barker O.B.E.

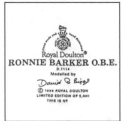

THE SAILOR

STYLE ONE: HANDLE — BINOCULARS

Designer: William K. Harper

VARIATION No. 1: Without "R.C.N." on binoculars

Statistics:	Doulton Number	Size	Height	Issued
	D6875	Small	4 ½", 11.9 cm	1991-1996

Handle: Binoculars
Colourway: White Royal Navy cap; light brown coat; white sweater
Backstamp: Doulton
Series: The Armed Forces

		Current Market Value		
Size	Variation	U.K. £	U.S. $	Can. $
Small	Var. 1	45.00	100.00	125.00

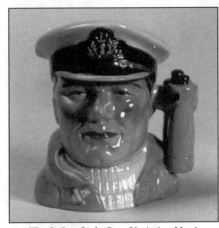

The Sailor, Style One, Variation No. 1

VARIATION No. 2: With "R.C.N." on binoculars

Variation Two of The Sailor was commissioned by The British Toby in a limited edition of 250 pieces. The set sold originally for $465.00 Canadian.

Statistics:	Doulton Number	Size	Height	Issued
	D6904	Small	4 ½", 11.9 cm	See below

Issued: 1991 in a limited edition of 250
Handle: R.C.N. binoculars
Colourway: White Royal Canadian Navy cap; dark brown coat; white sweater
Backstamp: Doulton / The British Toby
Series: The Canadians

		Current Market Value		
Size	Variation	U.K. £	U.S. $	Can. $
Small	Var. 2	150.00	300.00	350.00

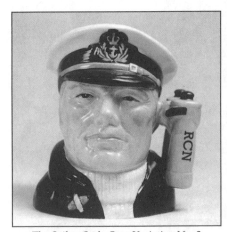

The Sailor, Style One, Variation No. 2

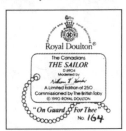

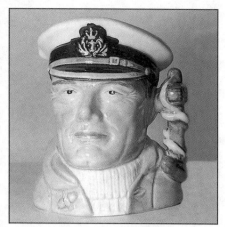

The Sailor, Style Two

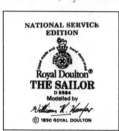

THE SAILOR

STYLE TWO: HANDLE — AN ANCHOR

Commissioned by Lawleys By Post, it was possible to have a National Service number incorporated within the accompanying certificate.

Statistics:	Doulton Number	Size	Height	Issued
	D6984	Small	4 ½", 11.9 cm	See below

Issued:	1994 in a special edition
Handle:	Anchor
Colourway:	White, black, brown and gold
Backstamp:	Doulton
Series:	National Service Edition

Size	Description	Current Market Value		
		U.K. £	U.S. $	Can. $
Small	Style Two	50.00	125.00	150.00

SAIREY GAMP

In Charles Dickens' 1843 novel, *Martin Chuzzlewit*, Sairey Gamp is a gossiping, gin-drinking midwife and nurse.

Misnumbered large-size jugs exist with the number D5528, which is the number allocated to the small-size jug. This does not add any premium to the price.

Designer: Leslie Harradine
Harry Fenton
Handle: Umbrella

VARIATION No. 1: **Colourway** — Black hair; light green band; dark green coat; yellow and burgundy bow
Handle — green umbrella

Statistics:	Doulton Number	Size	Height	Issued
1.	D5451	Large	6 ¼", 15.9 cm	1935-1986
2.	D5528	Small	3 ¼", 8.3 cm	1935-1986
3.	D6045	Miniature	2 ¼", 5.7 cm	1939-1986
4.	D6146	Tiny	1 ¼", 3.1 cm	1940-1960

Colourway: Black hair; light green band; dark green coat; yellow and burgundy bow; green umbrella with brown handle
Backstamp: A. Doulton
B. Doulton/Bentalls/
Souvenir From Bentalls. Jubilee Year, 1935.
Commissioned by Bentalls to commemorate the silver jubilee in 1935 of King George V
C. Doulton/Darley/
Souvenir from Darley & Son Sheffield & Rotherham

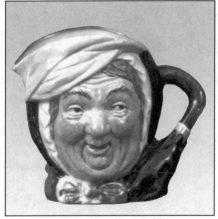

Sairey Gamp, Variation No. 1

Backstamp A - Doulton

Jug No.	Size	Comp.	Issued	Current Market Value U.K. £	U.S. $	Can. $
1A.	Large	EW	1935-1986	60.00	80.00	90.00
!A.		ETC	1968-1971	65.00	100.00	125.00
2A.	Small	EW	1935-1986	40.00	60.00	65.00
2A.		ETC	1968-1971	55.00	80.00	90.00
2B.	Small	EW	1935-1935	650.00	1,000.00	1,250.00
2C.	Small	EW	1936-1936	650.00	1,000.00	1,250.00
3A.	Miniature	EW	1939-1986	30.00	50.00	55.00
		ETC	1968-1971	40.00	70.00	80.00
4A.	Tiny	EW	1940-1960	55.00	80.00	90.00

Note: The Sairey Gamp small size jug is found in white gloss.

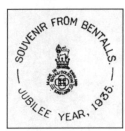

Backstamp B - Bentalls

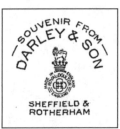

Backstamp C - Darley & Son

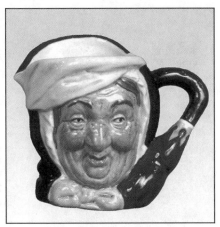

Sairey Gamp, Variation No. 2

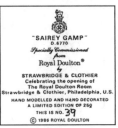

Backstamp A

SAIREY GAMP (cont.)

VARIATION No. 2: **Colourway** —Yellow band on hat; yellow bow
Handle — Maroon umbrella

Statistics:	Doulton Number	Size	Height	Issued
1.	D6770	Large	6 ¼", 15.9 cm	See below
2.	D6789	Small	3", 7.6 cm	See below

Issued: 1. Large — 1986 in a limited edition of 250
2. Small — 1987 in a limited edition of 500
Colourway: Yellow band on hat; yellow bow; maroon umbrella
Backstamps: A. Strawbridge and Clothier/Celebrating the opening of The Royal Doulton Room at Strawbridge and Clothier, Philadelphia, U.S.A. Commissioned by Strawbridge and Clothier, Philadelphia. Issued in 1986 in a limited edition of 250 pieces.
B. Strawbridge and Clothier/Made for the First Anniversary of the Royal Doulton Room at Strawbridge and Clothier. Commissioned by Strawbridge and Clothier in 1987 and issued in a limited edition of 500 pieces.

Jug No.	Size	Variation	Current Market Value U.K. £	U.S. $	Can. $
1A.	Large	Var. 2	225.00	350.00	400.00
2B.	Small	Var. 2	200.00	225.00	250.00

Sairey Gamp Derivatives

Item	Doulton Number	Height	Issued
Ash Bowl	D6009	3", 7.6 cm	1939-1960
Bookend	HN1625	3 ½", 8.9 cm	1934-1939
Bust	D6047	2 ¼", 5.7 cm	1939-1960
Napkin Ring	M62	3 ½", 8.9 cm	c.1935-1939
Sugar Bowl	D6011	2 ½", 6.4 cm	1939-1942
Teapot	D6015	7", 17.8 cm	1939-1942
Toothpick Holder	D6150	2 ¼", 5.7 cm	1940-1942

Doulton Number	Item	Current Market Value U.K. £	U.S. $	Can. $
D6009	Ash Bowl	85.00	150.00	175.00
D6011	Sugar Bowl	375.00	600.00	800.00
D6015	Teapot	900.00	2,000.00	2,500.00
D6047	Bust	75.00	100.00	125.00
D6150	Toothpick Holder	275.00	450.00	600.00
HN1625	Bookend	1,250.00	2,250.00	2,500.00
M62	Napkin Ring	375.00	750.00	900.00

SAM JOHNSON

A celebrated poet, essayist and lexicographer, Dr. Johnson (1709-1784) published his *Dictionary* in 1755, which was the first systematic study of the English language. His literary club met regularly at a London pub and included such famous figures as David Garrick, Oliver Goldsmith and Edmund Burke.

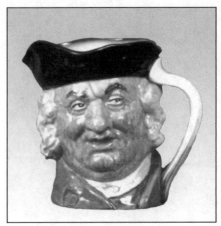

Samuel Johnson

Designer: Harry Fenton

Statistics:	Doulton Number	Size	Height	Issued
1.	D6289	Large	6 ¼", 15.9 cm	1950-1960
2.	D6296	Small	3 ¼", 8.3 cm	1950-1960

Handle: Plain
Colourway: Dark brown hat; light brown, maroon and white robes
Backstamp: Doulton

Jug No.	Size	Current Market Value		
		U.K. £	U.S. $	Can. $
1.	Large	200.00	350.00	400.00
2.	Small	125.00	200.00	300.00

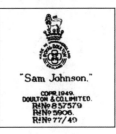

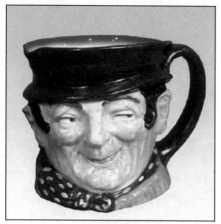

Sam Waller

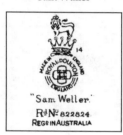

"Sam Weller."
R⁴Nº 822824
Rᴱɢᵉ IN AUSTRALIA

SAM WELLER

In the 1837 Charles Dickens novel, *The Pickwick Papers,* Sam Weller was a boots employed at the White Hart Inn. He became a faithful aide and valet to Mr. Pickwick and eventually married Napkins's housemaid.

This character jug is unusual in that its modelling changes dramatically between the large and smaller versions.

Designer: Leslie Harradine
Harry Fenton

Statistics:	Doulton Number	Size	Height	Issued
1.	D6064	Large	6 ½", 16.5 cm	1940-1960
2.	D5841	Mid	4 ½", 11.9 cm	1938-1948
3.	D5841	Small	3 ¼", 8.3 cm	1948-1960
4.	D6140	Miniature	2 ¼", 5.7 cm	1940-1960
5.	D6147	Tiny	1 ¼", 3.1 cm	1940-1960

Handle: Plain
Colourway: Dark brown hat; light brown coat; red kerchief with white spots
Backstamp: Doulton

Jug No.	Size	Current Market Value		
		U.K. £	U.S. $	Can. $
1.	Large	80.00	125.00	150.00
2.	Mid	125.00	200.00	225.00
3.	Small	60.00	100.00	125.00
4.	Miniature	45.00	70.00	75.00
5.	Tiny	65.00	90.00	110.00

Sam Weller Derivatives

Item: BUST
Height: 2 ½", 6.4 cm
Issued: 1939-1960

Item: NAPKIN RING
Height: 3 ½", 8.9 cm
Issued: c.1939-1939

Doulton Number	Item	Current Market Value		
		U.K. £	U.S. $	Can. $
D6052	Bust	75.00	100.00	125.00
M61	Napkin Ring	375.00	650.00	800.00

Note: The Sam Weller miniature size jug is found in white gloss.

SAMSON AND DELILAH

Samson was an Israelite judge from Biblical times, famous for his strength. Delilah, a Philistine, was paid to find the secret of Samson's strength, so that her people could overthrow their Israelite enemies. Samson fell in love with Delilah and told her that his strength lay in his hair. She shaved his head while he slept and the Philistines captured and blinded him. When his hair grew back, Samson avenged himself by pulling down a Philistine temple, killing himself and many of his enemies.

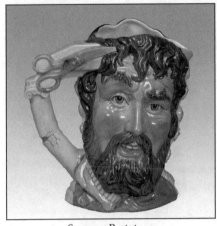

Samson, Prototype

PROTOTYPE

Designer: Stanley J. Taylor

Statistics:

	Doulton Number	Size	Height	Issued
	D —	Large	7", 17.8 cm	See below

Issued: Not put into production
Handle: Samson — Scissors; jawbone of an ass
Delilah — A broken column
Colourway: Reddish-brown, cream and green
Backstamp: Doulton

		Current Market Value		
Size	Description	U.K. £	U.S. $	Can. $
Large	Prototype	Sold November 21, 1999 Phillips, New Bond Street London, England, £8,500.00		

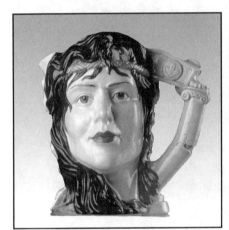

Delilah, Prototype

SAMSON AND DELILAH

REGULAR ISSUE

This jug was issued in 1988 in a limited edition of 9,500 pieces.

Designer: Stanley J. Taylor

Statistics:	**Doulton Number**	**Size**	**Height**	**Issued**
	D6787	Large	7", 17.8 cm	See below

Issued: 1988 in a limited edition of 9,500
Handle: Samson — Jawbone of an ass
Delilah — A broken column
Colourway: Brown, black and cream
Backstamp: Doulton
Series: The Star-crossed Lovers Collection (Two-faced jug)

Size	Description	Current Market Value		
		U.K. £	**U.S. $**	**Can. $**
Large	Regular Issue	100.00	150.00	175.00

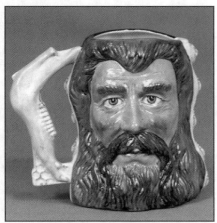

Samson, Regular Issue

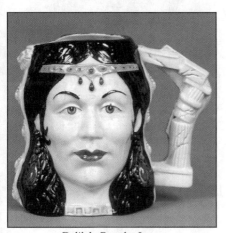

Delilah, Regular Issue

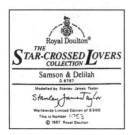

SANCHO PANÇA

This amiable peasant was employed as the squire to Don Quixote in Cervantes's 17th-century novel. Accompanying Quixote on many adventures, his down-to-earth common sense acted as a foil to his master's romantic musing.

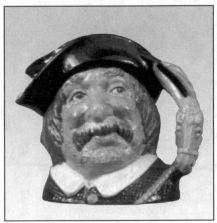

Sancho Pança

Designer: Geoff Blower

	Doulton			
Statistics:	**Number**	**Size**	**Height**	**Issued**
1.	D6456	Large	6 ½", 16.5 cm	1957-1983
2.	D6461	Small	3 ¼", 8.3 cm	1957-1983
3.	D6518	Miniature	2 ½", 6.4 cm	1960-1983

Handle: Light brown donkey
Colourway: Black hat with a white feather; black coat with a white collar
Backstamps: A. Doulton
B. Doulton/Sancho Panca/(A Servant to Don Quixote). Produced from 1957 to the early 1970s, with no cedilla.
C. Doulton/Sancho Pança
The spelling of the name Pança with the cedilla gives a soft "s" sound in pronunciation. Early versions of the backstamp included the cedilla, but it was dropped in the late fifties. The incised name shows that the cedilla was included in the modelling (1957-1959).

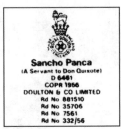

Sancho Panca
(A Servant to Don Quixote)
D 6461
COPR 1956
DOULTON & CO LIMITED
Rd No 881510
Rd No 35706
Rd No 7561
Rd No 332/56

Backstamp A - Doulton

Jug			**Current Market Value**			
No.	**Size**	**Comp.**	**Issued**	**U.K. £**	**U.S. $**	**Can. $**
1	Large	EW	1957-1983	85.00	150.00	175.00
		ETC	1968-1971	110.00	175.00	225.00
2	Small	EW	1957-1983	50.00	80.00	100.00
		ETC	1968-1971	60.00	90.00	125.00
3	Miniature	EW	1960-1983	45.00	70.00	90.00
		ETC	1968-1971	50.00	80.00	100.00

Note: The price differential between backstamps is no longer significant.

SANTA CLAUS

PROTOTYPES

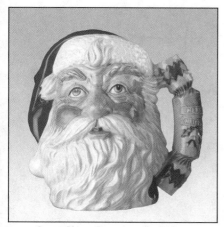

Santa Claus, Prototype, Style One

STYLE ONE: HANDLE — CHRISTMAS CRACKER

Designer: Michael Abberley

Statistics:

	Doulton Number	Size	Height	Issued
	D —	Large	7 ¾", 19.7 cm	See below

Modelled: 1987
Issued: Not put into production
Handle: A Christmas cracker
Colourway: Red and white
Backstamp: Doulton

VARIATION No. 1: **Colourway** — Yellow Christmas cracker

Doulton Number	Variation	Current Market Value U.K. £	U.S. $	Can. $
D —	Var. 1	Sold November 21, 1999 Phillips, London, England, £4,000.00		

VARIATION No. 2: **Colourway** — Green Christmas cracker

Doulton Number	Variation	Current Market Value U.K. £	U.S. $	Can. $
D —	Var. 2	Sold November 21, 1999 Phillips, London, England, £4,200.00		

STYLE TWO: HANDLE — CHRISTMAS TREE

Designer: Michael Abberley

Statistics:

	Doulton Number	Size	Height	Issued
	D —	Large	7 ¾", 19.7 cm	See below

Issued: Not put into production
Handle: A Christmas tree with "Happy Christmas" in banner
Colourway: Red and white
Backstamp: Doulton

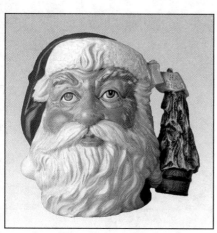

Santa Claus, Prototype, Style Two

VARIATION No. 1: **Colourway** — "Happy Christmas" in red, on cream background

Doulton Number	Variation	Current Market Value U.K. £	U.S. $	Can. $
D —	Var. 1	Sold November 21, 1999 Phillips, London, England, £6,000.00		

VARIATION No. 2: **Colourway** — "Happy Christmas" in green, on yellow background

Doulton Number	Variation	Current Market Value U.K. £	U.S. $	Can. $
D —	Var. 2	Sold November 21, 1999 Phillips, London, England, £6,000.00		

SANTA CLAUS

The Santa Claus jug was introduced in 1981 and was the first to undergo annual design changes. Featuring different well-known Christmas themes, the handle has changed several times since 1981.

STYLE ONE: HANDLE — A DOLL AND DRUM

Designer: Michael Abberley

Statistics:

Doulton Number	Size	Height	Issued
D6668	Large	7 ½", 19.1 cm	1981-1981

Handle: A doll stands on a drum
Colourway: Red, white and light brown
Backstamp: Doulton

		Current Market Value		
Size	Description	U.K. £	U.S. $	Can. $
Large	Style One	125.00	250.00	275.00

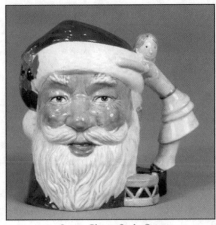

Santa Claus, Style One

STYLE TWO: HANDLE — THE HEAD OF A REINDEER

Designer: Michael Abberley

Statistics:

Doulton Number	Size	Height	Issued
D6675	Large	7 ¼", 18.4 cm	1982-1982

Handle: The head of a reindeer
Colourway: Red, white and brown
Backstamp: Doulton

		Current Market Value		
Size	Description	U.K. £	U.S. $	Can. $
Large	Style Two	150.00	350.00	375.00

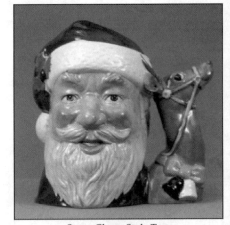

Santa Claus, Style Two

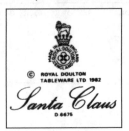

SANTA CLAUS

STYLE THREE: HANDLE — A SACK OF TOYS

Designer: Michael Abberley

	Doulton			
Statistics:	**Number**	**Size**	**Height**	**Issued**
	D6690	Large	7 ½", 19.1 cm	1983-1983

Handle: A sack of toys
Colourway: Red, white and light brown
Backstamp: Doulton

		Current Market Value		
Size	**Desription**	**U.K. £**	**U.S. $**	**Can. $**
Large	Style Three	200.00	375.00	425.00

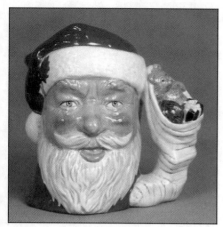
Santa Claus, Style Three

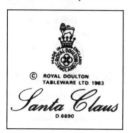

STYLE FOUR: HANDLE — PLAIN RED

Designer: Michael Abberley — Large, small, miniature
William K. Harper — Tiny

	Doulton			
Statistics:	**Number**	**Size**	**Height**	**Issued**
1.	D6704	Large	7 ½", 19.1 cm	1984-2000
2.	D6705	Small	3 ¼", 8.3 cm	1984-Current
3.	D6706	Miniature	2 ½", 6.4 cm	1984-1991
4.	D6950	Tiny	1 ¼", 3.1 cm	1984-Sp.ed.

Handle: Plain
Colourway: Red and white
Backstamps: A. Doulton
B. Doulton/Seaway China
Commissioned by Seaway China Marine City
MI U.S.A. Issued in a special edition of 2,500.

Jug			Current Market Value		
No.	Size	Description	U.K. £	U.S. $	Can. $
1.	Large	Style Four	80.00	165.00	230.00
2.	Small		50.00	100.00	150.00
3.	Miniature		75.00	125.00	135.00
4.	Tiny		45.00	65.00	90.00

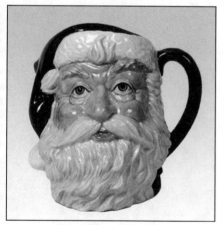
Santa Claus, Style Four

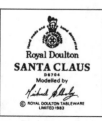
Backstamp A

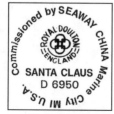
Backstamp B

346

SANTA CLAUS

STYLE FIVE: HANDLE — A HOLLY WREATH

Designer: Michael Abberley

Statistics:

	Doulton Number	Size	Height	Issued
1.	D6794	Large	7", 17.8 cm	See below
2.	D6900	Miniature	2 ½", 6.4 cm	See below

Issued: 1. Large — 1988 in a special edition of 5,000
2. Small — 1991 in a special edition of 5,000
Handle: A holly wreath
Colourway: Red, white and green
Backstamps: **A.** Doulton
Issued in a limited edition of 5,000 for
Christmas 1991.
B. Doulton/Home Shopping
Commissioned by the Home Shopping Network,
Florida. Issued in a special edition of 5,000.
Series: Christmas Miniatures

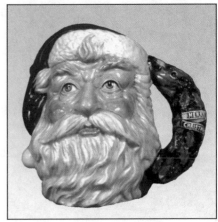

Santa Claus, Style Five

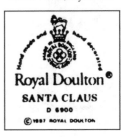

Jug No.	Size	Description	Current Market Value		
			U.K. £	**U.S. $**	**Can. $**
1A.	Large	Style Five	300.00	550.00	650.00
2B.	Miniature		65.00	100.00	120.00

STYLE SIX: HANDLE — A CANDY CANE

PROTOTYPE

Designer: Michael Abberley

Statistics:

Doulton Number	Size	Height	Issued
D6793	Large	7 ½", 19.1 cm	See below

Issued: Not put into production
Handle: Candy cane with green and white stripes
Colourway: Red and white
Backstamp: Doulton

VARIATION No. 1: Handle — Candy cane with green and white
stripes

Size	Variation	Current Market Value		
		U.K. £	**U.S. $**	**Can. $**
Large	Var. 1	Sold November 21, 1999 Phillips, New Bond Street London, England, £1,500.00		

VARIATION No. 2: Handle — Candy cane with light and dark
green stripes

Size	Variation	Current Market Value		
		U.K. £	**U.S. $**	**Can. $**
Large	Var. 2	Sold November 21, 1999 Phillips, New Bond Street London, England, £1,200.00		

Photograph
not available
at press time

Santa Claus, Style Six, Prototype

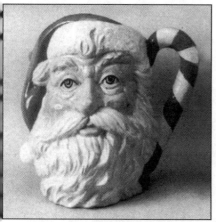

Santa Claus Style Six Regular Issue Var. No.1

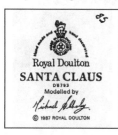

STYLE SIX (cont.)

STYLE SIX: HANDLE — CANDY CANE

REGULAR ISSUE

VARIATION No. 1: Handle — Candy cane with red and white stripes

Designer: Michael Abberley — Large
William K. Harper — Tiny

Statistics:	Doulton Number	Size	Height	Issued
1.	D6793	Large	7 ½"	See below
2.	D6980	Tiny	1 ¼"	See below

Issued: 1. Large — 1988 in a limited edition of 1,000
2. Tiny — 1995 in a limited edition of 2,500
Handle: Candy cane with red and white stripes
Colourway: Red and white
Backstamp: A. Doulton/Cable Value
Commissioned by the Cable Value Network.
Issued in a special edition of 1,000.
B. Doulton/Seaway China
Commissioned by Seaway China Marine City MI U.S.A.
Issued in a special edition of 2,500.

Jug No.	Size	Variation	Current Market Value		
			U.K. £	U.S. $	Can. $
1A.	Large	Var. 1	1,000.00	1,500.00	2,000.00
1B.	Tiny	Var. 1	45.00	60.00	90.00

VARIATION No. 2: Handle — Candy cane with red, white and green stripes

Designer: Michael Abberley

Statistics:	Doulton Number	Size	Height	Issued
	D6840	Large	7 ½", 19.1 cm	See below

Issued: 1989 in a special edition of 1,000
Handle: Candy cane with red, white and green stripes
Colourway: Red and white
Backstamp: Doulton/American Collectors Society
Commissioned by the American Collectors Society.
Issued in 1989 in a special edition of 1,000 pieces.

Size	Variation	Current Market Value		
		U.K. £	U.S. $	Can. $
Large	Var. 2	350.00	675.00	800.00

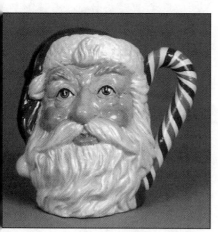

Santa Claus Style Six Regular Issue Var. No. 2

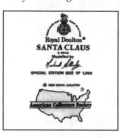

SANTA CLAUS

STYLE SEVEN: HANDLE — CHRISTMAS PARCELS

Designer: William K. Harper

Statistics:	**Doulton** **Number**	**Size**	**Height**	**Issued**
	D7020	Tiny	1 ¼", 3.1 cm	See below

Issued: 1996 in a special edition of 2,500
Handle: Blue and green Christmas parcels
Colourway: Red and white
Backstamp: Doulton/Seaway China
Commissioned by Seaway China Marine City MI U.S.A.
Issued in a special edition of 2,500.

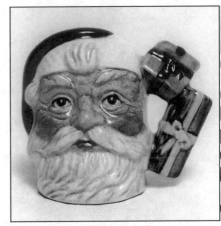

Santa Claus, Style Seven

		Current Market Value		
Size	**Description**	**U.K. £**	**U.S. $**	**Can. $**
Tiny	Style Seven	50.00	80.00	100.00

STYLE EIGHT: HANDLE — TEDDY BEAR

Designer: William K. Harper

Statistics:	**Doulton** **Number**	**Size**	**Height**	**Issued**
	D7060	Tiny	1 ¼", 3.1 cm	See below

Issued: 1997 in a limited edition of 2,500
Handle: Teddy bear
Colourway: Red and white
Backstamp: Doulton/Seaway China
Commissioned by Seaway China Marine City MI U.S.A.
Issued in a special edition of 2,500.

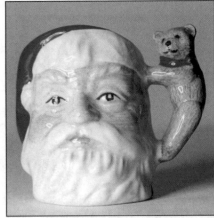

Santa Claus, Style Eight

		Current Market Value		
Size	**Description**	**U.K. £**	**U.S. $**	**Can. $**
Tiny	Style Eight	45.00	65.00	80.00

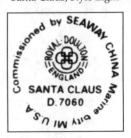

SANTA CLAUS

This jug was sold through the Home Shopping Network in the U.S.A. and was limited to 1,000 jugs.

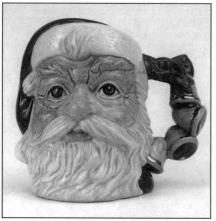

Santa Claus, Style Nine

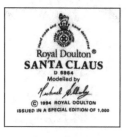

STYLE NINE: HANDLE — CHRISTMAS BELLS

Designer: Michael Abberley

Statistics:	Doulton Number	Size	Height	Issued
	D6964	Small	4 ½", 11.9 cm	See below

Issued: 1996 in a limited edition of 1,000
Handle: Christmas Bells
Colourway: Red and white
Backstamp: Doulton

| Size | Description | Current Market Value | | |
		U.K. £	U.S. $	Can. $
Small	Style Nine	375.00	700.00	850.00

SANTA CLAUS

This jug was commissione by Pascoe and Company in a special edition of 1,500 pieces.

STYLE TEN: HANDLE — CHRISTMAS TREE AND PARCELS

Designer: David B. Biggs

Statistics:	Doulton Number	Size	Height	Issued
	D7123	Large	7", 17.8 cm	See below

Issued: 1998 in a special edition of 1,500
Handle: Christmas tree and parcels
Colourway: Red, white, blue and grey
Backstamp: Doulton/Pascoe

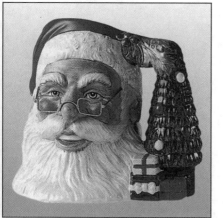

Santa Claus, Style Ten

| Size | Description | Current Market Value | | |
		U.K. £	U.S. $	Can. $
Large	Style Ten	75.00	125.00	200.00

SCARAMOUCHE

In the 17th-century comedy, written by Edward Ravenscroft, Scaramouche appears as a boastful, foolish character, dressed in the old Spanish style.

STYLE ONE HANDLE — A GUITAR WITH THE TWO MASKS OF COMEDY AND TRAGEDY

Designer: Max Henk

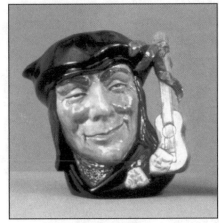

Scaramouche

Statistics:	Doulton Number	Size	Height	Issued
1.	D6558	Large	7", 17.8 cm	1962-1967
2.	D6561	Small	3 ¼", 8.3 cm	1962-1967
3.	D6564	Miniature	2 ½", 6.4 cm	1962-1967

Issued: 1962-1967
Handle: A guitar
Colourway: Blue-black, brown and green
Backstamp: Doulton

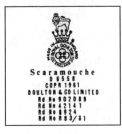

Jug No	Size	Current Market Value		
		U.K. £	U.S. $	Can. $
1.	Large	600.00	950.00	1,200.00
2.	Small	400.00	600.00	750.00
3.	Miniature	350.00	500.00	650.00

SCARAMOUCHE

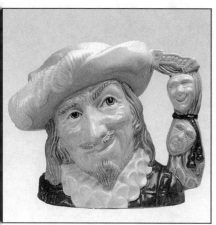

Scaramouche, Style Two, Variation No. 1

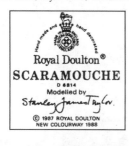

STYLE TWO: HANDLE —A CURTAIN WITH THE TWO MASKS OF COMEDY AND TRAGEDY

Designer: Stanley J. Taylor
Handle: The masks of tragedy and comedy rest against a curtain

Statistics:

	Doulton Number	Size	Height	Issued
	See below	Large	6 ¾", 17.2 cm	See below

VARIATION No. 1: **Colourway** —Yellow hat; turquoise tunic; white ruff; light brown hair
Handle — Lavender

Issued: 1988-1991
Colourway: Yellow hat; turquoise tunic; white ruff; light brown hair; lavender handle
Backstamp: Doulton
Series: Characters From Literature

Doulton Number	Variation	Current Market Value		
		U.K. £	U.S. $	Can. $
D6814	Var. 1	125.00	225.00	250.00

VARIATION No. 2: **Colourway** — Black hat; green tunic; white ruff; dark brown hair
Handle — Yellow

Issued: 1987 in a special edition of 1,500
Colourway: Black hat; green tunic; white ruff; dark brown hair; yellow handle
Backstamp: Doulton/Guild
Commissioned by the Guild of Specialist China & Glass Retailers in 1987 and issued in a special edition of 1,500 pieces.

Doulton Number	Variation	Current Market Value		
		U.K. £	U.S. $	Can. $
D6774	Var. 2	100.00	325.00	350.00

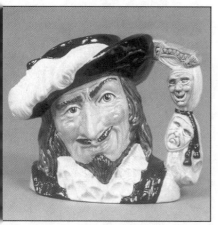

Scaramouche, Style Two, Variation No. 2

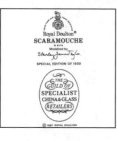

SCARLET PIMPERNEL

PROTOTYPE

In the 1905 novel by the Hungarian Baroness Orczy, the Scarlet Pimpernel was a group of Englishmen dedicated to the rescue of victims of the Reign of Terror in Paris. Sir Percy Blakeney, the group's leader, bested his opponents by clever wit and courage while disguising his identity from his friends back in England.

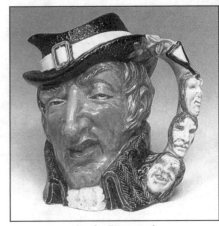

Scarlet Pimpernel

Designer: Geoff Blower

Statistics:	Doulton Number	Size	Height	Issued
	D —	Large	7", 17.8 cm	See below

Modelled: Unknown
Issued: Not put into production
Handle: Characters in assorted disguises
Colourway: Black, white and blue
Backstamp: Doulton

	Current Market Value		
Size	U.K. £	U.S. $	Can. $
Large		Unique	

SCHUBERT

Franz Schubert (1797-1828) was a prolific composer in his short life, and is best remembered for his songs and the famous "Unfinished" symphony.

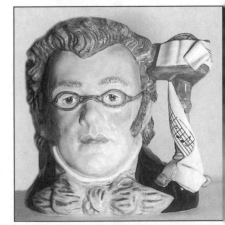

Schubert

Designer: Stanley J. Taylor

Statistics:	Doulton Number	Size	Height	Issued
	D7056	Large	6 ¾", 17.2 cm	1997-2001

Handle: Music rack and an excerpt from "Cradle Song"
Colourway: Black, green, brown and yellow
Backstamp: Doulton
Series: Great Composers

	Current Market Value		
Size	U.K. £	U.S. $	Can. $
Large	90.00	225.00	300.00

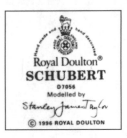

SCROOGE

For the character jug Scrooge see the "Charles Dickens Commemorative Set" page 143.

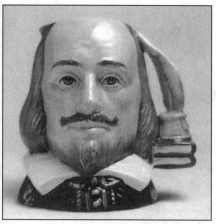

Shakespeare

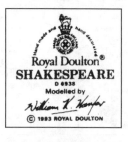

SHAKESPEARE

Designer: William K. Harper

	Doulton			
Statistics:	**Number**	**Size**	**Height**	**Issued**
	D6938	Small	3 ½", 8.9 cm	1993 to the present

Handle: Inkwell and books
Colourway: Black coat; yellow collar; light brown hair and beard; burgundy books; grey inkwell and quill
Backstamp: Doulton

	Current Market Value		
Size	**U.K. £**	**U.S. $**	**Can. $**
Small	60.00	100.00	150.00

Note: For William Shakespeare see page 395.

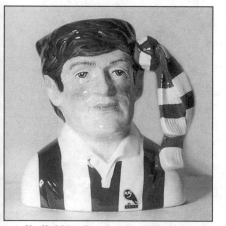

Sheffield Wednesday (Football Club)

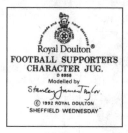

SHEFFIELD WEDNESDAY (FOOTBALL CLUB)

This jug was sold exclusively through John Sinclair of Sheffield, England.

Designer: Stanley J. Taylor

	Doulton			
Statistics:	**Number**	**Size**	**Height**	**Issued**
	D6958	Small	5", 12.7 cm	1993-1999

Handle: Team coloured scarf
Colourway: Blue and cream striped uniform
Backstamp: Doulton
Series: The Football Supporters

	Current Market Value		
Size	**U.K. £**	**U.S. $**	**Can. $**
Small	50.00	90.00	110.00

SHERLOCK HOLMES SET

These six tiny character jugs were issued in a tribute to Sir Arthur Conan Doyle, the creator of Sherlock Holmes. They were released by Lawleys By Post in a limited edition of 2,500. Each set has matching edition numbers and was issued with a presentation stand.

Designer: William K. Harper

Statistics:	Doulton Number	Size	Height	Issued
	See below	Tiny	1 ½", 3.8 cm	See below

Issued: 1995 in a limited edition of 2,500
Handle: Miscellaneous
Colourway:
1. **Sherlock Holmes** — Brown, white and grey
2. **Doctor Watson** — Brown, white and grey
3. **Mrs. Hudson** — Black, white and yellow
4. **Professor Moriarty** — Black, white and green
5. **Inspector Lestrade** — Brown, white and grey
6. **Jefferson Hope** — Black, white and red

Backstamp: Doulton

Jug No.	Doulton Number	Name	Current Market Value U.K. £	U.S. $	Can. $
1.	D7011	Sherlock Holmes	40.00	60.00	75.00
2.	D7012	Doctor Watson	40.00	60.00	75.00
3.	D7013	Mrs. Hudson	40.00	60.00	75.00
4.	D7014	Professor Moriarty	40.00	60.00	75.00
5.	D7015	Inspector Lestrade	40.00	60.00	75.00
6.	D7016	Jefferson Hope	40.00	60.00	75.00
		Complete set/stand	225.00	350.00	450.00

Note: For the toby jug Sherlock Holmes see page 79, and for the Sherlock Holmes and Dr. Watson bookends see page 406.

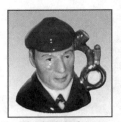
Sherlock Holmes

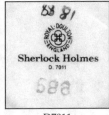
D7011

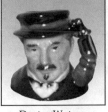
Doctor Watson

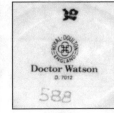
D7012

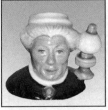
Mrs. Hudson

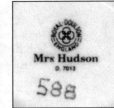
D7013

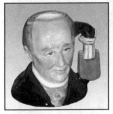
Professor Moriarty

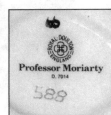
D7014

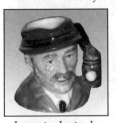
Inspector Lestrade

D7015

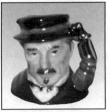
Jefferson Hope

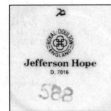
D7016

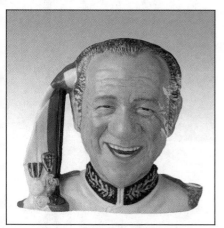

Sid James as Sir Sidney Ruff-Diamond

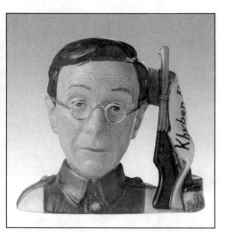

Charles Hawtrey as Private James Widdle

SID JAMES AS SIR SIDNEY RUFF-DIAMOND and CHARLES HAWTREY AS PRIVATE JAMES WIDDLE

These two models were issued as a pair with matching edition numbers. They were available from Doulton and Company Direct.

Designer: Sid James — Alexander Down
Charles Hawtrey — Davide Losi

Statistics:	Doulton Number	Size	Height	Issued
1.	D7162	Small	4", 10.1 cm	See below
2.	D7163	Small	4", 10.1 cm	See below

Issued: 2001 in a limited edition of 1,500
Handle: 1. Sid James — Medals of the British Governor
2. Charles Hawtrey — Rifle, "Khyber Pass"
Colourway: 1. Sid James — White jacket with black and gold collar
2. Charles Hawtrey — Brown and cream uniform; gold spectacles
Backstamp: Doulton
Series: Carry On Gang

Jug No.	Doulton Number	Description	Current Market Value U.K. £	U.S. $	Can. $
1.	D7162	Sid James	150.00	235.00	—
2.	D7163	Charles Hawtrey		Price for pair	

SIMON THE CELLARER

Simon was the subject of a 19th-century English folksong. The keys on the handle are those to his cellar, full of great wines and ales. He was always good for standing a drink for his friends.

The tiny version of Simon the Cellarer was one of a set of six tinies issued in 1994, in a limited edition of 2,500, to commemorate the diamond anniversary of the first character jug. The set, modelled by William K. Harper, was sold out within the first year. Other tinies in this series are Dick Turpin, Granny, the Jester, John Barleycorn and Parson Brown. The issue price was £150.00.

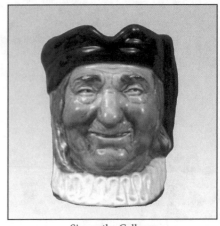

Simon the Cellarer

Designer: Charles Noke
Harry Fenton

Statistics:	Doulton Number	Size	Height	Issued
1.	D5504	Large	6 ½", 16.5 cm	1935-1960
2.	D5616	Small	3 ½", 8.9 cm	1936-1960

Handle: A bunch of keys
Colourway: Maroon hat; white ruff
Backstamps: A. Doulton
B. Doulton/Bentalls/Souvenir from Bentalls. 1936.

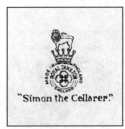

Backstamp A - Doulton

Jug No.	Size	Issued	Current Market Value		
			U.K. £	U.S. $	Can. $
1A.	Large	1935-1960	100.00	150.00	175.00
2A.	Small	1936-1960	50.00	75.00	85.00
2B.		1936-1936	425.00	725.00	875.00

Note: 1. Simon the Cellarer large and small size jugs are found in white gloss.
2. For the tiny version of Simon the Cellarer see the "Diamond Anniversary Set" page 164.

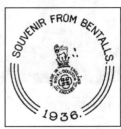

Backstamp B - Bentalls

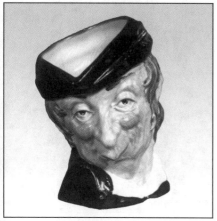

Simple Simon

SIMPLE SIMON

The subject of this jug dates back to a 17th-century nursery rhyme of Simon meeting a pieman.

Designer: Geoff Blower

	Doulton			
Statistics:	**Number**	**Size**	**Height**	**Issued**
	D6374	Large	7", 17.8 cm	1953-1960

Handle: Plain
Colourway: Green, brown and white
Backstamp: Doulton

	Current Market Value		
Size	**U.K. £**	**U.S. $**	**Can. $**
Large	400.00	625.00	750.00

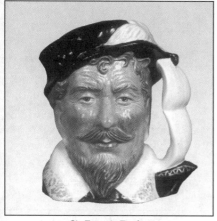

Sir Francis Drake

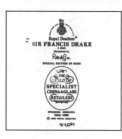

SIR FRANCIS DRAKE

This version of the Drake jug was produced to celebrate the 400th anniversary of the defeat of the Spanish Armada in 1588. Commissioned by the Guild of Specialist China & Glass Retailers, this jug was issued in 1988 in a special edition of 6,000 pieces.

Designer: Peter A. Gee

	Doulton			
Statistics:	**Number**	**Size**	**Height**	**Issued**
	D6805	Large	7", 17.8 cm	See below

Issued: 1988 in a special edition of 6,000
Handle: The *Golden Hind*'s bow and sails
Colourway: Black and white
Backstamp: Doulton/Guild of Specialist China & Glass Retailers

	Current Market Value		
Size	**U.K. £**	**U.S. $**	**Can. $**
Large	100.00	175.00	200.00

Note: For the character jug Drake see page 169 and for the toby jug Sir Francis Drake see page 80.

SIR HENRY DOULTON

In the mid 1830s, Henry Doulton (1820-1897) joined his father's firm just in time to capitalize on the expanding market that was developing in London for modern sanitation products. The manufacture of stoneware sewer and water pipes led Doulton and Company, as they were known after 1854, to become a large and flourishing concern. John Doulton retired around this time leaving Doulton and Company in the hands of his son Henry. In the 1860s, with decorative wares expanding, Henry Doulton was persuaded to hire students from the Lambeth School of Art as designers and decorators of the new ornamental wares his company was introducing. Their outstanding creations heralded the beginning of the studio-art pottery movement.

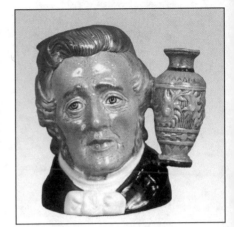

Sir Henry Doulton, Style One

STYLE ONE: SINGLE HANDLE — ART POTTERY VASE

Designer: Eric Griffiths

Statistics:	Doulton Number	Size	Height	Issued
	D6703	Small	4 ½", 11.9 cm	1984-1984

Handle: A Doulton art pottery vase
Colourway: Black coat; yellow cravat; grey hair; brown and blue vase
Backstamp: Doulton/RDICC
Series: RDICC

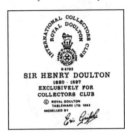

Size	Description	Current Market Value U.K. £	U.S. $	Can. $
Small	Style One	85.00	150.00	175.00

STYLE TWO: SINGLE HANDLE — ART POTTERY EWER

This was the Royal Doulton International Collector's Club Character Jug of the Year for 1997. The jug was issued in a limited edition of 1,997 and carries the special Sir Henry Doulton Centenary 1897-1997 backstamp.

Designer: William K. Harper

Statistics:	Doulton Number	Size	Height	Issued
	D7057	Small	5", 12.7 cm	1997-1997

Handle: Ewer and ribbon "Doulton & Co."
Colourway: Black, brown, yellow and gold
Backstamp: Doulton/RDICC
  Sir Henry Doulton Centenary 1897-1997
Series: RDICC

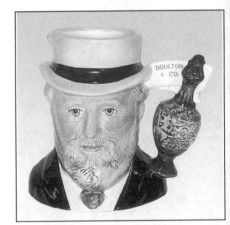

Sir Henry Doulton, Style Two

Size	Description	Current Market Value U.K. £	U.S. $	Can. $
Small	Style Two	75.00	125.00	150.00

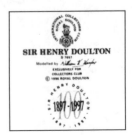

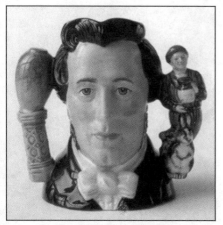

Sir Henry Doulton, Style Three

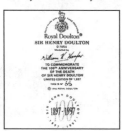

SIR HENRY DOULTON

This large size two-handled jug was issued to commemorate the 100th anniversary of the death of Sir Henry Doulton in 1897. The jug carries a special backstamp for the centenary year and was issued in a limited edition of 1,997.

STYLE THREE: TWO HANDLED JUG

Designer: William K. Harper

Statistics:	Doulton Number	Size	Height	Issued
	D7054	Large	7", 17.8 cm	See below

Issued: 1997 in a limited edition of 1,997
Handles: Lambeth product on the right and Burslem product on the left with Hannah Barlow and a rabbit modelled by Mark Marshall
Colourway: Blue, black, yellow and brown
Backstamp: Doulton/Sir Henry Doulton Centenary 1897-1997

		Current Market Value		
Size	Description	U.K. £	U.S. $	Can. $
Large	Style Three	125.00	250.00	375.00

SIR HENRY DOULTON
and
MICHAEL DOULTON

This two-faced jug was a special edition jug issued to mark Michael Doulton's personal appearances at retail locations. This piece is one of the few two-faced jugs made in the small size.

Designer: William K. Harper

Statistics:	**Doulton Number**	**Size**	**Height**	**Issued**
	D6921	Small	4 ½", 11.9 cm	See below

Issued: 1992 in a special edition
Handle: Flag bearing the lion and crown backstamp of Royal Doulton
Colourway: Henry — Grey hair; yellow cravat
Michael — Brown hair; dark blue suit; white shirt; light blue tie
Backstamp: Doulton

	Current Market Value		
Size	**U.K. £**	**U.S. $**	**Can. $**
Small	50.00	80.00	90.00

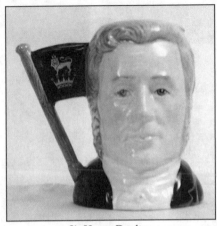

Sir Henry Doulton

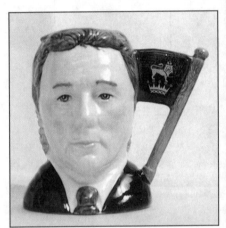

Michael Doulton

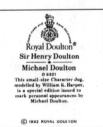

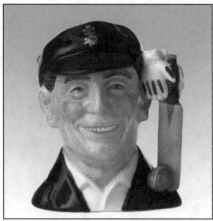

Sir Jack Hobbs

SIR JACK HOBBS

Sir Jack Hobbs was England's first-ever cricketer to be knighted.

Designer: Stanley J. Taylor

Statistics:	Doulton Number	Size	Height	Issued
	D7131	Small	4", 10.1 cm	See below

Issued: 1999 in a limited edition of 5,000
Handle: Cricket bat, ball and gloves
Colourway: Black hat and jacket; white shirt
Backstamp: Doulton
Series: Cricketers

Size	Current Market Value		
	U.K. £	U.S. $	Can. $
Small	65.00	110.00	—

SIR STANLEY MATTHEWS
"THE WIZARD OF DRIBBLE"

Sir Stanley Matthews, "The Wizard of Dribble", was known for his exemplary conduct. His impressive skills lead to the 1953 FA Cup Final being dubbed "The Matthews Final."

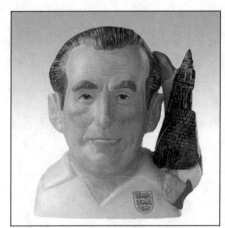

Sir Stanley Matthews, Variation No. 1

Designer: David B. Biggs

Statistics:	**Doulton**			
	Number	**Size**	**Height**	**Issued**
	D7161	Small	4", 10.1 cm	See below

Handle: Traditional Potteries bottle kiln and Blackpool Tower, with scarves in the red and white of Stoke City and the tangerine and white of Blackpool FC

VARIATION No. 1: Colourway — Cream jersey with blue and red crest (English national team shirt)

Issued: 2000 in a limited edition of 5,000
Colourway: Cream jersey with blue and red crest
Backstamp: Doulton

		Current Market Value		
Size	Variation	U.K. £	U.S. $	Can. $
Small	Var. 1	85.00	140.00	—

VARIATION No. 2: Colourway — Red and white striped jersey (Stoke City colours)

As part of a fundraising campaign to erect a statue of Sir Stanley at Stoke City's football ground (The Britannia Stadium in Stoke on Trent), Royal Doulton created a special colourway of Sir Stanley in his Stoke City colours. Three examples of this colourway exist: one is lodged in the Royal Doulton Museum, one in Sir Stanley Matthew's home club, Stoke City, and the third was auctioned with the proceeds going to the Sir Stanley Matthews Fund.

Issued: 2000 in a special edition of 3
Colourway: Red and white jersey
Backstamp: Doulton

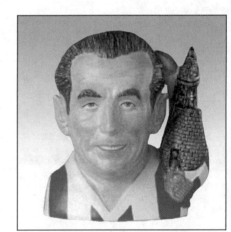

Sir Stanley Matthews, Variation No. 2

		Current Market Value		
Size	Variation	U.K. £	U.S. $	Can. $
Small	Var. 2	Sold June 11th, 2001 Louis Taylor Auctions £32,200.		

SIR THOMAS MORE

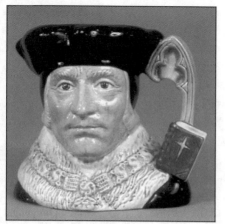

Sir Thomas More

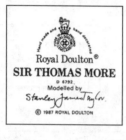

Thomas More (1478-1535) entered the service of King Henry VIII in 1518 as royal councillor. He was knighted and became Lord Chancellor after the dismissal of Cardinal Wolsey in 1529. At this time Henry was embroiled in a battle with Rome over his decision to divorce Catherine of Aragon. Unable to support his King, More resigned.

In 1534 More was arrested for high treason when he refused to swear an oath of supremacy, stating that Henry VIII ranked above all foreign leaders, including the Pope. He was beheaded in 1535 and canonized by the Catholic Church 400 years later, in 1935.

Designer: Stanley J. Taylor

Statistics:	**Doulton Number**	**Size**	**Height**	**Issued**
	D6792	Large	6 ¾", 17.2 cm	1988-1991

Handle: A window arch and a bible
Colourway: Dark green hat; brown fur-trimmed collar; gold chain of office
Backstamp: Doulton
Series: Henry and His Six Wives

	Current Market Value		
Size	**U.K. £**	**U.S. $**	**Can. $**
Large	125.00	275.00	300.00

SIR WINSTON CHURCHILL

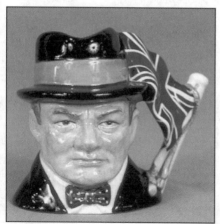

Sir Winston Churchill

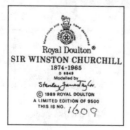

This Churchill jug was a new design, commissioned by Lawleys By Post. It was issued in 1989 as part of a set of three, and limited to 9,500 pieces.

Designer: Stanley J. Taylor

Statistics:	**Doulton Number**	**Size**	**Height**	**Issued**
	D6849	Small	3 ¼", 8.3 cm	See below

Issued: 1989 in a limited edition of 9,500
Handle: The Union Jack flag
Colourway: Black, grey and white
Backstamp: Doulton
Series: Heroic Leaders

	Current Market Value		
Size	**U.K. £**	**U.S. $**	**Can. $**
Small	135.00	275.00	300.00

Note: For the character jug Churchill see page 151, and for the character jug Winston Churchill see page 397. For the toby jug Winston Churchill see page 85.

THE SIX WIVES OF HENRY VIII

This set was commissioned by Lawleys By Post in a limited edition of 2,500.

STYLE TWO: HANDLES — INITIALS

Designer: William K. Harper

Statistics:

Doulton Number	Size	Height	Issued
See below	Tiny	1 ½", 3.8 cm	See below

Issued: 1996 in a limited edition of 2,500
Handle: Plain (initials)
Colourway:
1. **Catherine of Aragon** — Yellow and green
2. **Anne Boleyn** — Black and pink
3. **Jane Seymour** — Yellow and black
4. **Anne of Cleves** — Beige
5. **Catherine Howard** — Yellow and green
6. **Catherine Parr** — Brown and white

Backstamp: Doulton

Jug No.	Doulton Number	Name	Current Market Value U.K. £	U.S. $	Can. $
1.	D7041	Catherine of Aragon	45.00	70.00	90.00
2.	D7042	Anne Boleyn	45.00	70.00	90.00
3.	D7043	Jane Seymour	45.00	70.00	90.00
4.	D7044	Anne of Cleves	45.00	70.00	90.00
5.	D7045	Catherine Howard	45.00	70.00	90.00
6.	D7046	Catherine Parr	45.00	70.00	90.00
		Complete set with stand	250.00	425.00	550.00

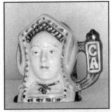

Catherine of Aragon

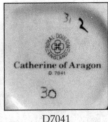

D7041

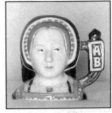

Anne Bolelyn

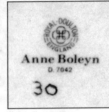

D7042

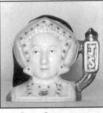

Jane Seymour

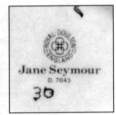

D7043

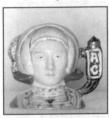

Anne of Cleves

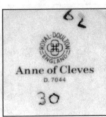

D7044

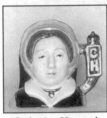

Catherine Howard

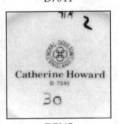

D7045

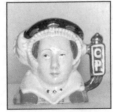

Catherine Parr

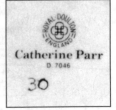

D7046

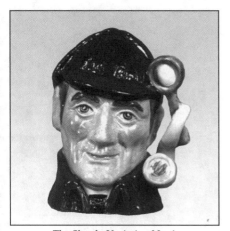

The Sleuth, Variation No. 1

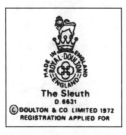

THE SLEUTH

Arthur Conan Doyle (1859-1930), an unsuccessful doctor, published the first of his widely popular detective stories in 1887. The amateur sleuth Sherlock Holmes shared rooms on Baker Street, as well as many adventures, with his friend and foil, Dr. Watson.

Designer: Alan Moore
Handle: A pipe and magnifying glass

VARIATION No. 1: **Colourway** — Dark green deerstalker hat; brown cloak

Statistics:	Doulton Number	Size	Height	Issued
1.	D6631	Large	7", 17.8 cm	1973-1996
2.	D6635	Small	3 ¼", 8.3 cm	1973-1996
3.	D6639	Miniature	2 ¾", 7.0 cm	1973-1991

Issued: See below

Colourway: Dark green deerstalker hat; brown cloak
Backstamp: Doulton

Jug No.	Size	Variation	Current Market Value U.K. £	U.S. $	Can. $
1.	Large	Var. 1	60.00	100.00	125.00
2.	Small		50.00	65.00	90.00
3.	Miniature		45.00	75.00	80.00

VARIATION No. 2: **Colourway** — Brown deerstalker hat; red cloak

Statistics:	Doulton Number	Size	Height	Issued
	D6773	Small	3 ¼", 8.3 cm	See below

Issued: 1987 in a limited edition of 5,000
Backstamp: Doulton/Lawleys/
This Limited Edition of 5,000 Commemorates The Centenary of the Publication of the First Sherlock Holmes story "A Study In Scarlet"
Commissioned by Lawleys By Post and issued in 1987 in a limited edition of 5,000 pieces.

Size	Variation	Current Market Value U.K. £	U.S. $	Can. $
Small	Var. 2	125.00	275.00	300.00

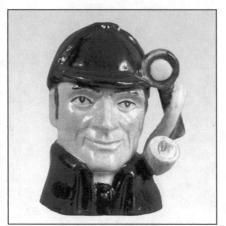

The Sleuth, Variation No. 2

SMUGGLER

The detailing on the barrel of the small-size jug is often less distinguishable than that on the large jug.

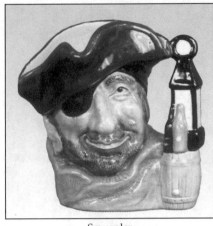

Smuggler

Designer: David B. Biggs

Statistics:	Doulton Number	Size	Height	Issued
1.	D6616	Large	7 ¼", 18.4 cm	1968-1981
2.	D6619	Small	3 ¼", 8.3 cm	1968-1981

Handle: Lantern above a barrel
Colourway: Green hat; red scarf
Backstamp: Doulton

Jug No.	Size	Comp.	Issued	Current Market Value U.K. £	U.S. $	Can. $
1.	Large	EW	1968-1981	125.00	200.00	225.00
		ETC	1968-1971	150.00	250.00	275.00
2.	Small	EW	1968-1981	60.00	90.00	110.00
		ETC	1968-1971	70.00	125.00	150.00

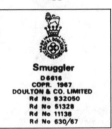

SMUTS

A South African attorney, military man and politician, Jan Christiaan Smuts (1870-1950) served as a member of the British War Cabinet in World War I and was one of the authors of the Covenant of the League of Nations. In 1945, after again serving the Allies in World War II, Smuts is credited with writing the preamble to the Charter of the United Nations. He became the Prime Minister of South Africa in 1919 and again in 1939.

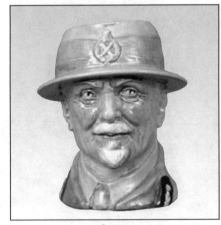

Smuts

Designer: Harry Fenton

Statistics:	Doulton Number	Size	Height	Issued
	D6198	Large	6 ½", 16.5 cm	1946-1948

Handle: Springbok
Colourway: See below
Backstamp: Doulton

VARIATION No. 1: Colourway — Tan Uniform

VARIATION No. 2: Colourway — Khaki Uniform

Size	Variation	Current Market Value U.K. £	U.S. $	Can. $
Large	Var. 1	1,000.00	1,750.00	2,250.00
Large	Var. 2	Extremely Rare		

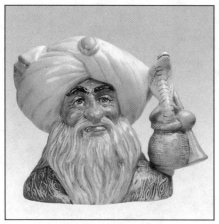

The Snake Charmer

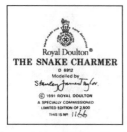

THE SNAKE CHARMER

This jug was issued in a limited edition of 2,500 pieces.

Designer: Stanley J. Taylor

Statistics:	Doulton Number	Size	Height	Issued
	D6912	Large	7", 17.8 cm	See below

Issued: 1992 in a limited edition of 2,500
Handle: Cobra, basket and pipe
Colourway: Yellow turban with blue and pink jewel; burgundy and yellow robes
Backstamp: Doulton

	Current Market Value		
Size	U.K. £	U.S. $	Can. $
Large	200.00	325.00	400.00

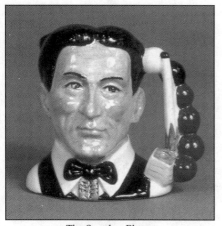

The Snooker Player

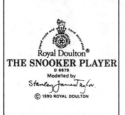

THE SNOOKER PLAYER

Designer: Stanley J. Taylor

Statistics:	Doulton Number	Size	Height	Issued
	D6879	Small	4", 10.1 cm	1991-1995

Handle: Cue with chalk and red and black cue balls
Colourway: Black hair; white shirt; black bow tie and vest
Backstamp: Doulton
Series: Characters From Life

	Current Market Value		
Size	U.K. £	U.S. $	Can. $
Small	50.00	100.00	150.00

SNOWMAN

STYLE ONE: HANDLE — A SCARF

This jug was commissioned by Royal Doulton (U.S.A.) Limited. It is also listed in the *Charlton Standard Catalogue of Royal Doulton Beswick Storybook Figurines*, under the Snowman series.

Designer: Graham Tongue
Modeller: Martyn C. R. Alcock

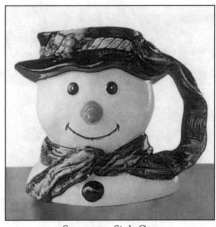

	Doulton			
Statistics:	**Number**	**Size**	**Height**	**Issued**
	D6972	Miniature	2 ¾", 7.0 cm	1994-1994

Handle: Scarf
Colourway: White, green and black
Backstamp: Doulton
Series: Christmas Miniatures

		Current Market Value		
Size	**Description**	**U.K. £**	**U.S. $**	**Can. $**
Miniature	Style One	125.00	200.00	250.00

Snowman, Style One

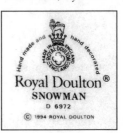

STYLE TWO: HANDLE — HOLLY AND BERRIES

A series of four snowman character jugs was commissioned by John Sinclair, England. One jug was to be issued each year in a special edition of 2,000 each, with a special gold edition being issued for the millennium in 2000.

Designer: William K. Harper

	Doulton			
Statistics:	**Number**	**Size**	**Height**	**Issued**
	D7062	Miniature	2 ¾", 7.0 cm	See below

Issued: 1997 in a special edition of 2,000
Handle: Holly and berries
Colourway: White; red hat; white and green striped scarf
Backstamp: Doulton/Sinclair
Series: Snowman Miniatures

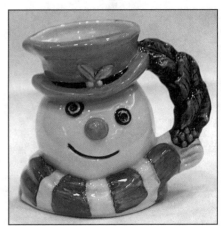

		Current Market Value		
Size	**Description**	**U.K. £**	**U.S. $**	**Can. $**
Miniature	Style Two	50.00	100.00	150.00

Snowman, Style Two

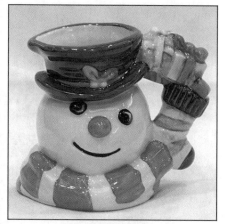

Snowman, Style Three

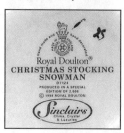

SNOWMAN

STYLE THREE: HANDLE — CHRISTMAS STOCKING AND PARCELS

This is the second jug in the Snowman series, issued in a special edition of 2,000.

Designer: William K. Harper

	Doulton			
Statistics:	**Number**	**Size**	**Height**	**Issued**
	D7124	Miniature	2 ¾", 7.0 cm	See below

Issued: 1998 in a special edition of 2,000
Handle: Christmas stocking and parcels
Colourway: White; blue hat; red and white striped scarf
Backstamp: Doulton/Sinclair
Series: Snowman Miniatures

	Current Market Value		
Size	**U.K. £**	**U.S. $**	**Can. $**
Miniature	50.00	100.00	150.00

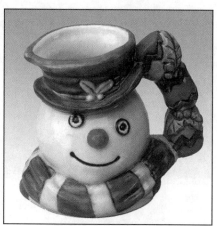

Snowman, Style Four

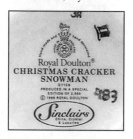

STYLE FOUR: HANDLE — CHRISTMAS CRACKER

The third in the series of Snowman jugs issued in a special edition of 2,000.

Designer: William K. Harper

	Doulton			
Statistics:	**Number**	**Size**	**Height**	**Issued**
	D7158	Miniature	2 ¾", 7.0 cm	See below

Issued: 1999 in a special edition of 2,000
Handle: Christmas cracker
Colourway: White; green hat; white and blue striped scarf
Backstamp: Doulton/Sinclair
Series: Snowman Miniatures

		Current Market Value		
Size	**Description**	**U.K. £**	**U.S. $**	**Can. $**
Miniature	Style Four	50.00	100.00	150.00

SNOWMAN

STYLE FIVE: HANDLE — WREATH AND ROBIN

This jug, to be issued in a special gold edition of 2,000, was issued to commemorate the millenium. It is the final jug in the Snowman series.

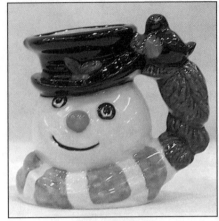

Snowman, Style Five

Designer: William K. Harper

Statistics:	Doulton Number	Size	Height	Issued
	D7159	Miniature	2 ¾", 7.0 cm	See below

Issued: 2000 in a special edition of 2,000
Handle: A wreath and a robin
Colourway: White; grey hat; olive and white striped scarf
Backstamp: Doulton/Sinclair
Series: Snowman Miniatures

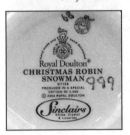

		Current Market Value		
Size	Description	U.K. £	U.S. $	Can. $
Miniature	Style Five	50.00	100.00	150.00

THE SOLDIER

STYLE ONE: HANDLE — BAYONET AND WATER CANTEEN

Designer: William K. Harper

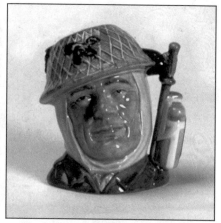

The Soldier, Style One, Variation No. 1

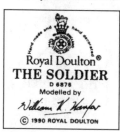

VARIATION No. 1: Desert rat patch on canteen

Statistics:	Doulton Number	Size	Height	Issued
	D6876	Small	4 ½", 11.9 cm	1991-1996

Handle: Bayonet and water canteen
Colourway: Army steel helmet with netting; khaki tunic
Backstamp: Doulton
Series: The Armed Forces

		Current Market Value		
Size	Variation	U.K. £	U.S. $	Can. $
Small	Var. 1	45.00	100.00	150.00

VARIATION No. 2: Red patch on canteen

Commissioned by The British Toby in a limited edition of 250 pieces, Variation Two originally sold in a set for $465.00 Canadian.

Statistics:	Doulton Number	Size	Height	Issued
	D6905	Small	4 ½", 11.9 cm	See below

Issued: 1991 in a limited edition of 250
Handle: Bayonet and water canteen with red patch
Colourway: Army steel helmet with netting; khaki tunic; red patch on canteen
Backstamp: Doulton/The British Toby
The backstamp illustrated shows an incorrect 'D' number
Series: The Canadians

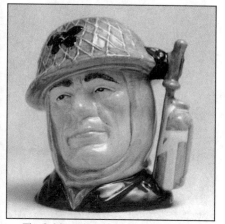

The Soldier, Style One, Variation No. 2

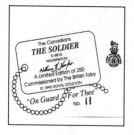

		Current Market Value		
Size	Variation	U.K. £	U.S. $	Can. $
Small	Var. 2	175.00	350.00	400.00

THE SOLDIER

The Soldier (Style Two) was a special edition for Lawleys By Post and paid tribute to all those who were called up for national service in the U.K.

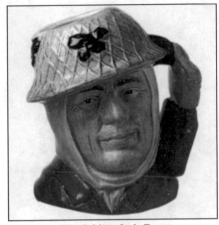

The Soldier, Style Two

STYLE TWO: HANDLE — JERRY CAN AND HAVERSACK

Designer: William K. Harper

Statistics:

Doulton Number	Size	Height	Issued
D6983	Small	4 ½", 11.9 cm	See below

Issued: 1994 in a special edition
Handle: A jerry can and haversack
Colourways: Black and brown
Backstamp: Doulton
Series: National Service Edition

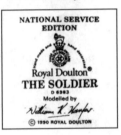

Size	Description	Current Market Value		
		U.K. £	U.S. $	Can. $
Small	Style Two	50.00	150.00	175.00

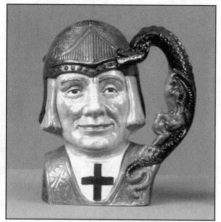

St. George, Style One

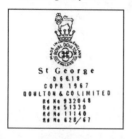

ST. GEORGE

The patron saint of England since the 13th century, George is the hero of a legend which describes him as a chivalrous knight who single-handedly slayed a huge dragon, saving the princess Melisande.

STYLE ONE: HANDLE — A DRAGON

Designer: Max Henk

Statistics:	Doulton Number	Size	Height	Issued
1.	D6618	Large	7 ½", 19.1 cm	1968-1975
2.	D6621	Small	3 ¾", 9.5 cm	1968-1975

Handle: A dragon
Colourway: Grey helmet; turquoise armour
Backstamp: Doulton

Jug No.	Size	Comp.	Issued	Current Market Value		
				U.K. £	U.S. $	Can. $
1.	Large	EW	1968-1975	225.00	350.00	500.00
		ETC	1968-1971	250.00	400.00	550.00
2.	Small	EW	1968-1975	150.00	275.00	400.00
		ETC	1968-1971	200.00	300.00	450.00

STYLE TWO: HANDLE — FLAG OF ST. GEORGE AND DRAGON

This jug was commissioned by Lawleys By Post and issued in a limited edition of 2,500.

Designer: Robert Tabbenor

Statistics:	Doulton Number	Size	Height	Issued
	D7129	Large	7 ½", 19.1 cm	See below

Issued: 1998 in a limited edition of 2,500
Handle: A dragon and the flag of St. George
Colourway: Grey-brown, gold and red
Backstamp: Doulton

Size	Current Market Value		
	U.K. £	U.S. $	Can. $
Large	125.00	200.00	300.00

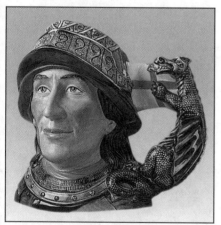

St. George, Style Two

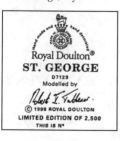

TAM O'SHANTER

In a poem written by Robert Burns in 1791, Tam O'Shanter is a drunken farmer who happens upon witches who pursue him and his horse. He escapes, but his horse doesn't quite make it — one witch pulls its tail off. The Scottish woollen cap is reputedly named after this poem's hero.

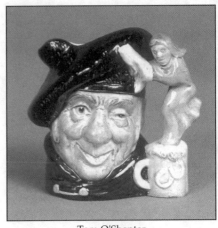

Tam O'Shanter

Designer: Max Henk

Statistics	Doulton Number	Size	Height	Issued
1.	D6632	Large	7", 17.8 cm	1973-1980
2.	D6636	Small	3 ¼", 8.3 cm	1973-1980
3.	D6640	Miniature	2 ½", 6.4 cm	1973-1980

Handle: Witch holding horse's tail above a mug of ale
Colourway: Dark blue tam; green cloak
Backstamp: Doulton

Jug No.	Size	Current Market Value		
		U.K. £	U.S. $	Can. $
1.	Large	100.00	150.00	175.00
2.	Small	65.00	100.00	125.00
3.	Miniature	60.00	100.00	100.00

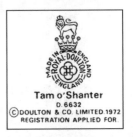

Tam o'Shanter
D.6632
©DOULTON & CO. LIMITED 1972
REGISTRATION APPLIED FOR.

TCHAIKOVSKY

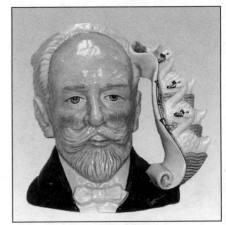

Tchaikovsky

Designer: Stanley J. Taylor

Statistics:	Doulton Number	Size	Height	Issued
	D7022	Large	7", 17.8 cm	1996-2001

Handle: Swans and music from Swan Lake
Colourway: Black, grey and white
Backstamp: Doulton
Series: Great Composers

Size	Current Market Value		
	U.K. £	U.S. $	Can. $
Large	100.00	225.00	300.00

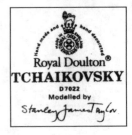

Royal Doulton®
TCHAIKOVSKY
D7022
Modelled by
Stanley James Taylor

TERRY FOX

Canadian Terrance Stanley Fox (1958-1981) was a student and athlete until diagnosed with a rare form of bone cancer. While recovering from the amputation of most of one leg, Fox conceived the idea of a "Marathon of Hope," a run across Canada to raise money for cancer research. He began on April 12, 1980, but had to abort his run on September 1, after being diagnosed with lung cancer. He raised over $24 million and became a source of inspiration for millions of people. Only three jugs were produced. One was given to his family, one resides in the Sir Henry Doulton Gallery and one was put up for auction at the International Royal Doulton Collectors Weekend, September 14 to 16, 1990, which realized $21,000 for charity.

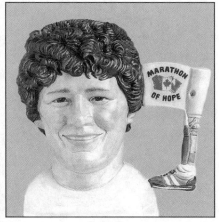

Terry Fox

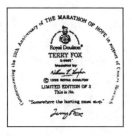

Designer: William K. Harper

Statistics:	Doulton Number	Size	Height	Issued
	D6881	Large	7", 17.8 cm	1990

Handle: Fox's artificial leg
Colourway: Brown and white
Backstamp: Doulton

	Current Market Value		
Size	U.K. £	U.S. $	Can. $
Large	Extremely rare. Only 3 known. Last sold at auction Toronto 1990, $21,000.00 Can.		

THOMAS JEFFERSON

This jug was issued in a limited edition of 2,500 to commemorate the 250th anniversary of Thomas Jefferson's birth in 1743. It was available only within the U.S.A., with an allocation of jugs for overseas members of the Royal Doulton International Collectors Club.

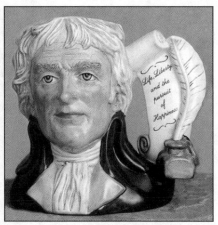

Thomas Jefferson

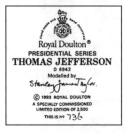

Designer: Stanley J. Taylor

Statistics:	Doulton Number	Size	Height	Issued
	D6943	Large	6 ¾", 17.2 cm	See below

Issued: 1994 in a limited edition of 2,500
Handle: "Life, Liberty and the pursuit of happiness" on scroll, feather quill and ink pot
Colourway: Grey hair; dark blue coat; grey cravat
Backstamp: Doulton
Series: Presidents of the United States

	Current Market Value		
Size	U.K. £	U.S. $	Can. $
Large	150.00	200.00	250.00

TOBY GILLETTE

Jimmy Saville's British television show, "Jim'll Fix It," invites public requests and it received one from Toby Gillette to have a character jug created in his likeness.

In 1984 three were produced: one was given to Toby Gillette, one remains in the Sir Henry Doulton Gallery, and the third was auctioned by Sotheby's, with the proceeds ($30,000) going to one of the charities Jimmy Saville supported. In 1986 Toby Gillette sold his own jug at a Sotheby's auction.

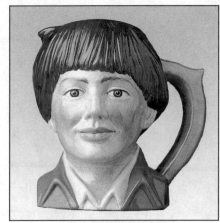

Toby Gillette

Designer: Eric Griffiths

	Doulton			
Statistics:	Number	Size	Height	Issued
	D6717	Large	7", 17.8 cm	1984

Handle: Plain
Colourway: Brown
Backstamp: Doulton

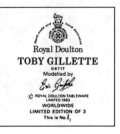

	Current Market Value		
Size	U.K. £	U.S. $	Can. $
Large	Extremely rare. Only 3 known.		

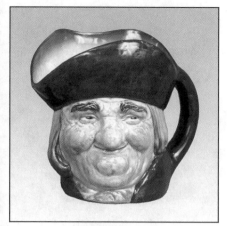

Toby Philpots

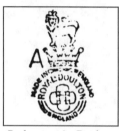

Backstamp A - Doulton

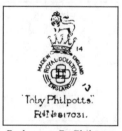

Backstamp B - Philpotts

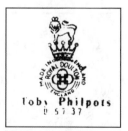

Backstamp C - Philpots

TOBY PHILPOTS

A "thirsty old soul" in an 18th-century drinking song, Toby is thought by some to be the source of the traditional British toby jug, in which a character sits astride a barrel of ale. Popular opinion suggests his name is a derivation of the French *topé*, to toast.

Designer: Charles Noke

Statistics:	Doulton Number	Size	Height	Issued
1.	D5736	Large	6 ¼", 15.9 cm	1937-1969
2.	D5737	Small	3 ¼", 8.3 cm	1937-1969
3.	D6043	Miniature	2 ¼", 5.7 cm	1939-1969

Issued: See below

Colourway: Green hat; brown coat; blue scarf with white spots

Handle: Plain

Backstamps: A. Doulton
B. Doulton/Toby Philpotts. (1937-1951)
Incised name on jug is "Toby Philpots," but on the backstamp "Toby Philpotts," which is incorrect.
C. Doulton/Toby Philpots (1952-1969)
Incised name on jug is "Toby Philpots," and the backstamp has been corrected to "Toby Philpots."

Jug No.	Size	Comp.	Current Market Value			
			Issued	U.K. £	U.S. $	Can. $
1.	Large	EW	1937-1951	80.00	125.00	150.00
		ETC	1968-1971		Rare	
2.	Small	EW	1937-1951	40.00	60.00	80.00
3.	Miniature	EW	1939-1951	35.00	55.00	70.00

Note: 1. Price differentials for the various backstamps are no longer significant.
2. The Toby Philpots miniature size jug is found in white gloss.

TONY WELLER

Designer: Leslie Harradine/Harry Fenton

Statistics:

	Doulton Number	Size	Height	Issued
1.	D5531	Extra Large	6 ½", 16.5 cm	1936-1942
2.	D5531	Large	5 ½", 14.0 cm	1936-1960
3.	D5530	Small	3 ¼", 8.3 cm	1936-1960
4.	D6044	Miniature	2 ¼", 5.7 cm	1939-1960

Handle: Plain
Colourway: Dark grey hat; maroon coat; grey-white bow with yellow spots
Backstamps: **A.** Doulton
B. Doulton/Darley & Son/Souvenir From Darley & Son/Sheffield & Rotherham Commissioned by Darley & Son, Sheffield and Rotherham.
C. Doulton/Bentalls/Souvenir From Bentalls Jubilee Year 1935
Commissioned by Bentalls to commemorate the silver jubilee in 1935 of King George V.
D. Doulton/Bentalls/Souvenir from Bentalls. 1936.

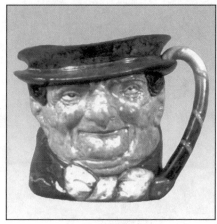

Tony Weller

Jug No.	Size	Issued	Current Market Value U.K. £	U.S. $	Can. $
1A.	Extra large	1936-1942	225.00	350.00	450.00
2A.	Large	1936-1960	125.00	200.00	225.00
3A.	Small	1936-1960	40.00	65.00	90.00
3B.		1936-1936	500.00	775.00	900.00
3C.		1935-1935	500.00	775.00	900.00
3D.		1936-1936	500.00	775.00	900.00
4A.	Miniature	1939-1960	40.00	60.00	75.00

Note: 1. The extra large jug has an opening of 6 ½", the large jug 5 ½".
2. The Tony Weller extra large, small and miniature size jugs are found in white gloss.

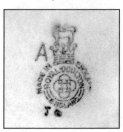

Backstamp A - Doulton

Tony Weller Derivatives

Item	Doulton Number	Height	Issued
Bookend	HN1616	4", 10.1 cm	1934-1939
Bust	D6051	2 ½", 6.4cm	1939-1960
Musical jug	D5888	6 ½", 16.5 cm	1937-1939
Napkin ring	M60	3", 7.6 cm	1935-1939
Sugar bowl	D6013	2 ½", 6.4 cm	1939-1960
Teapot	D6016	7", 17.8 cm	1939-1960

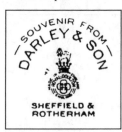

Backstamp B - Darley & Son

Doulton Number	Item	Current Market Value U.K. £	U.S. $	Can. $
D5888	Musical Jug	500.00	1,000.00	1,100.00
D6013	Sugar Bowl	500.00	800.00	1,000.00
D6016	Teapot	1,200.00	2,000.00	2,500.00
D6051	Bust	75.00	100.00	125.00
HN1616	Bookend	1,500.00	3,500.00	4,000.00
M60	Napkin Ring	350.00	625.00	750.00

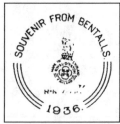

Backstamp D - Bentalls

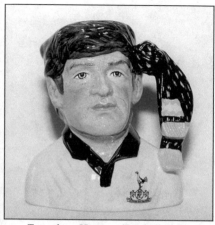

Tottenham Hotspur (Football Club)

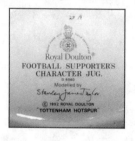

TOTTENHAM HOTSPUR (FOOTBALL CLUB)

Designer:	Stanley J. Taylor

	Doulton			
Statistics:	**Number**	**Size**	**Height**	**Issued**
	D6960	Small	5", 12.7 cm	1993-1999

Handle:	Team coloured scarf
Colourway:	White shirt with navy collar; navy scarf with yellow and white stripe
Backstamp:	Doulton
Series:	The Football Supporters

	Current Market Value		
Size	**U.K. £**	**U.S. $**	**Can. $**
Small	65.00	125.00	150.00

TOUCHSTONE

In Shakespeare's comedy, *As You Like It*, Touchstone is a jester to the court of the exiled Duke of Frederick. The Duke accompanies Rosalind and Celia into the Forest of Arden.

Designer:	Charles Noke

	Doulton			
Statistics:	**Number**	**Size**	**Height**	**Issued**
	D5613	Large	7", 17.8 cm	1936-1960

Handle:	Head of a clown
Colourway:	Maroon, green and light brown
Backstamp:	Doulton

	Current Market Value		
Size	**U.K. £**	**U.S. $**	**Can. $**
Large	200.00	325.00	425.00

Note: The Touchstone jug can be found in white gloss.

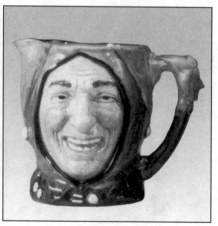

Touchstone

TOWN CRIER

STYLE ONE: HANDLE — BELL ON SCROLL

Designer: David B. Biggs

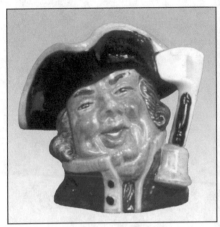

Town Crier, Style One

Statistics:	Doulton Number	Size	Height	Issued
1.	D6530	Large	7", 17.8 cm	1960-1974
2.	D6537	Small	3 ¼", 8.3 cm	1960-1974
3.	D6544	Miniature	2 ½", 6.4 cm	1960-1974

Handle: Bell on scroll
Colourway: Black hat trimmed with gold; scarlet coat trimmed with gold
Backstamp: Doulton

Jug No.	Size	Comp.	Issued	U.K. £	U.S. $	Can. $
				Current Market Value		
1.	Large	EW	1960-1973	150.00	250.00	275.00
		ETC	1968-1971	175.00	275.00	325.00
2.	Small	EW	1960-1973	100.00	150.00	175.00
		ETC	1968-1971	125.00	200.00	225.00
3.	Miniature	EW	1960-1973	125.00	200.00	225.00
		ETC	1968-1971	150.00	225.00	275.00

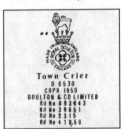

STYLE TWO: HANDLE — SCROLL WRAPPED AROUND BELL

Designer: Stanley J. Taylor

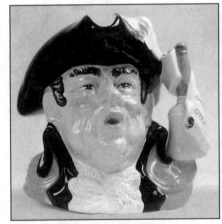

Town Crier, Style Two

Statistics:	Doulton Number	Size	Height	Issued
	D6895	Large	7", 17.8 cm	1991-1994

Handle: Scroll wrapped around bell
Colourway: Black, maroon and white
Backstamp: Doulton

Size	U.K. £	U.S. $	Can. $
	Current Market Value		
Large	110.00	200.00	225.00

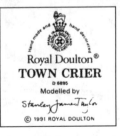

THE TRAPPER

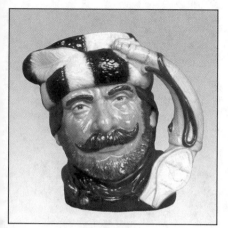

The Trapper

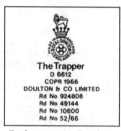

Backstamp A - Doulton

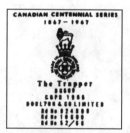

Backstamp B - Canadian
Centennial Series

An integral part of Canadian history, the early trappers, or voyageurs, were largely responsible for the early exploration of the country. In search of animal pelts for export to the European market, these rugged men spent the winter travelling by canoe, snowshoe and foot through the wild Canadian north.

The miniature version of the Trapper character jug was put into production briefly in 1983; however, before any quantity was produced, the decision was made to withdraw the character. Several dozen have appeared on the market.

The Trapper is one of three jugs that received a special backstamp in 1967. The other two, the Lumberjack and the North American Indian, complete the three-jug Canadian Centennial Series.

Designer: Max Henk
David B. Biggs

Statistics:

	Doulton Number	Size	Height	Issued
1.	D6609	Large	7 ¼", 18.4 cm	1967-1983
2.	D6612	Small	3 ¾", 9.5 cm	1967-1983
3.	D —	Miniature	2 ½", 6.4 cm	1983-1983

Handle: A horn and a pair of snowshoes
Colourway: Dark green and white hat; brown and green clothing
Backstamps: A. Doulton
B. Doulton/Canadian Centennial Series 1867-1967
Series: Canadian Centennial Series, 1867-1967

Jug No.	Size	Comp.	Issued	Current Market Value U.K. £	U.S. $	Can. $
1A.	Large	EW	1967-1983	70.00	100.00	125.00
		ETC	1968-1971	100.00	175.00	200.00
1B.		EW	1967-1967	175.00	325.00	375.00
2A.	Small	EW	1967-1983	50.00	70.00	90.00
		ETC	1968-1971	65.00	90.00	125.00
3A.	Miniature	EW	1983-1983	2,000.00	3,000.00	4,000.00

TUTANKHAMEN and ANKHESENAMUN

This pair of jugs was issued by Lawleys By Post in a limited edition of 1,500.

Designer: William K. Harper

Statistics:

	Doulton Number	Size	Height	Issued
1.	D7127	Small	4 ½", 11.9 cm	See below
2.	D7128	Small	4 ½", 11.9 cm	See below

Issued: 1. Tutankhamen — 1998 in a limited edition of 1,500
2. Ankhesenamun — 1999 in a limited edition of 1,500
Handle: 1. Tutankhamen — Horus, Hawk God of the Sun
2. Ankhesenamun — Feathered fan; coiled serpent
Colourway: 1. Tutankhamen — Blue, gold and coral
2. Ankhesenamun — Yellow, gold and red
Backstamp: Doulton

Jug No	Doulton Number	Name	Current Market Value		
			U.K.£	U.S. $	Can. $
1.	D7127	Tutankhamen	100.00	150.00	225.00
2.	D7128	Ankhesenamun	100.00	150.00	225.00

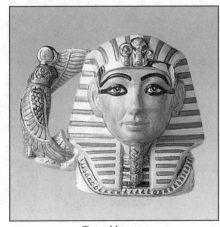

Tutankhamen

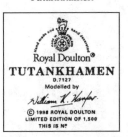

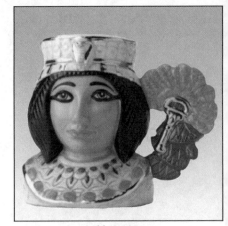

Ankhesenamun

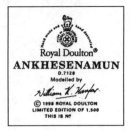

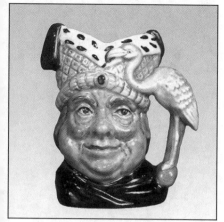

Ugly Duchess

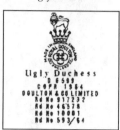

UGLY DUCHESS

The Ugly Duchess lives in Wonderland and plays croquet with the Queen. Alice found the game a curious one, with live hedgehogs for balls, flamingoes for mallets and playing-cards soldiers, who doubled over to serve as the arches.

Designer: Max Henk

Statistics:	Doulton Number	Size	Height	Issued
1.	D6599	Large	6 ¾", 17.2 cm	1965-1973
2.	D6603	Small	3 ½", 8.9 cm	1965-1973
3.	D6607	Miniature	2 ½", 6.4 cm	1965-1973

Handle: A flamingo
Colourway: Green, purple and pink
Backstamp: Doulton
Series: Alice In Wonderland

Jug No.	Size	Comp.	Issued	Current Market Value U.K. £	U.S. $	Can. $
1.	Large	EW	1965-1973	450.00	700.00	850.00
		ETC	1968-1971	500.00	850.00	950.00
2.	Small	EW	1965-1973	275.00	400.00	475.00
		ETC	1968-1971	300.00	475.00	525.00
3.	Miniature	EW	1965-1973	225.00	375.00	425.00

ULYSSES S. GRANT

PROTOTYPE

Designer: Unknown
Height: Unknown
Size: Large
Issued: Not put into production
Handle: Washington Monument
Colourway: Reddish-brown hair and beard; navy uniform
Backstamp: Doulton

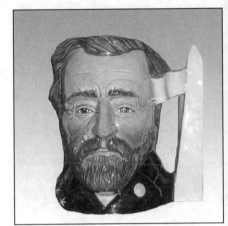

Ulysses S. Grant, Prototype

Size	Description	Current Market Value		
		U.K. £	U.S. $	Can. $
Large	Prototype	Extremely rare		

ULYSSES S. GRANT AND ROBERT E. LEE

PROTOTYPE

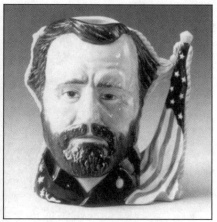

Ulysses S. Grant, Prototype

Differences between the prototype and issued jug — the eyes on the Grant prototype look ahead, while on the limited edition jug show the eyes looking to the left; the section of the flag bearing the stars is larger on the prototype jug and there are only four stripes on the prototype jug as apposed to seven on the limited edition jug.

Designer: Michael Abberley

Statistics:	Doulton Number	Size	Height	Issued
	D6698	Large	6 ½", 16.5 cm	See below

Modelled: 1983
Issued: Not put into production
Handle: Grant — Flag of the Union
Lee — Flag of the Confederacy
Colourway: Black, grey, brown and red
Backstamp: Doulton

		Current Market Value		
Size	Description	U.K. £	U.S. $	Can. $
Large	Prototype	Extremely Rare Sold at Sotheby's Auction New York, March 12, 1997, $2,415.00		

REGULAR ISSUE

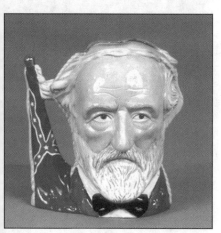

Ulysses S. Grant, Regular Issue

Ulysses Samuel Grant (1822-1885), a native of Ohio, was made Lieutenant-General by President Lincoln and put in command of the Union Army in the American Civil War. His successes led to his election as president in 1868.

Robert E. Lee (1807-1870) was the general in command of the Confederate Army. He was ruthlessly pursued by General Grant, who forced him to retreat from his defence of Richmond, Virginia, in 1865. Lee's troops were surrounded at the great battle of Appomattox, where he and the Confederate Army surrendered.

This jug was issued in 1983 in a limited edition of 9,500 pieces.

Designer: Michael Abberley

Statistics:	Doulton Number	Size	Height	Issued
	D6698	Large	7", 17.8 cm	See below

Issued: 1983 in a limited edition of 9,500
Handle: Grant — Flag of the Union
Lee — Flag of the Confederacy
Colourway: Black, grey, brown and red
Backstamp: Doulton
Series: The Antagonists' Collection (Two-faced jug)

		Current Market Value		
Size	Description	U.K. £	U.S. $	Can. $
Large	Regular Issue	225.00	400.00	475.00

Robert E. Lee

UNCLE TOM COBBLEIGH

PROTOTYPE

Designer: Robert I. Tabbenor

Statistics:

Model Number	Size	Height	Issued
2550	Large	6 ¾", 17.2 cm	See below

Modelled: 1975
Issued: Not put into production
Handle: Sheaf of wheat
Colourway: Brown hat with tan wheat in band; green smock; yellow neckerchief
Backstamp: Doulton

Size	Description	Current Market Value U.K. £ U.S. $ Can. $
Large	Prototype	Last sold November 21, 1999 Phillips, New Bond Street London, England, £5,000.00

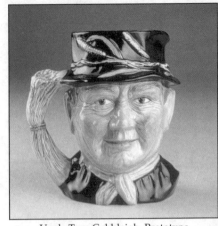

Uncle Tom Cobbleigh, Prototype

REGULAR ISSUE

In the popular 18th-century Devonshire song, Tom Cobbleigh and six friends borrow Tom Pearse's old mare to ride to the fair. Unable to support so many, the mare becomes sick and dies and still haunts the night-time moors to this day.

Designer: Max Henk

Statistics:

Doulton Number	Size	Height	Issued
D6337	Large	7", 17.8 cm	1952-1960

Handle: Horseshoe
Colourway: Dark brown hat; green coat; dark grey horseshoe
Backstamp: Doulton

Size	Description	Current Market Value U.K. £	U.S. $	Can. $
Large	Regular Issue	250.00	500.00	575.00

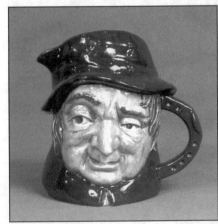

Uncle Tom Cobbleigh, Regular Issue

URIAH HEEP

For the tiny character jug Uriah Heep see the "Charles Dickens Commemorative Set" page 143.

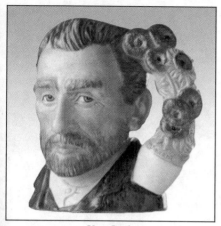

Van Gogh

VAN GOGH

Leader of the Post-Impressionist movement, Vincent Van Gogh (1853-1890) was one of the most influential painters of his time.

Designer: David B. Biggs

Statistics:	Doulton Number	Size	Height	Issued
	D7151	Large	7", 17.8 cm	2000 to the present

Handle: Sunflowers
Colourway: Cream shirt; green jacket
Backstamp: Doulton
Series: Famous Artists

Size	Current Market Value		
	U.K. £	U.S. $	Can. $
Large	120.00	205.00	—

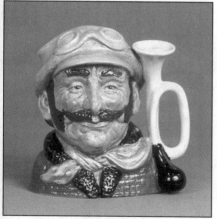

Veteran Motorist

VETERAN MOTORIST

Designer: David B. Biggs

Statistics:	Doulton Number	Size	Height	Issued
1.	D6633	Large	7 ½", 19.1 cm	1973-1983
2.	D6637	Small	3 ¼", 8.3 cm	1973-1983
3.	D6641	Miniature	2 ½", 6.4 cm	1973-1983

Handle: A horn
Colourway: Yellow hat; green coat; white scarf
Backstamp: Doulton

No.	Size	Current Market Value		
		U.K. £	U.S. $	Can. $
1.	Large	125.00	175.00	225.00
2.	Small	65.00	125.00	150.00
3.	Miniature	75.00	125.00	150.00

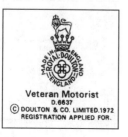

Veteran Motorist
D.6637
© DOULTON & CO. LIMITED.1972
REGISTRATION APPLIED FOR.

VICAR OF BRAY

In a popular song of the 18th century, this very adaptable parson boasted that he was able to accommodate himself to the religious views of Charles, James, William, Anne and George, and that "whosoever King may reign, he would always be the Vicar of Bray."

Prior to 1940 these jugs had a distinctive yellow rim.

Designer: Charles Noke
Harry Fenton

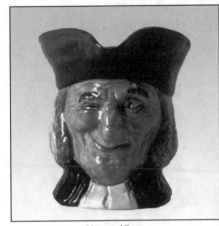
Vicar of Bray

Statistics:	**Doulton Number**	**Size**	**Height**	**Issued**
	D5615	Large	6 ¾", 17.2 cm	1936-1960

Handle: Plain
Colourway: Brown hat; green coat
Backstamp: Doulton

	Current Market Value		
Size	U.K. £	U.S. $	Can. $
Large	175.00	275.00	325.00

Note: The Vicar of Bray jug is found in white gloss.

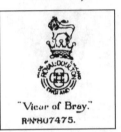

VICE-ADMIRAL LORD NELSON

This was the Character Jug of the Year for 1993. It was issued to commemorate the Battle of Trafalgar, on October 21, 1805.

Designer: Stanley J. Taylor

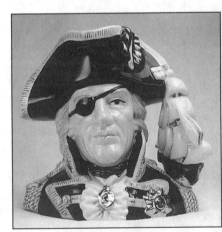
Vice-Admiral Lord Nelson

Statistics:	**Doulton Number**	**Size**	**Height**	**Issued**
	D6932	Large	8", 20.3 cm	1993-1993

Handle: The *Victory*
Colourway: Black, gold and cream
Backstamp: Doulton/Character Jug of the Year, 1993
Series: Character Jug of the Year

	Current Market Value		
Size	U.K. £	U.S. $	Can. $
Large	175.00	300.00	375.00

Note: For the character jug Lord Nelson see page 259, and for the character jug Nelson see page 287.

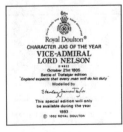

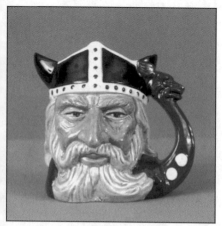

Viking

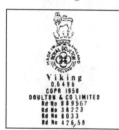

VIKING

Designer:	Max Henk			

	Doulton			
Statistics:	**Number**	**Size**	**Height**	**Issued**
1.	D6496	Large	7 ¼", 18.4 cm	1959-1975
2.	D6502	Small	4", 10.1 cm	1959-1975
3.	D6526	Miniature	2 ½", 6.4 cm	1960-1975

Handle: The prow of a Viking long ship
Colourway: Black, green and brown
Backstamp: **A.** Doulton
        B. Doulton / City of Stoke-on-Trent Jubille Year
        1959-1960 With the compliments of Lord Mayor
        and Lady Mayoress Alderman Harold Clowes
        O.B.E., J.P. and Miss Christine Clowes

Jug				Current Market Value		
No	**Size**	**Comp.**	**Issued**	**U.K. £**	**U.S. $**	**Can. $**
1A.	Large	EW	1959-1975	175.00	275.00	300.00
1A.		ETC	1968-1971	200.00	350.00	400.00
1B.		EW	1959-1960		Rare	
2A.	Small	EW	1959-1975	100.00	175.00	200.00
2A		ETC	1968-1971	125.00	200.00	250.00
3A.	Miniature	EW	1960-1975	125.00	200.00	225.00
		ETC	1968-1971	150.00	225.00	250.00

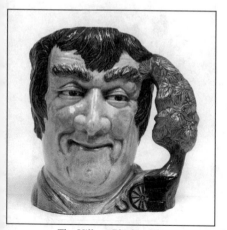

The Village Blacksmith

THE VILLAGE BLACKSMITH

PROTOTYPE

Designer:	Max Henk			

	Doulton			
Statistics:	**Number**	**Size**	**Height**	**Issued**
	D6549	Large	7 ½", 19.1 cm	See below

Modelled: 1961
Issued: Not put into production
Handle: Tree above anvil, wheel and horseshoe
Colourway: Blue, brown, black and green
Backstamp: None shown

	Current Market Value		
Size	**U.K. £**	**U.S. $**	**Can. $**
Large			

Only One Known
Sold at Philips, London
England,May 1993, £6,000.00

VISCOUNT MONTGOMERY OF ALAMEIN

This new design was specially commissioned by Lawleys By Post and was produced in a limited edition of 9,500 pieces. It was sold in a set of three: Montgomery, Mountbatten and Churchill.

Designer: Stanley J. Taylor

Statistics:	Doulton Number	Size	Height	Issued
	D6850	Small	3 ¼", 8.3 cm	See below

Issued: 1990 in a limited edition of 9,500
Handle: Imperial Army flag
Colourway: Black beret; khaki uniform; red flag
Backstamp: Doulton
Series: Heroic Leaders

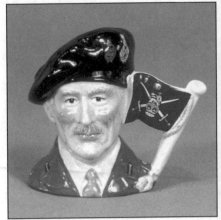

Viscount Montgomery of Alamein

	Current Market Value		
Size	U.K. £	U.S. $	Can. $
Small	125.00	200.00	225.00

Note: For the character jug Field Marshall Montgomery see page 184, and for the character jug Monty see page 278.

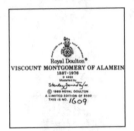

W. C. FIELDS

Born Claude William Dukenfield (1880-1946), W.C. Fields began his entertainment career at the age of 11 as a juggler. Much later he appeared in the Ziegfeld Follies and then in 1925 began his work in film. With his rasping voice and bulbous nose, he became a very successful satiric comedian.

The following quote appears on the base of the jug: "I was in love with a beautiful blonde once. She drove me to drink — 'tis the one thing I'm indebted to her for."

Designer: David B. Biggs

Statistics:	Doulton Number	Size	Height	Issued
A.	D6674	Large	7", 17.8 cm	1983-1986
B.	D6674	Large	7 ½", 19.1 cm	1983-Sp. ed.

Handle: A walking cane
Colourway: Black, grey and yellow
Backstamps: A. Doulton
 B. Doulton/American Express/ Premier Edition for American Express. Introduced in the U.S.A. as a promotional jug for American Express. Approximately 1,500 jugs bore the special backstamp.
Series: The Celebrity Collection

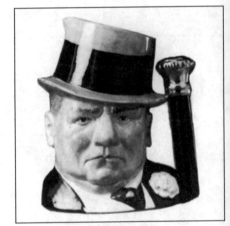

W. C. Fields

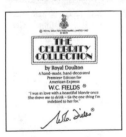

Jug No.	Size	Current Market Value		
		U.K. £	U.S. $	Can. $
A.	Large	125.00	225.00	250.00
B.	Large	200.00	350.00	400.00

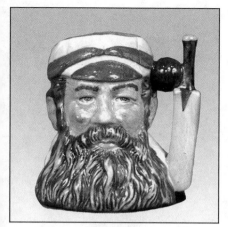

W. G. Grace

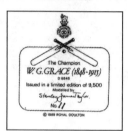

W. G. GRACE

William Gilbert Grace (1848-1915) began playing professional cricket at the age of 16 and rose quickly to the status of England's best batsman, earning the title of "The Champion." Throughout his long career, he set many records, retiring at the age of 60 after 44 seasons.

The small jug was commissioned by Lawleys By Post and issued in 1989 in a limited edition of 9,500 pieces.

Designer: Stanley J. Taylor

Statistics:	Doulton Number	Size	Height	Issued
1.	D7032	Large	7", 17.8 cm	See below
2.	D6845	Small	3 ¼", 8.3 cm	See below

Issued: 1. Large — 1996 in a limited edition of 9,500
2. Small — 1989 in a limited edition of 9,500
Handle: Cricket bat and ball
Colourway: Yellow and orange striped cap; black beard
Backstamp: Doulton
Series: Cricketers

Jug No.	Size	Current Market Value		
		U.K. £	U.S. $	Can. $
1.	Large	100.00	200.00	275.00
2.	Small	85.00	125.00	150.00

THE WALRUS & CARPENTER

On a beach in Wonderland, the walrus and carpenter invited a number of oysters for evening conversation, which the walrus promptly ate.

Designer: Max Henk
Handle: A walrus
Backstamp: Doulton

VARIATION No. 1: Colourway — Black hat; grey hair

Statistics:	Doulton Number	Size	Height	Issued
1.	D6600	Large	7 ¼", 18.4 cm	1965-1980
2.	D6604	Small	3 ¼", 8.3 cm	1965-1980
3.	D6608	Miniature	2 ½", 6.4 cm	1965-1980

Colourway: Black hat with yellow band, dark grey hair; pink neckerchief with yellow dots; Walrus wears green coat, yellow waistcoat and cream pants and
Series: Alice in Wonderland

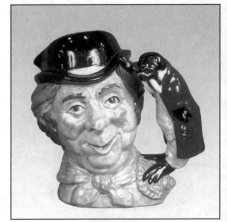

The Walrus and the Carpenter, Var. No. 1

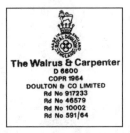

Jug No.	Size	Comp.	Issued	Current Market Value U.K. £	U.S. $	Can. $
1.	Large	EW	1965-1980	150.00	250.00	275.00
		ETC	1968-1971	175.00	275.00	300.00
2.	Small	EW	1965-1980	100.00	150.00	225.00
		ETC	1968-1971	125.00	175.00	250.00
3.	Miniature	EW	1965-1980	100.00	150.00	200.00
		ETC	1968-1971	125.00	175.00	225.00

VARIATION No. 2: Colourway — Black hat and hair

Statistics:	Doulton Number	Size	Height	Issued
	D —	Large	7 ¼", 18.4 cm	See below

Issued: Not put into production
Colourway: Black hat with white band; black hair; green neckerchief with yellow dots; Walrus wears green coat, yellow waistcoat and cream pants

Size	Variation	Current Market Value U.K. £	U.S. $	Can. $
Large	Var. 2	Extremely Rare		

VARIATION No. 3: Colourway — Green hat; red hair

Statistics:	Doulton Number	Size	Height	Issued
	D —	Large	7 ¼", 18.4 cm	See below

Issued: Not put into production
Colourway: Green hat with black band; ginger hair; yellow neckerchief; Walrus wears purple coat, pink waistcoat and yellow pants

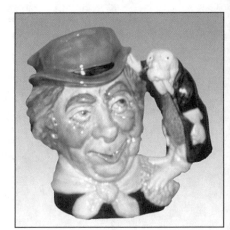

Walrus and the Carpenter, Var. No. 3

Size	Variation	Current Market Value U.K. £	U.S. $	Can. $
Large	Var. 3	Extremely Rare		

THE WIFE OF BATH

This jug was part of the proposed series "The Canterbury Tales."

PROTOTYPE

STYLE ONE : LARGE EYES; ROSY CHEEKS

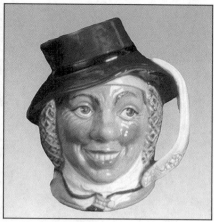

The Wife of Bath, Prototype, Style One

	Designer:	William K. Harper
	Height:	5 ¾", 14.6 cm
	Modelled:	1987
	Issued:	Not put into production
	Handle:	Folded linen
	Colourway:	Blue, green and white
	Backstamp:	Doulton

Doulton Number	Current Market Value		
	U.K. £	U.S. $	Can. $
D6778	Sold November 21, 1999 Phillips, New Bond Street London, England, £5,000.00:		

STYLE TWO: SMALL EYES, PALE COMPLEXION

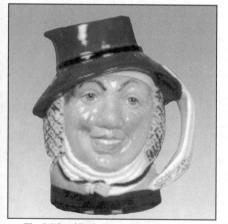

The Wife of Bath, Prototype, Style Two

	Designer:	William K. Harper
	Height:	5 ½", 14.0 cm
	Modelled:	October 1987
	Issued:	Not put into production
	Handle:	Folded linen
	Colourway:	Blue, green and white
	Backstamp:	Doulton

Model Number	Current Market Value		
	U.K. £	U.S. $	Can. $
3100	Sold November 21, 1999 Phillips, New Bond Street London, England, £5,500.00		

WILD BILL HICKOCK

After serving as a Union scout in the American Civil War, James Butler Hickock (1837-1876) became a marshall and then sheriff of several western frontier towns. An excellent gunman, he earned his nickname from his trigger-happy method of upholding the law at the many shootouts that erupted from poker games. He toured briefly with Buffalo Bill's Wild West Show (1872-1873) and was later murdered at Deadwood.

Designer: Michael Abberley

Statistics:

Doulton Number	Size	Height	Issued
D6736	Mid	5 ½", 14.0 cm	1985-1989

Handle: An upturned whiskey bottle flowing into a glass
Colourway: Black, brown and white
Backstamp: Doulton
Series: The Wild West Collection

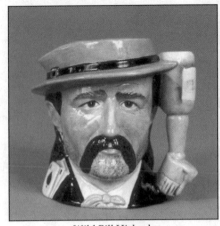

Wild Bill Hickock

Size	Current Market Value		
	U.K. £	U.S. $	Can. $
Mid	85.00	150.00	175.00

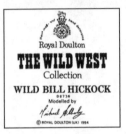

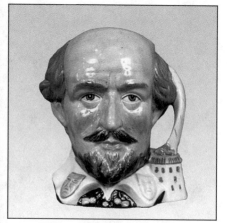

William Shakespeare, Style One

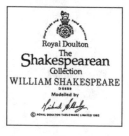

WILLIAM SHAKESPEARE

Shakespeare (1564-1616) was born in Stratford-upon-Avon. Apparently he moved to London in 1585 and by 1592 had emerged as a promising actor and playwright. He was a part of the theatre company, the King's Men of James I, throughout his London career, and in 1599, he became the new owner of the Globe Theatre. Immensely successful as a playwright, director, poet and actor, Shakespeare was said to have been quite wealthy by the time he returned to Stratford in 1613.

STYLE ONE: HANDLE — INK WELL WITH THE APPEARANCE OF THE GLOBE THEATRE

Designer: Michael Abberley

	Doulton			
Statistics:	**Number**	**Size**	**Height**	**Issued**
	D6689	Large	7 ¾", 19.7 cm	1983-1991

Handle: A feather quill with an inkwell of the appearance of the Globe Theatre
Colourway: White, grey and yellow
Backstamp: Doulton
Series: The Shakespearean Collection

		Current Market Value		
Size	**Desription**	**U.K. £**	**U.S. $**	**Can. $**
Large	Style One	100.00	150.00	175.00

STYLE TWO: HANDLE — CHARACTERS FROM DIFFERENT PLAYS

This jug was issued in a limited edition of 2,500 pieces.

Designer: William K. Harper

	Doulton			
Statistics:	**Number**	**Size**	**Height**	**Issued**
	D6933	Large	7", 17.8 cm	See below

Issued: 1992 in a limited edition of 2,500
Handle: Two handles, characters from different plays
Colourway: Brown
Backstamp: Doulton

		Current Market Value		
Size	**Description**	**U.K. £**	**U.S. $**	**Can. $**
Large	Style Two	300.00	450.00	600.00

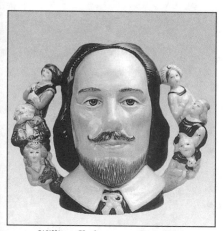

William Shakespeare, Style Two

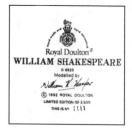

WILLIAM SHAKESPEARE

STYLE THREE: HANDLE — GLOBE THEATRE, MASKS OF COMEDY AND TRAGEDY

This jug was commemorates the 400th anniversary of the opening of William Shakepeare's Globe Theatre in London, England. The handle is fashioned from the masks of Comedy and Tragedy, as well as a replica of the Globe Theatre.

Designer: Robert Tabbenor

Statistics:	Doulton Number	Size	Height	Issued
	D7136	Large	7 ¾", 19.7 cm	1999-1999

Handle: Masks of Comedy and Tragedy; a replica of the Globe theatre
Colourway: Cream, brown, red and yellow
Backstamp: Doulton
Series: Character Jug of the Year

	Current Market Value		
Size	U.K. £	U.S. $	Can. $
Large	100.00	200.00	350.00

Note: For the character jug Shakespeare, see page 353.

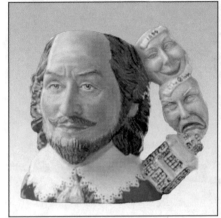

William Shakespeare, Style Three

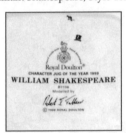

WILLIE CARSON O.B.E.

Born in Stirling in 1942, Willie Carson was the first Scotsman to become Champion Jockey. Among his many racing achievements are his first major Classic win in 1977 in the 2,000 Guineas; also in that year the Oaks and St. Leger; and in 1980, the Derby. This jug was issued by Lawleys By Post in a limited edition of 2,500 pieces.

Designer: Stanley J. Taylor

Statistics:	Doulton Number	Size	Height	Issued
	D7111	Small	4", 10.1 cm	See below

Issued: 1998 in a limited edition of 2,500
Handle: Riding crop, boot, horshoe and ribbon
Colourway: Blue and white jockey silks
Backstamp: Doulton

	Current Market Value		
Size	U.K. £	U.S. $	Can. $
Small	60.00	125.00	175.00

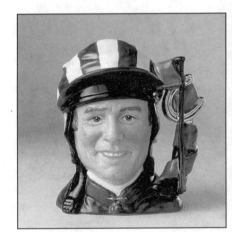

Willie Carson O.B.E.

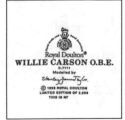

WINSTON CHURCHILL

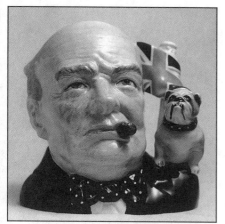

Winston Churchill, Style One

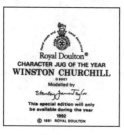

STYLE ONE: HANDLE — UNION JACK AND BULLDOG

This Winston Churchill jug was the Character Jug of the Year for 1992.

Designer: Stanley J. Taylor

Statistics:

Doulton Number	Size	Height	Issued
D6907	Large	7", 17.8 cm	1992-1992

Handle: Union Jack and bulldog
Colourway: Black, brown and white
Backstamp: Doulton/Character Jug of the Year, 1992
Series: Character Jug of the Year

	Current Market Value		
Size	U.K. £	U.S. $	Can. $
Large	175.00	350.00	500.00

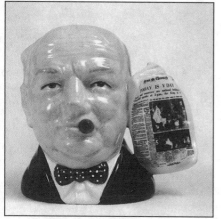

Winston Churchill, Style Two

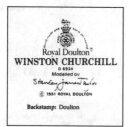

STYLE TWO: HANDLE — *NEWS CHRONICLE* VICTORY ISSUE

Designer: Stanley J. Taylor

Statistics:

Doulton Number	Size	Height	Issued
D6934	Small	4", 10.1 cm	1992 to the present

Handle: *News Chronicle* victory issue
Colourway: Black, grey, white and cream
Backstamp: Doulton

	Current Market Value		
Size	U.K. £	U.S. $	Can. $
Small	60.00	125.00	175.00

Note: For the character jug Churchill, see page 151, and for the character jug Sir Winston Churchill see page 363. For the toby jug Winston Churchill see page 85.

THE WITCH

Designer: Stanley J. Taylor

Statistics:	**Doulton** **Number**	**Size**	**Height**	**Issued**
	D6893	Large	7", 17.8 cm	1991-1991

Handle: Part of the witch's hat
Colourway: Black and greys
Backstamp: Doulton
Series: Mystical

Size	Current Market Value		
	U.K. £	**U.S. $**	**Can. $**
Large	150.00	275.00	350.00

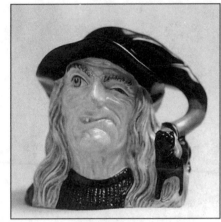

The Witch

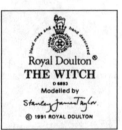

THE WIZARD

Designer: Stanley J. Taylor

Statistics:	**Doulton** **Number**	**Size**	**Height**	**Issued**
1.	D6862	Large	6 ¾", 17.2 cm	1990-1996
2.	D6909	Small	3 ¾", 9.5 cm	1992-1998

Handle: Black cat and a magic wand
Colourway: Blue-grey cap; black coat; red collar
Backstamp: Doulton
Series: Mystical

Jug No.	Size	Current Market Value		
		U.K. £	**U.S. $**	**Can. $**
1.	Large	95.00	200.00	275.00
2.	Small	50.00	85.00	125.00

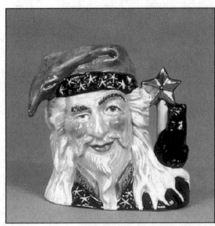

The Wizard

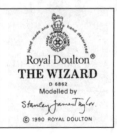

WYATT EARP

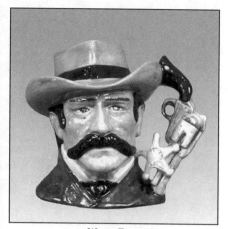

Wyatt Earp

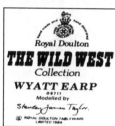

Wyatt Berry Stapp Earp (1848-1929) was an expert gunfighter. He worked as a police officer and armed guard and, in 1881, was involved in the famous shootout at the O.K. Corral. Later Earp travelled around the West, operating a number of saloons.

Designer: Stanley J. Taylor

Statistics:

	Doulton Number	Size	Height	Issued
	D6711	Mid	5 ½", 14.0 cm	1985-1989

Handle: A gun and sheriff's badge
Colourway: Brown coat; light brown hat with red band
Backstamp: Doulton
Series: The Wild West Collection

	Current Market Value		
Size	U.K. £	U.S. $	Can. $
Mid	100.00	175.00	200.00

YACHTSMAN

The small and miniature jugs of the Yachtsman were piloted, but never put into production.

STYLE ONE: YACHTSMAN WITH LIFE JACKET

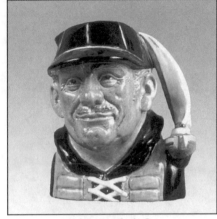

Yachtsman, Style One

Designer: David B. Biggs

Statistics:	Doulton Number	Size	Height	Issued
1.	D6626	Large	8", 20.3 cm	1971-1980
2.	D —	Small	Unknown	Unknown

Issued: See below
Handle: A yacht sailing from the front to back
Colourway: Blue cap and jersey; yellow lifejacket
Backstamp: Doulton

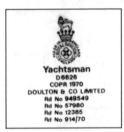

Jug No.	Size	Comp.	Issued	Current Market Value U.K. £	U.S. $	Can. $
1.	Large	EW	1971-1980	125.00	200.00	225.00
		ETC	1968-1971		Rare	
2.	Small	EW	Unknown	Extremely rare		

STYLE TWO: YACHTSMAN WITH PEAK CAP AND CRAVAT

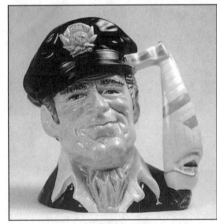

Yachtsman, Style Two

Designer: Stanley J. Taylor

Statistics:	Doulton Number	Size	Height	Issued
1.	D6820	Large	6 ½", 16.5 cm	See below

Issued: A. 1989-1991
B. 1988 in a special edition of 750
Handle: Sailboat with white sails and green trim sailing back to front
Colourway: Navy blue cap; dark blue jacket; yellow shirt; grey scarf
Backstamps: A. Doulton / For general release, 1989.
B. Doulton/Canadian Doulton Show and Sale Issued to commemorate the first Canadian Doulton Show and Sale at Durham, Ontario, July 29 to 31, 1988. Issued in a special edition of 750 pieces.

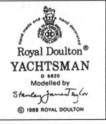

Backstamp A - Doulton

No.	Size	Current Market Value U.K. £	U.S. $	Can. $
1A.	Large	75.00	150.00	175.00
1B.		150.00	200.00	225.00

THE YEOMAN OF THE GUARD

In 1485 Henry VIII organized the Yeomen of the Guard, bodyguards to the monarch of England. Today the Yeomen, or Beefeaters as they are more commonly known, serve only as ceremonial guards.

Designer: Stanley J. Taylor

Statistics:	Doulton Number	Size	Height	Issued
A.	D6873	Large	7", 17.8 cm	1991-1997
B.	D6883	Large	7", 17.8 cm	1990-Ltd.ed.
C.	D6882	Large	7", 17.8 cm	1990-Ltd.ed.
D.	D6885	Large	7", 17.8 cm	1990-Ltd.ed.
E.	D6884	Large	7", 17.8 cm	1990-Ltd. ed.

Handle: Raven and tree trunk
Colourway: Black hat; white frills; red jacket
Backstamps: See below
Series: The London Collection

The jugs bearing backstamps B, C, D and E were released in the U.S.A. to commemorate the anniversaries of the opening of the four Royal Doulton Rooms in the U.S.A. They were issued in a limited edition of 450 pieces total and bore a special backstamp.

Backstamp:

A. Doulton

B. Doulton/Dillards/
To Commemorate the third anniversary of the opening of the Royal Doulton Room Dillards, New Orleans, Louisiana, U.S.A.
Issued in a limited edition of 50 pieces.

C. Doulton/Joseph Horne/
To Commemorate the third anniversary of the opening of the Royal Doulton Room Joseph Horne, Pittsburgh, Pennsylvania, U.S.A.
Issued in a limited edition of 75 pieces.

D. Doulton/Strawbridge and Clothier/
To Commemorate the fourth anniversary of the opening of the Royal Doulton Room Strawbridge and Clothier, Philadelphia, Pennsylvania, U.S.A.
Issued in a limited edition of 75 pieces.

E. Doulton/Higbee/
To Commemorate the fifth anniversary of the opening of the Royal Doulton Room Higbee Cleveland, Ohio, U.S.A.
Issued in a limited edition of 250 pieces.

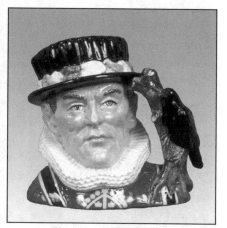

The Yeoman of the Guard

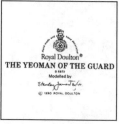

Backstamp A - Doulton

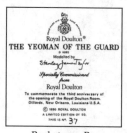

Backstamp B - Doulton/Horne

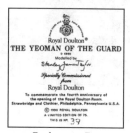

Backstamp D - Doulton/Strawbridge

Jug No.	Size	Issued	Current Market Value U.K. £	U.S. $	Can. $
A.	Large	1991-1997	80.00	125.00	175.00
B.		1990-Ltd. ed.	225.00	350.00	425.00
C.		1990-Ltd. ed.	200.00	325.00	400.00
D.		1990-Ltd. ed.	200.00	325.00	400.00
E.		1990-Ltd. ed.	175.00	275.00	375.00

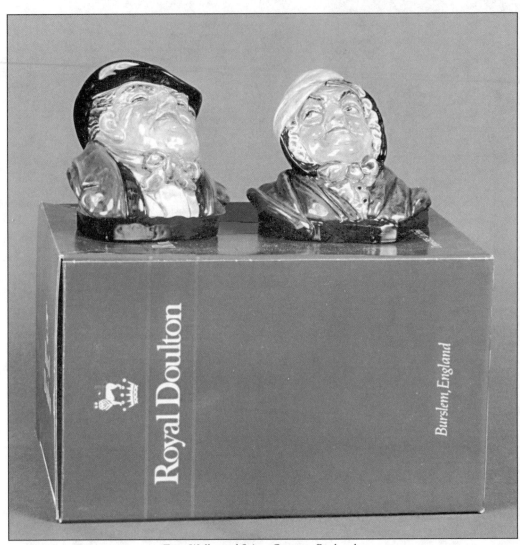

Tony Weller and Sairey Gamp — Bookends

BOOKENDS

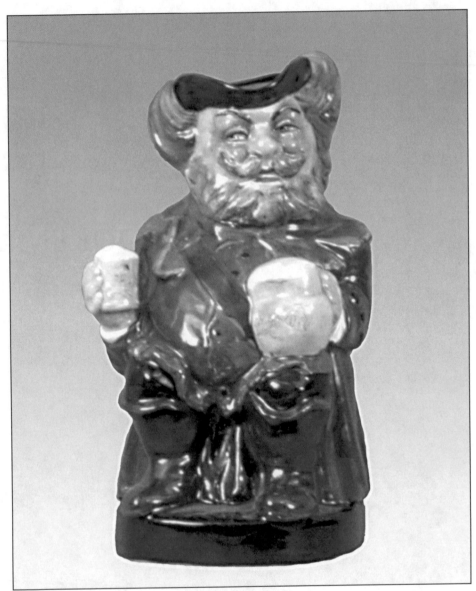

Falstaff Toby Jug

HENRY V and FALSTAFF

Designer: David B. Biggs

Statistics:	Doulton Number	Name	Height	Issued
1.	D7088	Henry V	7 ½", 19.1 cm	1997-2001
2.	D7089	Falstaff	7 ½", 19.1 cm	1997-2001

Colourway:
1. Henry V — Grey maroon, yellow and gold
2. Falstaff — Maroon, white, grey and gold
Red book covers

Backstamp: Doulton

No.	Name	Current Market Value		
		U.K. £	U.S. $	Can. $
1.	Henry V	75.00	175.00	275.00
2.	Falstaff	75.00	175.00	275.00

Note: For the toby jug Falstaff see page 49 and for the character jug Falstaff see page 181.

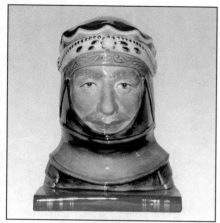

Henry V

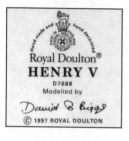

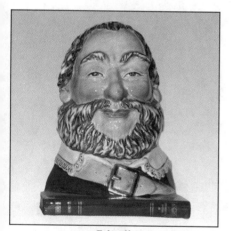

Falstaff

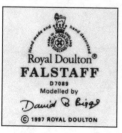

SHERLOCK HOLMES
and DR. WATSON

Designer: Martyn C. R. Alcock

Statistics:

	Doulton Number	Name	Height	Issued
1.	D7038	S. Holmes	7 ½", 19.1 cm	See below
2.	D7039	Dr. Watson	7 ½", 19.1 cm	See below

Colourway:
1. Sherlock Holmes — Brown coat and deerstalker
2. Dr. Watson — Grey jacket and tie; brown hat Green book covers

Backstamp: Doulton

VARIATION No. 1: BOOK TITLES
Sherlock Holmes — "The Adventures of Sherlock Holmes" / "The Hound of the Baskervilles"
Dr. Watson —"The Adventures of Sherlock Holmes " "The Last Problem"

Issued: 1996-1997

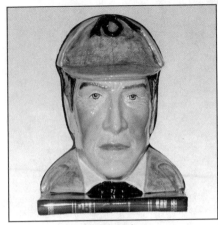

Sherlock Holmes

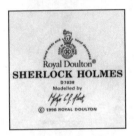

No.	Name	Variation	Current Market Value		
			U.K. £	U.S. $	Can. $
1.	Sherlock Holmes	Var. 1	100.00	200.00	325.00
2.	Dr. Watson		100.00	200.00	325.00

VARIATION No. 2: BOOK TITLES
Sherlock Holmes — "The Memoirs of Sherlock Holmes"
Dr. Watson — "The Memoirs of Sherlock Holmes" "The Final Problem"

Issued: 1997-2001

No.	Name	Variation	Current Market Value		
			U.K. £	U.S. $	Can. $
1	Sherlock Holmes	Var. 2	75.00	175.00	275.00
2.	Dr. Watson		75.00	175.00	275.00

Note: For the toby jug Sherlock Holmes see page 79, and for the character jug Sherlock Holmes see the "Sherlock Holmes Set" page 354.

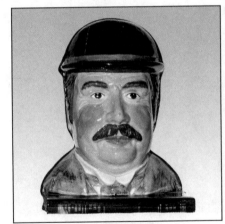

Dr. Watson

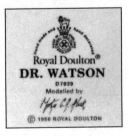

STAN LAUREL AND OLIVER HARDY

These bookends were issued in a limited edition of 2,500.

Designer: William K. Harper

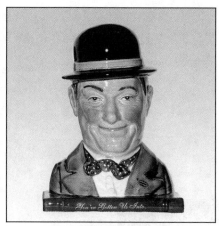

Stan Laurel

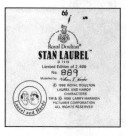

Statistics:

	Doulton Number	Name	Height	Issued
1.	D7119	S. Laurel	7 ¾", 19.7 cm	See below
2.	D7120	O. Hardy	7 ¾", 19.7 cm	See below

Issued: 1998 in a limited edition of 2,500

Colourway: 1. Stan Laurel — Grey jacket; black bow tie with white spots; black bowler with grey band "You've Gotten Us Into."

2. Oliver Hardy — Grey jacket; red tie with white spots; black bowler with grey band "Here's Another Nice Mess"

Backstamp: Doulton/TM & © 1998 Larry Harmon Pictures Corporation All Rights Reserved

		Current Market Value		
No.	Name	U.K. £	U.S. $	Can. $
1.	Stan Laurel	75.00	150.00	200.00
2.	Oliver Hardy	75.00	150.00	200.00

Note: For the character jugs Laurel and Hardy see page 248.

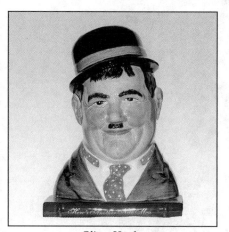

Oliver Hardy

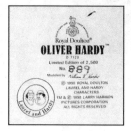

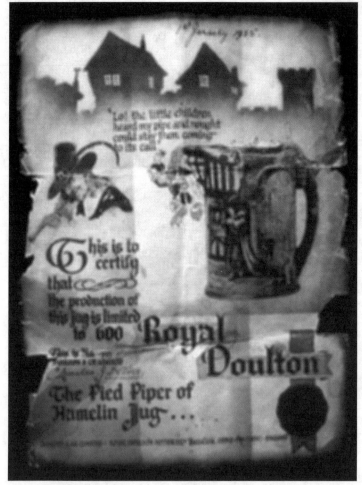

Certificate issued for The Pied Piper of Hamelin Jug

LIQUOR CONTAINERS AND JUGS

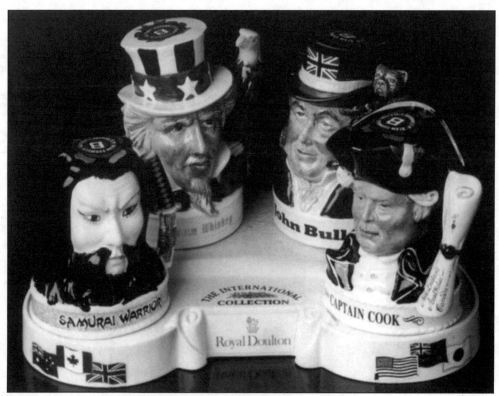

Samurai Warrior, Uncle Sam, John Bull, Captain Cook

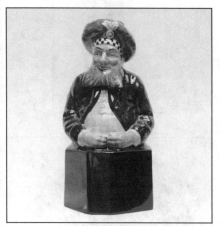

Irishman

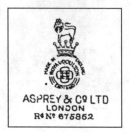

Scotsman

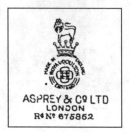

ASPREY & CO. LTD.

WHISKEY DECANTERS

Two whisky flasks, one depicting an Irishman and the other a Scotsman, were made in the 1920s for Asprey and Co. Ltd, New Bond Street, London, England. Each was set within a wooden tantalus, and the head of the flask was detachable. The Irishman contained Irish whiskey, and the Scotsman, Scottish whisky. These two flasks are usually traded as a set.

Designer: Harry Fenton
Height: 9 ½", 24.0 cm
Issued: 1920-1930
Colourway: Black hat and coat; green cravat; maroon vest
Backstamp: Doulton

Doulton Number	Name	Current Market Value		
		U.K. £	U.S. $	Can. $
D —	Irishman	900.00	2,000.00	2,500.00
D —	Scotsman	900.00	2,000.00	2,500.00

CAPTAIN COOK

LIQUOR CONTAINER

This Captain Cook liquor container was commissioned by Pick-Kwik Wines and Spirits in a limited edition of 2,000 pieces.

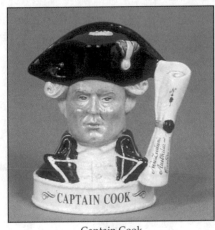

Designer:	Harry Sales
Modeller:	Graham Tongue
Height:	4 ¾", 12.1 cm
Size:	Small
Issued:	1985 in a limited edition of 2,000
Handle:	Scroll
Colourway:	Black hat; black and yellow uniform
Inscription:	"Captain Cook" "The World's Finest Bourbon since 1795"
Backstamp:	Doulton/Pick-Kwik
Series:	The International Collection

Captain Cook

Doulton Number	Current Market Value		
	U.K. £	**U.S. $**	**Can. $**
D —	65.00	125.00	150.00

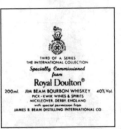

FALSTAFF

LIQUEUR CONTAINER

The Falstaff, Poacher and Rip Van Winkle character jugs were adapted by Royal Doulton as liqueur containers for Bols liqueur for the bottling firm of W. Walklate Ltd. The small-size jugs were commissioned circa 1960 by W. Walklate Ltd.

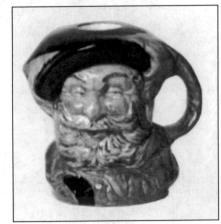

Designer:	Harry Fenton
Height:	4", 10.1 cm
Size:	Small
Issued:	c.1960-c.1960
Handle:	Plain
Colourway:	Rose tunic; black hat trimmed with rose plumes; grey beard
Backstamp:	Doulton

Falstaff

Doulton Number	Current Market Value		
	U.K. £	**U.S. $**	**Can. $**
D6385	60.00	125.00	150.00

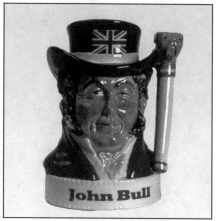

Variation 1 - Inscription "John Bull"

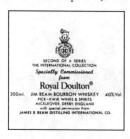

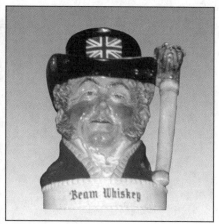

Variation 2 - Inscription "Beam Whiskey"

JOHN BULL

LIQUOR CONTAINER

Designer: Harry Sales
Modeller: Graham Tongue
Height: 5", 12.7 cm
Size: Small
Handle: Cane with bull dog head

VARIATION No. 1:   **Colourway** — Red coat with white edging
        Inscription around base — John Bull

The John Bull liquor container was commissioned by Pick-Kwik Wines and Spirits in a limited edition of 2,000 pieces.

Issued: 1985 in a limited edition of 2,000
Colourway: Black hat with yellow band; red coat with white edging; white shirt points, yellow shirt/bow tie; dark grey hair
Inscription: "John Bull" in red lettering
Backstamp: Doulton/Pick-Kwik
Series: The International Collection

Doulton Number	Variation	Current Market Value		
		U.K. £	U.S. $	Can. $
D —	Var. 1	85.00	175.00	200.00

VARIATION No. 2:   **Colourway** — Red coat with yellow edging
        Inscription around base — Beam Whiskey

Issued: Unknown
Colourway: Black hat; red coat with yellow edging; white shirt; grey hair
Inscription: "Beam Whiskey" in green lettering
Backstamp: Unknown

Doulton Number	Variation	Current Market Value		
		U.K. £	U.S. $	Can. $
D —	Var. 2	85.00	175.00	200.0

MR. MICAWBER

This liquor container was commissioned by Pick-Kwik Wines and Spirits.

STYLE ONE: LIQUOR CONTAINER

Designer: Harry Sales
Modeller: Graham Tongue
Height: 5", 12.7 cm
Size: Small
Backstamp: Doulton/Pick-Kwik

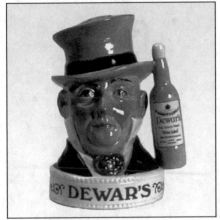

Mr. Micawber, Style One, Variation No. 1

VARIATION No. 1: **Colourway** — Brown hat; dark blue blazer; maroon cravat
Handle — Dewar's
Inscription on Base —"Dewar's"

Issued: 1983 in a limited edition of 2,000
Handle: Dewar's
Colourway: Brown hat; dark blue blazer; maroon cravat
Inscription: "Dewar's"

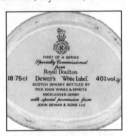

Doulton Number	Variation	Current Market Value		
		U.K. £	U.S. $	Can. $
D —	Var. 1	70.00	150.00	175.00

VARIATION No. 2: **Colourway** — Grey hat; green blazer; light blue cravat
Handle — Pickwick Deluxe
Inscription around Base — "Pickwick Deluxe Whiskey"

Issued: 1983 in a limited edition of 2,000
Handle: Pickwick Deluxe
Colourway: Grey hat; green blazer; light blue cravat
Inscription: "Pickwick Deluxe Whiskey"

Doulton Number	Variation	Current Market Value		
		U.K. £	U.S. $	Can. $
D —	Var. 2	65.00	125.00	150.00

VARIATION No. 3: **Colourway** — White
Handle — Pickwick Deluxe
Inscription around Base — "Pickwick Deluxe Whiskey"

Issued: 1985 in a limited edition of 100
Handle: Pickwick Deluxe
Colourway: White
Inscription: "Pickwick Deluxe Whiskey"

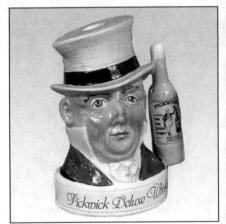

Mr. Micawber, Style One, Variation No. 2

Doulton Number	Variation	Current Market Value		
		U.K. £	U.S. $	Can. $
D —	Var. 3	150.00	250.00	300.00

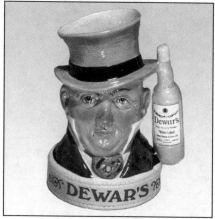

Mr. Micawber, Style Two, Variation No. 1

MR. MICAWBER

STYLE TWO: CHARACTER JUG

This jug was commissioned by Pick-Kwik Wines and Spirits.

Designer: Harry Sales
Modeller: Graham Tongue
Height: 4", 10.1 cm
Size: Small

VARIATION No. 1: **Colourway** — Brown hat; blue blazer; maroon cravat
Handle — Dewar's
Inscription around Base — "Dewar's"

Issued: 1985 in a limited edition of 100
Handle: Dewar's
Colourway: Brown hat; blue blazer; maroon cravat
Inscription: "Dewar's"
Backstamp: Doulton/Pick-Kwik

| Doulton Number | Variation | Current Market Value | | |
		U.K. £	U.S. $	Can. $
D —	Var. 1	150.00	250.00	275.00

VARIATION No. 2: **Colourway** — White
Handle — Dewar's
Inscription around Base — "Dewar's" in red

Issued: 1985 in a limited edition of 100
Handle: Dewar's
Colourway: White
Inscription: "Dewar's"
Backstamp: Doulton/Pick-Kwik

| Doulton Number | Variation | Current Market Value | | |
		U.K. £	U.S. $	Can. $
D —	Var. 2	150.00	275.00	300.00

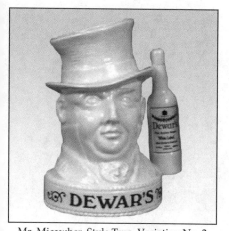

Mr. Micawber, Style Two, Variation No. 2

MR. MICAWBER

VARIATION No. 3: **Colourway** — Grey hat; green blazer; light blue cravat
Handle — Pickwick Deluxe
Inscription around Base — "Pickwick Deluxe Whiskey"

Issued:	1985 in a limited edition of 100
Handle:	Pickwick Deluxe
Colourway:	Grey hat; green blazer; light blue cravat
Inscription:	"Pickwick Deluxe Whiskey"
Backstamp:	Doulton/Pick-Kwik

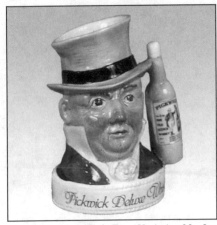

Doulton Number	Variation	Current Market Value		
		U.K. £	**U.S. $**	**Can. $**
D —	Var. 3	150.00	275.00	300.00

Mr. Micawber, Style Two, Variation No. 3

VARIATION No. 4: **Colourway** — White
Handle — Pickwick Deluxe
Inscription around Base — "Pickwick Deluxe Whiskey"

Issued:	1985 in a limited edition of 100
Handle:	Pickwick Deluxe
Colourway:	White
Inscription:	"Pickwick Deluxe Whiskey"
Backstamp:	Doulton/Pick-Kwik

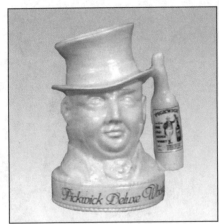

Doulton Number	Variation	Current Market Value		
		U.K. £	**U.S. $**	**Can. $**
D —	Var. 4	150.00	275.00	300.00

Mr. Micawber, Style Two, Variation No. 4

MR. PICKWICK

CHARACTER JUG

Pick-Kwik Wines and Spirits commissioned the Mr. Pickwick jug.

Designer: Harry Sales
Modeller: Graham Tongue
Size: Small
Backstamp: Doulton/Pick-Kwik

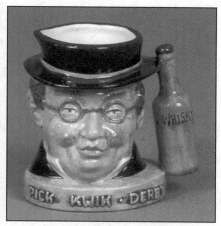

Mr. Pickwick, Variation No. 1

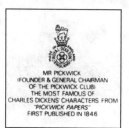

MR PICKWICK
(FOUNDER & GENERAL CHAIRMAN
OF THE PICKWICK CLUB)
THE MOST FAMOUS OF
CHARLES DICKENS' CHARACTERS FROM
"PICKWICK PAPERS"
FIRST PUBLISHED IN 1846

VARIATION No. 1: Colourway — Green hat; black coat
Handle — No label / "Whisky"
Inscription around Base — "Pick Kwik
Derby Whiskies Wines Ales"

Height: 4", 10.1 cm
Issued: 1982 in a limited edition of 2,000
Handle: "Whisky"
Colourway: Green hat; black coat
Inscription: "Pick Kwik Derby Whiskies Wines Ales"

Doulton Number	Variation	Current Market Value		
		U.K. £	U.S. $	Can. $
D —	Var. 1	85.00	150.00	175.00

VARIATION No. 2: Colourway — Brown hat; dark brown coat
Handle — Jim Beam
Inscription around Base — "Pick-Kwik
Derby Sells Jim Beam Whiskey"

Height: 4", 10.1 cm
Issued: 1984 in a limited edition of 2,000
Handle: Jim Beam
Colourway: Brown hat; dark brown coat
Inscription: "Pick-Kwik Derby Sells Jim Beam Whiskey"

Doulton Number	Variation	Current Market Value		
		U.K. £	U.S. $	Can. $
D —	Var. 2	75.00	175.00	200.00

VARIATION No. 3: Colourway — Beige hat; brown coat
Handle — Beam's White Label
Inscription around Base —"Beam Whiskey"
"The World's Finest Bourbon"

Height: 5 ¼", 13.3 cm
Issued: 1984 in a limited edition of 1,000
Handle: Beam's White Label
Colourway: Beige hat; brown coat
Inscription: "Beam Whiskey" "The World's Finest Bourbon"

Doulton Number	Variation	Current Market Value		
		U.K. £	U.S. $	Can. $
D —	Var. 3	75.00	175.00	200.00

MR. PICKWICK

VARIATION No. 4: Colourway — Beige hat; brown coat
Handle — Beam's Black Label
Inscription around Base — "Beam Whiskey"

Height: 5 ¼", 13.3 cm
Issued: 1984 in a limited edition of 1,000
Handle: Beam's Black Label
Colourway: Beige hat; brown coat
Inscription: "Beam Whiskey"

| Doulton | | Current Market Value | | |
Number	Variation	U.K. £	U.S. $	Can. $
D —	Var. 4	75.00	175.00	200.00

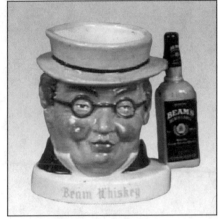

Mr. Pickwick, Variation No. 4

VARIATION No. 5: Colourway — White
Handle — No label / "Whiskey"
Inscription around Base — "Pick Kwik Derby"

Height: 5 ¼", 13.3 cm
Issued: 1985 in a limited edition of 100
Handle: Whiskey
Colourway: White
Inscription: "Pick Kwik Derby"

| Doulton | | Current Market Value | | |
Number	Variation	U.K. £	U.S. $	Can. $
D —	Var. 5	125.00	275.00	300.00

VARIATION No. 6: Colourway — White with red transfers
Handle — Jim Beam
Inscription around Base — "Pick Kwik Derby Sells Jim Beam Whiskey"

Height: 5 ¼", 13.3 cm
Issued: 1985 in a limited edition of 100
Handle: Jim Beam
Colourway: White with red transfers
Inscription: "Pick Kwik Derby Sells Jim Beam Whiskey"

| Doulton | | Current Market Value | | |
Number	Variation	U.K. £	U.S. $	Can. $
D —	Var. 6	125.00	275.00	300.00

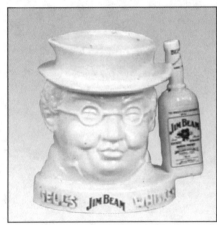

Mr. Pickwick, Variation No. 6

VARIATION No. 7: Colourway — Brown hat; green coat
Handle — Beam's White Label
Inscription around Base — "Pick Kwik Derby Sells Jim Beam Whiskey"

Height: 4", 10.1 cm
Issued: 1985 in a limited edition of 2,000
Handle: Beam's White Label
Colourway: Brown hat; green coat
Inscription: "Pick Kwik Derby Sells Jim Beam Whiskey"

| Doulton | | Current Market Value | | |
Number	Variation	U.K. £	U.S. $	Can. $
D —	Var. 7	125.00	275.00	300.00

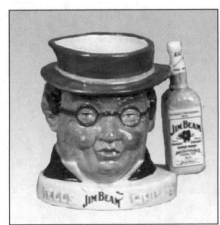

Mr. Pickwick, Variation No. 7

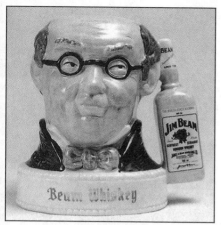

Mr. Pickwick

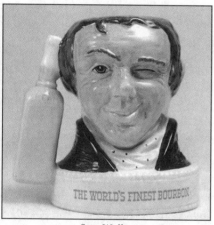

Sam Weller

MR. PICKWICK and SAM WELLER

LIQUOR CONTAINER

This two-faced liquor container was commissioned by Pick-Kwik Wines and Spirits in a limited edition of 2,000 pieces.

Designer:	Harry Sales
Modeller:	Graham Tongue
Height:	5", 12.7 cm
Size:	Small
Issued:	1985 in a limited edition of 2,000
Handle:	Jim Beam, plain bottle
Colourway:	Mr. Pickwick — Dark green coat; pink bow tie
	Sam Weller — Dark green coat; yellow cravat with red dots
Inscription:	"Beam Whiskey" and "The World's Finest Bourbon"
Backstamp:	Doulton/Pick-Kwik
Series:	The Pickwick Collection

Doulton Number	Current Market Value		
	U.K. £	**U.S. $**	**Can. $**
D —	75.00	200.00	225.00

OLD MR. TURVERYDROP

LIQUOR CONTAINER

Commissioned by Pick-Kwik Wines and Spirits, Old Mr. Turverydrop was produced in a limited edition of 2,000 pieces.

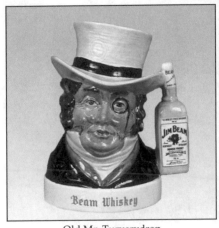

Designer:	Harry Sales
Modeller:	Graham Tongue
Height:	5", 12.7 cm
Size:	Small
Issued:	1985-1985
Handle:	Jim Beam
Colourway:	Yellow hat; dark brown coat
Inscription:	"Beam Whiskey" "Famous for quality since 1795"
Backstamp:	Doulton/Pick-Kwik

Doulton Number	Current Market Value		
	U.K. £	U.S. $	Can. $
D —	65.00	175.00	175.00

Old Mr. Turverydrop

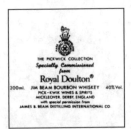

THE POACHER

LIQUEUR CONTAINER

The Falstaff, Poacher and Rip Van Winkle character jugs were adapted by Doulton to liqueur containers for Bols liqueurs for the bottling firm W. Walklate Ltd. The small-size jugs were commissioned about 1960 by W. Walklate Ltd.

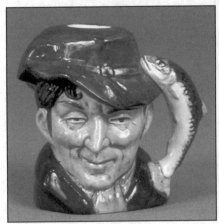

Designer:	Max Henk
Height:	4", 10.1 cm
Size:	Small
Issued:	c.1960-c.1960
Handle:	A salmon
Colourway:	Green coat; red scarf; light brown hat
Backstamp:	Doulton

Doulton Number	Current Market Value		
	U.K. £	U.S. $	Can. $
D6464	60.00	125.00	150.00

The Poacher

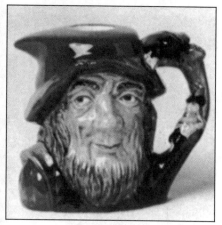

Rip Van Winkle

RIP VAN WINKLE

LIQUEUR CONTAINER

The Falstaff, Poacher and Rip Van Winkle character jugs were adapted by Doulton to liqueur containers for Bols liqueurs for the bottling firm W. Walklate Ltd. The small-size jugs were commissioned about 1960 by W. Walklate Ltd.

Designer:	Geoff Blower
Height:	4", 10.1 cm
Size:	Small
Issued:	c.1960-c.1960
Handle:	A man resting against a tree
Colourway:	Grey-blue cap; brown robes; figure resting against tree dressed in blue
Backstamp:	Doulton

Doulton Number	Current Market Value		
	U.K. £	**U.S. $**	**Can. $**
D6463	60.00	125.00	150.00

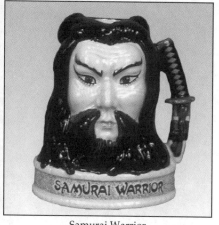

Samurai Warrior

SAMURAI WARRIOR

LIQUOR CONTAINER

Commissioned by Pick-Kwik Wines and Spirits, the Samurai Warrior was produced in a limited edition of 2,000 pieces.

Designer:	Harry Sales
Modeller:	Graham Tongue
Height:	5", 12.7 cm
Size:	Small
Issued:	1986-1986
Handle:	Sword
Colourway:	Black hair; white face
Inscription:	"Samurai Warrior" "Famous for quality since 1795"
Backstamp:	Doulton/Pick-Kwik
Series:	The International Collection

Doulton Number	Current Market Value		
	U.K. £	**U.S. $**	**Can. $**
D —	75.00	150.00	150.00

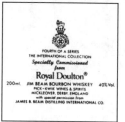

FOURTH OF A SERIES
THE INTERNATIONAL COLLECTION
Specially Commissioned
from
Royal Doulton®
200ml.   JIM BEAM BOURBON WHISKEY   40% Vol.
PICK-KWIK WINES & SPIRITS
MICKLEOVER, DERBY, ENGLAND
with special permission from
JAMES B. BEAM DISTILLING INTERNATIONAL CO.

SGT. BUZ FUZ

CHARACTER JUG

This character jug was commissioned by Pick-Kwik Wines and Spirits.

Designer:	Harry Sales
Modeller:	Graham Tongue
Height:	4", 10.1 cm
Size:	Small
Backstamp:	Doulton/Pick-Kwik

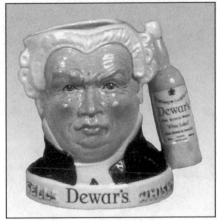

Sgt. Buz Fuz

VARIATION No. 1: **Colourway** — White hair; black coat
Handle — Dewar's
Inscription around Base — "Pick-Kwik Derby Sells Dewar's Whisky"

Issued:	1982 in a limited edition of 2,000
Handle:	Dewar's
Colourway:	White hair; black coat
Inscription:	"Pick-Kwik Derby Sells Dewar's Whisky"

Doulton Number	Variation	Current Market Value		
		U.K. £	**U.S. $**	**Can. $**
D —	Var. 1	75.00	200.00	200.00

VARIATION No. 2: **Colourway** — White with red transfers
Handle — Dewar's
Inscription around Base — "Pick-Kwik Derby Sells Dewar's Whisky"

Issued:	1985 in a limited edition of 100
Handle:	Dewar's
Colourway:	White with red transfers
Inscription:	"Pick-Kwik Derby Sells Dewar's Whisky"

Doulton Number	Variation	Current Market Value		
		U.K. £	**U.S. $**	**Can. $**
D —	Var. 2	125.00	275.00	300.00

VARIATION No. 3: **Colourway** — White
Handle — Plain bottle
Inscription around Base — "Pick-Kwik Derby Sells Whisky"

Issued:	1985 in a limited edition of 100
Handle:	Dewar's
Colourway:	White
Inscription:	"Pick-Kwik Derby Sells Whisky"

Doulton Number	Variation	Current Market Value		
		U.K. £	**U.S. $**	**Can. $**
D —	Var. 3	125.00	275.00	300.00

TOWN CRIER OF EATANSWILL

LIQUOR CONTAINER

This Town Crier was commissioned by Pick-Kwik Wines and Spirits and was issued in a limited edition of 2,000 pieces.

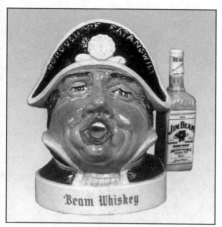

Town Crier of Eatanswill

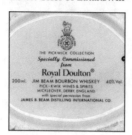

Designer:	Harry Sales
Modeller:	Graham Tongue
Height:	5", 12.7 cm
Size:	Small
Issued:	1986 in a limited edition of 2,000
Handle:	Jim Beam
Colourway:	Black hat; maroon coat with yellow trim
Inscription:	"Beam Whiskey"
Backstamp:	Doulton/Pick-Kwik

Doulton Number	Current Market Value		
	U.K. £	U.S. $	Can. $
D —	85.00	175.00	200.00

UNCLE SAM

STYLE ONE: HANDLE — JIM BEAM BOTTLE

Commissioned by Pick-Kwik Wines and Spirits, Uncle Sam was issued in a limited edition of 2,000 pieces.

Designer:	Harry Sales
Modeller:	Graham Tongue
Height:	5 ¼", 13.3 cm
Size:	Small
Issued:	1984 in a limited edition of 2,000
Handle:	Jim Beam bottle
Colourway:	Red, white and blue hat, blue brim
Backstamp:	Doulton/Pick-Kwik
Series:	The International Collection

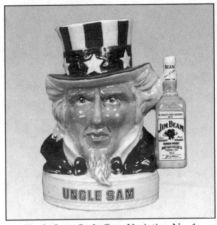

Uncle Sam, Style One, Variation No. 1

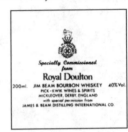

VARIATION No. 1:   Inscription around Base — "Uncle Sam"
"Famous for quality since 1795"

Doulton Number	Variation	Current Market Value		
		U.K. £	U.S. $	Can. $
D —	Var. 1	75.00	175.00	200.00

VARIATION No. 2:   Inscription around base — "Beam Whiskey"

Doulton Number	Variation	Current Market Value		
		U.K. £	U.S. $	Can. $
D —	Var. 2	75.00	175.00	200.00

STYLE TWO: HANDLE: EAGLE

Commissioned by Pick-Kwik Wines and Spirits, Uncle Sam was issued as promotional item in a limited edition of 500 pieces.

Designer:	Harry Sales
Modeller:	Graham Tongue
Height:	5 ¼", 13.3 cm
Size:	Small
Issued:	1986 in a limited edition of 500
Handle:	Eagle
Colourway:	Red, white and blue hat, white brim
Backstamp:	Doulton/Pick-Kwik

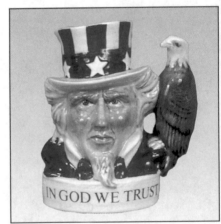

Uncle Sam, Style Two, Variation No. 1

VARIATION No. 1:   Inscription around base — "In God We Trust"

Doulton Number	Variation	Current Market Value		
		U.K. £	U.S. $	Can. $
D —	Var. 1	100.00	250.00	300.00

VARIATION No. 2:   Inscription around base — "Beam Whiskey"
"The World's Finest Bourbon"

Doulton Number	Variation	Current Market Value		
		U.K. £	U.S. $	Can. $
D —	Var. 2	100.00	250.00	300.00

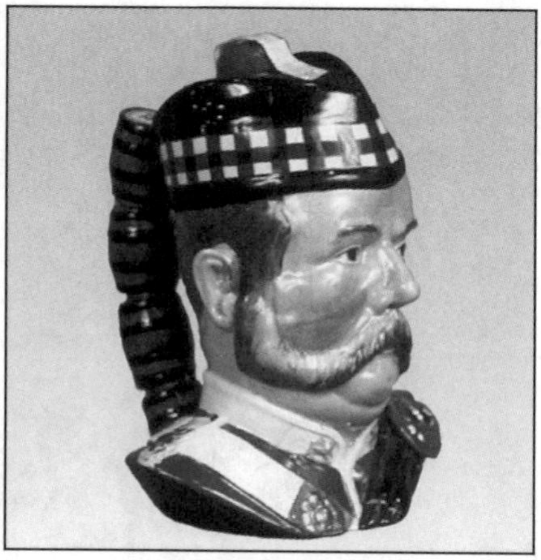

William Grant, Style One

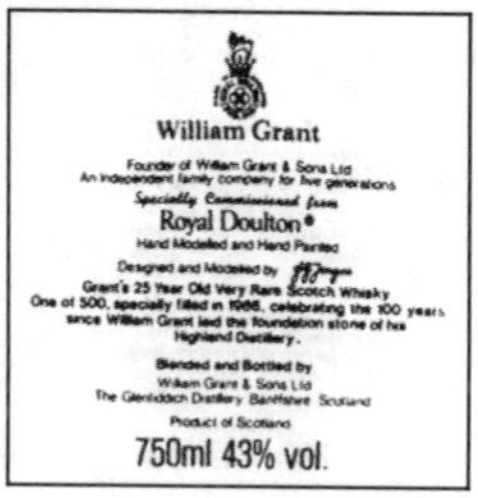

Backstamp A - 100th Anniversary Foundation Stone

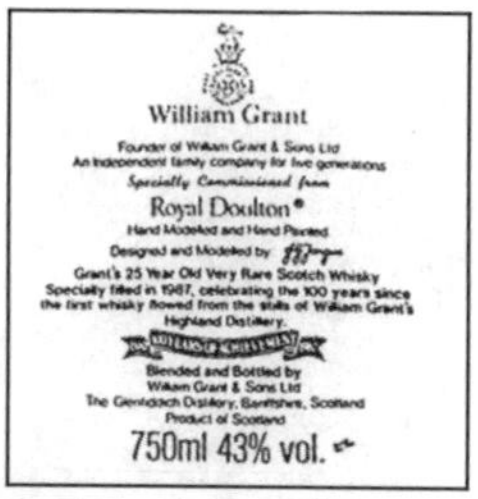

Backstamp B - Christmas 1987

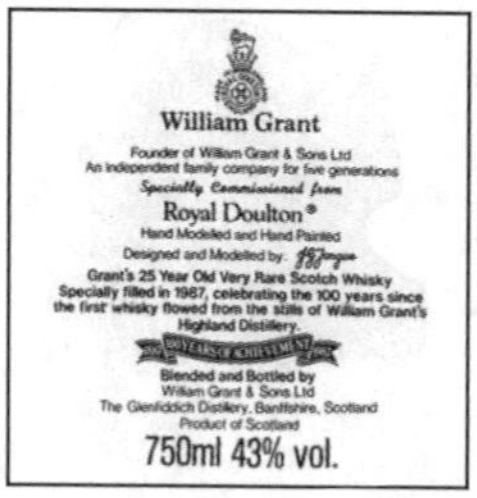

Backstamp C - 100th Anniversary of Production

WILLIAM GRANT

LIQUOR CONTAINER

STYLE ONE: HANDLE — FOUR OAK CASKS

Issued to commemorate the centenary of the founding of the Glenfiddich Distillery, this jug contains 750 ml of 25-year-old Grants Whisky. The uniform is that of a major of the 6th Volunteer Battalion of the Gordon Highlanders. The Glengarry cap features the symbol of a stag's head, which also appears on all of the company's bottles of whisky.

Designer: Graham Tongue
Height: 7", 17.8 cm
Size: Large
Issued: See below
Handle: Four oak casks
Colourway: Scarlet
Backstamps: A. Doulton/William Grant 100th Anniversary
Issued in 1986 in a limited edition of 500 pieces to commemorate the 100th anniversary of the laying of the foundation stone.
B. Special commission by Grant & Sons for employees on Christmas 1987.
C. Doulton / William Grant 100 Years
Issued in 1987 in a limited edition of 2,500 pieces to celebrate the 100 years since whisky first flowed from the stills.

Doulton Number	Backstamp	Issued	Current Market Value U.K. £	U.S. $	Can. $
D—	A	1986-Ltd. ed.	300.00	500.00	550.00
D—	B	1987-Ltd. ed.		Rare	
D—	C	1987-Ltd. ed.	200.00	375.00	375.00

WILLIAM GRANT

LIQUOR CONTAINER

STYLE TWO: HANDLE — FIELD OFFICERS' SWORD

Commissioned by Grants Glenfiddich Distillery, this liquor container was issued in 1988 in a limited edition of 5,000 pieces.

Designer: Graham Tongue
Height: 7", 17.8 cm
Size: Large
Issued: 1988 in a limited edition of 5,000
Handle: Field officers' sword
Colourway: Scarlet
Backstamp: Doulton/William Grant

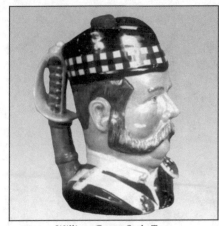

William Grant, Style Two

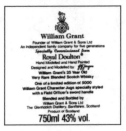

Doulton Number	Backstamp	Current Market Value		
		U.K. £	U.S. $	Can. $
D —	Doulton/Grant	250.00	525.00	600.00

LOVING CUPS
AND JUGS

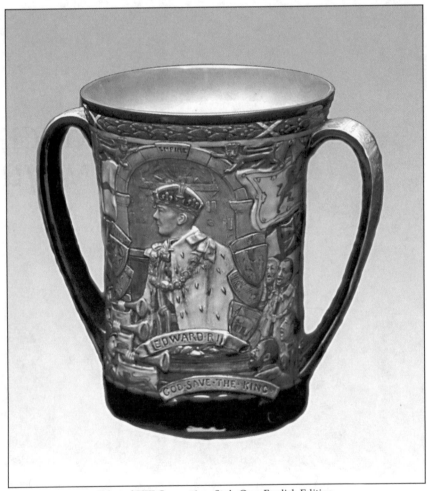

Edward VIII Coronation, Style One, English Edition

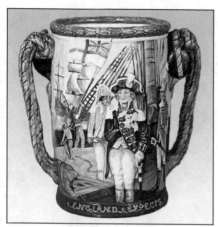

Admiral Lord Nelson

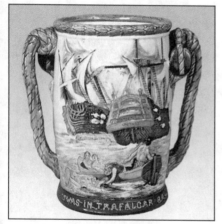

Admiral Lord Nelson

ADMIRAL LORD NELSON

This cup was issued in a limited edition of 600 pieces.

Designer: Charles Noke/Harry Fenton
Height: 10 ½", 26.7 cm
Issued: 1935 in a limited edition of 600
Handles: Block and tackles
Colour: Brown, blue, yellow and green
Inscription: "England Expects" and "It was in Trafalgar Bay"
Backstamp: Doulton

Doulton Number	Type	Current Market Value U.K. £	U.S. $	Can. $
—	Cup	1,250.00	2,000.00	2,250.00

THE APOTHECARY

The Apothecary was issued in a limited edition of 600.

Designer:	Charles Noke/Harry Fenton
Height:	6", 15.0 cm
Issued:	1934 in a limited edition of 600
Handles:	Distorted faces
Colour:	Green, red and yellow
Backstamp:	Doulton

Doulton Number	Type	Current Market Value U.K. £	U.S. $	Can. $
—	Cup	800.00	1,350.00	1,500.00

Note: Sold (factory proof) Phillips, New Bond Street, London, England, November 1999, £800.00.

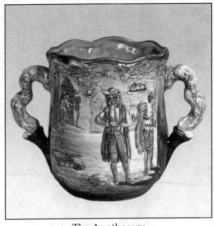

The Apothecary

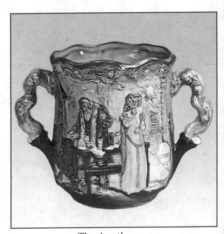

The Apothecary

CAPTAIN COOK

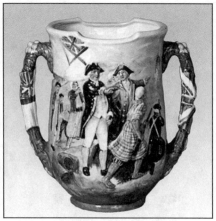

Captain Cook

The Captain Cook loving cup was issued in a limited edition of 350 pieces.

Designer:	Charles Noke/Harry Fenton
Height:	9 ½", 24.0 cm
Issued:	1933 in a limited edition of 350
Handles:	Coconut palms with the flags of St. George and the Union Jack
Colour:	Green, blue, yellow and red
Backstamp:	Doulton

Doulton Number	Type	Current Market Value		
		U.K. £	**U.S. $**	**Can. $**
—	Cup	3,000.00	5,000.00	6,000.00

Note: Sold (factory proof) Phillips, New Bond Street, London, England, November 1999, £2,600.00.

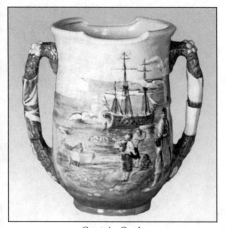

Captain Cook

CAPTAIN PHILLIP

This jug was issued in a limited edition of 350 pieces.

Designer: Charles Noke/Harry Fenton
Height: 9 ¼", 23.5 cm
Issued: 1938 in a limited edition of 350
Handle: Eucalyptus tree trunk
Colour: Yellow, blue, red and green
Spout: Face of Captain Phillip
Inscription: "Colony New South Wales founded January 1788 Sydney"
Backstamp: Doulton

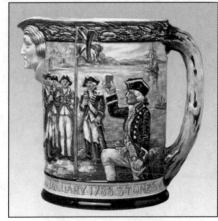

Captain Phillip

Doulton Number	Type	Current Market Value		
		U.K. £	U.S. $	Can. $
—	Jug	3,000.00	4,750.00	6,250.00

Note: Sold (No. 1 of 350) Phillips, New Bond Street, London, England, November 1999, £4,500.00.

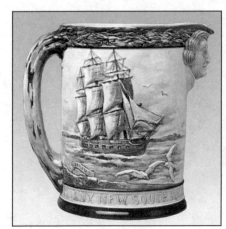

Captain Phillip

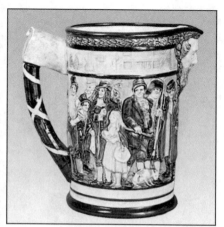

Charles Dickens

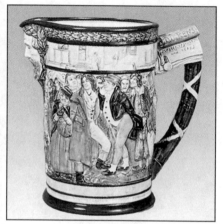

Charles Dickens

CHARLES DICKENS

This jug was issued in a limited edition of 1,000.

Designer: Charles Noke/Harry Fenton
Height: 10 ½", 26.7 cm
Issued: 1936 in a limited edition of 1,000
Handle: Open book
Spout: Face of Charles Dickens
Colour: Brown, green and red
Backstamp: Doulton

Doulton Number	Type	Current Market Value		
		U.K. £	U.S. $	Can. $
—	Jug	1,000.00	1,650.00	2,250.00

DICKENS DREAM

Although Dickens Dream was issued in an unlimited edition, probably only 1,000 pieces were produced.

Designer: Charles Noke
Height: 10 ½", 26.7 cm
Issued: 1933-Unknown
Handle: Poor Jo
Colour: Brown, green and red
Backstamp: Doulton

Doulton Number	Type	Current Market Value		
		U.K. £	U.S. $	Can. $
—	Jug	1,500.00	2,500.00	3,500.00

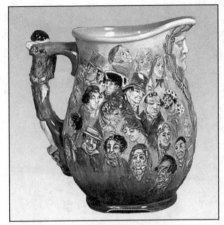

Dickens Dream

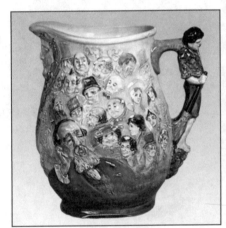

Dickens Dream

GEORGE WASHINGTON

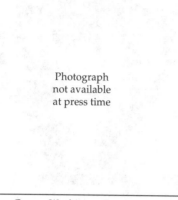

Photograph
not available
at press time

George Washinton, Prototype

PROTOTYPE

The handle of this prototype differs from the production model in that the stars are moulded in relief and set atop a striped background.

Designer: Charles Noke
Harry Fenton
Height: 10 ¼", 26.0 cm
Issued: 1932-1932
Backstamp: Doulton
Handle: Stars and Stripes
Colour: Brown, blue, red and cream
Spout: Face of George Washington
Inscription: "Declaration of Independence"

Doulton Number	Type	Current Market Value		
		U.K. £	U.S. $	Can. $
—	Jug	Extremely rare		

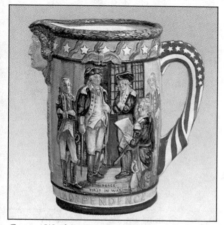

George Washington, Regular Issue, Style One

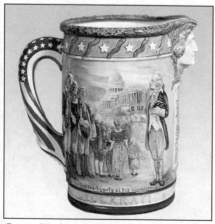

George Washington, Regular Issue, Style One

REGULAR ISSUE

STYLE ONE: JUG

This jug was issued in a limited edition of 1,000 pieces.

Designer: Charles Noke/Harry Fenton
Height: 10 ¼", 26.0 cm
Issued: 1932 in a limited edition of 1,000
Handle: The Stars and Stripes
Colour: Brown, blue, red and cream
Spout: Face of George Washington
Inscription: "Declaration of Independence"
Backstamp: Doulton

Doulton Number	Type	Current Market Value		
		U.K. £	U.S. $	Can. $
—	Jug	7,000.00	12,500.00	14,500.00

Note: Sold (No. 1 of 1,000) Phillips, New Bond Street, London, England, November 1999, £9,000.00.

GEORGE WASHINGTON

This George Washington loving cup was issued to commemorate the 200th anniversary of his birth.

STYLE TWO: LOVING CUP

Designer:	C. J. Noke
Height:	8 ¼", 21.0 cm
Issued:	1932-Unknown
Handle:	Laurel leaves
Colour:	Browns, green and red
Backstamp:	Doulton

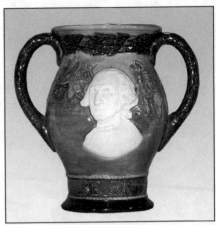

George Washington, Regular Issue, Style Two

Doulton Number	Type	Current Market Value		
		U.K. £	U.S. $	Can. $
—	Cup	Extremely rare. Only four known. Sold October 29, 1998 Phillips, London, England, £6,325.00		

Note: A pitcher, 9" high, with the same design as the George Washington, Style Two, loving cup is known.

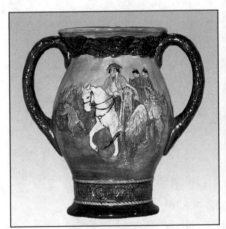

George Washington, Regular Issue, Style Two

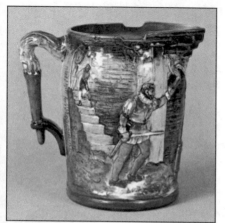

Guy Fawkes

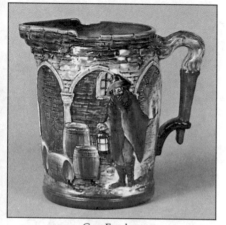

Guy Fawkes

GUY FAWKES

The Guy Fawkes jug was issued in a limited edition of 600 pieces.

Designer: Harry Fenton
Height: 7 ½", 19.1 cm
Issued: 1934 in a limited edition of 600
Handle: Flaming torch
Colour: Green, brown and red
Backstamp: Doulton

Doulton Number	Type	Current Market Value U.K. £	U.S. $	Can. $
—	Jug	1,000.00	1,500.00	1,750.00

I. T. WIGG BROOM MAN

PROTOTYPE

Designer:	Unknown
Height:	20.5 cm
Issued:	c.1935
Handles:	Tree branch
Spout:	Broom
Colour:	Browns, green and marron
Backstamp:	Doulton

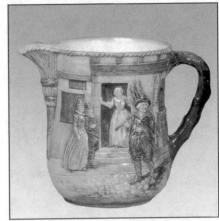

I. T. Wigg Broom Man, Prototype

Doulton Number	Type	Current Market Value U.K. £ U.S. $ Can. $
—	Jug	Sold November 21, 1999 Phillips, New Bond Street London, England, £5,500.00

JACKDAW OF RHEIMS

PROTOTYPE

This jug is believed to have been a trial piece only. No evidence exists that this jug actually went into production.

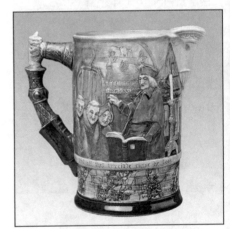

Jackdaw of Rheims, Prototype

Designer:	Unknown
Height:	11", 27.9 cm
Issued:	c.1934, not put into production
Handle:	Candle, candlestick and candle-snuffer
Colour:	Brown, red and green
Backstamp:	Doulton

Doulton Number	Type	Current Market Value U.K. £ U.S. $ Can. $
—	Jug	Extremely rare Sold November 21, 1999 Phillips, New Bond Street London, England, £20,000.00

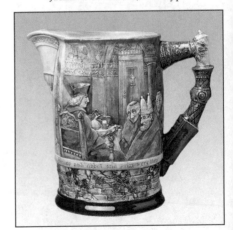

Jackdaw of Rheims, Prototype

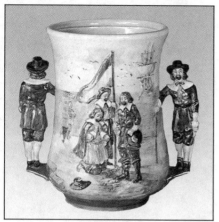

Jan Van Riebeeck

JAN VAN RIEBEECK

This cup was issued in limited edition of 300 pieces.

Designer:	Charles Noke/Harry Fenton
Height:	10 ¼", 26.0 cm
Issued:	1935 in a limited edition of 300
Handles:	Van Riebeeck figures
Colour:	Yellow, green, blue and red
Backstamp:	Doulton

Doulton Number	Type	Current Market Value U.K. £	U.S. $	Can. $
—	Cup	4,000.00	6,000.00	7,000.00

Note: Sold (No. 1 of 300) Phillips, New Bond Street, London England, November 1999, £3,800.00.

Jan Van Riebeeck

JOHN PEEL

The John Peel cup was issued in a limited edition of 500 pieces.

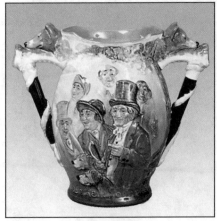

John Peel

	Designer:	Unknown
	Height:	9", 22.9 cm
	Issued:	1933 in a limited edition of 500
	Handles:	Fox heads on riding whips
	Colour:	Green, red and brown
	Backstamp:	Doulton

Doulton		Current Market Value		
Number	Type	U.K. £	U.S. $	Can. $
—	Cup	1,250.00	2,250.00	2,500.00

Note: Sold (factory proof) Phillips, New Bond Street, London, England, November 1999, £1,200.00.

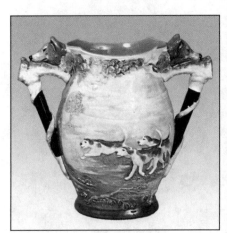

John Peel

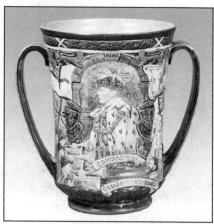

Edward VIII Coronation, Style One

Edward VIII Coronation, Style One

KING EDWARD VIII CORONATION

STYLE ONE: ENGLISH EDITION, LARGE SIZE

This coronation cup was issued in a limited edition of 2,000 pieces, of which 1,080 were sold.

Designer:	Charles Noke/Harry Fenton
Height:	10", 25.4 cm
Issued:	1937 in a limited edition of 2,000
Handle:	Names of Commonwealth countries
Colour:	Green, yellow and red
Backstamp:	Doulton

Doulton Number	Type	Current Market Value U.K. £	U.S. $	Can. $
—	Cup	700.00	1,100.00	1,500.00

KING EDWARD VIII CORONATION

STYLE TWO: ENGLISH EDITION, SMALL SIZE

Designer: Charles Noke
Height: 6 ½", 16.5 cm
Handle: Names of Commonwealth countries
Backstamp: Doulton

VARIATION No. 1: Portrait of Edward VIII in white

This small cup was issued in a limited edition of 1,000 pieces, of which only 454 were sold because the coronation never took place.

Issued: 1937 in a limited edition of 1,000
Colour: Green, red and yellow

Doulton Number	Type	Current Market Value U.K. £	U.S. $	Can. $
—	Cup		Extremely rare	

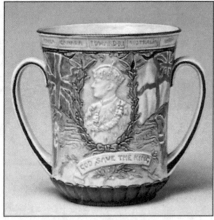
Edward VIII Coronation, Style Two, Var. 1

VARIATION No. 2: Portrait of Edward VIII fully coloured

Issued: 1937 in a limited edition of 2,000
Colour: Green, red and yellow

Doulton Number	Type	Current Market Value U.K. £	U.S. $	Can. $
—	Cup		Extremely rare	

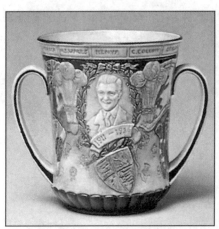
Edward VIII Coronation, Style Two, Var. 1

Note: Variation No. 2 (number 413 of a limited edition of 2,000) was sold at Christie's, 7.5.99.

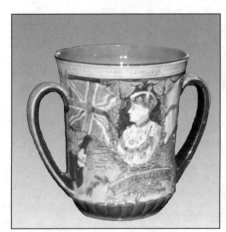
King Edward VIII Coronation Cup, Var. No. 2

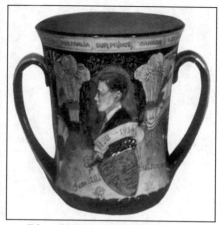

Edward VIII Coronation, Style Three

KING EDWARD VIII CORONATION

STYLE THREE: WELSH EDITION, SMALL SIZE

Style Three was issued in a limited edition of 2,000 pieces and was made especially for the Welsh market. The portrait of Edward, Prince of Wales, differs from that on the previous cup. The words "I am still the same man" appear on the jug, taken from a speech Edward made while on his first visit to Wales as sovereign.

Designer:	Charles Noke
Height:	6 ½", 16.5 cm
Issued:	1937 in a limited edition of 2,000
Handle:	Names of Commonwealth countries
Colour:	Green, red and brown
Backstamps:	Doulton

Doulton Number	Type	Current Market Value		
		U.K. £	**U.S. $**	**Can. $**
—	Cup	1,200.00	1,800.00	2,250.00

KING GEORGE V AND QUEEN MARY SILVER JUBILEE

This jubilee cup was issued in a limited edition of 1,000 pieces.

STYLE ONE: CROWNED CONJOINED PORTRAITS

Designer: Charles Noke/Harry Fenton
Height: 10", 25.4 cm
Issued: 1935 in a limited edition of 1,000
Handles: Names of Commonwealth countries and provinces
Colour: Green and brown
Backstamp: Doulton

| Doulton Number | Type | Current Market Value | | |
		U.K. £	U.S. $	Can. $
—	Cup	800.00	1,250.00	1,500.00

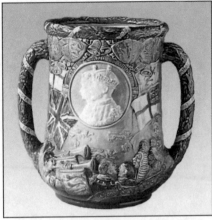

Style One - Crowned Conjoined Portraits

STYLE TWO: UNCROWNED CONJOINED PORTRAITS

Designer: Charles Noke/Harry Fenton
Height: 10 ½", 26.7 cm
Issued: 1935-Unknown
Handles: Plain
Colour: Yellow, red and green
Backstamp: Doulton

| Doulton Number | Type | Current Market Value | | |
		U.K. £	U.S. $	Can. $
—	Cup	800.00	1,250.00	1,500.00

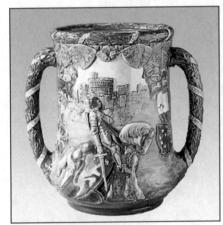

Style One Reverse

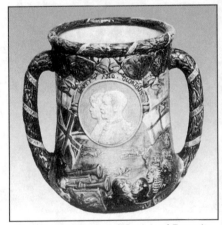

Style Two, Uncrowned Conjoined Portraits

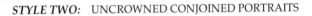

KING GEORGE VI AND QUEEN ELIZABETH CORONATION

STYLE ONE: LARGE DESIGN — CROWNED
CONJOINED PORTRAITS

Style One was issued in a limited edition of 2,000 pieces.

Designer: Charles Noke/Harry Fenton
Height: 10 ½", 26.7 cm
Issued: 1937 in a limited edition of 2,000
Handles: Plain
Colour: Yellow, red and green
Backstamp: Doulton

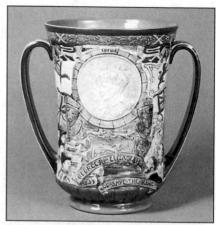

Style One, Large design, 10 ½", 26.7 cm

Doulton Number	Type	Height	Current Market Value		
			U.K. £	**U.S. $**	**Can. $**
—	Cup	10 ½", 26. 7 cm	750.00	1,300.00	1,500.00

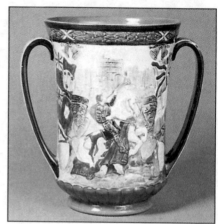

Style One, Large design, 10 ½", 26.7 cm

KING GEORGE VI AND QUEEN ELIZABETH CORONATION

STYLE TWO: SMALL DESIGN — CROWNED
SINGLE PORTRAITS

Style Two was issued in a limited edition of 2,000 pieces.

Designer:	Charles Noke/Harry Fenton
Height:	6 ½", 16.5 cm
Issued:	1937 in a limited edition of 2,000
Handles:	Plain
Colour:	Yellow, green, blue and red
Backstamp:	Doulton

Doulton Number	Type	Height	Current Market Value		
			U.K. £	U.S. $	Can. $
—	Cup	6 ½", 16.5 cm	600.00	900.00	1,200.00

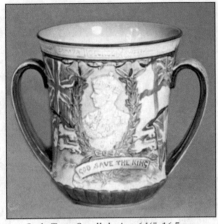

Style Two, Small design 6 ½", 16.5 cm

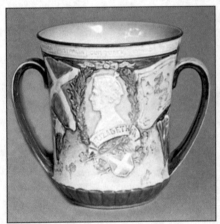

Style Two, Small design 6 ½", 16.5 cm

MASTER OF FOXHOUNDS

PROTOTYPE

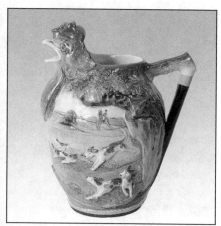

Master of Foxhounds, Prototype

Designer: Charles Noke
Height: Unknown
Issued: Unknown
Handle: Whip
Spout: Rooster's head
Colour: Green, red and brown
Backstamp: Doulton

Doulton Number	Type	Current Market Value		
		U.K. £	U.S. $	Can. $
—	Jug		Extremely Rare	

Master of Foxhounds, Prototype

MASTER OF FOXHOUNDS

REGULAR ISSUE

This presentation jug was issued in a limited edition of 500 pieces.

Designer:	Charles Noke
Height:	13", 33.0 cm
Issued:	1930 in a limited edition of 500
Handle:	Whip
Spout:	Rooster's head
Colour:	Green, red and brown
Backstamp:	Doulton

Doulton Number	Type	Current Market Value		
		U.K. £	**U.S. $**	**Can. $**
—	Jug	1,000.00	1,500.00	2,000.00

Note: Sold (No. 1 of 500 [damage to spout]) Phillips, New Bond Street, London, England, November 1999, £380.

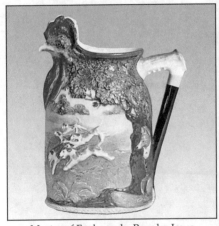

Master of Foxhounds, Regular Issue

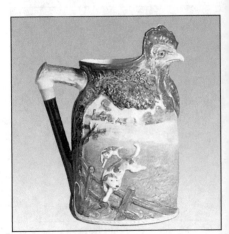

Masater of Foxhounds, Regular Issue

THE PIED PIPER OF HAMELIN

The Pied Piper jug was issued in a limited edition of 600 pieces.

Designer:	Charles Noke/Harry Fenton
Height:	10", 25.4 cm
Issued:	1934 in a limited edition of 600
Handle:	Tree
Spout:	Window
Colour:	Yellow, brown and green
Backstamp:	Doulton

Doulton Number	Type	Current Market Value		
		U.K. £	**U.S. $**	**Can. $**
—	Jug	1,250.00	1,850.00	2,250.00

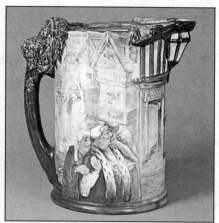

The Pied Piper of Hamelin

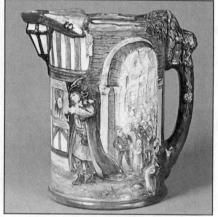

The Pied Piper of Hamelin

POTTERY IN THE PAST

The Pottery in the Past cup was issued exclusively for the members of the Royal Doulton International Collectors Club.

Designer: Graham Tongue
Height: 6", 15.0 cm
Issued: 1983-1983
Handles: Plain
Colour: Brown and green
Backstamp: Doulton/RDICC

Doulton		Current Market Value		
Number	Type	U.K. £	U.S. $	Can. $
D6696	Cup	150.00	250.00	275.00

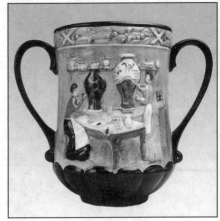

Pottery in the Past

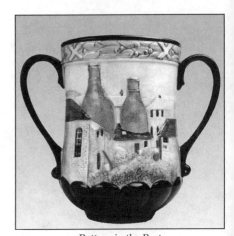

Pottery in the Past

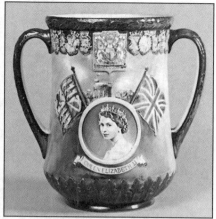

Queen Elizabeth II Coronation - Loving Cup

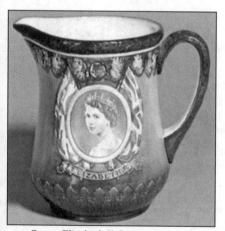

Queen Elizabeth II Coronation - Loving Cup

QUEEN ELIZABETH II CORONATION

Elizabeth became Queen of England on February 6, 1952. This commemorative cup features depictions of both Queen Elizabeth II and Elizabeth I. The handles are plain. It was issued in a limited edition of 1,000 pieces.

LOVING CUP

Designer:	Cecil J. Noke/Harry Fenton
Height:	10 ½", 26.7 cm
Issued:	1953 in a limited edition of 1,000
Handles:	Plain
Colour:	Brown
Backstamp:	Doulton

Doulton Number	Type	Current Market Value		
		U.K. £	U.S. $	Can. $
—	Cup	500.00	750.00	1,000.00

JUG

This small jug features a portrait of Queen Elizabeth II flanked by the Union Jack and the royal standard, with "Elizabeth R" underneath. A scene of Windsor Castle is on the other side. This piece was not issued in a limited edition.

Designer:	Unknown
Height:	6 ¼", 15.9 cm
Issued:	1953-1953
Handles:	Plain
Colour:	Brown
Backstamp:	Doulton

Doulton Number	Type	Current Market Value		
		U.K. £	U.S. $	Can. $
—	Jug	150.00	300.00	350.00

Queen Elizabeth II Coronation - Jug

QUEEN ELIZABETH II SILVER JUBILEE

Designer: Reg Johnson
Height: 10 ½", 26.7 cm
Handles: Lion heads
Backstamp: Doulton

VARIATION No. 1: PLAIN INNER RIM

This Queen Elizabeth II Silver Jubilee cup was issued in a limited edition of 250 pieces.

Issued: 1977 in a limited edition of 250
Colour: Red, brown, green and yellow

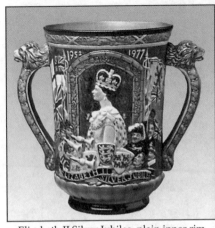

Elizabeth II Silver Jubilee, plain inner rim

Doulton Number	Type	Current Market Value		
		U.K. £	U.S. $	Can. $
—	Cup	1,250.00	1,850.00	2,250.00

Note: Sold (No. 1 of 250) Phillips, New Bond Street, London, England, November 1999, £850.00

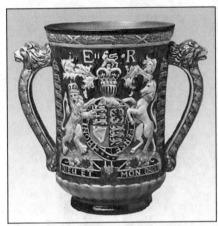

Elizabeth II Silver Jubilee, plain inner rim

VARIATION No. 2: FLORAL INNER RIM

Issued: 1977
Colour: Red, brown, green and yellow

Doulton Number	Type	Current Market Value		
		U.K. £	U.S. $	Can. $
—	Cup		Extremely Rare	

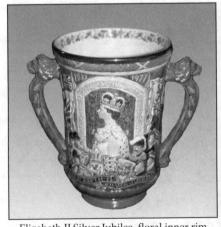

Elizabeth II Silver Jubilee, floral inner rim

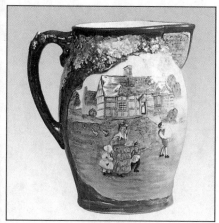

Regency Coach

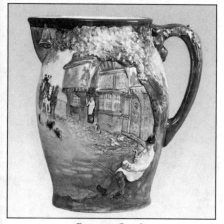

Regency Coach

REGENCY COACH

The Regency Coach jug was issued in a limited edition of 500 pieces.

Designer: Charles Noke
Height: 10", 25.4 cm
Issued: 1931 in a limited edition of 500
Handle: Tree branch
Spout: A parchment and inn sign
Colour: Green and brown
Backstamp: Doulton

Doulton Number	Type	Current Market Value U.K. £	U.S. $	Can. $
—	Jug	1,250.00	1,850.00	2,250.00

ROBIN HOOD

This cup was issued in a limited edition of 600 pieces.

Designer: Charles Noke/Harry Fenton
Height: 8 ½", 21.6 cm
Issued: 1938 in a limited edition of 600
Handles: Plain, incised names of "The Merry Men"
Colour: Green, red and brown
Backstamp: Doulton

| Doulton Number | Type | Current Market Value | | |
		U.K. £	U.S. $	Can. $
—	Cup	1,400.00	2,000.00	2,500.00

Note: Sold (No. 1 of 600) Phillips, New Bond Street, London, England, November 1999, £1,700.00.

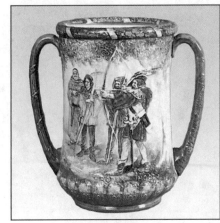

Robin Hood

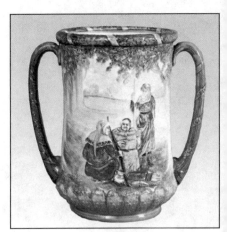

Roin Hood

ROGER SOLEMEL, COBBLER

PROTOTYPE

This is believed to have been a trial piece only. There are no production pieces known to exist.

Designer: Geoff Blower
Height: 10 ½", 26.7 cm
Issued: Unknown
Handle: Pair of shoes; "Cobbler" inscribed
Spout: Twine
Colour: Brown, tan, green, grey and white
Backstamp: Doulton

| Doulton Number | Type | Current Market Value | | |
		U.K. £	U.S. $	Can. $
—	Jug	Sold November 21, 1999, Phillips, New Bond Street, London, England, £3,000.00		

Note: Jug sold at auction had damage to the spout.

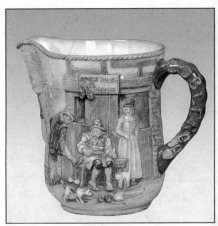

Roger Solemel, Cobbler

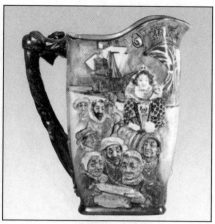

Sir Francis Drake

Sir Francis Drake

SIR FRANCIS DRAKE

The Sir Francis Drake jug was issued in a limited edition of 500 pieces.

Designer:	Charles Noke/Harry Fenton
Height:	10 ¼", 26.0 cm
Issued:	1933 in a limited edition of 500
Handle:	Rope and lantern
Colour:	Brown, red, green and blue
Backstamp:	Doulton

Doulton Number	Type	Current Market Value		
		U.K. £	**U.S. $**	**Can. $**
—	Jug	1,200.00	1,850.00	2,250.00

THE THREE MUSKETEERS

This cup was issued in a limited edition of 600 pieces.

Designer: Charles Noke/Harry Fenton
Height: 10", 25.4 cm
Issued: 1936 in a limited edition of 600
Handles: Trophies of war and the accoutrements of pleasure
Colour: Yellow, green, brown and red
Backstamp: Doulton

Doulton Number	Type	Current Market Value		
		U.K. £	U.S. $	Can. $
—	Cup	800.00	1,250.00	1,850.00

Note: Sold (No. 1 of 600) Phillips, New Bond Street, London, England, November 1999, £1,200.00.

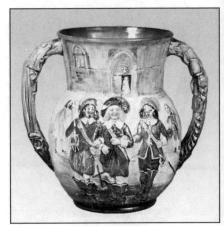

The Three Muskateers

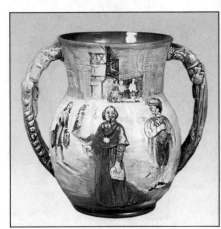

The Three Muskateers

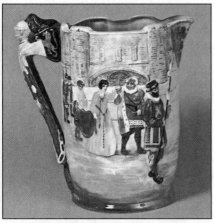

Tower of London, Variation No. 1

Tower of London, Variation No. 1

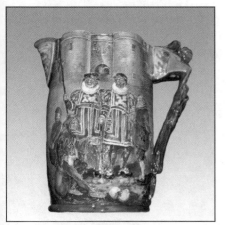

Tower of London, Variation No. 2

TOWER OF LONDON

This jug was issued in a limited edition of 500 pieces.

Designer: Charles Noke/Harry Fenton
Height: 10", 25.4 cm
Issued: 1933 in a limited edition of 500
Handle: Axes, pikes, chains and armour
Spout: Shield bearing the lions of England

VARIATION No. 1: **Colourway** — Jester wears green, yellow and brown; Royal Standard: purple and red

Colour: Red, yellow, green, grey and brown
Backstamp: Doulton

Doulton Number	Type	Current Market Value U.K. £	U.S. $	Can. $
—	Jug	1,000.00	1,500.00	1,850.00

VARIATION No. 2: **Colourway** — Jester wears green, purple and brown; Royal Standard: yellow and red

Colour: Red, yellow, green, purple and brown
Backstamp: Doulton

Doulton Number	Type	Current Market Value U.K. £	U.S. $	Can. $
—	Jug	Extremely Rare		

TREASURE ISLAND

The Treasure Island jug was issued in a limited edition of 600 pieces.

Designer: Charles Noke/Harry Fenton
Height: 7 ½", 19.1 cm
Issued: 1934 in a limited edition of 600
Handle: Palm tree
Spout: Palm leaves
Colour: Yellow, green and brown
Backstamp: Doulton

Doulton Number	Type	Current Market Value U.K. £	U.S. $	Can. $
—	Jug	850.00	1,275.00	1,575.00

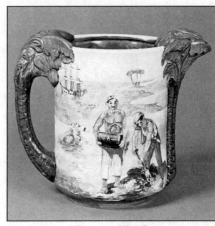

Treasure Island

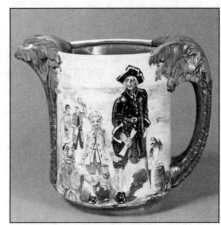

Treasure Island

THE VILLAGE BLACKSMITH

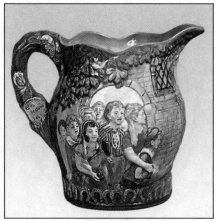

The Village Blacksmith

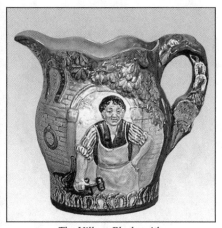

The Village Blacksmith

This jug was issued in a limited edition of 600 pieces.

Designer: Charles Noke
Height: 7 ¾", 19.7 cm
Issued: 1936 in a limited edition of 600
Handle: Branch with milestone at base of handle; milestone incised "Longfellow" on one side and "Long-fellow 1842" on the other
Spout: Leaves
Colour: Brown, green and red
Backstamp: Doulton

Doulton Number	Type	Current Market Value U.K. £	U.S. $	Can. $
—	Jug	1,000.00	1,500.00	1,850.00

Note: Sold (No. 1 of 600) Phillips, New Bond Street, London, England, November 1999, £1,000.00.

THE WANDERING MINSTREL

The Wandering Minstrel cup was issued in a limited edition of 600 pieces.

Designer:	Charles Noke/Harry Fenton
Height:	5 ½", 14.0 cm
Issued:	1934 in a limited edition of 600
Handles:	Trees
Colour:	Green, brown and yellow
Backstamp:	Doulton

Doulton Number	Type	Current Market Value U.K. £	U.S. $	Can. $
—	Cup	1,000.00	1,500.00	1,850.00

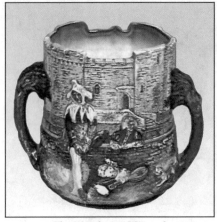

The Wandering Minstrel

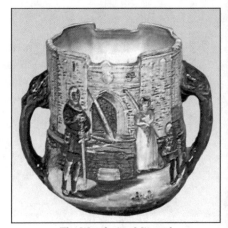

The Wandering Minstrel

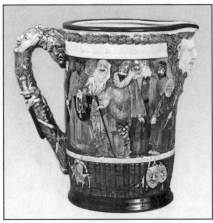

William Shakespeare

WILLIAM SHAKESPEARE

The William Shakespeare jug was issued in a limited edition of 1,000 pieces.

Designer: Charles Noke
Height: 10 ½", 26.7 cm
Issued: 1933 in a limited edition of 1,000
Handle: Masks of tragedy and comedy; swords
Spout: Face of Shakespeare
Colour: Green, brown and red
Backstamp: Doulton

Doulton Number	Type	Current Market Value U.K. £	U.S. $	Can. $
—	Jug	1,100.00	1,650.00	2,000.00

William Shakespeare

WILLIAM WORDSWORTH

This cup was issued in an unlimited edition, but few are known to exist.

Designer: Charles Noke
Height: 6 ½", 16.5 cm
Issued: 1933-Unknown
Handles: Tied vines
Colour: Green, yellow and red
Backstamp: Doulton

Doulton Number	Type	Current Market Value U.K. £	U.S. $	Can. $
—	Cup	2,000.00	3,250.00	4,000.00

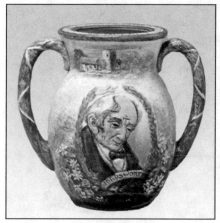

William Wordsworth

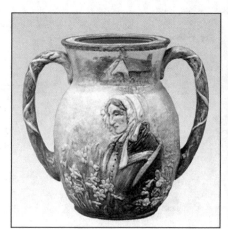

William Wordsworth

COLLECTING BY SERIES

DOULTON
NUMBER
INDEX

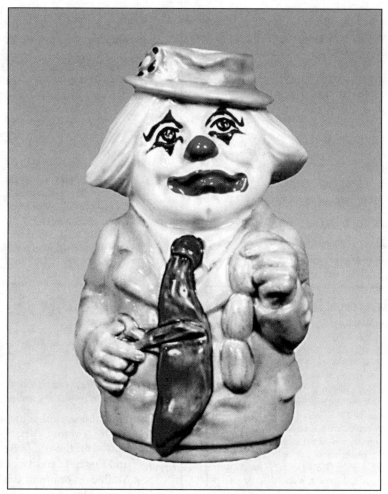

Charlie Cheer the Clown (The Doultonville Collection)

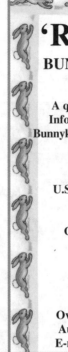

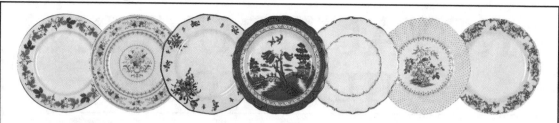
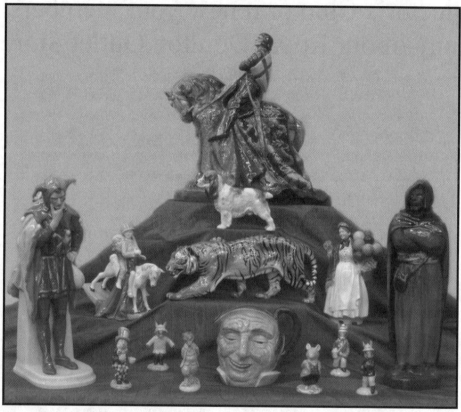
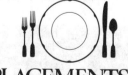

ROYAL DOULTON
OUTLET STORES

Join our Royal Doulton International Collector's Club or renew your membership at any of our Royal Doulton Outlet Stores.

Cabazon, **CA** . . . . . . (909) 849-4222	Smithfield, **NC** . . . . . (919) 934-0101
Camarillo, **CA** . . . . . (805) 987-6208	Flemington, **NJ** . . . . . (908) 788-5677
Carlsbad, **CA** . . . . . . (760) 804-0159	Las Vegas, **NV** . . . . . (702) 260-4192
Gilroy, **CA** . . . . (408) 842-1653	Central Valley, **NY**. . . . (845) 928-2434
Lake Elsinore, **CA** . . (909) 674-5884	Riverhead, **NY**. . . . . . (631) 369-6940
Vacaville, **CA**. . . . . . (707) 448-2793	Jeffersonville, **OH**. . . (740) 948-9200
Castle Rock, **CO**. . . . (303) 660-1601	Lincoln City, **OR** . . . (541) 996-5065
Clinton, **CT**. . . . . . . (860) 669-3496	Lancaster, **PA** . . . . . . (717) 291-9370
Rehoboth, **DE**. . . . . . (302) 226-9335	Grove City, **PA** . . . . . (724) 748-4990
Ellenton, **FL**. . . . . . . (941) 729-2076	Tannersville, **PA** . . . . (570) 619-4020
Estero, **FL**. . . . . (941) 947-5200	Hilton Head , **SC**. . . . (843) 837-9157
Orlando, **FL** . . . . (407) 352-5578	Myrtle Beach, **SC** . . . (843) 236-5703
St. Augustine, **FL**. . . (904) 824-9700	Pigeon Forge, **TN** . . . (865) 428-0977
Calhoun, **GA**. . . . . . . (706) 602-2066	Conroe, **TX** . . . . (936) 856-7383
Dawsonville, **GA** . . . (706) 216-1480	San Marcos, **TX** . . . . (512) 754-0555
Michigan City, **IN** . . (219) 872-7916	Prince William, **VA**. . (703) 497-6845
Kittery, **ME** . . . . (207) 439-4770	Williamsburg, **VA**. . . (757) 565-0752
Birch Run, **MI** . . . . . (989) 624-1011	Burlington,**WA** . . . . . (360) 757-6660
Blowing Rock, **NC**. . . (828) 295-9230	

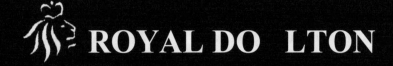

ROYAL DO LTON

V

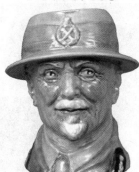

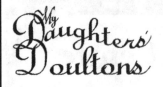

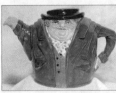
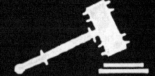

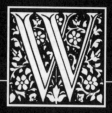

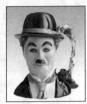
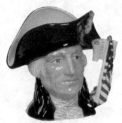
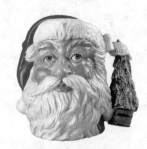

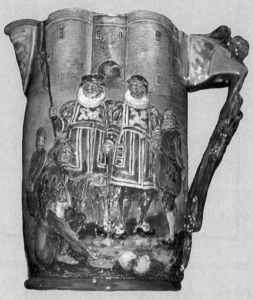
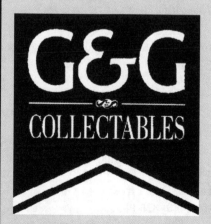

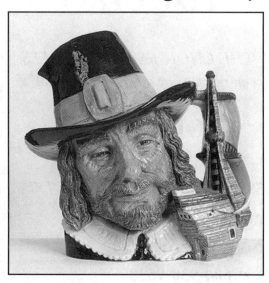

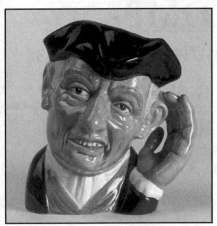